Level Up!

Third Edition

Level Up!
The Guide to Great
Video Game Design

Third Edition

Scott Rogers

WILEY

Additional Copyright Information:

To everyone around the world who has read the first two editions of Level Up! and gone on to dream about, learn about and make their own games.

And always, to Brenda, Evelyn and Jack.

Acknowledgments

WHEW. FINALLY DONE. I'm not gonna lie, this was a tough one to get through. But there were so, so many people to help get me through it. First of all, a huge thank you for my team at Wiley & Sons: Jim Minatel, Brad Jones, Pete Gaughan, Sara Deichman and Ashley Edwards. I always appreciate your collective patience and support. You are all the best!

To the guy who runs the GDC bookstore, thanks for <u>not</u> carrying my book in 2023 and saying to me, "I don't carry programming books that are over ten years old." Your words provided me with the ammunition I needed for Wiley & Sons to say "yes" to this long overdue third edition. (I was told that the bookstore carried *Level Up!* in 2024.)

Next, a huge thank you to Dr. Alex Herrera, Dr. Yi-Ping Wen, Tracey Sutton, Dr. Warren Lok, the infusion staff at Kaiser Permanente, Woodland Hills and the Day Hospital staff at City of Hope, Duarte. You collectively and literally saved my life, which was threatened from Hodgkin's Lymphoma. Here's to hoping that the bone marrow transplant is a success. Jim, sorry that my long illness interrupted the production of this book.

As a result of this near-death experience, I have received the greatest out-pouring of love and support I might ever receive in my life. Readers of *Level Up!* from around the globe wrote to tell me about their experience with the book, how much they loved it, and how it helped many of them take their first steps into the world of video game design. Manuel Moavero from Italy, who told me there are still no design courses in Italy and how *Level Up!* helped him start his career path. Daniel de Sant'anna who uses *Level Up!* in his game design classes in Chile. Mr. Nelson, who says *Level Up!* helped him get his first game design job. Sham and Jana AlBdour from Turkey, who created an entire YouTube video series about *Level Up!* Patrick Schnorbus from Germany, who organized a fundraiser and an entire day of game design lectures, many of which were based around *Level Up!* and its teachings. I heard from so many other people—too many to count. It was an absolutely astonishing and humbling experience. I now know that *Level Up!* has made a difference in the lives of so many around the world. As my wife reminds me, "I am the richest person in Bedford Falls."

And speaking of my wife, thank you and I love you to all my family and friends who are always so supportive during the writing process: Brenda Lee Rogers, Evelyn Lee Emma Rogers, Jack Blackwood Montgomery Rogers, Jackie Rogers, Brett Rogers, Jen Trebby, Elinor Trebby-Rogers, Dr. Christopher Rogers, Patti Rogers, Hardy LeBel, Marvin Jones, Ethan Schaeffer, Peter Vaughn, Manny Vega, Michael Floyd, Drew Massey, Daniel McGuffey, Chad

Jones, Ryan Prast, Todd Martens, Danny Bilson, Richard LaMarchand, Jeff Luke, Jaclyn Luke, Seth Johnson, Jeremy Gibson-Bond, Mike Heath. David Abzug, Andy Ashcraft, Dru Erridge, Taylor Hellem, Min Htet, all my co-workers at Gamebreaking Studios, Eric Eikmeier, Donna Ricci, and the entire staff at Geeky Teas and Games.

Apologies if I have forgotten anyone. There's always the fourth edition.

About the Author

AFTER DISCOVERING THAT game designers have more fun, **Scott Rogers** embarked on a 30 year plus career as a video game designer, author, educator, imagineer and cartoonist.

He has designed many video games that you have heard of and maybe even played, including *Pac-Man World*, the *Maximo* series, *God of War*, the *Drawn to Life* series, *Darksiders*, and many *Spongebob Squarepants* games (but not the good one). In addition to the two editions of this book, Scott wrote *Swipe This! The Guide to Great Touchscreen Game Design* and *Your Turn! The Guide to Great Tabletop Game Design*. He also contributed an essay to *Level Design: Processes and Experiences*.

He is the creator of the comic book *Bedbug: Single Father Superhero* and a designer of board games including *ALIEN: Fate of the Nostromo*, *Pantone the Game*, *The Texas Chainsaw Massacre Game*, *Rayguns and Rocketships*, and a couple of expansions for the game *Marvel Villainous*. His board game knowledge and career have been featured on the History Channel's *The Toys that Build America* and in the 2020 documentary, *Gamemaster*.

Scott is an adjunct professor at USC's prestigious School of Interactive Media and a former instructor at the New York Film Academy. He was a Principal Imagineer for Walt Disney Imagineering R&D and is now trying to figure out what to do for an encore.

Scott lives just outside Los Angeles with his wife, two children, and more games than he has time to play.

Why not visit him online at www.mrbossdesign.com or follow him on Insta, X, Facebook or whatever. Oh, and review this book. It really helps us authors!

Contents

Foreword

WHEN SCOTT ROGERS first released *Level Up! The Guide to Great Video Game Design*, our industry was on the cusp of a revolution. Indie developers were beginning to rise, new platforms like mobile, cloud gaming, and VR were still finding their footing, and the concept of games as a mainstream cultural force was just starting to solidify. Scott's book became an essential addition to the library of aspiring game designers, offering a treasure trove of insights, practical advice, and a deep understanding of what makes games resonate with players.

In the past 15 years, the gaming landscape has continued to evolve. Our industry is bigger than ever in terms of both revenues and global reach, our audiences are more diverse and inclusive, and technology continues to push the boundaries of what's possible. Despite all these changes, good game design is still about understanding players, crafting compelling experiences, and telling stories that matter.

This latest edition of *Level Up!* doesn't just update the content for today's technologies and trends; it also reflects the growth and maturation of the industry itself. Scott has expanded earlier topics to move from early inception to broader use (VR/XR/AR/MR/LBE). He's also investigated the vital connection between playtesting and systems design, even providing processes and materials to up your design game.

As a game designer, I've always found Scott's approach to be both practical and inspirational. His writing demystifies the complexities of game design without losing sight of the creative spark that drives us to make games in the first place. As you make your way through the pages of this literal treasure trove, you'll find yourself engaged by how downright approachable it all is.

I've been fortunate enough to know Scott personally for more years than either of us will readily admit. Professionally, we've shared many of the same experiences and shared our hopes and dreams for what could be accomplished through games when we were both at The Walt Disney Company. I've always envied his role as an Imagineer as it was the perfect title for someone who has always dreamed big and then worked incredibly hard to bring those dreams to life. This book is one of those dreams that we all benefit from having become real.

Enjoy - and, as always, Keep Gaming!

Bill Roper

Co-Founder, Lunacy Games // Creative executive on over 20 titles including the *Warcraft, Diablo, and StarCraft franchises, Hellgate: London, Champions Online, Star Trek Online, and Disney Infinity*

Press Start!

"The only thing that is constant is change"
—Heraclitus of Ephesus

WHEN I STARTED working in the video game industry, games were coded in assembly language, specifically 68009. The 16-bit artwork and character sprites were created using two commercial products published by Electronic Arts: Deluxe Paint and Deluxe Animator. They were clunky to use, and it took time and skill to create anything that looked good, let alone looked like art. The most popular game genres on consoles were fighting games and character-based platformers, while adventure games and flight sims were still popular on PCs.

By the time I wrote the first edition of *Level Up! The Guide to Great Video Game Design*, games were being coded in C#, and Maya and Photoshop were being used to create the 3D artwork. This software was expensive AND complicated to use, and the most popular genres were 3D shooters and motion-controlled sports games. It was a totally different way to design and develop games, and if you couldn't keep up, you were out.

It's been almost 15 years since I wrote *Level Up! 2e* and the game industry has changed again and again by leaps and bounds. During that time, games on mobile phones have become ubiquitous, virtual reality (VR) has come and mostly gone (again), and streaming video games have replaced most physical media. The tools, platforms, and architectures have evolved. Unity and Unreal—the most popular game creation platforms—used to cost thousands of dollars for professionals to license but are now free for students and novice creators. Creating 2D art can be as simple as typing a few words into AI tools like Midjourney or NightCafe. There are literally thousands of YouTube tutorials available on a variety of topics from coding to game design theory. There is so much to choose from, how can we even know where to start?!?

Adaptability is the key to a long career in video games. It's also the key to having your book still stocked on the shelves! So, it's time for a new edition of *Level Up! The Guide to Great Video Game Design*! Over the time since I wrote the second edition, I've realized that the book needs to refocus. The first two editions were from the perspective of the games I created during my career, which were third-person action games.

In this new edition, I take a broader view and address as many different topics and game genres as the book's page count allowed. I wanted to make sure that you feel like you're getting your money's worth, even if you've bought the previous editions of *Level Up! The Guide to Great Video Game Design*. More importantly, my goal is to make this book as up-to-date and as relevant as possible with content that will hopefully be relevant for the next 10 years or more!

That's not to say that we aren't going to cover the material in the other editions of *Level Up! The Guide to Great Video Game Design*. We're still going to talk about action games, boss fights, chili, dynamic game difficulty balancing, ergonomics, fun, gender representation, haunted mansions, islands and alleys, jump distances, keys and doors, leitmotifs, Mexican pizzas, non-player characters (NPCs), one-sheet design, pitch presentations, quick timer events, roguelikes, skill trees, the Triangle of Weirdness, unfun, virtual reality, walking simulators, XR, y-axis and zombies, but we're going to look at them through a more defined lens, to help you apply the knowledge to making games, not just theorize about making games. This book will teach you the who, what, where and most importantly, the how of designing video games.

I have always thought of *Level Up! The Guide to Great Design* as a handbook, something that a game developer can refer to from time to time or find inspiration in during their regular workday. Heck, there are times I find myself referring back to it. However, my viewpoint on some subjects has matured, evolved, refined, even changed! There might be some contractions in this edition. That's okay; it's good to grow. I've grown a lot as a game creator having worked on a wider variety of games and projects in the intervening years as well as spending many years as a game design educator on a wide variety of topics.

Before we start, keep in mind that there are many ways to approach game design. Most of them are valid, but they must first and foremost COMMUNICATE the designer's ideas to the team. We'll talk about many ways to do this further on. Many of these are techniques I have personally used, so I know that they work. I want to make sure you have the best tools possible to help you with your own design efforts.

Another quick reminder: when I say "I designed a game" this is an oversimplification. Video games are created by many, many, many talented people (you'll be introduced to them shortly) and to give the impression that I did all the work myself is not only incorrect, but it is wrong. Credit always needs to be given to those who deserve it. There is no "I" in team.

You'll find that many of the concepts found in this book are relevant to many different types of game design—whether it's console, mobile, computer, or XR. These design concepts will also work when designing theme parks, museum installations, ARGs, location based experiences (LBEs), and even analog games like tabletop games. It shouldn't be too hard for you to translate the design lessons from one game medium to another.

Another thing before we get started. If you are looking for a single chapter about gameplay design, don't bother. EVERY chapter in this book is about gameplay. You should be thinking about gameplay all the time and how the experiences and systems you create affect the player, even when designing passive elements like cutscenes, monetization models, pause screens, and passive gameplay systems.

Since you've made it this far, I may as well start by telling you the bad news up front. While **making video games is the best job in the world**, it can be thrilling, frustrating, rewarding, nerve-wracking, hectic, boring, vomit-inducing, and just plain fun. BUT, making video games is ALWAYS very hard work. As my former boss used to say, "Video games is a hard business."

This is why I feel fortunate that I have survived 30 years as a game developer. I have experienced the industry as a developer on AAA games, as a developer on Indie games, as a developer on VR games, as a game developer at a major theme park, as a producer at a major video game publisher, and as a business director at a small developer. I have seen the video game business from just about every side...and it is always difficult. You won't always succeed. You'll make dumb mistakes, but I'm here to help you with that. I've already made the mistakes. Follow my advice, and hopefully you won't make them yourself.

No, You Can't Have My Job

All of the experience I have gained over my career, I will list for you in the section at the end of each chapter called **Clever Ideas and Universal Truths.** That way, you can reference insights quickly when you are designing your own games. These clever ideas and universal truths are things that I know to be true because I have experienced them and wrestled with them again and again and again.

In the main body of the text, I will call out **very important things** for you to note. It might be a term, a concept, or a theory. **Very important things** are always in **bold text**. For example, the first very important thing I learned on my career journey as a game designer was:

GAME DESIGNERS HAVE MORE FUN!

My first job in the video game industry was as an artist. Back in those very early 16-bit days, video games artists drew images pixel by pixel. Now there are several amazing 16 bit artists who have passed through the industry, but I was not one of them. To me, drawing images out of pixels was like...laying bathroom tile—boring, and definitely not making art. For example, here is a picture that I drew out of pixels.

It's fine, but it's not going to win me any awards. As I was "pushing pixels," I heard the sound of raucous laughter coming from the adjacent cubicles. Like a prairie dog, I peered over the wall of my cubicle to see all the game designers in the company yucking it up and having a good ol' time. I thought "those designers are having more fun making games than I am!" Making video games should be fun! I want to have fun, too! I want to become a game designer!"

I got my shot and learned how to map levels, design characters, and write a game design document. With some help and some opportunities, I eventually worked my way up the ladder at several companies to become a lead game designer and then design director! However, while working as a game designer, I quickly learned another very important thing:

NO ONE WANTS TO READ YOUR GAME DESIGN DOCUMENT

This is a sad truth for a game designer to discover because writing a game design document is the primary way to communicate your ideas to your teammates. Remember how I said that communication was the most important skill as a game designer? Let me put that very important thing in bold:

COMMUNICATION IS THE MOST IMPORTANT GAME DESIGNER SKILL

Imagine my dilemma. Here I was, a brand-new game designer, ready to share all of his game design ideas with the world but no one would read them! How frustrating! Fortunately, I had a secret weapon. I drew my game design documents as cartoons. And guess what, people like looking at cartoons more than they like reading text. The cartoons conveyed the ideas I wanted to get across. I've been designing games this way ever since. Here's an example of one of my cartoon designs.

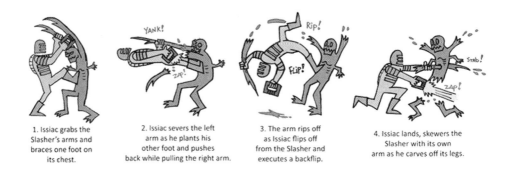

1. Issiac grabs the Slasher's arms and braces one foot on its chest.

2. Issiac severs the left arm as he plants his other foot and pushes back while pulling the right arm.

3. The arm rips off as Issiac flips off from the Slasher and executes a backflip.

4. Issiac lands, skewers the Slasher with its own arm as he carves off its legs.

This is why you will find *Level Up!* packed with many cartoon pictures that illustrate and explain game design concepts. Maybe they'll motivate you to keep reading this book because you think the cartoons are funny. Whatever it takes to keep your reader engaged and communicate your ideas. Give it a try; it doesn't even matter if you're good at drawing.

Who is This Book For?

Why *you*, of course. Provided you are one of the following people:

A working video game professional. Even though you are a working professional, you can't be expected to remember *everything*. I've been making games for 30 years, and I forget stuff all the time! This is where *Level Up!* comes in. If you've forgotten all the options on how an enemy can interact with a player character, you can just flip to that page. If you need to remind yourself how a camera can be used for dramatic effect, just go to that chapter. *Level Up!* is filled with lots of practical tips and information to help you make your game better. There are lots of other good video game design books out there, but most of them concentrate on THEORY. Now, there's nothing wrong with designing a game theoretically, but when I am working on a game, with my sleeves rolled up and the blood is splattered on the walls, I find that I need practical nuts n' bolts advice and information about how to solve a problem. I hope you find the techniques and tips in the book useful in your day-to-day game design work.

A future video game designer. Hey, I'm talking to you! The programmer who knows they can do a better job designing your game's combat system. The artist who is tired of hearing the game designers yucking it up in the other cubicles. The tester who wants to move up in the company but doesn't quite know how. You're the person who dreams of being a videogame designer. And why not? It's an awesome job! Remember the story I just told about being a pixel pusher; the point of that story is that *I was just like you*. Someone who dreamed of a better life, a better career, who wanted something more fun to do for a living. When I wanted to become a videogame designer, there were no books on the subject, no classes, or degrees in video game design. I had to learn everything from my peers—provided they were willing to share their knowledge. I was lucky to have a mentor and an opportunity to work as a game designer. If you don't have either of those things, don't fret. *I will be your mentor.* All you need to do is read this book, follow my advice, and be prepared to take advantage of any opportunity when it finally arrives!

A students of game design. You're in luck. In addition to designing video games for 30 years, I've also taught game design at some of the best universities! I've spent a lot of time determining how best to help someone learn how to make games. Earlier editions of *Level Up! The Guide to Great Video Game Design* are used as textbooks in classrooms all over the world! You'll be learning all of these lessons in this book. It's like getting a game design degree without all the homework!

Finally, this book is for **anyone who loves video games**. I love video games. I love to play them. I love to make them. I love to read about making them. I love to talk about making them. I think they're the coolest thing in the world! If you want to make video games, then you must love them, too. Ironically, I've met people who work in video games but freely admit they do not like to play video games. This does not make any sense to me. Why would you work in video games if you do not love video games? Those people are fools. They should step aside and let someone who loves video games make video games.

Someone like you.

Level 1

Welcome N00bs!

OKAY, "N00BS" MIGHT not set the right tone. You might be new to gaming and want to learn how they are made; that's no reason to be insulting. You might have been making games for years, you might be in school to learn how games are being made, or you might have been making games all on your own. Forget that I called you a N00b.

But if you are new to gaming, then this chapter is for you. In it, I talk about what is a game, who makes them, and what kind of games there are. It's pretty basic stuff, so if you aren't a N00b, then feel free to skip this. However, you are going to be missing out on a lot of great stuff. Don't say I didn't warn you.

First off, let's address "*What is a Game*"?

Within the academic gaming community there are many different definitions for what qualifies as a game. Here's one from USC professor Tracy Fullerton: "a game is a closed, formal system that engages players in a structured conflict and resolves its uncertainty in an unequal outcome."

Here's another from designer Chris Crawford that states "a game needs to be a closed formal system that subjectively represents a subset of reality." Here's another from Roger Lewis that says that a game needs to have "players in conflict with each other."

Bernard Suits says, "a game is the voluntary attempt to overcome unnecessary obstacles." Author Jesse Schell calls them "a problem-solving activity, approached with a playful attitude." Designer Sid Meier writes "a game is a series of interesting decisions."

Let's consider bouncing a ball against a wall. You only need one player to play this, but does this activity qualify as a game? There're no other players to be in conflict with as in Roger Lewis' definition. Bouncing a ball against the wall is hardly Crawford's "subset of reality"— unless you lead a very boring life. Let's face it, bouncing a ball against a wall is just a ball bouncing against a wall. It's not a game, it's an activity.

Doing the activity of bouncing a ball might seem like a timewaster, but a timewaster can become a game when you add rules and an objective. A rule might be that you throw the ball with your right hand and catch it with your left. A rule might be that you can't drop the ball until you reach a predetermined number of wall-hits. A victory condition could be that you must catch the ball ten times in a row. A failure condition would be if you've violated any of those rules or objectives. You can even add a second player to try to keep the ball bouncing back and forth for as long as possible. These might be simple rules and objectives, but they were enough of a game to inspire William Higinbotham, the creator of one of the earliest video games: *Tennis for Two*.

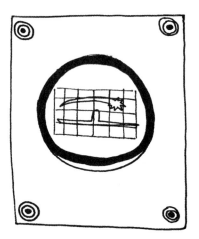

Tennis for Two

So, let's ask this basic question:

Q: What is a Game?

A: A Game is an activity that

- Has gameplay
- Has rules
- Has a win/lose condition

That's pretty much it.

If it doesn't have all of these, it is either an activity (like bouncing a ball), or a toy (like *The Sims 4* or the beta version of *Minecraft* (before Notch added the Ender level).

OK, you ask, "What is gameplay?" Gameplay is the interaction of the player with the game. This can also be between two or more players and the game. Gameplay is also dictated by the rules…but I'm getting ahead of myself; I'm so excited to tell you about this stuff!

Now that you know what a game is, you might ask:

Q: What is a video game?

A: A video game is a game played on a video screen.

Sure, you can start complicating the definition and add requirements about devices, peripherals, control schemes, player metrics, monetization, boss fights and zombies (there are always zombies). But by my reckoning, that is pretty much as simple as it gets.

Oh, there's one other thing to consider when discussing what is essential to a game. A game needs a clear **objective** so that the player knows what the goal of the game is! You should be able to sum up a game's objective quickly and clearly. If you can't, then you have a big problem.

Danny Bilson, the current head of USC's Interactive Media Department, has a great rule of thumb when it comes to a game's objective. He says that you should be able to sum up a game's objective as easily as an old Milton Bradley board game. These objectives are taken from the front of those old game boxes:

- *Battleship:* Sink all of your opponent's ships.
- *Operation:* Successful operations earn "Money." Failures set off alarms.
- *Knock Out:* Have more stoppers in the grid at the end of the game.
- *Mouse Trap:* Players turn crank A, which rotates gears B, causing lever C to move and push stop sign against shoe D. Shoe tips bucket holding metal ball E. Ball rolls down

rickety stairs F and into rain-pipe G, which leaps it to hit helping hand rod H. This causes bowling ball I to fall from top of helping hand rod through thing-a-ma-jig J and bathtub K to land on diving board L. Weight of bowling ball catapults diver M through the air and right into wash tub N causing cage O to fall from top of post P and trap unsuspecting mouse.

OK, let's just ignore that last one. The lesson is you need to keep your game objectives simple. Speaking of simple games, let's take a moment to travel back to the dawn of video games. They had to start somewhere, right?

A (Somewhat) Brief History of Video Games

Welcome to the 1950's. The dawn of television, 3D movies, Disneyland, and rock n' roll!

Didja know video games were invented in the 1950s, too? They were, but they were only played by very few people on very large computers. The first video game programmers were students in the computer labs of large universities like MIT or the employees of the military facility, the Brookhaven National Laboratory.

Early games like *Tennis for Two* (1958) and *Spacewar!* (1962) had very simple or even no graphics at all. These earliest games weren't even displayed on video screens as we know them today. Some used small black and white oscilloscope screens to play their games.

Some game genres are older than you think! The first multiplayer, first person shooter was *Maze* (also known as *Maze War*), which was programmed in 1973 by Steve Colley, Greg Thompson, and Howard Palmer at NASA's Ames Research Center. The adventure game genre started with 1976's *Colossal Cave Adventure* (also known as *Adventure*) and the first VR "game" was GE's simulator that was created to train aircraft pilots in 1973—15 years before the term virtual reality was coined!

After playing *Spacewar!* at the University of Utah's computer lab, future Atari founders Ted Dabney and Nolan Bushnell were inspired to create *Computer Space*, the first **commercial arcade game** in 1971. Atari followed up with *Pong* (1972), which was a huge smash hit. These first arcade games could be found in bars and gyms! Actual video game arcades dedicated to video games didn't start to appear until the late '70's.

Early arcade games were rendered using either **vector graphics** (images constructed from code-generated lines) that created bright, striking images like *Asteroids* (1979), *Battlezone* (1980) and *Tempest* (1981), or **raster graphics** (images created by artists using pixels) that allowed artists to create cartoon-inspired creatures and characters like *Space Invaders* (1978), *Pac-Man* (1980), and the cast of *Donkey Kong* (1981). These early characters became pop culture icons overnight, appearing on everything from t-shirts to bed sheets, Saturday morning cartoons to breakfast cereal.

Asteroids
(Vector Graphics)

Galaxian
(Raster Graphics)

During the early 1980s, video games were played in **arcades.** The arcades were filled with **arcade cabinets** that housed the individual games. There were three styles of arcade cabinets: **uprights** (cabinets the player stood in front of while playing), **cocktail tables** (arcade games set into the top of a small table, allowing the player to sit down while playing) and **cockpits** (elaborate cabinets designed to look like the cockpit of an airplane, race car or spaceship, which allowed the player to lean or sit in to further enhance the gaming experience).

Arcade Cabinet   Cocktail Table   Arcade Cockpit

In the mid-1980s, arcades began springing up everywhere, and video games took the world by storm! Game genres and themes became more imaginative and varied, while the game's controls became more complicated and realistic. The cabinets themselves became more artistic with beautiful graphics decorating their marquees and cabinet sides. You could sit back-to-back in a two-player spaceship cockpit while playing *Tailgunner* (1979), battle Klingons from a replica of Captain Kirk's command chair in *Star Trek* (1982) or "drive" a miniature Ferrari Testarossa that moved, tilted and shook in *Out Run* (1986).

The technology that played the games improved, too. Gameplay that originally kept to single screen, now **scrolled** in all directions. **Laser discs** allowed *Dragon's Lair* (1983) and *Space Ace* (1983) to display Disney-quality animation and games like *Berzerk* (1980) and *Gorf* (1981) "spoke" to the player using **synthesized speech**.

Into the 1990s, many arcade games evolved to resemble single-rider theme park attractions complete with gyroscopically moving virtual **simulators** (*R360*, 1990), rideable rubber rafts (*Rapid River*, 1996) and racehorses (*Final Furlong*, 1997) and fighting booths that allowed players to battle virtual foes using real punches and kicks (*Street Fighter II* on Holoplex's Combatica system, 1999).

The most elaborate of these arcades was Virtual World's BattleTech Center—steampunk themed lounges with linked "battle pods" that allowed eight players to fight each other while stomping around in giant virtual "mechs." The few remaining arcade game manufacturers strived to compete, creating epic gaming experiences like Namco's *Deadstorm Pirates* (2009), *Star Wars Battle Pod* (2014) and Raw Thrills' *Jurassic Park Arcade* (2015). These games are more like theme-park dark rides than arcade games. But these elaborate arcade systems required lots of floor space and were very expensive to maintain.

Home systems began to rival and then eventually surpass the graphics seen in most arcade games. Video games in arcades were replaced by more lucrative redemption machines and games of skill like Skee-Ball, Whack-A-Mole, and basketball hoops. The golden age of video game arcades is over.

But you can't keep a good idea down. In the late '90s, LAN gaming centers combined retail and social space to allow players to play on a computer and console on a per-hour basis. Some upgraded to feature large-scale gaming experiences held in movie theater-sized venues. Internet cafes cultivated a cafe-style environment.

Historians and academics have realized the impact and importance of video gaming. Museums have sprung up around the world, such as the Strong Museum of Play in upstate New York, the Computerspielemuseum in Berlin, Germany, and the Museum of Art and Digital Entertainment in Oakland, California.

In the mid-2010s, nostalgia for arcades resurged and "barcades" started to spring up, places where adult gamers could play classic arcade games and pinball while enjoying an adult beverage. Even "retro" arcades are making a comeback, complete with glo-in-the-dark carpet and token dispensers, offering players another chance to play their favorite vintage arcade and pinball games and revisit their favorite old-school home system games.

Speaking of home systems, a **console** is a gaming platform that can be used at home. A microprocessor runs the electronic device, which sends a video display signal to the user's TV set or monitor. Unlike the dedicated controllers of an arcade cabinet, a home console controller has enough buttons, triggers, and analog controls to allow for a variety of games to be played. These controllers can also be switched out for more specialized controllers such as light guns, steering wheels and even the controls of a giant mech. And unlike the dedicated motherboards of arcade games, which could only hold one game, console games used cartridges, CDs, and DVD media to allow players to quickly swap and play a variety of games.

The first commercial home console was the Magnavox Odyssey (1972) invented by gaming pioneer Ralph Baer. The games were programmed by Jerry Lawton, the first African American game developer. Technologically, the Odyssey was pretty far ahead of its time. It featured an analog controller, games that were on removable ROM cartridges and, thanks to a deal with Japanese game developer Nintendo, a light gun rifle—the first gaming peripheral.

From the late 1970s onward, there have been many home consoles. Some of the most popular and/or well-known consoles include the Atari 2600, the Mattel Intellivision, the ColecoVision, the Nintendo Entertainment System, The Super Nintendo Entertainment System, The Sega Genesis, The Sega Dreamcast, the PlayStations 1-5, The Atari Jaguar, the 3DO interactive player (one of the first CD game systems), the XBOX (and XBOX 360 and XBOX One), the Nintendo Wii, WiiU and Switch. Virtual Reality systems include the Oculus Rift and Quest 3, the PlayStation VR, and the Apple Vision Pro.

Atari 2600

Nintendo Entertainment
System (NES)

Playstation One (PSX)

Like arcade games, **handheld games** have a visual display, processor, and a controller but are small enough to fit in the hand or even the pocket of the player. The first handheld games were dedicated to only one game per unit. *Auto Race* (1980) used a digital display much like a calculator while the Game & Watch series (1980) features a more appealing liquid crystal display that allowed the game creators to have the player control cartoon characters Jumpman and Popeye. Microvision (1979) was one of the earliest handheld systems to have switchable cartridges.

Handheld gaming really took off when Tetris became a phenomenon on the Nintendo Game Boy (1989). Created by Gunpei Yokoi, the Game Boy became the form-factor for all of Nintendo's hardware for the next 30-plus years. Tiger Electronics dominated the handheld market for years with their licensed LED games based on Aladdin, Duke Nukem 3D, Goosebumps, Harry Potter, and Batman. The SEGA Nomad owners could play their existing library of Genesis games. The processor of the Sony PlayStation Portable (PSP) ran the equivalent of a PlayStation 1. Nintendo had another hit with the DS (dual screen) systems: the DS and 3DS. These systems featured innovative touchscreens, two screens and digitally downloaded content. This continued with the newest portable gaming systems such as the Playdate, which provides old-school fun with its novel crank controller while the Nintendo Switch provides state-of-the-art entertainment for players on the go.

Nintendo Game Boy

Sega Nomad

Playstation Portable (PSP)

The Brave New World of Gaming: Mobiles, Online Distribution and Touchscreens

Handheld gaming, especially on **mobile devices**, is the main way many people play games today. With the advent of digital-only content, you can carry an entire gaming library around in your pocket. Touchscreens have enabled the creation of new control systems and increased the popularity of genres such as strategy games, role-playing games, and **hyper-casual** puzzle games.

Mobile gaming has changed not only the way we play games but also the way they are made. By the 1990s and early 2000s, games required large teams and larger budgets to make. Thanks to greater access to inexpensive and even free tools, game developers can make games quicker and for less money than their console and computer counterparts. Mobile games are built around shorter play sessions and repeated play. This is similar to how arcade games were in the earliest days of the industry. As they say, everything old is new again.

Another impact to gaming is the advent of **digital distribution**. Originally used to sell add-ons and expansions, now entire games can be purchased and downloaded at any time of the day or night via the internet. Gamers are able to **stream** content whenever they want, resulting in a severe reduction in the demand for physical media. In the past, the size of the game was limited because of the media, now games can be as large as the player's hard drive can hold. Game developers can have their mistakes and imperfections **"patched"** with a simple download. Season passes and micro-transactions can generate revenue for the developer and publisher, giving them more ways to earn money. It's fair to say that modern mobile gaming and **downloadable content** has forever changed the way we game and make games.

As of this writing, there are still a few publishers who sell games on disc and cartridges like Sony, Nintendo and boutique companies like Limited Release, but most gamers get their games from digital stores such as Steam, the PlayStation Store, Nintendo eShop and the Microsoft Store. Of course, digital distribution has caused retailers and publishers to react with incentives—sweetening the deal with physical goods such as collectibles and exclusive digital content.

As **personal computers** (or **PCs**) became accessible and affordable in the late 1970s, both video game programming and video game playing became more common. An entire generation of game developers started off in their bedrooms and garages, programming games on their PC's. Those early games were stored on cassette tapes used in tape drives. Later, floppy discs replaced tape drives. The young game devs would seal their game discs and tapes in Ziplock bags and sell them at their local computer store. Some of the biggest names in early gaming like Jordan Mechner, Warren Spector, Noah Falstein and Lord British got their start this way.

While early video game consoles were emulating games from the arcades with varying degrees of success, those computer game developers of the 1970s and 1980s took advantage of what computers like the Atari VCS, Apple II, and ZX Spectrum had to offer—more memory, text, and most importantly, keyboards. The keyboard allowed greater user input and created unique-to-the-computer genres including the **text adventure game** like 1976's *Colossal Cave Adventure*.

Since computer gamers could spend more time gaming (and would be more comfortable sitting down while playing!), computer games necessitated a different gaming experience. Story-based adventure games, strategy games, and construction and management games provided longer play experiences than their arcade counterparts…and gave players more perceived value for their money. I distinctly remember determining how much play time I was getting for my money back in the early 1980s. Let's see, an average arcade game costs a quarter for a few minutes of play while *Temple of Apshai* for the Commodore 64 costs $39.95 and takes several hours to explore its 200 rooms. Hmmm. Which one is the better bargain?

As the computer hardware, memory, graphics processors and storage increased, computer games became even more visually detailed, featured more involved designs and unique gaming controllers were created to play them. The rise of the **first-person shooter** (**FPS**) can be attributed to the popularity of the **mouse controller**. By the mid-1990s, the computer was the ultimate gaming platform, thanks to leaps in technology including CD ROM and DVD media. Several gaming genres, particularly strategy, FPS, and **massively multiplayer online** games (or **MMOs**) emerged and have remained very strong on the computer platform.

Computers also became host to virtual reality systems such as the Oculus Rift and Oculus Quest, creating new ways for players to put themselves into the game. Digital distribution is even more common on computer systems, with gamers having access to (as of this writing) 73 thousand games on the Steam platform alone! Where will computer gaming go in the future? If I knew that, I'd be rich!

What's the Difference Between AAA and Indy?

A lot of my students ask me "what's the difference between AAA games and independent (indie) games? Currently, there are actually three different classifications of games: AAA games, AA games and indie games. So, what is the difference?

AAA games are created by large studios with hundreds or thousands of employees. Their budgets are exceeding tens or even hundreds of millions of dollars to pay for top-of-the-line graphics, and voice actors. They are the "blockbusters" of the game industry—cinematic cutscenes, gorgeous visuals, often based on well-known IP like *Mario*, *Legend of Zelda*, *Grand Theft Auto*, *Call of Duty*, or the *Batman Arkham* games. Or, they are franchised sports games like *Madden* and *FIFA*. They are tried-and-true genres, predictable and often have slight variations on a theme. They get global distribution, physical and digital releases and extensive marketing before and during their release, which generates significant hype for the game.

AA games are titles created by medium sized teams. They have modest budgets compared to AAA games—usually in the tens or hundreds of thousands of dollars, but sometimes in the low millions. They have more varied genres—RTS, RPG, simulations, action-adventure—and they often are original IP. They might get a physical release, but more often they are digitally distributed.

Indie games are made by a small but passionate team. They have a limited budget, often relying on crowdfunding or other methods to raise funds. They can be any genre—indies have complete creative freedom to make any type of game that looks and plays however they want. They are mostly released through streaming services such as Twitch and Switch, and on mobile. They have no marketing budget, so they rely on reviews and word-of-mouth for publicity.

Commodore 64 (C64)   Macintosh Plus   Personal Computer (PC)

Game Genres

The term **genre** is used to describe a category of something—often the categories used to describe books, movies, or music. For example, music can be rock and roll, gospel, or country. Movies can be action, romance, or comedies. Books can be drama, biographies, or horror; you get the idea.

Video games are classified into genres, too, but here's where it gets a little tricky. Games actually have two types of genres: **story genre** and **game genre**. *Story genre* describes the type of story, theme or narrative: fantasy, historical, sports, horror, etc. *Game genre* describes the type of *gameplay*: First person shooter, MOBA, match three, simulator, etc. Simple enough, right? We will talk about story genre later, but for now let's look at some of the different types of game genres:

- **Action:** Games that rely on hand/eye coordination and player skill. There are lots of stylistic variations, making it one of the most diverse genres. Some of the earliest arcade games are action games.

- **Adventure:** Games that focus on characters (like in a role-playing game) but often don't have the characters evolve in skill or ability. This genre is about story and lore, inventory management and often puzzle solving.

- **Augmented Reality (AR):** Games that incorporate peripheral devices like cameras and global positioning systems (GPS) into gameplay. They create a "layer of unreality" over the real world for the player to interact with.

- **Auto Battler:** A game where the player constructs a "build" of cards, characters, etc., which are then tested against an adversary. Players merely observe the interaction to see how well their build did.

- **Card Battler:** Digital version of analog card game where the game automates several aspects of the setup and maintenance for the player. Often there are other elements such as music and effects to enhance the play experience.

- **Educational:** A game with the primary intention is to educate while entertaining. These games are often aimed at a younger audience.

- **MOBA** (Multiplayer Online Battle Arena): A strategy game where two players (or teams of players) compete on a single battlefield. Players control characters while being supported by "creeps," lesser strength helpers controlled by the computer.

- **MMO** (Massively Multiplayer Online): Games that are primarily role-playing games that support many players at once. The gameplay often centers around character progression, quests, and "grinding," doing several menial tasks over and over again for points or money.

- **Party:** A game specifically designed for several players who compete in a variety of styles of gameplay: from quizzes to games of skill.

- **Platformer:** Games where the player controls a character (often a publisher's "mascot") who runs and jumps their way across a series of hazardous landscapes to reach the other side of the playfield. This game genre is often viewed in a side-view perspective. A **Metroidvania** is a platformer subgenre that focuses on non-linear progression and exploration.

- **Puzzle:** Games based on logic, observation, and pattern completion. Sometimes they are slow and methodical, other times they require quick hand/eye coordination like an action game.

- **Real Time Strategy:** A strategy game where the action takes place in real-time. Players must quickly respond to the action on screen or suffer the consequences.

- **Rhythm:** A game where the player must use a controller (or their body) to match a rhythm or beat to score points.

- **Rogue-Like:** Named after the 1980 computer game, a rogue-like is a role playing game (RPG) that takes place in a procedurally generated dungeon, often has grid or turn-based gameplay and the players suffer permanent death upon the loss of their character.

- **Serious:** At first glance, serious games seem similar to educational games but with a focus on social issues. But the genre is more diverse than that! Serious games are used to provide job training, advertise products or even to just exist as art!

- **Shooter:** Games that focus primarily on firing projectiles at other players or enemies. There are sub-genres such as SHUMPs (a contraction of "shoot 'em up") and "Bullet Hells." It's still one of the most popular genres (at least here in the West).

- **Simulation:** Games that focus on creating and managing a world. Or a theme park. Or a farm. Or the life of an adorable monster or a princess. Many simulations cross over into the realm of **"toy games"**—games that provide tools for creativity but have no rules or win/lose conditions.

- **Sports:** Games based on athletic competitions—from traditional sports to extreme ones. Like action games, there are many stylistic forms with this genre ranging from ultra-realistic simulations to fantasy variants. There is a subgenre of **Sports Management** games where you play as the sports team owner rather than the players.

- **Strategy:** Thinking, planning and executing are the hallmarks of strategy games. This is one of the oldest genres of games: strategy games' roots are in **ancient games** like Senet, Mancala, Chess and Go.

- **Survival Horror:** Players of this genre are generally helpless against a supernatural threat. Jump scares, stealth, inventory management, and puzzle solving are key components to this genre.

- **Turn-Based:** Where the players take turns between actions. The pace of a turn-based game is slower and allows the player time to think and strategize.

- **Traditional:** These are games based on (but not always) games that existed in other, often physical, formats. Card games, board games and casino games fall into this genre.

- **Vehicle simulation:** Games where players simulate piloting or driving a vehicle, from a race car to a star fighter. There are a variety of stylistic and control options for the player, which can result in a fast-paced arcade-style experience or a slow-paced realistic simulation.

- **Virtual Reality:** Games where players use headsets and special controllers to see and navigate an all-encompassing virtual environment. Many genres of games fit within this genre, but there are special rules and control considerations that need to be made for this genre...as we shall see.

This list is just the tip of the iceberg! In addition to the genres on this list, there are all types of subgenres and **hybrid games**. New genres are constantly being created. For example, 2015's *Crypt of the Necrodancer* combines a rogue-like dungeon crawler with a rhythm game where players can only move or attack to the beat of the music! What's next? What will be the most popular game genre in the future? Who knows? Perhaps you will create it!

Who Makes This Stuff?

Just as there are many genres of games, there are many types of people who make them. Video game creators are known as **developers** or **development teams**. They are similar to a production team that creates a film or a television show—several creative people who are responsible for different parts of the game, all working together to create entertainment.

In the earliest days of video game development, games were created almost solely by individuals—primarily programmers. For example, the original *Prince of Persia* (1989) was created primarily by Jordan Mechner, who programmed, designed, and animated the entire game. He even composed the game's music!

However, not everyone was as talented. As computer's and console's graphic capabilities improved, game creators realized that better looking games sold well and had to keep up. These programmers teamed up with digital artists who could create beautiful art and animation for their games.

Video games were initially designed by whichever team member had the best idea for a game. When game content became too involved for the programmers and artists to deal with, a dedicated design position was created to make the gameplay. Both Mario creator Shiguru Miyamoto and I started as artists who moved into the field of game design. Although team members can wear many different hats, specialization is commonplace on larger production teams.

Nowadays, only the biggest AAA games have large development teams. I'm talking about hundreds of employees—if not more. On the other hand, currently, most game development is being done by smaller indie developer teams. The initial versions of *Minecraft* (2009), *Undertale* (2015), *Stardew Valley* (2016) were each created by one person! Creative teams are no longer reliant on huge budgets and publishing organizations to make and sell games. The power is back in the hands of the developers!

Let's take a look at who makes up a development team.

Programmer

A programmer must be proficient in coding with languages such as C++, Lua, Java, Objective C, and others, depending on the project and the target platform. They create the code that draws the game's graphics and on-screen text. They develop control systems that allow the player to interact with the game. They code the camera systems that allow the player to see the game world. They program physics that affects the player and objects in the world. They write the artificial intelligence (AI) that controls the enemies. They write the scripting to allow designers to manipulate objects in the world...and much, much more!

One programmer may work exclusively on **tools** to help the team members build the game more efficiently. Another programmer may write code to simulate real-world physics to make water act and look realistic. A third could be developing **inverse kinematics** to make a character move and react realistically. Yet another may be working solely on the sound tools needed to play music and effects in the game. Programmers could be working on graphics, or **backend systems** like networking. There are plenty of tasks required to make a game, which is why programmers are usually in such high demand.

Regardless of the position, a programmer needs to have an excellent understanding of mathematics, creating 2D and 3D graphics, know how to code physics, particle systems, user interface displays, artificial intelligence, input devices and computer networking. Programmers can make a good living as contractors, moving from project to project as "hired guns," writing code and providing solutions to beleaguered development teams.

Artist

In the early days of video games, programmers created all of the game art. Because much of that early art was crude, developers will sometimes call placeholder art "programmer art." Thank goodness trained artists came along. One of the first artists working in video games was Shigeru Miyamoto, who created Mario, Donkey Kong and Link He was able to create these memorable characters on an 8-bit CPU using only 2-bit pixels—that means background elements have four colors and sprites only have three. That's a lot of personality per pixel!

There were a few exceptions in the early days, such as *Dragon's Lair* (1983) and *Space Ace* (1983), beautifully animated games created by a team lead by ex-Disney animator Don Bluth. Those games were a rare exception because they needed to be run on laser discs, expensive technology in the early 1980s. Eventually, new, and better hardware with more memory, color depth and the ability to display larger resolution graphics meant that artists could create more detailed characters, images, and backgrounds.

As high-end computer software like Maya and Softimage became more affordable to developers, 3D graphics, which had been limited to the movies like *Tron* (1982) and *Toy Story* (1995) began appearing in games thanks to a deal between graphics tool creator Silicon Graphics and game publisher Nintendo. Eventually other developers followed suit, pushing the limits of what a game could look like.

True 3D graphics have been in video games for a long time, ever since the 1980 arcade game *Battlezone*. The move to bring 3D into homes started on the 3DO game system with games *Crash and Burn* (1993) and *Total Eclipse* (1993). *Wolfenstein 3D* (1993) and *Doom* (1993) allowed players to navigate in 3D space, while *Myst* (1993) and *Donkey Kong Country* (1994) used pre-rendered graphics. The success of these games meant that 3D was here to stay.

At some development studios, art has become a specialized job. A **concept artist** draws what the game characters, environments and enemies look like. These images are translated by **modelers** who create the 3D models of the characters and environments in a computer. **Texture artists** "paint" these models with 2D textures. **Riggers** make it possible for the character models to be moved by **animators**. Visual effects artists create spectacular visual effects using a combination of 2D and 3D art. **User interface (UI) artists** design the icons and elements that communicate important information to the player. **Storyboard artists** illustrate the game's cinematics and cutscenes and sometimes elements of the gameplay to be passed on to programmers, artists and animators to work from. **Technical artists** help every artist on the team by doing a variety of tasks or sometimes creating tools to help the artist work better. The **art director** supervises all of the work created for the game to make sure it is consistent with the artistic vision of the entire project. Regardless of what kind of art position you are interested in, make sure you study the basics (anatomy, perspective, color theory) and keep drawing!

Designer

Designer, planner, lead designer, senior designer, principal designer—no matter what the job title is, a designer's role is the same: create the ideas and rules that comprise a game. A game designer needs to possess many skills and must love to play games. As a game designer, you should be able to tell the difference between a good and bad game and, more importantly, communicate why. "Because it sucks" is *never* an acceptable answer.

Within the title of designer, there are many subtitles depending on the task the designer does. **Level designers** create environments that players will navigate. They can start in a variety of ways: paper maps, "gray box" environments; I knew a game designer who would sculpt levels in clay, and designer Hideo Kojima would build his environments out of Legos. We'll talk more about the term "level" later, but it doesn't just refer to 3D environments; it can be the environments of an adventure game or a physics-based puzzle game. **System designers** develop how the game's elements relate to one another, whether it is the game's economic system or a technology tree. They design the pace of player progression and balance the availability and usefulness of in-game items, ensuring meaningful player choices. **Combat system designers** focus solely on the attacks and interactions of a game's main character and its enemies. They "balance" the player's controls and interactions to create the optimal exciting gameplay. A **UI designer** creates the visual layout and functionality of menus, pause screens, as well as the HUD (heads up display) of the main game screen with the intention of clearly communicating the players' options and abilities. The **creative director** maintains the game's vision while supervising the other designers, often offering suggestions for improving their work.

There is one other task that a designer is responsible for: ensuring that the game is "fun." However, I will leave this can of worms unopened until later in the book. I hope you can stand the suspense!

Producer

Overseeing the entire game's development is the **producer**. Originally, producers were members of the development team who also managed the work of their team members. They had the authority to make all final decisions, including creative ones. A producer's role on a game has expanded dramatically over the years, in some cases requiring several producer roles on one game. In this case, an **executive producer** is required to oversee the overseers!

A producer's responsibilities include hiring and building the development team, writing contracts, contributing to the game's design, managing the team's work schedule, maintaining good work/life balance, balancing the game's budget, resolving disputes between creative and programming leads, acting as the team representative to upper management and publishers, coordinating the creation of outside resources including art, music and cinematics and arranging testing and localization! It's a lot of responsibility to be a producer!

Producers are usually the first team in a game and the last one off the game's production. More often than not, you will find a producer acting as the public face of the game, talking to the press and public about the game.

Because a producer has so many things to do, often you will find **assistant producers** and **associate producers** helping with the day-to-day tasks. Sometimes, the tasks may seem "trivial" such as ordering dinner for a team that is working late or creating team t-shirts to help create a sense of comradery on the team. Believe it or not, some of those "menial" chores are some of the most important that a producer can provide to a team.

Regardless of how helpful producers can be, some studios consider producers an unnecessary part of development. Others feel that producers should not have any creative control, but just manage the game's production and schedule. As with designers the role and influence of the position of producer varies wildly across the industry.

Tester

Do you like to play games? Do you like to play games over and over and over? Do you like to play the same level over and over and over and over and over and over and over and over and over and over and over again? Then testing is for you!

While **testers** work long hours and have to play to a degree that some would classify as mind-numbingly boring; being a tester requires more skills than this description might imply. Good testers have patience, persistence, and great communication skills to report any problems (also known as **bugs**) that they find in a **build** of a game. It's not a glamorous job, but without testers games would be far more "broken." We'd be plagued with games that crash upon loading, have crappy camera systems or unplayable controls and unfair balance. Let's take a moment to thank the testers of video games.

Quality assurance (or **QA**) is crucial to the successful completion of a game. Publishers hold games to a rigorous quality standard so the game that you buy is (mostly) free of bugs and problems. The standard can be met only by thoroughly testing a game for weeks, if not months. Only after it has passed muster with a QA department, can it be offered for submission or certification with a publisher. Then after the submitted version of the game is approved, it is truly ready to be released to the public. Sometimes, several submissions are needed before a game is ready for release. No one wants to release a buggy game!

Being a tester is a great gateway job for newcomers to the game industry. I have seen testers go on to be great designers, artists, producers and even the heads of studios! You can find out a lot about games in a short time by working first as a tester.

Composer

In the earliest days of video games, game music was nothing more than crude bleeps and bloops to accompany the game's action. Very quickly, technology evolved to allow, for example, audio engineer Yukio Kaneoka to create the memorable tunes of *Donkey Kong* (1981) and *Mario Bros.* (1983).

Music is extremely important to the gaming experience, and it is a **composer** who creates that music. Game music is created digitally and is integrated into the game either by the composer or the programmer. To be a composer, you need a keyboard, microphones, maybe instruments and, of course, you should know how to play them! You'll need software to create the music; Pro Tools is a popular option. Another useful tool is a sound library that contains a good mix of orchestral and synthesized instruments.

As the sound technology has improved in games, many composers have created "live" and orchestral pieces for games; this requires a whole new set of skills, including conducting an orchestra. It's not just waving a baton around!

For you amateur composers, home versions of modern audio software are powerful enough to mix and master professional sounding samples. If you want to become a composer, you should write some music, record it, and then get it into the hands of a game producer. Or, you could present it on YouTube, TikTok, or some other social media platform for game creators to see.

As someone who has reviewed lots of composer's audio portfolios, I can tell you that the designer has a specific idea for the style or feel of the type of music in their mind. If your music sample matches what the designer wants, they will contact you for the job. What matters most is that your music style is unique and diverse so it will be appealing to game developers and fit a variety of game genres.

Oh, one more note, writing music for games is somewhat different than writing music for movies. Most game themes are either very short or have to repeat over and over again. Being able to compose powerful and exciting music with these limitations in mind will make your music more appealing than someone who just composes "songs." I will cover more about music in a future chapter.

Sound Designer

Unlike the composer who creates music for a game, the **sound designer** creates all of the sound effects (and sometimes the voices) that are used in the game. Go ahead and fire up a game, turn off the sound and try playing it. Do you notice that the game just isn't the same without sound effects? A lot of information is delivered to the player via sound. These audio cues are the sound designer's responsibility to create.

Personally, I think creating sounds is a lot of fun. I've done it for several games I've worked on. Games come to life when sound is added to them. That's why it is important to have placeholder sound effects even when creating your game. Sound design requires a lot of creativity. Mixing and blending sounds to create something no one has ever heard before is pretty cool. However, a good sound designer needs to understand the game they are working on and how to create sounds that help the player.

Some sound effects need to sound "positive" to encourage players that they are doing something correct or have collected something valuable. Other sounds warn the player of danger or that they are about to make a bad move. A sound designer can make a sound effect sound happy, deadly, scary, or valuable—and sometimes all of the above!

If you want to be a sound designer, you need to know how to take direction from game developers who may or may not know what they want, or they have unreasonable or ridiculous requests. For example, they might ask for a "creature that sounds like a phlegmy cougar from hell but make it sound more shriek-y than growly." If you can create that, then congratulations, you are on your way to becoming a video game sound designer!

Narrative Designer/Writer

Unlike in Hollywood where **writers** come up with the initial idea for a movie with a screenplay, in video games, writers are often hired late into the process, which I feel is a mistake. Getting a writer on-board as early as possible just makes sense to me.

A writer or narrative designer does more than just write the story and lore. They need to understand how games work and how games are made in order to contribute to the team. Too often I have seen writers (including big-name ones) who have no idea how to write for games. It's a very different beast than writing for movies or comic books, and not everyone can do it.

Writing for games requires the writer to not just write dialogue, but variations of that dialogue so the player doesn't read or hear the same dialogue over and over again. They need to write **"barks"**—short vocal snippets for when the player completes a task, interacts with an object, responds to a situation in the game or gets injured during battle. Writing a dozen variations of "aarrgh!" is a fun challenge.

They need to write for a variety of forms of communication—a hastily written note is very different from a correspondence letter for example—and they need to be able to write in many different "voices" so that each character sounds unique. In this era of story-driven games, a lot of content needs to be created by the writer, depending on the game. Some games have scripts that run as long as hundreds of pages!

I have encountered many people who want to get into the game industry, and when I ask them what they want to do, they tell me they want to be a narrative designer. They want to write a story! They want to write lore! What I tell them is, if you want to write a narrative, you really need to have a different position on the team—most likely as a game designer or a tester. Any job to get your foot in the door, and when the opportunity comes to write something, you take it.

You see, the need for a writer on a game isn't very consistent. A writer is often brought in late in the process to write a script or to fix or "punch up" what some other team member wrote. This means that you won't be working the entire life cycle of the game's development. This is why many writers are freelance contractors rather than employees of a game company. We'll talk more about all of this and much more in Level 3.

Well, now you know all the different employment opportunities in the video game industry, right? Wrong! People don't generally think of this, but there is an entire second career path in video game publishing.

Community Manager

A community manager is a position that you often find at game studios that make MMOs or other games with large player counts. They interact with the public to find out what they like and don't like about the game. They often help create events with the game designers for the players to experience in the world. They help settle problems that happen within the game world. They are the wielders of the all-mighty ban-hammer! So, stay on their good side!

Have You Thought About Publishing?

Publishers provide the funding for game development teams, manage the game's production, handle any legal issues (like securing IP rights or writing contracts), manufacture physical media, provide promotions at trade shows and handle public relations and marketing for the game. They even distribute the finished game via streaming or at brick-and-mortar stores. The following sections describe some of the more common positions found at a game publisher.

Product Manager

Much like game producers, **product managers** work with the development team and manage them based upon an agreed production schedule. They help determine production priorities, act as an intermediary between the studio and the publisher, manage contracts and other issues from the publisher's legal department, review and approve milestones, and make payments to the studio. They talk to licensors to ensure that they approve of how the game is turning out. They work with the ESRB to secure a rating for the game. Needless to say, they're pretty busy people.

Creative Manager

When people ask me what I did as a **creative manager** at THQ, I tell them "I had the job that people think of when they think of someone working in video games." Working as a creative manager wasn't just "thinking up games and playing games all day," but sometimes it was.

Creative managers are usually game designers who, after being worn down by the long hours of game development, seek more stable employment with publishers. I kid. I kid. Like a product manager's involvement with a game developer, a creative manager's involvement on the game can vary from developer to developer. In some cases, I flew to the developer (usually in another country) and helped them design their game from the ground up while I just left others to their own devices; played their builds and gave them occasional feedback. Mostly, my job was to do this...give a developer feedback, keep them true to the game's core idea, and make sure that their game was "fun" (there's that word again!)

The best benefit that a creative manager can provide is what I call the **"thousand-foot view"** (as if I were looking down on the game from a thousand feet in the air, not looking at thousands of feet!)—an unbiased viewpoint on a game that can help root out weaknesses in the game design and execution. When games aren't "solid," it was my job to provide the team clear feedback on how the gameplay can be improved or to give advice on how the team can explore another creative direction.

Creative managers may also work with the marketing or public relations teams to provide marketing or press materials to make sure the game is shown in the very best light. Often, it was me playing those games that you saw videos of online or on giant monitors at E3. I won't tell you how many times I wrote what was on the backs of game boxes while I was at THQ!

Art Director

An **art director** is similar to a creative manager but deals only with the game's art. Art directors can help a team create a visual style for the game and take it in directions that the team hadn't previously considered. An art director can even create examples to help the team understand what a licensor or publisher wants. Art directors often also work with the marketing teams to create packaging materials (such as the cover of a game's case) or wrangle or create assets like screenshots and concept art that is used to publicize the game.

Technical Director

Technical directors come from a programming background. They review and recommend tools and software to game development teams to help them create their games more efficiently or to solve a problem they were wrestling with. They provide technical support and advice when there are deficiencies in the team's programming staff. They also perform **due diligence** on a new team to help assess whether they can make the game they are being hired to make.

Marketing Team

The marketing team promotes the game to the world. They work with magazines (the few that are left), websites, YouTubers, and other influencers to promote the game. They help design packaging materials (when applicable) and write copies for the back of the box—when they aren't having the creative manager doing it for them. They work with advertising firms to create promotional material or even create stunts and events for trade shows. Those t-shirts have to come from somewhere!

When working with a marketing team, make sure that someone on the team plays your game (sadly, I've found that many marketing teams don't play your game! It happens more often than you'd think). They need to understand what's great about your game so they can market and sell it in the best way.

And the Rest...

Other publishing positions aren't directly involved in making games but are important in creating and selling a game, nonetheless. **Business development** staff build relationships with studios, hold game pitch meetings, and review prospective game demos. They make deals with external studios and find emerging studios to acquire or partner up with. If you ever own your own game development studio, you will eventually meet a lot of business developers. A **lawyer** negotiates all the contracts and makes sure the production team isn't creating content that will get the publisher into any legal trouble, such as copyright infringement.

A **brand manager** creates a marketing strategy to promote and advertise a game. This person works with internal or external marketing teams to develop print materials such as case covers, billboards or magazine materials. A **public relations manager** talks to influencers and the public and organizes press events to show off the game in the best light. A **quality assurance manager** runs the **game testing department** (also known as the QA department) organizing play sessions and relaying bugs back to the developer.

In addition to production and publishing staff, many others interact with development teams and publishers. A **talent recruiter** searches for new (and old!) talent and helps them get employment. **Game reviewers** and **influencers** play games before they come out and create videos and other content for gamers to read and watch, helping form an opinion of the game and building hype before it comes out. **Licensors** work for major entertainment companies and make sure their brands are properly represented in the games based on their IP.

As you can see, there are plenty of options if you want a career in games. But, I say forget all of those other jobs. You want to find out how to make great game designs, right? Trust me, game design is where the real fun is!

But to make great games, you need great ideas. Where do you get them? Let's find out!

Level 1's Universal Truths and Clever Ideas

- A game has rules, gameplay, and a win/lose condition.
- Your game objective should be simple.
- Game genres come in all shapes and sizes. Don't be afraid to mix and match.
- Gaming technology is always evolving. Adapt or get left behind.
- It takes all kinds of people with all kinds of skills to make video games.

Level 2
Ideas

LET'S TALK ABOUT making video games. To most people, how to make a video game is a complete mystery. The average party conversation goes something like this:

So, you program video games? Is it hard to write all of that code?

No, I said I *design* games.

Oh, so you draw the characters? That must be fun.

No, I don't draw them. That's what an artist does.

I don't get it. If you don't code the games or draw the games what *do* you do?

Apparently nothing.

At this point in the conversation, I tell the person that games are made by elves. (Sometimes it's just easier to tell someone a fantasy answer than explain what I do for a living.) However, a question people ask that *is* easier to answer is: "Where do your **ideas** for games come from?"

Ideas: Where to Get Them and Where to Stick Them

Every good idea borders on the stupid
   - Michel Gondry

I like this quote because many game ideas often sound stupid. Try these on for size:

- A plumber jumps on the heads of mushrooms as he looks for his girlfriend.

- A prince rebuilds stars by rolling balls of junk into bigger balls of junk.

- The player moves candy around to create matching lines of candy that destroys the candy.

All those stupid-sounding ideas ended up being games that made lots and lots of money. Flappy Bird was making around $50,000 a day before the developer took it down. I guess stupid sounding ideas don't end up being so stupid. To me, the lesson is, never dismiss a game idea, even if it does sound stupid.

So, where do I get my own stupid ideas to turn into video games? They[1] often say you just have to wait for inspiration to hit. But as they say, "inspiration is for amateurs." We want to be professional game designers, which means we need to come up with good ideas at the drop of a hat, anytime, anywhere. The good news is that a good game idea can come from anywhere. Here's a list of things I do to get those creative juices flowing. I suggest you try them yourself the next time you need to come up with an idea.

- **Cram your head.** I find the process of creation goes something like this: watch/read/listen to a lot of stuff. Consume as much as you can. Then, let all those images, stories, sounds, ideas and thoughts percolate in your head. Apply your own perspective on life to them. New ideas will form. Make sure you have a pencil and paper (or a voice recorder) to catch those ideas when they pop up.

- **Read something you normally wouldn't read.** Don't just cram your head with the same old stuff. For example, I once attended a roundtable discussion with the famous game designer Will Wright. He was asked where he got his inspiration from. Mr. Wright said that he got his inspiration for his games from Japanese gardening, architectural design, and biology. I replied that all those things were great to be inspired by, but what about "normal nerds like me" who are into comic books, sci-fi movies, television shows, and video games? But I realized that I knew the answer to my question even as I asked it.

  One of the reasons why so many video games feel the same is that many game developers love the same stuff. There's nothing wrong with liking movies, comic books and video games; however, when developers only get their ideas from them, the games start to feel the same.

  What can you do? Take the time to expand your educational horizon, even just a little. You don't have to get a degree in the subject, just take some time to search for a new topic on the internet or spend an afternoon researching at the library. I find that research can be one of the most fun parts of creating something new! In other words, stop reading the same old crap and learn something new!

- **Take a walk, drive or take a shower.** Sometimes our brain is our worst enemy. We tend to overthink our ideas and second-guess ourselves. But when the active part of

---

[1] Who are these "they" and why do they have so many opinions?

your brain is being occupied by a familiar activity like walking or driving, your subconscious is free to start wandering, making connections it would normally never make. These connections sometimes lead to great ideas. Besides, many game developers could stand to take an occasional shower. Please make sure that if you do come up with a great idea while driving, pull over to the side of the road before you start writing it down!

- **Attend a lecture.** I love the Game Developers Conference (GDC) because I get so inspired by the lectures and discussions. Even the conversations in the hallways are fantastic. After the show, I often end up with a notebook full of ideas. You don't have to attend a big event like GDC, but you can check in with your local community groups to see if there are game designer events in your area.[2]

Or, join a group on a social media site such as Discord and talk to other designers there. Make sure you share your ideas with them; don't be afraid of anyone stealing your idea. It's always good to test the strength of your idea to find out where an idea bends and where it breaks. Just be prepared to be told that your ideas might be stupid.

- **Play a game, preferably a bad one.** Playing a good video game can be beneficial, but I find it more educational to play a bad game. As you play a bad game, look at all of the things done poorly. Then think about what you would do to improve them. Consider how many people "invented" the airplane before the Wright Brothers built and flew their plane. Sometimes it takes several iterations on an idea before it works successfully.

- **Play a different game.** Your mom was right when she told you not to play video games all day, so why not change it up and play a tabletop game instead? Many video games have been inspired by board and card games. The first adventure game *Colossal Cave Adventures* was inspired by the game *Dungeons & Dragons*. *Sid Meir's Civilization* was inspired by Avalon Hill's *Civilization* board game. *Among Us* is just a reinterpretation of the party game *Mafia*.

Not into board games? How about Tag, Capture the Flag or Cops and Robbers? They might inspire you to create the next *Pac-Man*, *Team Fortress*, or *Grand Theft Auto*.

- **Follow your passions.** Satoshi Tajiri's love for collecting insects led to him inventing *Pokemon* (1996). David Jaffe turned his love for Ray Harryhausen action movies into *God of War* (2005). Follow your passion and make them a part of your game. If you really love something, that love will shine through in your work. If you follow your passions, designing your game won't even feel like work.

---

[2] I attend a developer meet-up lunch every month in Culver City. It's a great opportunity to socialize with game industry professionals of all experience levels.

It's one thing to have a good idea, it's another to have a *marketable* one. During the course of my career, I have been told many times (usually by my colleagues in the marketing department) that my game idea was a "designer's idea," which means they think my idea is one that I (a game designer) would love to play, but the game wouldn't be marketable to the general public.

Personally, I am torn about this assessment.[3] On the one hand, I can understand the desire to make a game that will sell. If your game sells, that means you can make more games.

On the other hand, before I am ready to give in to the opinion of "the suits," I am reminded of all the innovative games that have been created over the years. I am sure that at one point, those game designers were told by someone that their ideas were too weird, too unmarketable, too stupid. If that were the case, innovative games like *PUBG*, *Dota Auto Chess*, *Inscryption* or *Balatro* would never have been made.

Getting Ahead of the Game

If you think something is innovative, it just means you haven't been paying enough attention.
- Scott Rogers

Although I am sure there are still completely original ideas out there in the galaxy of ideas, the majority of gameplay design works by each game building on its predecessors. I truly believe this strategy is one of the keys to creating great game design. Even games like the aforementioned *PUBG*, *Dota Auto Chess*, *Inscryption* and *Balatro* had their predecessors in *Call of Duty* multiplayer, *Pokemon Defense*, *Magic the Gathering* and *Poker*.

Here's another secret. My idea isn't even original. Designer Raph Koster charts the evolution of the shoot 'em up genre in his book *A Theory of Fun for Game Design* (Paraglyph, 2004). Taking Raph's chart as inspiration, I will show you the evolution of gameplay design within the platformer game genre.

- *Space Panic's* (1980) walking character climbed ladders and dug holes to temporarily stun enemies.

- *Donkey Kong* (1981) adding jumping and a power-up that could defeat enemies.

- *Popeye* (1982) introduced moving health collectibles and environmental mechanics that the player could interact with.

---

[3] In retrospect, that statement was a pretty dismissive thing to say from a person who didn't really play games!

- *Pitfall!* (1982) added alternate movement including vine swinging and hopping on alligator's heads.

- *Mario Bros.* (1983) added a second player and enemies that could be defeated by player skill rather than just a power-up.

- *Pac-Land* (1984) featured a world map, a variety of themed levels and dynamic hazards.

- *Ghosts N' Goblins* (1985) features multiple weapons, including projectiles. It also has health (in the form of armor that shatters off), and "boss" monsters.

- *Super Mario Bros.* (1985) launched a wave of imitators that were inspired by its tight controls, whimsical environments and creative level design.

- *Dark Castle's* (1986) hero, Duncan, could "hide" from enemies. It was also the first game where players didn't immediately die from falling, but rather ended up in a dungeon.

- *Mega Man* (1987) introduced themed stages that ended with similarly themed bosses whose powers could be taken by the player once they were defeated.

- *Crash Bandicoot* (1996) used 3D character models and environments to create the camera view known as "2 and a half D."

- *Mario 64* (1996) brought all of the gameplay of the Mario series platform games into the third dimension.

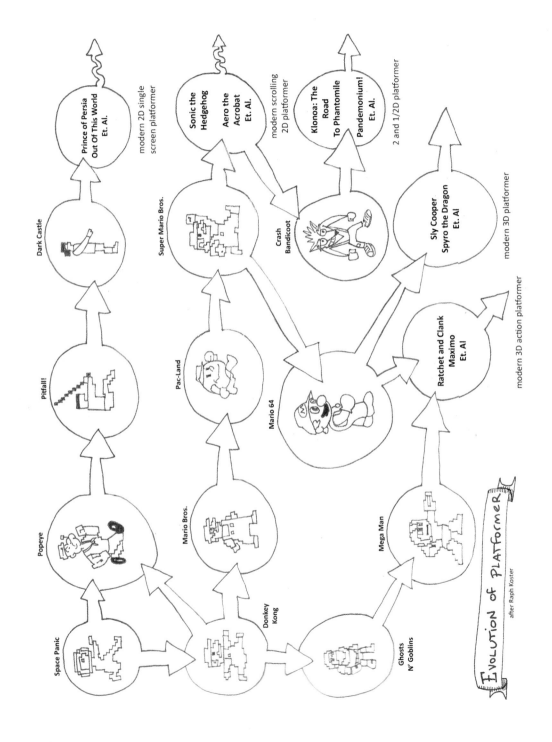

Evolution of Platformer

after Raph Koster

Space Panic

Popeye

Dark Castle

Pitfall!

Prince of Persia
Out Of This World
Et. Al.

modern 2D single
screen platformer

Donkey Kong

Mario Bros.

Pac-Land

Super Mario Bros.

Sonic the
Hedgehog

Aero the
Acrobat
Et. Al.

modern scrolling
2D platformer

Mario 64

Crash
Bandicoot

Klonoa: The
Road
To Phantomile

Pandemonium!
Et. Al.

2 and 1/2D platformer

Ghosts
N' Goblins

Mega Man

Ratchet and Clank
Maximo
Et. Al.

modern 3D action platformer

Sly Cooper
Spyro the Dragon
Et. Al

modern 3D platformer

As you can see, each idea builds on the next. Each game designer inspires the one that comes after them. Or as Pablo Picasso once said, "Bad artists copy. Good artists steal."

Now that you have a great game idea to start with, you have to ask yourself the question posed in the following heading.

What Do Gamers Want?

Automobile inventor Henry Ford once said, "If I had asked people what they wanted, they would have said faster horses." The same is true with video games.

I believe that most gamers don't know what they want until it is shown to them. That is why it is important for game designers to have ideas born of passion. To have a vision of their game.

Gamers can feel when developers are passionate about their game designs. They can smell it like a dog smells fear. Don't be afraid to hold onto your unique vision: Just be aware that it may not always end up exactly how you envisioned it. Because game design is a team sport and that means compromise.

But that didn't answer the question. What do gamers want? Here's the simple answer:

GAMERS WANT GOOD GAMES

Of course, there is no guarantee that your game will be good. I've made many games that ended up just being okay. While no one sets out to make a bad game, bad games still end up getting made.[4]

Tim Schafer, the designer of *Psychonauts* and *Broken Age*, says that all good games provide **wish fulfillment**. Playing as characters they wish they could be gives players a chance to be something they aren't in the real world. I think the same is true about games in *general*. Regardless of the genre, games should *make players feel something that they aren't in the real world*: rich, powerful, smart, skillful, sneaky, bad, heroic or successful.

As you are developing your idea, you need to ask: "Who is my game for?"

You need to decide who your game idea is for. Is it for the casual or the hardcore player? The rise in casual gaming has created renewed interest in shorter play sessions. Games for players who don't otherwise have time for longer, traditional games.

---

[4] You can lay the blame for a bad game at the feet of multiple reasons, which we will cover later.

You can rule out certain design decisions early by deciding who your audience is. Some designers will say "my game is for everybody!" but that's just uninformed thinking. No game is for everybody. Pick your audience and make the best game for them.

Don't forget to ask this important question: "What is the age of my audience?" Having made dozens of "kids" games, I have observed this useful fact about kids and games. Kids always want what is made for an audience older than their own age group.

An 8-year-old wants to play what's been made for a 10-year-old. A 10-year-old kid wants to play what's been made for a 13-year-old. A 13-year-old wants to play what's aimed at a 16-year-old. Many kids aren't interested in playing games directly targeting their age group. They'll tell you "I wouldn't play this game, but it'd be good for my little brother." Ouch! What a stinging insult! In kid language, there's no greater put-down!

Developers, especially ones who have never made a game for kids or have little to no experience with children, tend to oversimplify and talk down to younger audiences. They say, "We don't want this game to be too hard because it's for kids."

What they don't know is that kids are far better game players than adults. It's the adults we should be making the easier games for! Kids pick up on things faster than adults. They have quicker eye-hand coordination (unless you are making a game for very young children, then it's the opposite).

But there are limitations that you must consider when making games for very young children. Their hands can't perform overly complex control schemes. A first-grader or younger (6 or 7 years old) may not even be able to read many complex words or long amounts of text. And please, no swearing.

Brainstorming

Brainstorming is technically a group discussion to generate ideas or solve a problem. To brainstorm properly, you need the following:

- A working brain

- Something to write with

- Something to write on

- A place to work, preferably quiet

- Collaborators, preferably ones who also have working brains

Before you start brainstorming, you need to set some ground rules. First, there is no such thing as a stupid or bad idea. Say yes to everything at this stage. Make sure you are collaborating with people from other disciplines than just game design. This can include programmers, artists, writers and even testers. The more diverse your brainstorming group is, the better. You want as many different perspectives as possible at this stage. Besides, some of the best ideas can come from unexpected people. People always surprise me with what they bring to the idea creation process.

Think about all the things you want your game to be, then write them down. Your goal is to freely associate an idea as far as it can go. When you have reached the ridiculous, it's time to stop. Here is an example of notes from a brainstorming session:

As you can see, the topics didn't exactly relate to each other. Sure, they are all features you might expect a combat/racing game to have. The ideas don't have to be original at this stage either; you are merely cataloging ideas or concepts. As you design them further, you can start thinking of trying to make them unique or even fun.

When I am brainstorming, I like to write the ideas down on a big whiteboard or use sticky notes and cover a wall with them. Index cards spread out over a table can work, too. It doesn't matter what you use. What matters is that the ideas get recorded and are available for everyone in the brainstorm meeting to see. That way, even if an idea doesn't work, you can save it for another game.

An excellent exercise you can use to brainstorm your game is to create a mock-up for the front and back of a box as well as create the manual. What would the cover image be? How would the bullet-points on the back of the box read to get a customer excited? How would you communicate your game in a 16-page black-and-white manual? By placing these limitations on your idea, you can strip your idea to the bare essentials in order to find the true heart of the game. Here's a template you can use when designing the back of a game's box:

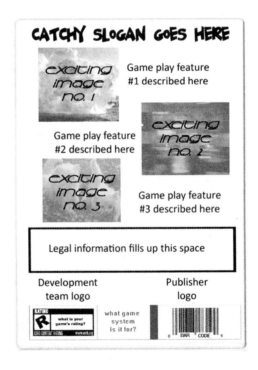

Breaking Writer's Block

Oh no! All of this creative strain and stress has caused you to develop **writer's block**!

What do you do when the ideas just won't come? Everyone's creativity dips from time to time. Here are a few tricks to try when dealing with writer's block:

- **Narrow your focus.** Maybe you are trying to think of too many things at once. Tackle problems one by one by making an outline or breaking things down to a minute level. Give yourself a timeline to complete each of these tasks, but don't take days. Try to get them done in hours.

- **Take a walk or exercise.** Everyone knows that the brain is fueled by blood. Don't let that blood coagulate in your butt! Get up and move around! Get outside and take a walk. When your blood starts circulating again, the new ideas will be coming back in no time.

- **Deal with the thing that may be distracting you.** Sometimes when I am stuck, the reason is that I'm worrying about something else. It may be an unfilled expense report or a floor that needs vacuuming. Take a break, deal with that problem, and then get back to work! Once you deal with it, it won't be a concern anymore!

- **Jump ahead to the good stuff.** Sometimes you have to come up with ideas for a game feature that might not excite you as much as another part of the game. If these game features are slowing you down, go ahead and jump to the good part and get that done. Take some time to design a boss fight rather than stressing over UI design. However, I recommend this trick ONLY as a last resort because it can be very dangerous to your schedule. The truth is, games are built around schedules, deadlines and budgets. If you don't get your work done on time and choose the fun stuff over the drudge work, then the game, the whole team and even the company can suffer. Don't procrastinate. Time management is very important, so be responsible.

- **Learn from others.** Sometimes when you are trying to think of an answer to a problem, it's a good idea to look at other video games to see how they solved it. Maybe you'll solve your problem the same way, or maybe their solution will provide inspiration for a new and unique idea!

- **Change your environment.** I find that my office is full of distractions. E-mail, Facebook and Instagram beckon. Video games call out to be played and game design documents won't write themselves. When this happens, I get out of my workspace and go to the nearest quiet space to work. It can be an empty conference room or another room in your house like a kitchen or patio. Go outside and sit in the sun and get some "vitamin Duh" to recharge your batteries.

When you have your list of ideas, it's time to get critical. Start narrowing down your list. Some items will immediately jump out as keepers, where others are clear losers. Be merciless. It is better to have too many good ideas that you can get rid of rather than have a game full of bad ones.

Present these ideas to another team member who wasn't in on the brainstorming. Shiguru Miyamoto has his "wife-o-meter." He presents his idea to his wife and if she hates it, they get thrown away.[5]

I used to have the executive assistants, game testers and even the janitors at the companies I'd work for take a look at my ideas. Someone who has no vested creative interest in your idea will often give you the clearest and most honest feedback.

Why I Hate "Fun"

"Is it fun?" is the question that I dread the most while coming up with a new game idea. Many gaming academics have attempted to define what fun is. Designer Marc LeBlanc breaks down fun into eight categories: Sensation, Fellowship, Fantasy, Discovery, Narrative, Expression, Challenge and Submission. Although the classification of fun is an interesting exercise, I don't find it very helpful "in the field." There are always problems with the term fun.

For example, a game idea (or a mechanic or boss fight or whatever) can sound fun on paper but when you get it in the game, it might not be as much fun as you imagined. Or it may work, but only you find it fun.

---

[5] A good lesson for all of you married game developers. Always listen to your spouse!

The problem with fun is that just like with humor, sexy or scary, it is completely subjective. Everyone has a completely different idea of what fun is.

Some people think riding a roller-coaster is fun while others find it terrifying. You can try to skew the odds in your favor by basing your gameplay mechanic (or boss fight or whatever) on a pre-existing, proven game. Copying something is a perfectly fine way to start, as long as whatever you are making isn't a complete rip-off of that thing. You don't want to end up with a "clone" game of another title.

Comparisons can be deadly, especially when it comes to reviewers talking about your game. Look at how many lousy first-person shooters and horror games have been made. Often those developers were just copying another, more successful game and failing to capture what made it great in the process.

Even if I find something fun the first time I play a game, it will almost certainly not be fun on the hundredth go. This ultimately happens to all game designers while working on a game. You will play the same level hundreds of times over the course of the production. Then you will start to lose all objectivity. I distinctly remember several times when a producer of the game I was working on came into my office and asked:

When it comes to fun and games, I have found that there is only one truth:

YOU HAVE NO GUARANTEE THAT YOUR GAME IDEA IS GOING TO BE FUN

See how I wrote that in big bold letters? Because developers *always* lose their objectivity during the course of production. And due to the laws of entropy, things will go from order to chaos.

Problems will creep into your game, making things even worse. I've seen it happen! To help you (and developers all over the world) with this, I have created **The Theory of Un-Fun**, which states:

Start with a "fun" idea, as you develop the game, remove the "un-fun." All that should be left is the fun.

Seems like common sense, right? And yet I have encountered many developers who have left bad gameplay mechanics and ugly art and broken cameras in their games because they either got used to them ("That's just the way it is" is a poor answer) or they didn't recognize the un-fun as a problem. They didn't possess the objectivity to see that something in their game just wasn't fun.

The theory of un-fun must be applied many times during a game's development. Stop what you are doing and look at your game, make a list of all the things making your game un-fun and then fix them!

How do you recognize un-fun? Usually, it is something that is pretty obvious. It could be laggy controls that make the player feel like they are moving too "floaty." It could be a character animation that takes too long to play after the player presses a button, and it impacts the timing of an attack. It could be puzzles that are too arcane or difficult to solve. It could be an enemy or a boss that is too easy to defeat. The list goes on and on.

While removing un-fun from your game might seem obvious, you are going to have to remove some un-fun things in your game that you might have gotten used to. You might even have to change something that took a fair amount of work to get done.

A producer I once worked with gave me a great piece of advice when it came to ideas as well as content in a game. He said, "Don't be too dear." What he meant was, "don't become too attached to your ideas that you lose objectivity about your game." Don't be afraid to kill bad ideas. Don't be afraid to kill a few good ones, too. If un-fun is ruining your game, kill the un-fun. That's the priority. Don't worry, there are plenty more ideas where those came from.

Now that you have your good ideas, let's put them to good use!

Level 2's Universal Truths and Clever Ideas

- All gamers want are good games.
- You have no guarantee that your game is going to be fun.
- Start with a "fun" idea, as you develop the game, remove the "un-fun." All that should be left is the fun.
- Be willing to throw out bad ideas. Throw out some good ideas along with the bad ones if they don't fit into your game or you have more than you need.
- Ideas are cheap. It's how you use them that matters.
- If you're stuck, take a break—but don't procrastinate.

Level 3
Writing the Story

ALMOST SINCE THE dawn of gaming, designers have debated which is more important: story or gameplay? Some designers believe games require a story to engage the players. Other designers think a story is what people use to describe the play when it is finished.[1] Pro-story designers reply that games are an artistic medium used to tell a story. Anti-story designers counter that a story is what you watch while the game loads.

In the old days, you know, back in the 90s, designers at Game Developer Conferences all around the world faced off against each other.

Some would yell "*BioShock*!" while others shouted back "*Doom*!" Silly game designers. They are both right and wrong. A game doesn't need to have a story, and yet it always has a story. Perplexing?

While you are chewing over that concept, let's look at the classical definition of "story" as taught by everyone from Aristotle to famous screenwriters.

---

[1] They're wrong. That's known as "narrative," which we will be talking about in a moment.

Once Upon a Time...

Here's the most basic structure of a story:

1. First, there is a **hero** who has a **desire**.

2. Our hero encounters an **event** that throws his life into disarray and interferes with obtaining the desire. This event causes a **problem** for the hero.

3. The hero tries to **overcome the problem**...

4. ...but **his method fails**.

5. There is a **reversal of fortune,** which causes more trouble for the hero.

6. An **even greater problem** is created for the hero that puts the hero at greater risk.

7. Finally, there is **one last problem** that threatens the hero with the **most risk of all.**

8. The hero must resolve the final problem...

9. ...in order to gain his **object of desire.** And everyone lives happily ever after. Well, until the sequel anyway.

Remember that no matter what your story is about, a story ALWAYS has a beginning, a middle and an end. Hollywood has spent many years analyzing and deconstructing the story.

Don't feel that you need to reinvent the wheel; learn what those in Hollywood have. Read screenwriting books, take classes, visit screenwriting websites. But you don't have to feel chained to a standard story structure like Joseph Campbell's "Hero's Journey," Syd Field's "Three Act Structure," or even Dan Harmon's Story Circle.[2]

Try using another medium's structures to tell your story. How is a story told in a song? In a TV news report? In a Homeric poem? Try looking at other forms of storytelling for inspiration, like "Kishōtenketsu," which contains four acts: introduction, development, twist, and reconciliation and was the inspiration for Nintendo planner Koichi Hayashida's designs of the later Mario games.

Or you could use the "Repetition-Break Structure," which is a classic format used in fairytales like *The Three Little Pigs* and *Goldilocks and the Three Bears*. Just remember that video games are an interactive medium, and as William Shakespeare[3] reminds us, "The play's the thing." That was one guy who knew the story, and he was pretty smart for someone who never played a video game.

If gameplay is the meat of the game, then story should be the salt: just enough will add flavor, but too much can ruin everything and even kill you.

Narrative Design

Some games don't have stories. Games like *Balatro*, *Candy Crush Saga* or the classic *Pac-Man* arcade game don't need a story to be engaging for the player. However, they still generate a **narrative,** which literally means "an order of events."

Because we humans perceive time as a linear sequence of events, we express our experiences linearly as well, even if they aren't presented in a traditional story structure. Let's look at it this way: every time you play a game, you create a narrative.

---

[2] Which, by the way, is fantastic, and you can learn all about it at www.studiobinder.com/blog/dan-harmon-story-circle/.

[3] Or as I like to call him, the 17th Earl of Oxford.

A player can create an infinite number of narratives. As a designer, you need to look at all[4] the possible narratives and find out how to make them ALL fun. The goal is to create multiple narratives that the player will enjoy playing.

In a narrative, the player (you) are the "hero" of the game. The designer needs to look at the game from the player's perspective and be aware of the ordering of the events and experiences that will eventually help the player create the narrative. As each experience builds on the next, the goal is to create rising emotional states for the player. Then the designer can design systems to choreograph these interesting experiences, which in turn create emotions. Savvy? How about an example?

Left 4 Dead uses an **artificial intelligence** called the "Director" to control the game's pacing. Depending on the player's "stress level," which is calculated using many variables, including health, skill and location. The Director then adjusts the number of zombies that attack, what items such as ammo and health are generated, and even the music. In the end, the game itself generates a unique and dynamic play experience for the player. However, because most developers don't yet have technology like *Left 4 Dead*'s Director, it is up to designers to create these situations as best they can within their games.

When you are designing a game, it is extremely important to plan the narrative that the player will experience. You'll find that the player's narrative can end up quite different from the game's story. **Remember to never mistake story for gameplay and similarly never mistake gameplay for story.**

The art of **narrative design** combines the story (the authored content) and the narrative (the interacted content) to create the overall experience of the game. To be a good narrative designer, you first need to be a good game designer.

Remember that the player's experience is the most important part of the game. If your game design centers around a story, then it might not be a good game. The player's interaction with the mechanics should be foremost in the design.

Narrative design is NOT game writing. As a narrative designer, you aren't creating the script, nor are you writing the cutscenes, dialogue, or character barks, but it's up to you to use these pieces in conjunction with the game play. A narrative designer brings plot to life through gameplay. If you want to be a good narrative designer, you have to:

- Put the gameplay first

---

[4] Or as many as you can guess will happen. It's like a massive series of "what if." However, because these possibilities can stretch on to infinity, predicting everything might not be worth the time investment. That's why when something happens that the designer didn't expect and doesn't break the game, we're more than happy to call it a "feature" and embrace it!

- ■ Have the story match the players' motivation

- ■ Create storyline arcs

Put gameplay first – We are making a game; therefore, gameplay is the most important thing. If the story isn't working for the gameplay, then change the story! It's easier to change the skin of the story than the bones of the game. You can always make the story work within the confines of the game.

Have the story match the player's motivation – What the player does should match who the character is. Here's a bad example: in the *Uncharted* series, protagonist Nathan Drake comments on how much he dislikes violence. Yet over the course of the game, the character kills dozens of enemies. This disconnect between what the player says (or what the game tells us about the character) and what the character does is known as **ludonarrative dissonance**. The story and the gameplay don't match.

Ludonarrative dissonance can take the player out of the game, ruining the experience.[5] To avoid this, you want actions to be thematic and true to the characters. Good examples of thematic gameplay can be found in the *Batman Arkham* series, the *Assassins Creed* series, the *God of War* series, and games like *ALIEN: Isolation* (2014) and *Red Dead Redemption 2* (2018). *The Stanley Parable* (2013) is practically a lesson in narrative design.

Create Story Arcs – Story arcs are a tool to visualize progression and pacing. They can be very useful to spotting problems in your narrative. Let's create one as an example. In our game, we have a player character—let's call him Thorn—who enters the dungeon where he is attacked by enemies. He then searches around for treasure and is attacked by more enemies. Thorn finally fights more enemies and then the big boss of the level. If we are looking at these from an emotion perspective, the story chart would look like this:

Notice how flat this "arc" is. There's no arc to it at all. A good storyline has **rising action**. Things get more exciting as they go. Let's redesign this story arc with this in mind. Thorn enters the dungeon, where he searches around for treasure. He then encounters some enemies. Thorn looks around for more treasure, which he finds, but he also encounters

---

[5]Developers Naughty Dog recognized this and have an achievement in *Uncharted 4* called "Ludonarrative Dissonance" if you kill 1000 enemies!

a wandering wizard that warns him of the dangers ahead. Thorn then encounters more enemies to fight. He then finds the entrance to the temple of evil and after dodging a few traps, he finally confronts the big boss.

Do you see how this story rises in intensity over time? It will keep the player engaged by alternating between searching and avoiding traps (low energy) and fighting against enemies and the boss (high energy). This makes for a much better narrative for the player.

Anything is Gameplay

I am a firm believer that almost ANY TOPIC can be made into gameplay. Don't feel as though you are limited by subject matter. Look at games like *Mr. Mosquito* (the player is a mosquito who drinks the blood of a human family), *Turnip Boy Commits Tax Evasion* (a turnip battles against a corrupt system), *Untitled Goose Game* (a goose makes people angry), or *Donut Country* (you are a hole in the ground that sucks up trash).

Still don't believe me? Let's look at the classic and simple story *Little Red Riding Hood*. This children's story has all the elements you need to make a great video game:

1. Little Red Riding Hood walks through the forest to Grandma's house = classic player exploration. Give Red some goodies to collect to fill up her picnic basket (inventory system) and have her jump over a fallen log or two on her way.

2. Red meets the Big Bad Wolf = the player has her first enemy encounter. Of course, you can't kill off the wolf yet…(unless the enemies are "wolf minions").

3. Carrying a full basic set of goodies (gating mechanism), Red reaches Grandma's house (next level), where she finds "Grandma" waiting in bed.

4. Red questions "Grandma's" true identity ("what big eyes you have"). This can take the form of a quiz, a puzzle or even a rhythm game.

5. "Grandma" is revealed as the Big Bad Wolf, and Red and the wolf battle to the death = boss fight! [6]

See? Even a "simple" classic story can still offer all the elements to make an exciting and varied video game! [7]

The Triangle of Weirdness

I am sure you have heard of the famous production triangle, shown here:

One of the best things about video games is that, technical restraints of your chosen platform aside, you are limited only by your imagination.

Developers can craft virtual worlds that feature unrealistic physics, bizarre characters, and absurd quests. However, it is possible to go too far with creativity. This is why I created the **"Triangle of Weirdness."** Notice the difference in the choices on the triangle of weirdness: characters, activities, and world.

---

[6] Everyone knows that Little Red Riding Hood ends with Red nearly being eaten by the wolf and having the woodcutter save her, but where is the fun in that? Why watch a cutscene when you can have a boss fight? It's not my fault that boss fights weren't invented when Little Red Riding Hood was written. Personally, I think that my ending is better!

[7] Okay, the story of Little Red Riding Hood might not make for a very LONG video game, but it can be made into a game, nonetheless.

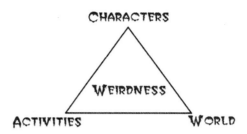

Unlike the production triangle where you can have any two points, you can choose only **one** corner on the triangle of weirdness. Choose any more than that and you risk alienating your audience.

Let's look at three examples of how to apply the Triangle of Weirdness to your story and world.

While the *Wizard of Oz* features weird characters such as the Tin Man, the Lion and the Scarecrow, the land of Oz was a pretty typical fairy tale location when it was created in the 1900s. The characters of the *Wizard of Oz* have desires readers can relate to: courage, love and the wish to return home.

While the main characters of *Star Wars* are familiar (the young hero, the princess in distress, the charming rogue), and their desires are familiar (join the war effort, defeat the villains, get the girl), it is the world of *Star Wars* that is weird with its Jawas, Wookiees, Jedis, and a cantina populated by the craziest-looking scum in the galaxy.

Monty Python and the Holy Grail feature typical (if not archetypical) characters: King Arthur and his knights of the round table. These stalwart knights travel through medieval England on their quest for the Holy Grail. However, that quest is filled with weird activities like designing shrubs for the knights who say "Ni!" or getting massacred by a killer rabbit.

It is possible to go too far. Movies like *Dune* (1984) and *The City of Lost Children* (1995), or video games like *SkullMonkeys* or *Muscle Man March*, while incredibly unique and creative, left many audiences feeling like they just "didn't get it." And nobody likes to feel stupid.

What do these games and movies have in common? They all violate the Triangle of Weirdness. Character, Activity, World. Pick only one to be weird. Do more at your own peril...

A Likely Story

When developing a game story, you will find you have three different types of people in your audience:

1. Players who are into your story as it happens

2. Players who want to get into your story in depth

3. Players who don't care what the story is at all[8]

Making your story appealing to all three types of players can be a challenge. The best rule of thumb is to always make the story be in service of the gameplay and not the other way around. Here are some tips on involving story into the game:

- To satisfy players who are looking for a deeper experience, provide details but make sure they don't get in the way of the story. For example, *Alien: Isolation* and *Mass Effect 3* both have non-mandatory collectible audiotapes that reveal deeper story details to players without intruding on the main story.

- Because players who are just along for the ride will indiscriminately press the "A" button to get through audio cues and cutscenes that reveal story points, make sure your game's story is also revealed through gameplay and level design to prevent players from skipping it entirely. Otherwise, they will get lost and confused.[9] You can also introduce story as gameplay by making stories playable flashbacks or puzzles.

- Another option is to start your story as late into the action as possible. This can be in the middle of a boss fight, at the end of a level, or during a car chase. Keep in mind that your story will still have to have a beginning; you are just choosing to start the game before showing it. You can flash back or tell the story in a non-chronological order.

  This change in structure works better in story-based games. I'm not sure it's such a good idea to start a puzzle game of *Tetris* with dozens of tiles raining down on the players.

- Always keep your stories lively and moving. Professional screenwriters may introduce a change in the plot or action every 15 minutes. Even with non-story games, play sessions are becoming "bite-sized" so they're short enough for players to enjoy in short bursts.

Speaking of surprises, there is a trend in game stories that I blame squarely on Hollywood: the twist/surprise ending. "It was all a dream." "He was really dead the whole time." "He was really the murderer and not my friend." These kinds of O. Henry endings have become more and more common as video game creators try to tell what they consider a "mature" story.

While audiences like to be taken by surprise, more and more often these twist endings wind up feeling like a predicable cliché. There is merit to a predictable ending. Why? Because people also like it when the good guys win and the bad guys lose, even though that's the oldest

---

[8] I can't take credit for this observation. This statement was made by Ken Levine, the director of *BioShock*, during his excellent 2009 GDC speech.

[9] Yeah, I know. It's their own darn fault if they get confused for skipping the cutscenes in the first place but remember the first rule of responsible game design: love thy player.

story in the book. While you want to have some surprises to keep things interesting, don't sacrifice consistency. If everything in your story (or game for that matter) is a surprise, the player won't have anything to latch onto and will constantly be thrown off-balance.

Take, for example, the James Bond movies of the 1980s. When I was growing up, I loved to go see those films. Even before I saw them, I knew that Bond was going to use a cool new gadget and drive an awesome car, defeat the villain's scheme, save the world and end up with the hot girl. So, if I knew all these things, then why did I bother watching the movie? For me, the fun was the twists and turns the story took. I knew the WHO, the WHAT and the WHY, but I didn't know the HOW.

There is a delight in predicting how things will turn out. It makes the players feel smart, as if they "called it" in an election or solved a mystery. Besides, life is unpredictable enough as it is; why not give your audience a little predictability? The point I am making is you don't have to be especially clever when writing your story, just entertaining.

Conversely, something that I don't find very clever is a video game story in which the main character has amnesia. Amnesia ranks as the number one video game cliché of all time, but I understand why game writers use it. It's an attempt to approximate the lack of information about the characters and the world as a player begins the game. However, it ultimately becomes an excuse for the writer to construct an "unreliable narrative" and intentionally omit information to the player to be able to create a "shock ending." It feels forced and, frankly, isn't fair to the player.

Classic director Alfred Hitchcock presented a great theory about the value of surprise versus suspense. Imagine that two men are sitting at a table talking about baseball. The conversation lasts about five minutes, when suddenly there is a huge explosion! This shocks the audience, but that surprise lasts only a few seconds.

But Hitchcock discovered how to get a greater impact. He started the scene by showing the bomb under the table. The bomb is set to explode in five minutes. The two men discuss baseball while the audience members are squirming in their seats thinking, "Don't just sit there talking about baseball! There's a bomb under the table! Get out of there!" When you make the audience aware of the danger the characters are in, they get emotionally involved. By the time your scene reaches its climax, you have created more excitement with your audience than just the surprise of the bomb exploding.[10]

---

[10] Hitchcock also recommends that you don't actually kill the characters in this scenario. It's even less desirable in the case of video games; the game would be over!

Some people believe that **theme** is even more important than story to a game. Why is that? Because theme is the central topic of the game. A theme can often be summed up in a statement like "love conquers all," "order is better than chaos," or "with great power comes great responsibility." Your game can have a theme without even having a story. *Pac-Man's* theme? "Eat or be eaten." *Dark Souls'* theme? "Good versus evil." *Journey's* theme? "Life is a journey that is better with others." Gameplay should be centered around the game's theme. If the gameplay doesn't support the game's theme, maybe it doesn't belong in the game.

Another question to consider when developing your story is "what is at stake?" Many video games are about saving the world from evil or destruction. But just like every movie doesn't have to be a slam-bang blockbuster, not every video game has to be about saving the world. Small themes can be just as important as big ones. In my opinion, using a theme for your story other than "violence solves all problems" is a worthwhile pursuit. It worked for games like *Crossy Road*, *Stray* and *Stardew Valley*.

Time to Wrap It Up

Ending games can be just as hard as starting them. In the good old days, there wasn't an end to a game, just a kill screen.[11] Or games just ran forever, frequently wrapping their scores around like your car's odometer. Then along came *Dragon's Lair*, and everyone wanted to know whether or not Dirk rescued the Princess and players spent lots of money to find out.[12]

---

[11] A *kill screen* originally wasn't the "game over" screen, but rather a screen that appeared due to a programming error or design oversight. The most famous kill screen from classic gaming is the 256th level of *Pac-Man*. At this point, due to a bug, half the screen becomes garbled data, which keeps the player from collecting all the dots and clearing the board to move on. Arcade owners had to unplug or "kill" the game to start it back up again.

[12] Since *Dragon's Lair* cost twice the money of an average arcade game to play (a whopping 50 cents!), my brother and I would observe the other players at our local arcade and write down the patterns required to get through each of the game's trap- and monster-laden rooms. When it was our turn to play, one of us would man the joystick while the other called out which way to go. We managed to save the princess without spending more than five dollars. The world's first cooperative player gaming experience!

How long should a game be? In the old days, the average was 20 hours. In the really old days, it was 40. For modern story-based console games, playtime averages 8-12 hours. Contrast that with mobile games with play sessions that can last minutes but still offer dozens of hours of gameplay for a single title. Multiplayer games can offer years of gameplay. Even after logging more than 860 hours on *Team Fortress 2* (Valve, 2007), I still enjoy playing it.

I recommend ending the game when you feel you have left the players feeling satisfied. If you leave plot points dangling open up storylines for sequels, your players will feel like they are missing something or not getting the whole story. I always suggest that you play fair with the players. Let them feel as though they accomplished everything they needed to during the game.

Some games even offer extra experiences so the players can continue playing after the story has ended. Multiple endings, minigames, and unlockable and downloadable content of entirely new adventures, or "deleted levels" (akin to deleted scenes on a DVD) will let your players experience new stories in your established world.

This advice is particularly true with the living world of an **MMORPG** (massively multi-player online role-playing game), which needs long-term, evolving storylines to keep players engaged (and paying monthly subscription fees). Blizzard's *World of Warcraft* has been continuously running since 2004 thanks to the addition of quests and even new worlds that add more content for the players.

Or you can just throw away all the previous advice and write your story at the last minute. Some development teams concentrate solely on the gameplay and create the storyline last. They claim this approach works. Personally, I think it would make me nervous.

A Note About "Lore"

I meet many potential game developers who want to get into games to write "**lore**"—which is just another name for "world-building." **World-building** is creating all of the intricate details about a place from the creatures that inhabit it to the food the people eat to the places they travel.

When I first started working in games, a lot of this world building was created by the game's artists, especially the concept artist. They worked with a designer or a creative director to create these kinds of details; or they simply made something up! Nowadays, a lot of creators concentrate on the "lore" of their world, and to be honest, I couldn't care less about it because the world is not the story. As someone[13] smart once said: *"If you are a tour guide, then*

---

[13]That person was Abraham Mireles, a writer for Cracked.com.

the world is the most important thing, but if you are a storyteller, then it's the characters." Focus on the characters. Focus on who the player is playing. After all, you are playing a character, not the world.

Since I have been privileged to create a few worlds, here is my advice for you and all potential world-builders:

- **Start with a character (preferably the player).** The DC multi-verse didn't start as a massively sprawling place inhabited with thousands of heroes and villains; it started with Superman. A single character. Once you know about that character, you start to understand the world they live in. You will then understand what they want. And then, you'll understand who stands in their way...

- **Who is the opponent?** Granted not all games have villains, and some games don't need villains, but if your game *does* have one, make sure their presence is known to the players. An antagonist literally translates to "The Opponent" so make sure they get in the player's way early on. An opponent doesn't need to be a human, monster, or even physical. It can be a timer or a condition that has to be met by the player, otherwise they don't succeed. We will learn more about making opponents in Level 11.

- **What are the rules?** There are many different ways that magic and technology work in a game's world. Some magic can be simple, useful spells or they can be wildly dangerous and dramatic ones. Your world might not have discovered gunpowder and only uses swords. Players might shoot miniature nukes at enemies. When I was creating the pulp sci-fi world of *Rayguns and Rocketships*, I didn't have technology like holograms, teleporters, or energy shields. Everything was powered by atomic, electric, or magnetic like in the stories of the 1930's that was the inspiration for the game. Knowing what is and isn't in your world will help you craft your world easier and make it cohesive for the player.

- **Start at "home."** Many world-builders want to start with epic battles or grand locations, but that can get too overwhelming or may only be mildly relevant to the players and their adventures. Start with a small location instead. If it's a fantasy roleplaying game, perhaps starts with where the characters meet: a tavern, a king's chambers, the lobby of the adventurer's guild. If it's sci-fi, the deck of a spaceship, the hanger of a base, or an outpost on a fall-flung world. You get the idea.

- **Who lives here (other than the players?)** Think about what kind of people live in the player character's neighborhood. There might be a tavern. Who runs it? Who goes to it? Who doesn't like going to it? There might be a church up the street. Who runs it? Who attends it? Who or what are they worshipping? Does the church have any influence on the town? Who runs the town? Do they have a martial presence? Are they friendly or hostile to the players? Do they have better weapons/skills than the players... As you can see, just by answering these questions you are building your world, bit by bit.

- **Make sure the world is relatable.** I've already introduced you to the Triangle of Weirdness. This is where it comes into play. There is a reason why in fantasy and sci-fi movies you see the characters eat a meal. All of us eat a meal; we can relate to it. It makes things less weird if the player is doing relatable things like gathering chickens, shopping, or cooking a meal. This extends to creatures, places, and things in the world. It helps if they have real-world analogies so the player can quickly understand what they are. If your player can look at a monstrous steed and say "Oh, it's just like a camel" then it's relatable.

- **Keep it in the world**. Lore is best when it is discovered by the players during game-play, not in cutscenes or cinematics. Even overly long pieces of text can get to be too much for an average player. Let the world tell the story through level design, puzzle design, and encounters with other characters; both good and bad. See if you can have that pesky sword wielding goblin tell the players something about the world and not just the good-looking bar keeper.

In the end, "lore" is fine, but a little goes a long way. Lore is the spice, not the main meal.

A Game by Any Other Name

Oh, I almost forgot to address one of the most important things about your game's story: the title! There are several ways to approach naming your game.

- A **literal title** makes it easy to figure out where the title came from. It can be the name of your main character, like *Sonic the Hedgehog* or *Hollow Knight*. It can be the main location of your game, like *Castle Wolfenstein* or *Saint's Row*. Or you can name your game after a gameplay activity or component like *Command and Conquer* or *Boom Blocks*.

- The **action/cool title** is one that captures the spirit of the game without mentioning any of the game characters or locations. Games like *Darksiders*, *Brütal Legend*, and *Gears of War* all have cool titles.

- The **punny title** is one that makes you appreciate its cleverness. *System Shock*, *Half Life*, and *Dead Space* are all good examples of punny titles. As puns are word play, you have to be careful because your audience may not get the reference or think the pun is funny. As columnist Doug Larson said, "A pun is the lowest form of humor, unless you thought of it yourself."

- A **purple cow title** is one that makes your audience stop in their tracks and wonder why the title was chosen.[14] It is a title that captures your curiosity and begs your attention. Purple cow titles include *LittleBigPlanet*, *Resident Evil 2*, and *Naughty Bear*.

---

[14] The term "purple cow" comes from the poem by Gelett Burgess, who wrote: "I never saw a purple cow, I never hope to see one. But I can tell you anyhow, I'd rather see than be one."

The advantage to a purple cow title is that it becomes strongly associated with the game because the title is so unique.

- The **dramatic title** is one that sounds more like a movie than a game. Typically, it's a phrase that sounds dramatic rather than a title. It often refers to the theme of the game or tries to connote the feeling of the game. Examples include *The Sum of All Fears, The Binding of Isaac,* and *The Last of Us.*

- The **referential title** refers to something in the game that you have no idea what it is about unless you have played the game. After players have played the game, they understand the significance of the title. For example, if you were to hear the word "halo" before playing *Halo,* you might have thought of that glowing circular band over an angel's head. Now that everyone has played the game, it's going to be a long time before anyone thinks of using the word halo in a game title; it's just too strongly associated with that game. Other examples include *Unreal, Portal,* and *Spore.*

- A **subtitle** is used in some games to communicate ideas and themes that the main title might not do. In those cases, usually the name of the franchise or IP comes first followed by a colon and then the new idea as seen in games like *Maximo: Ghosts to Glory, Ace Combat 7: Skies Unknown,* and *Adventure Time: Explore the Dungeon Because I Don't Know!*

No matter what naming convention you use, I think that shorter titles are better than longer ones. First of all, they are easier to remember and say. I like to keep them to two or three syllables like *Star Wars, Don-kee Kong, Pac-Man,* or *Hey-lo.* I think this started because of marquee sizes on arcade cabinets: they needed to attract the players' attention, create some mystery, and describe the gameplay. "Defender" is still one of the best names ever: it perfectly sums up the game in one three-syllable word.

Second, shorter titles are easier to make into logos for your game's start screen and read on the cover of a game's box. Don't forget to consider marketing aspects when you are creating your game's title. If you have to use a longer title or a subtitle, still try to keep it short. *Uncharted 3: Drake's Deception* combines a couple of purple cows to make a pretty good title. *Uncharted* gives you the image of exploring or sailing into unknown and dangerous territory. Players will want to know who Drake is and what his deception is. *Batman: Arkham City* lets you know who you are playing (Batman) and where the action takes place (Arkham City).

This title is especially good because it adds a bit of the "what the?" factor, since most Batman fans know that Batman lives in Gotham City and Arkham is the asylum home of his greatest villains! The title alone compels you to play the game!

Try to name your game sooner than later. I have always preferred the titles created by the game's developers over those made up by someone else such as the marketing team. And publishers have a bad habit of vetoing developers' suggested names or outright name the game themselves. The larger the budget, the more power the publisher will have over the name. However, I believe that the developer knows what is important about the game and often knows best who they are making the game for. Trust their instincts.

I once worked on a game that was pitched with a great purple cow title: *Mr. Hong's Violent Orchestra*. The title drew our attention and really made people sit up and take notice. People wanted to know who Mr. Hong was. They were delightfully confused to what a "violent orchestra" could be. What kind of music did a violent orchestra play? Because it was a silly musical fighting game, the title was very appropriate. Sadly, the management didn't agree. As the game was transformed into a music-centric rhythm game (rather than a musical combat game), the title was changed to the more forgettable *Battle of the Bands*. Needless to say, the game didn't do very well, and I feel the lackluster title was part of the reason why.

When you have finally named your game, you may discover that your great title is already in use by someone else. A thorough Google search will help validate your question pretty quickly. Or a title may be trademarked by someone else. In the U.S., you can check for patents on U.S. Patent and Trademark Office web site: http://uspto.gov. Be sure you check with your publisher's legal department to make sure you can use your title before you become too attached to it. Even a quick word search on the Internet will help get you started.

Creating Characters Your Players Care About

My friend and fellow designer Andy Ashcraft believes that video game developers don't care about telling the second act of their story. He points out that developers love telling the setup and background of their game, and they love getting to the big finish of the game. What they neglect to concentrate on is the middle of the story, the second act, where character and story development happens. I tend to agree with Andy.

However, games that skip the second act are missing an important part of the storytelling process.[15] In games, the first act is usually told with a cutscene or, even worse, the game's manual, which no one ever reads![16] The second act is the grind that moves the player toward the third act, which is the completion of the story, usually the last level and a boss fight.

This is a mistake.

---

[15] Remember, all stories have what? A beginning, a middle, and an end.

[16] Maybe I am exaggerating a little, but c'mon. When was the last time you really read a game manual? Then again, when was a game manual worth reading? Are there even game manuals anymore?

In the first act, the player should be given an opportunity to find out about and care about the character. See what "normal life" is like for the character. You need that first act to bond with the character, even if you kill off that character repeatedly (common in video games) or radically change him into a killing machine. Case in point, you don't need to look any further than the 1986 movie *Robocop*.

In the film *Robocop*, the audience is introduced to police officer Alex Murphy. He's an honest cop and a decent guy fighting crime in futuristic Detroit. By page 25 of the script, you actually care about the guy and feel bad when he's gunned down by criminal scumbags. The second act kicks off when Murphy is rebuilt as the cyborg Robocop. Several video game adaptations of this movie have been made, and in all of them, Murphy's death is shown only as a cutscene. Players start the game as Robocop, and the killing of bad guys commences immediately.[17]

But in our hypothetical Robocop game, why not start with Murphy as a cop? The first level of the game would have Murphy tracking down the bad guys and end with his death. The players should have time to bond with him, making his death and resurrection have much more of an impact.

In that vein, death should mean something to the players, especially when it isn't the main character dying. When was the last time you cried when a game character died? (Other than when you accidently deleted your save file?) Aerith from *Final Fantasy 7*? Arthur from *Red*

---

[17] Just so you realize that I'm not a complete idiot, I do know why the developers of Robocop began the player as Robocop. (1) It's more appealing to play as a criminal-blasting cyborg than as a fragile human; (2) game carts in 1988 didn't have the memory to store two completely different player character models, and why would you go through all the work to create them, especially if you were only going to be the human player character for one level; and (3) the game is called *Robocop*, not "Guy who gets shot and eventually becomes *Robocop*."

Dead Redemption 2? Aunt May in Insomniac's *Spider-Man*? Writers forget that you have to care about a character first if it is going to mean anything when you kill him. And the solution isn't to make the character a relative or part of a meaningful relationship, especially if that character is killed off in the first cutscene. I remember playing a game that opened with the player's relative getting murdered after interacting with him for one level. I didn't feel the righteous anger that the player felt for the rest of the game because I knew the character for such a short time. Invest the time in these characters, even if the ultimate goal is to kill them off.

A tried-and-true way to get players to care about a video game character is to use what I call the **Yorda Effect.** Named after the non-player character (NPC) from *Ico* (SCEA, 2001), Yorda is a young girl that Ico has to protect from enemies and help traverse the environment as the pair attempt to escape a mysterious castle. Yorda is portrayed as a (mostly) helpless character, and her survival is critical to the player's success. If Yorda dies, so do you.

But your Yorda character cannot be completely helpless. The character needs to offer limited assistance to the player in the form of healing, assisting in combat, providing extra ammo, or solving puzzles. If designed correctly, this co-dependency between characters creates a protective relationship in which the player comes to genuinely care about the welfare of the NPC. This allows the storyteller to solicit stronger emotions between the characters over the course of the game. One particularly brilliant mechanic from *Ico* is that the ever-distracted Yorda runs only when Ico holds her hand. It might seem like a small detail, but it is a lovely way of illustrating the relationship between the two characters.

If you want to get players to care about a character, make sure the players spend some time with that character, even if it's only for a little while. *Heavy Rain's* (Quantic Dream, 2010) protagonist Ethan spends a (playable) day with his son Shaun before the boy is kidnapped by the Origami Killer. By the time you get to the scene where you are trying to find Shaun in a crowd, you have built up a relationship and genuinely care about his welfare.

The *Uncharted* series' Victor "Sully" Sullivan, *BioShock Infinite's* Elizabeth, Shadow the dog from *Dead to Rights*, and Ellie from *The Last of Us* all offer examples of the Yorda Effect because the respective games attempt to make you care about these NPCs...with varying degrees of success.

Creating a Yorda-type character for your game takes a lot of design time and effort...that you just might not have. The point is you must make the characters in your game important somehow to the players. A character can provide information on how to play the game, represent the game's economic system (like the proprietor of the game's store) or provide health power-ups to the player on a regular basis. When that character is taken out of the game, the player will feel the impact.

Because of this, the only game character whose death ever felt impactful to the player was Aerith from *Final Fantasy VII*.

Aerith filled many roles for the player: she was a damsel in distress, one part of the hero's love triangle, a character who contributed solutions to the problems in the plot, and a "playable" part of the gaming party. When she died, her loss to the player was felt on many levels. You lost a love interest, the party's healer, and an interesting character. The point is to build up your game characters before you tear them down. Make their loss count.

Your party members don't have to be human: the deaths of Agro the horse in *Shadow of the Colossus* and Dogmeat the dog in *Fallout 3* have similar effects on players. All that matters is that your players have a bond with these characters to feel the loss when it happens.

All this talk about death has bummed me out. So, what about humor in games? Most writers agree that comedy is harder than drama. However, I believe that the secret to humor is a funny character.

My favorite first person shooter is *Team Fortress 2,* and I believe it is one of the funniest games I have ever played. The game doesn't feature humor like other games have; you won't find physical gags, "hilarious" jokes, or burping and farting like some games resort to. What makes the game so funny is how true the characters are to themselves. From the wry Australian sniper who has to defend his occupation to his parents, to the Russian heavy gunner who is overly fond of "sanviches." All the game characters' appearances, animations, and vocal barks reinforce their personalities, raising them from stereotypes to truly original (and funny) characters.

Your game character's actions should be defined by their personality. When we were creating *Maximo*, we decided that he was an impatient guy, always in a hurry to rescue the princess or get into a fight. He didn't even stop to open a treasure chest; he just kicked it open, collected the treasure, and kept moving.

If you start with your character's personality, you will end up with some interesting animations and gameplay. Characters can have many motivations: the desire for success or revenge, they could be seeking love or acceptance. Many characters have more than one and often conflicting motivations. Knowing their motivations will help you determine what your characters will say and do. The result will be much richer characters.

Speaking of characters, just like giving your game the right title is important, it is equally important to name your characters correctly. Would you name a strapping barbarian hero Mortimer? Only if your hero is a parody or it's a comedy game. Names carry great weight. It is important to give your characters the right name. Baby books are a great place to start.

Mortimer!
It's short for Mort...
Which is latin for death..

I like names that have some significance to a character's personality or what their occupation is. *Star Wars* has some of the best names. What does the name Luke Skywalker tell you about the character? Luke feels like a simple, homespun name fitting for a farm boy who yearns to "walk among the stars."[18]

---

[18] Did you know that Luke Skywalker's original name was Luke Starkiller? This name change provides a great lesson: never give your character a name that gives away the ending of your story!

It's also fun to have characters' names juxtaposed to each other. Two of my favorite character names are from *When Harry Met Sally*. Billy Crystal's character is named Harry Burns. It's a curmudgeonly, burned-out name if ever there was one. Meg Ryan's character is Sally Albright. She's positive, romantic, and a little naïve. These names are blatantly obvious, and they give you a quick snapshot of each character's personality.

Comedic characters need appropriate names too. Guybrush Threepwood, SpongeBob Squarepants, and Larry Laffer aren't heroic-sounding names, but they are totally appropriate for the humorous games they are in. The only rule of thumb is that when you look at an image of the character, the name should fit what you see.

Games Are About Everyone

For a long time, there was an unfortunate trend in gaming: women, people of color, and disabled people were under-represented in games. If they weren't Pac-people, anthropomorphic animals, or space aliens, the lead character in video games tended to be white and male. If women, people of color or disabled people did show up in games, they were the love interest, the NPC, or a villain character. They were almost never the hero.

Fortunately, that has changed...albeit slowly. It is more common to see women, people of color and people with disabilities as the protagonists in modern games. It's important that we, as game creators, represent all types of people in our games. Not only is it a true reflection of the world around us, but it provides a good message to the players: "You are all welcome here."

It is important for you to have representation in your game. While it can be a challenge to create characters of an ethnicity or gender that "isn't you" here are some pointers to make sure you do it respectfully and responsibly:

- If your game has a character customizer, offer a wide range of skin colors, body sizes, and hair styles.

- Create stories or plots that feature culturally diverse characters—but treat them as people, not as stereotypes.

- Treat women (and all of your characters) as people. Maybe we should just ditch the whole "rescue the princess" trope once and for all; they aren't prizes to be won. I'm looking forward to playing a game about being the princess for a change!

- If you are writing about a character from a different culture, consult someone who is from that culture to make sure that what you are creating is sensitive, authentic, and culturally correct.

- Strive to create more realistic body types for your characters. *Tomb Raider's* Laura Croft started as a buxom model and evolved into a realistic body type over the years. She's still the same character, but she's now less offensive to women who would want to play as her.

- Avoid sexist costuming. The "chainmail bikini" that was a trope of sword & sorcery stories is now considered offensive (and completely impractical!) Instead, create costumes that are more functional rather than an excuse to show off skin.

- Avoid the "blue is for boys; pink is for girls" trope. Offer more and better color choices for your characters? How about green? Or purple? Or plaid? Give your players a wider palette to choose from. You don't have to use those colors to signify gender.

- Provide more representation for LBGTQ+ characters. *Baldur's Gate 3* (2023), *Stardew Valley* (2016) and *Cyberpunk 2077* (2020)—three very different genres of games—all give players the option of what kind of romantic relationship they want to pursue without "making a statement" or framing it as a negative. Again, it's about giving players a choice on how they want to play the game.

The more inclusive you are when creating your game, the more people will be interested in playing it. We can all do better if we only put in the effort.

A Few Pointers on Writing for Kids of All Ages

Here's some advice when writing games for kids: just because you are writing game stories for kids doesn't mean the story has to be simplistic. The most common mistake kid-game writers make is trying to make the story too simple.

I have often heard developers protest overusing complex ideas and themes because "it's for kids!" But think about children's literature. Children's classics like *Where the Wild Things Are, Heidi,* and *The Chronicles of Narnia* are full of complex themes, interactions, and emotions. If it's good enough for kids' books, it should be good enough for kids' games. Coming of age doesn't only mean that your main character can fight in a war or can cast their vote.

According to literary scholars, a **bildungsroman** or coming-of-age story, has four stages that aid the young protagonist on their journey: The first stage is a significant loss at the beginning. This is like how Harry Potter's parents have been murdered or the disappearance of Rachel in *Life is Strange.*

The second stage is a journey, where the protagonist tries to understand the world better. This can be a metaphorical journey or a physical journey like Ellie's trip across the ruined United States in *The Last of Us.*

The third stage has the protagonist encounter conflict. This is the most common part of a video game! Opponents and obstacles bar the main character's way, but as the protagonist overcomes them, they mature and learn how to take control of their situation.

Finally, in the fourth stage, the protagonist matures—mentally or physically. They have changed and they have a positive outlook on the future.

Another great thing about kids' games (heck, this applies to all games) is that you can teach your players things without their even knowing it. I'm not talking about "edutainment," but the type of entertainment you used to find in movies and comic books.

As a kid, I remember a *Batman* comic book in which I learned about famous comedians of the 1940s, the opera *Pagliacci*, African masks, and how paraffin wax discolors with age.[19] That's some pretty impressive knowledge to gain from a "kiddie story." Don't be afraid to educate as well as entertain. Who knows, your players may learn something while they are having fun... and you may learn something as you are writing your story.

Writing for Licenses

A **licensed game** is one you create based on a pre-existing intellectual property (or *IP*), such as a character or world first seen in a movie, comic book, real life, television, or even another video game.[20] *Star Wars, Batman, Harry Potter*, and *SpongeBob Squarepants* are all licensed characters and worlds, known as **properties.** The property is licensed by a publisher or developer, which means that a fee is paid to use the property for a game (or several games). The group or individual who owns the original property is called the **licensor.**

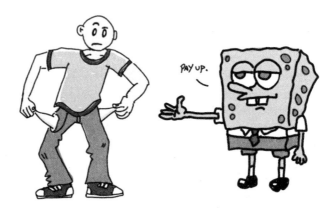

---

[19] This is all from the now classic story from Batman #73 "The Joker's Utility Belt."

[20] There are also plenty of IPs that exist in the public domain: *Cinderella, The Wizard of Oz, Dracula, The Three Musketeers, The Bible, Dante's Inferno,* to name a few. Remember to base your own work on the original material and not on someone else's interpretation.

Licensors include organizations such as Lucasfilm, DC Comics, Pottermore Publishing, or Nickelodeon (to use the preceding examples). However, just because the **licensee** has paid to make a game using the character, that doesn't mean they can make any game they want.

A licensee must work with the licensor to adhere to the brand. For example, a licensor may not want a character to kill enemies. Therefore, the developer must design the game around these "brand limitations." Some properties are lenient about what developers can do with them, whereas others are very strictly moderated.

Don't be dismayed about having to stay within the confines of a license. With a good licensing partner, you can design a game that allows room for creativity.

For example, my team was working on a licensed game that had seen more than ten games previously based on it. Not looking forward to making just "another installment" of the property, we discussed making the new game a genre that wasn't just a standard platformer. After we made our pitch, the licensor confessed to being tired of creating the same style of game over and over but had never considered taking the gameplay in another direction. The licensor gave us a lot more freedom than we had previously thought we would have, and, in the end, we produced a solid game. Just because you are working on a licensed game, don't assume that you are locked in to the "same old, same old." It never hurts to ask.

Here are a few tips I've picked up from working on licensed games:

- Find out about the license inside and out. Read, watch, and play everything you can on it. Go deep whenever possible. If you go in directions that aren't obvious or use characters that are more obscure, the fans of the brand will appreciate it. Every licensed game should be a celebration of the license and a big "thank you" to the fans.

- Uncover the "big issues" early. Talk to your licensor and find out what the big "no-no" issues are. Doing this will save you a lot of headaches and prevent you from making resources that will have to be changed later in production. For example, one game used hamburgers as a power-up. When the character ate them, he became invulnerable. However, even though it was never mentioned in any of the license's episodes, one of the main characters (one that was a playable character in our game) was a vegetarian. We had to change the power-up because the show's creators didn't like that we had their character eating meat.

- Remember that licensors can have final approval and working with them can be very tricky. On one project, the licensor would repeatedly reject the project because a rock was the wrong color blue.[21] But unfortunately, there's often not much you can do about this behavior. If it's not important, follow their request and move on.

---

[21] Seriously, this happened. It happened so much on one project my teammates started calling this kind of request "blue rocking." The term has stuck in my personal vocabulary.

- Get as much material as possible from the licensor. Television shows and other IP often have "bibles"—detailed documents—that outline the show's characters and worlds. Established comic books have years of back issues that make great reference material. If your license is still in production (for example, if you are making a game for a movie with a simultaneous release), get hold of scripts, animatics, storyboards, and production photos as soon as possible.

- If you are working on a game based on a movie or TV show, try to go to the set (if applicable) and take your own reference pictures. Try to get all the reference material you might need to help you replicate the world of the license as closely as possible.

- Respect the license but find ways to make it your own. A two-hour movie may not have enough material to allow you to create an eight- to ten-hour game. Work with the licensor to expand the fiction to help you fill in the gaps. Don't be afraid to bring your own interests to the party; those interests may fit in better with the brand's license than you may think.

Now that we have our story ready to go, let's talk about getting our game design down "on paper" by creating a game design document!

Level 3's Universal Truths and Clever Ideas

- Some games need a story. Some games don't. All games need gameplay.
- A story always has a beginning, a middle, and an end.
- Never mistake story for gameplay.
- A narrative designer brings plot to life through gameplay.
- Almost ANYTHING can be made into gameplay.
- Create a world that players will want to play in, and they will come back to play.
- Lore is the spice, not the meal.
- Make death matter.
- Players care about NPCs when those characters contribute something to the gameplay.
- Keep names short and descriptive.
- Representation is important.
- Don't underestimate kids: they're smarter than you think.
- Stay true to a license, but don't be afraid to "make it your own."

Level 4

You Can Design a Game, but Can You Do the Paperwork?

A JAPANESE GAME director once visited the studio where I worked to impart his wisdom to our team about his philosophy of game design, which mainly had to do with how much money his latest game had made. As he was leaving, he asked our team a cryptic question: "I believe making games is like fishing," he said. "When I return, you will tell me why this is so." If he had been wearing a cape, I'm sure he would have swooshed it mysteriously as he left.

He never did come back to tell us the answer, but in the meantime, I spent a lot of time thinking about just exactly how making games was like fishing. Fishing is quiet and slow and boring and involves waiting for something to happen that may never happen.[1] In the end, I decided that making games is **nothing** like fishing. I also decided that this game director was full of crap, so, I developed my own analogy.

Instead, I realized that making games is like making chili. When you make chili, you first need a recipe. Games need a recipe too, and that recipe is the game's design. Having the right recipe is important. You want to make sure that your

---

[1]You may be able to tell from this statement that I do not enjoy fishing.

game's **documentation** covers not only what is in your game, but how your game is to be made—just like a recipe. Be sure to follow the recipe as you make your game, but be mindful that it might have to change, especially if something doesn't go right. You know the saying "season to taste?" Well, that might happen during the creation of your game.

The next step is to assemble the ingredients. Just as a chili needs ingredients, a game's design needs gameplay mechanics, hazards, obstacles, puzzles, and enemies (depending on the game!) I believe that game developers are the chefs. The best ones make sure that everything is prepared for cooking. You need the right tools—the right game code and scripting tools to create the gameplay—just like you need spoons, pots and pans, and a stove to make your chili. However, you might not have exactly what you need at hand. Sometimes you might have the team and resources you want, and sometimes you must improvise with what is available. That's okay; I hear cowboys made some pretty good chili using nothing more than a campfire and a tin can. Prepare and add the ingredients in the right order. Simmer the beans and the vegetables first. Brown the meat **before** you add it to your pot. (I learned that one the hard way.) If it needs more of a specific ingredient—a type of gameplay is more fun—then add more of it! The goal is to make something pleasing to the audience.

In chili, everything is brought to a boil and then left to simmer. The **game's production** reminds me of boiling—a burst of energy and effort to get everything in and running. However, if you leave the pot boiling too hot for too long, you can ruin the chili, burn the pot, and catch the stove (and the chefs) on fire. I find it funny and appropriate that when your little developers in *Game Dev Story* (1997) work too hard, they burst into flame!

Games and studios have been destroyed by too much **crunch time**, so be responsible. **Game polishing** and **bug squashing** remind me of chili simmering. Chili isn't ready the moment you finish cooking it. You need to take the time to make it just right, to adjust the flavor, to add a little more seasoning and give the chili time to let the ingredients blend together to create a richer taste. Games, just like chili, need time to be iterated on, improved, and seasoned. **Bugs, features,** code, art, and design problems with the game need to be found and fixed. That takes time. Allow for that time, just like you need to allow for cooking time with chili. Sometimes it's good to let the team play with a part of the game to find out what works and what doesn't. I find that chili always tastes better the day after you have made it.

You may need to add something to your chili at the last minute to make it work. Unless you've royally screwed it up, chili can usually be salvaged. However, I don't recommend making games this way. It can lead to an upset stomach. Chili can also deceive. It may look horrible but taste delicious. Some games may not be perfect or even pretty, but if they have good gameplay, they can still entertain. Good games satisfy the soul as well as the stomach. Good games should do so as well.

You see? Making games is **exactly** like making chili. Take that, Japanese game director![2]

---

[2] I don't blame him for his bad analogy. After all, they might not have very good chili in Japan.

The Game Design Document

So, you've learned how to make chili, but what about making games? Many game designers start by creating a **game design document,** or **GDD** for short. A GDD is a blueprint for your game that details *everything* that is in your game. Sounds like a tall order! It is!

But a GDD has to do more than that. You are *selling* your game design. You are selling it to your team members, to your publisher, and to anyone who reads the GDD. It's not easy to write a clear, let alone interesting GDD, but here are a few pointers courtesy of my friend Armando Soto, who has read hundreds of game design documents and makes these observations:

- **A good GDD gets to the point:** Don't worry about character or world lore or detailed environment descriptions; keep these descriptions short and punchy. Providing illustrations of these things in your GDD is even better.

- **A good GDD fosters curiosity:** As you read through the GDD, you are carried through the "story" of the game. A good GDD *tells a story* that flows from the player. Start with what the player wants to achieve. Move into how the player interacts with the world, its obstacles, and enemies. Finally, tell how they overcome them. If you write your GDD in this way, the reader will want to know what happens next. They will *have* to know what comes next!

- **A good GDD has a clear emotional intent:** The great game designer Shigeru Miyamoto once said, *"When I create a game, I try to focus more on the emotions that the player experiences during the game play."* What emotions are you trying to stir? Fear? Wonder? Excitement? Tension? Describing gameplay and the game in these emotional terms will help keep your reader engaged. Imagine yourself in a situation that will make you feel that emotion and then determine the game play that evokes it. Remember visuals also help convey emotion to the reader.

- **A good GDD is rooted in player motivation:** All gameplay stems from the player. What does the player want? What does the player need? What do they have to do to get it? Nathan Drake wants Drake's treasure and every decision and action he does in *Uncharted: Drake's Fortune* leads toward that goal. In *Tetris*, every action the player does is to prevent the blocks from filling up the screen.

These points should all be answered as you write your GDD. If you do this, then you will have something that not only clearly conveys your game design but will actually be worth reading. Strive not just to inform with your GDD, but also to entertain. After all, you are designing a game. It should be fun!

Game Design Document (again)

A game design document can be a daunting thing—but don't be scared, there are actually four documents that will guide you through preproduction as you build toward making your GDD:

1. The one-sheet

2. The ten-pager

3. The beat chart

4. The game design document

While each of these documents has a specific use during the preproduction/production, the first three each build upon the content from the previous document and eventually compose the content found in the GDD.

NOTE   Check out Bonus Levels 1, 2, and 3 for templates of these documents.

The length of your GDD is going to be dictated by the complexity of your game. A GDD for a mobile game might only need a few pages while a console game might require a document that is 300 pages or more! Game designers have struggled with just how long a game design document should be. There is a movement within the game development community to keep the game design document as short as possible, for a variety of reasons. In the end, I believe a GDD should be just long enough to accurately describe what is going on in the game. However, don't let that intimidate you. The other documents—the one-sheet, the ten-pager, and the beat chart—are all steps that help you reach your goal of a complete GDD.

Speaking of the basics, you should make sure your document is readable. I'm not just talking about using proper grammar or using correct spelling and punctuation—all of which are very important in making your documents look professional. I'm referring to using the right body font. **Font** refers to a particular style of typeface. Fonts can be used to convey feeling when you only have words to play with, and I will explain how to do that later in this chapter. What I'm referring to is the main body of text of your document—much like the words in a book. In general, you should avoid using fancy fonts; otherwise, your readers won't be able to read your document. Keep things simple and legible.[3]

Speaking of fonts, I recommend never using more than two font styles in a single document unless you absolutely have to. You can use a fancy (but legible) font for the title page and things like headings, which can be 18 pts **(points)** or larger. For the body text of your document, the font size should be 12 pts. Anything smaller can be hard for some people to read. If you are creating a PowerPoint presentation for your game, I suggest using body text no less than 24 pts.

By the way, there is no official format for any of these game design documents. What I'm showing you here is just one way to present the information. For example, video game consultant Mark Cerny presents his GDD material in a single page per topic, bullet point format. He claims this simple presentation is easier for his teammates to read and digest. Use what works best for you. Just remember, the goal of great game design documentation is **communication**—communication to the player, your team members, and your publishing partners. The clearer the communication, the easier it is to get your coworkers excited about your ideas. Got it? Good. Let's start writing!

Writing the GDD, Step 1: The One-Sheet

The one-sheet is a simple overview of your game. A variety of people will read it, including your teammates and publisher, so you need to keep it interesting, informative, and most importantly, short. It should be no longer than...you guessed it...a single page. Here's an example.

---

[3] I suggest clear and easy-to-read fonts like Arial, Calibri, Helvetica, or Times New Roman.

A Compelling Story, A mystery that unfolds thru cinematic and puppet story sequences

The Second Saga Begins...
Eight months have passed since Ghosts to Glory and Maximo and Grim have searched in vain for Sophia. Their search is suddenly interrupted when they encounter a maiden menaced by a strange "clockwork" monster....

Excitement! Fun! Heroic!

MAXIMO VS The ARMY of ZIN

A Single Player Combat / Action Game!

The Sequel to Maximo: Ghosts to Glory

Maximo's appearance reflects his status!

MAXIMO: TEEN (Violence) Rated

- **More Heroic** - Maximo has to save others not just his own skin!
- **More attack moves!** Cool Combat Motions & combos, simple to command!
- **Get Stronger!** - Build up your character with the new experience system to gain effective and powerful abilities, armor and new weapons!
- Responsive movement and combat feel - Satisfying to play controls
- Customize your character with unique boxers and abilities!

Maximo's character image:
- He's Brave, Heroic and Impulsive!
- He's a man of action! Physical in nature.
- Will always do the right thing even if it's to his disadvantage.

Maximo's telling character traits:
- He is always holding a sword
- He fights even in his underwear
- He has Death as a companion

THE ARMY OF ZIN

Unique, marketable and Very Cool
- **Created by the famous artist Susumu Matsushita**
- **Enemy Variety** - Different size, shape, movement and method of attack and defeat.

FUN TO PLAY AND EASY TO GET INTO!

The Zin Legend...
500 years ago the Army of Zin attacked! The forces of man rallied and in a great and terrible battle the Zin were defeated and placed in the Great Vault. There they tick away the centuries waiting to freed so they can march once more.

Innocent and not so innocent characters for Maximo to interact with and rescue!

Collect Death Coins to play as DEATH!

Grim finally shows his true nature as the reaper, an invulnerable and unstoppable floating force!!

Keep collecting Koins to buy unique items!

Unexpected game play situations, enemies and story twists!

Jump over obstacles and beat the crap out of stuff with style!

The Besieged village:
This once peaceful village is bombarded into ruin by the army of Zin. Maximo must search out the mysterious Gearmaster who lives in the dark forest.

Cool dark atmospheric stylized creepy environments!

The Haunted Forest:
Maximo must brave the horrors of the haunted forest where even the trees don't want him to leave alive. Maximo learns about the Zin from Tinker, the cute and intelligent Gearmaster, before being abducted by Lord Bane.

Hazardous obstacle courses and physical puzzles!

The Crystal Mountains:
Maximo will have to cross teetering bridges and crumbling paths to reach Castle Hawkmoor and the great Vault. Maximo duels with his old rival, the Baron, to gain access to the Great vault.

Active environments that move and change as you smash stuff!

The Dead Sea:
The Dead Sea has been sucked dry by the Zin Fortress and the mysteries of the deep uncovered. Maximo must battle his his way to the Soul crusher.

The Zin Fortress:
Maximo must survive the grinding gears to rescue Tinker, destroy the soul crusher and the soul stones that power the Army of Zin.

You will find two more examples of one-sheets in Bonus Level 1. You can create them any way you like, just as long as you include the following information:

- Game's working title
- Intended game systems
- Target age of players
- Intended Entertainment Software Rating Board (ESRB) rating
- Overview of the game – story and gameplay
- The game's core loop
- Unique selling points
- Competitive products

Most of these terms are self-explanatory, but the following sections describe a few you may not know.

ESRB Ratings

The ESRB is a self-regulatory organization that enforces a rating system as well as advertising and online privacy principles for software in the United States and Canada.[4] The ESRB's creation is similar to the comic book industry's Comics Code Authority, which was created to enforce content and morality guidelines in conjunction with concerned parent groups. However, the ESRB's rating system more closely resembles that of the MPAA's movie rating system (G, PG, PG-13, R, X). Games are reviewed and assigned a letter rating according to content.

Currently, the ESRB can assign six ratings:

- **E (Everyone)**: May contain fantasy, cartoon or mild violence, and infrequent use of mild language.
- **E10 (Everyone 10+):** May contain more fantasy, cartoon or mild violence, and mild language and suggestive themes.
- **T (Teen):** May contain violence, suggestive themes, crude humor, minimal blood, and infrequent use of strong language.

---

[4]The ESRB is the American rating system. There are several other international systems including the Pan-European Games Information (PEGI), the UK's British Board of Film Classification (BBFC), and Germany's Unterhaltungssoftware Selbstkontrolle (USK). Their age and content restrictions vary by country.

- **M (Mature 17+):** May contain intense violence, blood and gore, sexual content, and strong language.

- **AO (Adults Only 18+):** Not suitable for people under 18; may contain prolonged scenes of intense violence, graphic sexual content, and nudity.

- **RP (Rating Pending):** This is when the ratings board is still trying to figure out what rating the game should be. It's only used on advertisements and product mock-ups.

Although the ESRB's guidelines are effective in informing parents to what titles are appropriate for their children, stigma is attached to some of the ratings within the development community and fanbase.

Many gamers consider E to be for "baby games" because this rating most frequently appears on edutainment and licensed titles for young audiences. At the other end of the scale, no brick-and-mortar retailer in America will carry a game with the AO rating. It's the industry's equivalent of an X rating in film. Therefore, most publishers and developers won't even consider making games for this rating and will take great pains to prevent their titles from having this rating.[5]

An advantage to publishing iOS and Android games is that developers don't need to submit their games to the ESRB to sell them. However, Apple, Google, and Microsoft have best practices and guidelines on certain content such as pornography, so you can forget about selling your X-rated platformer on the iPhone. In recent years, with the rise of streaming games, the ESRB has lost some of its jurisdiction. Games published on Steam or Apple's App store don't require an ESRB rating to be published.

The Core Loop

A game's **core loop** is the heart of the game. It's the thing the player does the most during the game. It's the gameplay. In *Fortnite*, it's building and shooting. In *Dorfromatik*, it's placing tiles. In *Alien: Isolation*, it's sneaking and hiding. In *Pac-Man*, it's not "eating," it's "moving." As you move through the maze, you eat dots. You move away from ghosts. You move toward an energizer. You move toward the blue ghosts. See how every action flows from the character's main action? Everything in your game should support this core loop. If it doesn't, it doesn't belong in your game. If your reader understands what the core loop is, they'll understand the game.

---

[5]This situation happened on *The Punisher* (THQ, 2005), where players could curb-stomp and feed criminals into a woodchipper during interrogations. The scenes were so graphic that the developer changed the camera angles and displayed the action in black-and-white to bring the AO rating down to an M.

Unique Selling Points

Unique selling points (or **USPs**) are the bullet points found on the back of the box. As a rule of thumb, you should have around five USPs. This is a number I developed when I realized I could really fit only five bullet points on the back of a game box. Remember that "amazing graphics" and "awesome story" or "sequel to the award-winning game" don't count. All games should have or be these things (though only if your game actually is a sequel in the case of the last one). Besides, gamers can spot that marketing lingo a mile away. USPs should be the unique features that make your game stand out from the crowd. Here are some examples. Let the spin begin!

- "Multiple gameplay modes, including the mind-blistering 256-player death match!"

- "Over 1,000 tunes from the universe's greatest bands!"

- "Explore gaming's biggest open world, where players can go anywhere!"

- "Mow through your enemies using the blastinator, the skull-defiler, and the awesome fire-ant extinguisher!"

- "Experience better-than-reality physics and eyeball-numbing special effects with the new Realitech engine!"

As you can see, USPs should get readers excited about the features of a game without going into lengthy detail about them. Exposing more of that detail is what the ten-pager is all about.

Competitive Products

Competitive products (or **"comps"**) are games that are similar to your game design idea that have already been released. Listing comps in your one-sheet helps your readers understand what your game is going to be about. However, make sure that when you choose your comps, you pick games that (a) people are very familiar with or (b) are successful. Publishers and marketers are very aware of how well or poorly a game sold. If you choose a comp of a game that did badly, a potential publisher may get scared off. Compare yourself to winners, only pick successful games.

Writing the GDD, Step 2: The Ten-Pager

Now that you have completed your game overview, it is time to expand that information and flesh out the details.

The **ten-pager** is a "broad stroke" design document that lays out the spine of your game. The intent is for readers to quickly understand the basics of the final product without going into excruciating detail. Keeping your ten-pager interesting may be the most important part of your document. Remember, important people may be reading this document including teammates, producers, and investors.

Be sure to provide plenty of visuals but keep them relevant. I like to have my ten-pagers look good so I will often commission concept artists to create art for my ten-pagers. In fact, if I can create a ten-pager that doesn't use words at all to convey my game, that's even better.

If you don't go all-out with visuals, you should avoid going overboard with fancy fonts and ornate layouts. Readability is the key. Creating your ten-pager in PowerPoint or a similar program will assist you with formatting and will enable you to present it electronically during a pitch meeting or print it out as a "leave behind" handout.

No matter which document you are creating, the goal is to make it interesting enough, so your readers want to continue reading it. As you write your ten-pager, ask yourself, "Who is my audience?" There is a big difference between a ten-pager that is being circulated around your team versus one that will be presented to the marketing department. Here are some examples of how you should skew the information in your ten-pager for each audience type:

Production Team	Marketing/Executives
Provide clear diagrams of gameplay.	Show exciting conceptual images.
Use short, punchy sentences.	Organize text in bullet-point form.
Use specific terminology to get your intention across clearly.	Use vivid, descriptive examples.
Compare gameplay to appropriate games, even vintage titles.	Use successful, modern games as comparative titles.

Although the examples in the table show two different audiences for a ten-pager, that doesn't mean you have to write two different documents. Just remember that both audiences will be reading it.[6]

Keep in mind that the ten pages of a ten-pager are more what you might call "guidelines" than actual rules. Feel free to go over or under[7] the ten-page count as long as you succinctly communicate the basics of your game design. By the way, you will find an example of a ten-pager in Bonus Level 2.

---

[6]Then again, sometimes you might want to make a version that caters to one audience over another...it never hurts to be prepared.

[7]Preferably under.

The Rule of Threes

Before you start writing, here is a **very important rule of thumb** I use when creating a ten-pager:

THREE IS A MAGIC NUMBER

History has observed that all good things come in threes. Don't believe me? Observe:

- The Hindu Trimurti
- The *Back to the Future* trilogy
- *Romance of the Three Kingdoms*
- Arthur C. Clarke's three laws of Robotics
- The saying "The third time's a charm"

This rule will come up again later in this book, but for now, my point is that people like things in threes, especially when you are providing examples.[8] The logic behind the **rule of threes** is this:

- The first example gives readers an idea of what you are talking about but can still mislead them.
- The second example gives readers something to compare or contrast the first example with.
- The third example can complement or contrast the other two, keeping your examples from feeling binary or contrived.
- Anything past three just gets too long and boring: never be boring.

Now that you know the rule of threes, use this power for good! When you are listing your examples in your ten-pager, group them in threes. History will thank you.

Everything that you've created for your one-pager migrates over to create...

The Ten-Pager Outline

If the one-pager is the heart of your game design, the ten-pager is the bones. Everything important about your game should be in the ten-pager. Remember that it doesn't have to be 10 pages, if you need more or use less, then that's fine. I've included an example of one of my own ten-pagers in Bonus Level 2. Check it out!

---

[8]Unlike the above. Sheesh.

Page 1: Title Page

Your title page should include the following items:

- Game working title
- Logo (optional, but recommended)
- Genre
- Target audience and rating

Working title: Give your game a name, any name so that way people can refer to it by something. You could even call it *"Untitled Zombie Game"* if you think your marketing department will want to come up with the title, but I'm not a fan of those kind of "flavorless" titles.

Logo: I also suggest that you have a placeholder logo. Pick a font that matches your game's genre, but make sure it's legible. If you use Photoshop, create the logo as a .PNG,[9] which will allow you to place it on any image because of its transparent background.

Choosing the proper font for your title allows you to convey the genre of your game quickly without the need for pictures. Here's a fun game! See if you can guess the game genres suggested by the following fonts:

SUPER MAGIC WORLD

VERY FAST CARS

DUDE WITH SWORD

You figured it out, didn't you? That's because a logo is a great way to convey a game's genre.

Genre: We talked about a whole list of genres earlier. Pick one. Pick two. Or mash a few together. Just don't overdo it, otherwise your game will sound "too busy."

Target Audience and Rating: Who is your game for? Kids? Adults? Soccer Moms? (Soccer Moms play games more often than you think!) What is the rating of your game? Even if you plan to submit your game via web-browser or on the Apple App store, which doesn't require an ESRB rating, it's good to know who your target audience is.

---

[9]To make a .PNG in Photoshop, go into "layers" create a new layer, put it underneath the layer with your artwork and then click the "eye" to make it invisible. Then in the pull-down menu select "Discard hidden layers." You will be left with your image on a transparent layer that you can save as a .PNG.

Page 2: Game Overview

Your game outline page should include two elements:

- An overview of the gameplay
- A short outline of the gameplay story and/or the gameplay experience

Overview: This is your "elevator pitch" of the game. Your game is summed up in a sentence.

Gameplay story/experience overview: Describe the beginning, middle, and end of your game's story. It helps if you approach this description from the direction of gameplay. Use action words (verbs) when writing. Keep in mind, this overview shouldn't be more than a few paragraphs long, but that limitation shouldn't stop you from telling the entire story. Your readers want to know whether your hero rescues the princess! (She does.)

Or you could briefly describe the outline of the game's action in the context of the player's experience. For example:

> *"Shadow of the Tomb Raider (2018) In the spectacular action-adventure puzzle game and thrilling finale to the Tomb Raider origins trilogy, Lara Croft must save the world from a Mayan apocalypse and shape her destiny to become the Tomb Raider."*

This brief game experience tells players who they are playing (Lara Croft), and the genre of gameplay (action-adventure puzzle); plus, it paints a picture of game locations (the Mayan jungle) and the players' goals (save the world). Here are some other questions that should be answered by the game experience:

- What are the challenges players encounter and the methods by which they can overcome them? Again, use verbs to describe these actions.
- How does the gameplay tie into the story? Do players encounter puzzles that grant access to new areas when solved? Do players have to fight bosses that bar their progression?
- How does the player win? Save the universe? Kill all the enemies? Collect 100 stars? All of the above?

If your game doesn't feature a singular character or has no character at all, then concentrate on the player's actions. For example, *Candy Crush Saga (2012)* is all about matching three or more candies to create combos and spectacular chain-reactions. If you are creating a sports game, are there any special events like the Super Bowl or March Madness? Are there special locations where players can compete? If you are making a driving game, concentrate on tracks or races. If you are making an Olympic game, what are the events the player will be participating in? The key is always to take your audience through the gameplay experience while creating vivid (but brief) images of the game's locales and gameplay.

Page 3: Player Character

On page 3, you want to highlight who the player is playing as or controlling. As a player, I might be a soccer player or a soccer mom. A pilot or a pirate. Batman or game designer man. If applicable list the character's age, gender, and other dossier-style background materials...as long as you feel this information does your character justice. Don't bother listing your character's blood type if this detail doesn't add anything to your game. But if it does, mention it!

Concept art is a must when dealing with characters. What does your character look like? What is the character's backstory? How did they end up in this predicament? What is their personality type? How do they respond to the challenges in the game? For example, when I worked on *God of War*, we were constantly referring to Kratos as "brutal," and everything he did in the game, from killing enemies to opening treasure chests, had to reflect that brutal personality.

How does all this information about the character relate back to gameplay? Does the character have any signature moves, abilities, weapons, or attacks? For example, Mario has his jump-and-stomp attack, whereas Simon Belmont from *Castlevania* has his whip. What other gameplay does the character do? Driving, flying, or swimming? Make sure you mention every action that your player can perform during the course of your game. If you can customize the character; change their costume, armor, physical appearance, etc., make sure to mention it here. If you don't have a player character – like in an abstract or card game or puzzle game—or if the player is YOU (a game where the player character IS the player), you can skip this page.

Page 4: Core Gameplay Loop

Here is where you elaborate on the core gameplay loop you created for the one-pager. What is the main action of the player and how is it used over the course of the game?

You also want to outline how your game is going to be structured. Are there multiple story chapters? Or is your game divided into levels or rounds? You are trying to paint a complete picture of the game and how it is played without going into a lot of details. I find that a graph or pie-chart showing a breakdown of the gameplay (for example, 10% exploring, 15% puzzle solving, 75% shooting) works well here. Anything to convey the information about your gameplay quickly to the reader is a big help.

Page 5: Visual and Audio Style

The German word **"gestalt"** translates as "the whole" of something. "Gestalt" is often used by stuffy film and art critics to describe the overall feeling of a work of art or the ambiance of a restaurant. The concept of gestalt is fantastically useful when applied to video games. To make a game feel like a complete experience, you want to show and explain examples of the look and feel of your game world...in other words, the whole, or the gestalt of your game.

To communicate your game's gestalt, present some images of the game world. They can be original art or inspirational images taken off the internet or from other sources. How do these locations or characters tie into your story? What mood is being invoked in each world? What style of music will you have? Now that you know what "gestalt" means, what is the overall gestalt of your game? Humorous? Horrific? Thrilling? Hardcore? Foreboding? Sexy? How is this feeling going to be presented to the players from the beginning of your product?

Page 6: Game World Fiction

Page 6 is where you detail more of your world. What makes your world interesting and more importantly, how does it support the type of play that the players will be doing? Remember, it's easy to get seduced into writing lore, but it's the game play that the player will be doing. Too much of the story can get boring to a reader.

Describe how your story will be told. Will you have **cutscenes** in your game? How will they be used to tell your story? How will they be presented to players? Describe the method by which they will be created including (but not limited to) CG cutscenes or in-game animation.[10] Describe when and how players will be seeing these such as during the game, at the headers and footers of levels, and so on.

Page 7: Objectives and Progression

Page 7 is where you tell the reader the WHY of the game. Why is the player playing? Why is it fun? Why will the player want to keep playing? Why will they keep them coming back for more?

Many games have role-playing elements, called **progression** wherein the character gains abilities, skills, and weapons as they get more experienced. Here's where you can describe that progression and what the player gains as they master the game—strength, health, wisdom, dexterity, accuracy—that type of thing.

Detail the player's objectives. Is it to slay a dragon and free the princess? Is it to slay the princess and free the dragon? Do the objectives keep changing over the course of the game (they should otherwise you might have a short game!)? How will the game present these changes to the player? Are there items and tools to help the player achieve their objectives?

Collectibles are items that are collected (well, duh) by the player. They can be coins, puzzle pieces, or trophy items. What do players collect? What is the benefit of collecting them? Can they be used to buy items, access new abilities, unlock material later in the game? Will they earn players trophies or achievements?

---

[10]Don't fear; I cover all these in a later Levels.

Some collectibles are **power ups!** These are temporary collectibles that give the player immediate powers and abilities, whether it's moving really fast, making the character invulnerable for a brief time, or restoring a hurt character's health.

If your game has an in-game **economy system**, briefly touch on that as well. Describe how players will be able to collect money (or gems, credits, or smurfberries) and buy things in the game. Briefly describe the shopping experience (is it via an interface, a store, or the character of Owner Smurf, etc.?).

Page 8: Examples of Game Play

Page 8 is where you will describe gameplay in more detail. You want to describe the interesting interactions and challenges the player will be doing. It helps to write these descriptions like a story, covering the beginning, middle, and end of an example. Like this:

After the last level's space pirate attack, Betty Blair has found herself stranded in space, amid the wreckage of the Star's Pride. Tapping on the X button, she activates her jetpack to maneuver carefully through the razor-sharp debris. As a pirate cruiser slowly passes by, she moves the analog stick to flatten herself against a large chunk of the shattered hull. A searching beam sweeps by, but she manages to avoid detection. Once the rocketship passes, she continues jetting toward the floating escape pod which will carry her home...hopefully.

See how this describes the actions of the game—jetting through space, hiding from enemies, avoiding dangerous environments? Try to paint a colorful image for your readers.

Does your gameplay use any unique interfaces? These can be modes that enhance existing gameplay like "detective vision" in the *Batman: Arkham* games, for example. Here's a good place to highlight it. Does your game have any minigames? Make sure you provide a brief description explaining how to play them. Does your game have an additional play mode such as driving, flying, or swimming? Describe that mode. Does your game have a different play style like *League of Legends' Teamfight Tactics* auto battler? Describe it. Does your game have unique gameplay mode like the "Battlemode" in *Doom Eternal*? Describe it. Describe it. Describe it. If your game has *anything* that will get readers excited about your gameplay, make sure to describe it.

Page 9: Monetization

This is the part where you describe your game's monetization plan. **Monetizing** a game is the action of getting players to give you real-world money. It is the act of making money from players but giving them the opportunity to buy content from within the game or by paying to add content (new levels, new characters, new skins, etc.) to an existing game.

For example, *Kingdom Rush 5: Alliance* players can buy power-ups to give their character more health, upgradable hero characters, and the ability to freeze and explode enemies. *Monopoly Go* lets players buy dice that extend gameplay time. *Marvel Snap* can purchase limited release cards with art by famous comic artists and monthly subscription packages that give players a leg up on the game. *Team Fortress 2* players can buy new weapons, gear, and amusing hats. *Fortnite*'s customers can buy skins to turn their avatar into characters as diverse as Marvel's Spider-Gwen, Metal Gear Solid's Solid Snake, Teenaged Mutant Ninja Turtles, or Star Wars' Boba Fett.

Developers use downloadable content (DLC) as an opportunity to expand the core mechanics to their game. *LittleBigPlanet* added an entire fluid dynamics mechanic to the game with its *Pirates of the Caribbean*-themed DLC.

Monetization is critical to many game developers and publishers. Does your game have a "free-to-play" system where the players can freely download the core game but have the option to pay to extend their play experience? Describe it! Does your game charge a nominal fee to allow players to buy extra content to improve their chances of victory? Describe it!

What are your players spending, and how does it thematically tie into the game? *Marvel Snap* (2022) allows players to buy gold, which they can use to buy cards—or credits. These can then be used to upgrade cards and unlock more content. In an attempt to sweeten the deal, developers can offer **season passes** that bundle together unique content. Season passes provide an opportunity to buy episodes or content at a "reduced" price. Make sure you mention these monetization methods because they will impact your game's content creation time and your game's release plan.

Monetization doesn't stop with virtual goods. *Skylanders'* and *Disney Infinity's* publishers sold physical toys and "power discs" that add characters, environments, and gameplay mechanics when used with an electronic interface. If these physical goods are important to your game, make sure you describe how they work! We're going to dive deeper into monetization later in Chapter 16.

Page 10: Platform, Technology and Scope

Page 10 is where you go into detail about platform-specific features. What platform is your game going to be available on? A console? Computer? Mobile? Or unique hardware of your own creation? Does it use a camera or a motion controller? Does it use AR or is it VR? Is your multiplayer mode played split screen or on individual screens? Cover these details because they will be important for readers to understand what technology requirements will be needed to produce your game.

Writing the GDD, Step 3: The Beat Chart

Now that you have your ten-pager written, let's start the beat chart.

The **beat chart** is a handy-dandy tool that not only helps you develop the content of your GDD but also provides a "map" of the structure of your game; this is extremely important when examining the gameplay progression. The example that follows is a beat chart of a third-person action game. The elements you list for your own beat-charts will differ from genre to genre. In this example, the beat chart requires the following elements:

- Level/environment name
- File name (level/environment designation)
- Time of day (in context of the game)
- Story elements for level
- Progression: gameplay focus of the level
- Estimated play time of level
- Color scheme of level/environment
- Enemies/bosses introduced and used
- Mechanics introduced and used
- Hazards introduced and used
- Power-ups found in level/environment
- New abilities, weapons, or gear introduced/unlocked
- Treasure amount and type the players can find
- Bonus material found in level/environment
- Music track(s) to be used in this level/environment

Here is an example of a beat chart for a couple of levels from *Maximo: Ghosts to Glory*.

Level: World 1-1 Name: Grave Danger (Boneyard)	Level: World 1-2 Name: Dead Heat (Boneyard)
TOD: Night	**TOD:** Night
Story: Maximo enters the graveyard, fighting his way through undead creatures that bar his way.	**Story:** Achille's drill has cracked open the earth, causing lava pits to open up throughout the graveyard.
Progression: Player taught basic movement, combat, and defensive moves. Player learns how to collect and map abilities.	**Progression:** Player masters hazardous jumps and more intense combat.
Est. play time: 15 min	**Est. play time:** 15 min
Color map: Green (trees), brown (trees/rock), purples (tombstones)	**Color map:** Red (lava), brown (trees/rock), purples (tombstones)
Enemies: Skeleton (basic), sword skeleton (red), skeleton (axe), ghost, zombie (basic), wooden coffin, chest mimic	**Enemies:** Skeleton (basic), skeleton (axe), sword skeleton (red), sword skeleton (blue), skeleton (guardian), zombie (basic), raven, ghost
Mechanics: Holy ground, breakable tombstone, breakable torch, breakable crypt lid, breakable rocks, Achille key statue, key lock, opening gate (door), opening gate (cave), prize wheel, treasure chest, locked chest, hidden chest, end plinth	**Mechanics:** Holy ground, breakable tombstone, breakable torch, breakable crypt lid, key statue, key lock, opening gate (door), enemy coffin, floating platform, prize wheel, treasure chest, locked chest, hidden chest, end plinth
Hazards: Unholy ground, Achille statue, fall-away ground, skull tower, breakaway bridge, deep water, lava pit	**Hazards:** Unholy ground, swinging gate, skull tower, flame jet, lava pit
Power-ups: Koin, koin bag, diamond, death koin, spirit, life up, flametongue, shield recharge, sword recharge, half health, full health, iron key, gold key, armor up	**Power-ups:** Koin, koin bag, diamond, death koin, spirit, life up, flametongue, shield recharge, sword recharge, half health, full health, gold key, armor up
Abilities: Second strike, mighty blow, magic bolt, doomstrike, foot cheese	**Abilities:** Second strike, mighty blow, magic bolt, doomstrike, throw shield
Economy: 200 koins, 2 death koins	**Economy:** 200 koins, 1 death koin
Bonus materials: N/A	**Bonus materials:** N/A
Music track: Graveyard 1	**Music track:** Graveyard 2

When you compare two or more columns of a beat chart, certain patterns start to emerge regarding the introduction of new enemies, mechanics, items, and abilities. You can then identify deficiencies in the design and start to move elements around. Filling in holes here, shifting bloated areas there.

Here are a few things to watch for:

- Beware of "clumping" such as too many new enemies or mechanics being introduced at once. Spread these out over the course of the game. Remember, the first level of the game always has several elements, so technically it doesn't count.

- Also beware of "samey-ness" such as too many identical combinations of enemies and mechanics. You want to mix things up to keep interaction fresh.

- Alternate your time of day and color schemes. If you have too many of the same lighting or color schemes in a row, things are going to feel and look repetitive. It's easier for players to notice change and feel progression in the world if things are colored differently.

- Alternate your music tracks. Players will get bored listening to the same music over and over again.

- Watch out for deficiencies and excesses in your in-game economy. Make sure players have enough money to buy items to use in the world. Also, make sure players don't have so much money that it becomes worthless, or it allows the player to buy so much stuff that the game becomes too easy.

- Introduce mechanics and enemies in conjunction with the items and abilities required to defeat them.

- Determine when players will have "everything" in the game such as all weapons, all skills, all vehicles, or all armor upgrades. Make sure players have time to play with them. I try to make sure players have everything by three-fourths of the way through the game, so the last quarter lets players use all their cool stuff.

- Introduce elements in a reasonable way. As a rule of thumb, I try to introduce two or three new mechanics, enemies, and rewards per level.

- Look out for too much story. How long have the players gone without playing? Modern gamers don't have the patience to watch anything more than a minute or two. A game is a game because you play it. Otherwise, it's a movie. Keep it short.

Writing the GDD, Step 4: The Game Design Document

The Game Design Document can be a lengthy work. I've created GDDs that are hundreds of pages long. Sometimes it takes several months to create one. Rather than make this Level much longer by outlining the game design document, you can find the outline of a GDD in Bonus Level 3 near the end of this book. I find that having a framework can be helpful when you are writing a GDD. There's a lot to cover and sometimes you might forget something. I hope you find it useful. Just remember this above all else:

THE MOST IMPORTANT PART OF A GAME DESIGNER'S JOB IS COMMUNICATION

As you write your GDD, keep that in mind. Do your best to communicate your game's ideas to your reader. Make sure you provide very specific examples and terms for the elements in your game design, especially when referring to characters and game mechanics. If an accurate term doesn't exist, go ahead, and make one up!

For example, when I was working on *Maximo vs. Army of Zin*, I first referred to the game's enemies, the Zin, as robots. I quickly learned that everyone on my team had a different mental image of what a robot was, ranging from Star Wars' See-Threepio to the Iron Giant. I realized that my team would be on the wrong page unless I provided a clearer description for them. The image I had in my head of the Zin was of a metal skeleton made out of riveted brass with turning gears for guts. I started using the term "clockwork undead" to describe the Zin. I found that when I focused my language on something very specific, my teammates were able to better visualize the image I had in my head.

ROBOT   ZIN

My advice is to keep it short, interesting and use pictures whenever possible.

Writing the GDD, Step 4.1: Now, Unlearn What You Have Learned

I just spent half of this Level teaching you how to create a game design document. While I find that creating a GDD is a useful exercise for a game designer to go through, times have changed. I challenge you to *ditch the GDD*. It's long. It's cumbersome. It's too much of an "ask" to have your teammates read a large document. It can be self-indulgent. It can lead to feature creep. There's as much bad about a game design document as there is good. We modern designers need an alternative.

All of the following alternate methods are meant to allow the game designer to communicate with their audience. Different methods work for different teams. The first step is to TALK to your teammates about how they like to work. Some teams like reading documents while others want nothing to do with them. Here are some alternative methods of communicating your game design:

- **One-Sheets Only:** I know many game designers who only write their designs as one-sheets. They believe that everything you should know about a feature or character action, or mechanic should fit on a single piece of paper—otherwise it is too long and involved. The good thing about this is that it is quick for your teammates to read and easy to replace in case the design is changed.

- **Storyboards:** Just like movies, gameplay can be storyboarded. It doesn't matter whether you can draw detailed images or stick figures; there is truth to the old saying "a picture is worth a thousand words." If you are having trouble coming up with ideas, you can use published movie storyboards, comic books, or even the gameplay diagrams in this book for inspiration.

- **Diagrams:** If you are worried about your art skills (you shouldn't be, even a stick figure conveys information), you can always diagram your gameplay examples. Use consistent shapes and colors to represent elements of your game. Make sure you include a **legend** (a guide to all of the elements shown on a map) so your readers know what your icons and shapes mean.

- **Animatics:** Using your storyboards or diagrams as a starting point, you (or an artist friend) can animate them with programs like ProCreate, Lightwave, or even PowerPoint. Although this approach takes more time, seeing your gameplay examples in motion leaves very little room for misinterpretation. Or you could assemble them from movie scenes or other games using video editing tools like Adobe Premier Pro or Apple Final Cut Pro. This type of "clip-show" is called a **rip-a-matic**.

- **The beat chart:** A beat chart is a document that covers the entire span of the game. The advantage is that it allows readers to grok[11] a lot of information on one page, as well as compare and contrast the flow of information within the game.

- **Whiteboard program:** In a recent project, my team and I used an in-program whiteboard tool to brainstorm and write down our game design. What was great about it was that we could paste inspirational images and links to videos and websites. You'll need a moderator to make sure things don't get too cluttered, but it was easy for others to quickly understand the design of our game.

- **The team wiki:** Rather than killing trees, why not publish your GDD electronically on a wiki or in a Google doc? It's a great way for your team members to be kept up to date on the latest and greatest game material, especially because they can contribute to its creation. But be careful; as preproduction moves into production, the design team can very easily neglect a wiki so that it becomes out of date.

It doesn't matter how you communicate your ideas, as long as you are clear. There are plenty of techniques you can use to get this information across, but when creating a game design, always keep this **very important thing** in mind:

EVERYTHING IS LIQUID

This means that game designs are living things. Game designs change: they flow, they mutate, they evolve. If you don't let your game idea simmer (like chili!), you may not think of a great idea, or you may miss an opportunity to create some truly great gameplay. Eventually, many of the things you write in your design will become obsolete. At a certain point, writing things down becomes counterproductive, and it all becomes about finishing the game. But you need a starting point, and a GDD gives you that launching pad from which your game design can soar.

There is some debate as to which is better: a shorter, "bite-size" play experience or a longer, more involved one. To be honest, the choice totally depends on your game genre, but now that mobile games have exploded onto the market, players are getting used to shorter gameplay experiences (averaging around 15 minutes a session). Even longer games like

---

[11]"Grok" means "to understand completely" and is a slang term created by sci-fi writer Robert Heinlein. Now do you grok?

RPGs and action-adventure games are carving up their game experiences into encapsulated sessions. Whichever way you go, what matters most is that you give your players their money's worth.

I usually advise teams making a big, single player action game to aim for a minimum of ten to twenty hours of gameplay, depending on the gameplay. For readers of older editions, you'll notice that this number has changed. That's because gamers expect way more for their money than in the old days. It's also why you'll notice that so many games are multiplayer; because a multiplayer game can offer "endless" gameplay, while a single character action or platformer game is limited by story and levels, which are much more expensive to make, especially when they require more unique content.

I advise teams making mobile games to aim for no more than 2 to 5 minutes per level. If you are creating a racing game, try not to make a round last 30 to 40 minutes. If you are making an adventure game, make sure the player does something interesting every 12 minutes. This doesn't include replay time, time spent watching cutscenes, or time spent reading dialogue. Remember, it never hurts to have more content; however, if you must cut a level, remember that you still need to integrate that content (mechanic, item, enemy, etc.) someplace else. If it's just hanging out at the start of the next level for no apparent reason other than it was needed, the player will be left with a feeling that the game is shoddy. You will learn about some tricks to help determine playing time and avoid cutting features in Level 9.

Writing the GDD, Step 5: Be Responsible

Creating all these design documents is important, but your designs mean nothing if you aren't a responsible game designer. Some of the following advice may seem like common sense, but I've also learned that common sense isn't always that common:

- **A good idea can come from anywhere.** I have seen many teams suffer from what I call the **"not invented here syndrome,"** a belief that any idea from someone who isn't on the design team isn't valid. Pardon my French, but only a colossally arrogant idiot would believe that. Good designers always have their ears to the ground for great suggestions from others. Always share your ideas and designs with others. They may disagree with you, but you don't always have to take their advice either.

- **Decide and stick with it.** Although game designs are always changing, the worst thing you can do is keep redoing and redoing work. It's no crime to be a perfectionist, but many design issues can be thought out and designed on paper first, before a single pixel is rendered or a line of code typed. I have seen many projects drain away time, resources, and team morale when design leads are unable to commit to a direction.

- **Update often.** Send out e-mails, make comments on documents, use a version control system, and include in-document comments or text highlighting to make sure your colleagues are kept up to date when changes occur.

- **Talk to your teammates.** I'm a big believer in "face time." Get up out of your chair and go talk to a teammate in person...or video chat with a team mate to get their opinion on something. You never know what great idea might arise during the course of a conversation.

- **Tackle the tough ones first.** Talk to your art and programming leads ahead of time about how they work and what issues in your design they think are going to be trouble spots. Don't leave these difficult design issues until the last minute. Sort them out first. If they don't work, you will still have time to make course corrections with your design.

- **Trust your instincts....** There are moments when you are going to have an idea for something in your game that no one else is going to believe will work. Sometimes you just must dig in and fight for it. Don't be afraid to fight for a good idea. You may be right in the end.

- **...Or don't.** First make sure your idea is a good one and worth fighting for. Shop it around to other teammates. Get opinions. Try using someone else's idea for a change. Better to let Darwinism—the strongest ideas—weed out the bad ideas. You don't want to end up fighting for a bad idea. It's a waste of time and energy and makes you look foolish.

- **Don't make everything a drama.** If something makes you mad or get loud, or angry, take a break. Get some air. There's nothing worse for a team than shouting and arguing. If you genuinely care about a feature or level or character that other teammates want to change or cut, make a reasonable case for why it should be kept. But be prepared for it not to work. In the words of one of my colleagues "Don't be so dear."

- **Respect the abilities of your peers and be mindful of their limitations.** Certain team members are better at certain things. Work with your producer to find out who would be the best person for the job. The last thing you want is a teammate working on an aspect of your design that they don't have the talent for or interest in. Conversely, talk to your teammates about what they'd like to work on. Everything else being equal, you will always get better results if your teammates are into what they are working on.

- **Games are made by people.** Vacations are taken, grandparents die, babies are born during the course of production. Any of these things can cause designers not to be around at a critical moment in production. Make sure your designs are accessible to all the pertinent team members, especially your producer. Be sympathetic to your coworkers if something happens or if they need some time off.

- **Save often and always.** Accidents happen and sometimes people forget to save their work. Or they overwrite someone else's work. Or a hard drive fails. Use version control programs such as Git, Perforce, Alien Brain, Google Documents, WorkSpace, Dropbox, or Subversion to store documents on a drive that is backed up regularly. Save to the cloud or server. Don't keep the contents of your game on your local drive. Don't keep the contents of the game in your head. Write those things down. Make sure you have some system of filing so you can find your work, too!

- **Stay organized.** When creating files and documents, use naming conventions that humans can understand. For example, if you have a forest level, make sure the word "forest" or at least the letter "f" is part of the name. Add the YEAR-MONTH-DAY to the end of your documents, especially when multiple documents exist. It's easier to sort and find your documents using this numbering convention. Naming files by date is helpful, especially when your project spans longer than a single calendar year. Make sure you use consistent naming of everything in your game.

- **Be prepared.** Eventually, you will need ways for others to get around your game. Have your game include level skips; a flexible cheat camera so others can take screenshots of your gameplay; and cheat codes that enable invulnerability, grant power-ups and money, and so on. Talk to your publishing/marketing partners about their needs early in the development of your game. Sometimes they will want additional content such as extra levels, costumes, or bonus materials to market and sell the game. Be prepared to create this material; don't leave it until the last minute of production. Be aware that you may have to make a demo of your game. Think about what you want to have in your game demo to show the game in the best possible light. Earmark potential content such as specific levels or experiences that may be used for a demo later down the line.

Arm yourself with this advice, and I guarantee you, your project will go a lot smoother in the long run.

Writing the GDD, Step 6 – Other Game Genres

The GDD that I've described so far has been for first-person or third-person games played on a home console or computer; but there are so many more different types of games with their own design requirements. While I can't cover all genres, here is advice for some of the more popular ones.

Role-Playing Games

Inspired by the pen and paper game *Dungeons and Dragons (1973)*, role-playing games (RPGs) were some of the earliest computer games including *dnd (1975)* and *Dungeon (1975)*. Game designer James Portnow[12] says that all RPG designs have the following: Mystery, mastery, mental challenge, narrative, novelty, and flow.

A good RPG GDD should not only focus on lore, the world, and enemies, but should focus on progression. The character's growth is the most important part of a role-playing game. Here are some design elements to focus on:

- **Clear objectives:** Guidance is important, especially in the open world environments common to RPGs. Explain how the story or NPCs (non-player characters) might guide the player, or how the character's progression (wants and needs) will guide them through the game. Remember that giving the player too many objectives can be overwhelming, or it devalues them from being special or important. It's better to have a player achieve an objective deliberately than by accident. An accident removes all of an achievement's importance and the player's celebration of achieving it.

- **Meaningful choices:** Outline what kinds of choices the player will be making and how they are meaningful to the character. The best choices are when both choices are appealing.

- **Useful progression system:** RPGs are all about characters improving. Whether it's core stats (like strength, speed, health, or even ammo capacity) or a weapon or spell that gets stronger (more damage, wider area of effect, shorter cooldown) you should explain how each level of a player's progression improves the character and affects gameplay.

- **Engaging environments:** RPGs are best at transporting players to exciting and exotic realms. Exploring the world is a big part of the appeal of an RPG. Describe these places, why the character is there, and what they will be doing. We'll talk more about this when we discuss level design.

- **Diverse challenges:** RPGs allow players to be all different types of characters such as wizards, barbarians, rangers, druids, etc. Explain how each character class can resolve an encounter or solve a puzzle related to their class: the barbarian smashes a massive troll, the wizard charms the troll with magic, and the rogue is sneaky and avoids the troll altogether. Show that each class gets their "hero moment"—a situation that only they can solve.

Real-Time Strategy Games

Starting with *Herzog Zwei* (1989), **real-time strategy** games (or RTS) came into their own in the 90's with *Dune II: The Building of a Dynasty* (1992), *Warcraft: Orcs & Humans* (1994), *Command and Conquer* (1995) and *StarCraft* (1998), which became a global phenomenon. RTS's

---

[12]You can listen to James' thoughts on RPG game design at www.youtube.com/watch?v=tWtvrPTbQ_c.

influence can be felt in popular modern games such as *Rise of Kingdoms* (2019) or *Total War: Warhammer III* (2019).

Real-time strategy games are very different than the first-person and third-person games we've been talking about. Sure, they share some traits like player objectives and progression, but they have their own unique design challenges that you should be aware of:

- **Camera:** Strategy games are often viewed from **"god view,"** which is a position above the battlefield to give the player a wider field of view of the action. You will want to refer to environments in general terms as players won't see details as easily as they would in a first-person or third-person view. Characters are smaller, too, so keep player actions broad and general—like shooting, mining, or moving.

- **Unit management:** Explain how RTS players manage their units, whether as an army or an individual unit. Describe the actions (such as resource gathering, combat, repair, etc.) they can do and how they perform them when they are alone. (This is the start of how their AI will work).

- **Player agency:** Explain how players can create their own strategies by "creating their own rules" within the established rules of the game. Provide scenarios that illustrate how the player can "bend the rules" to convey this greater sense of freedom during the game.

- **Rock, Paper, Scissors:** Many of the interactions in strategy games are based on the classic "Rock, Paper and Scissors" where something always beats something else. Map out the relationship between the player's abilities and the obstacles in the game. There should always be an exception to this rule, but the player should have to figure out what it is. This leads to some great "ah-ha" moments for the player.

First-Person Shooters

The earliest **first-person shooters** (or FPS) were a player, armed with weapons, usually guns, battling against other players or AI bots in a **death match**. FPS soon added other game play modes including **capture the flag**, **area control**, and **escort missions**.

The "first person" comes from the camera view. The first FPS was *Maze War* (1973) but the genre boomed in popularity with *Wolfenstein 3D* (1992) and the subsequent games: *Doom* (1993) and *Quake* (1996). Here are a few pointers when designing for an FPS:

- **Control schemes:** Detail your control scheme. How does a player use the controller or keyboard to play the game? Many FPS use what are called HALO[13] controls.

---

[13]Named after the popular FPS game *HALO: Combat Evolved* (2001)

Using controls that players are already familiar with will allow players to quickly learn how to play.

■ **List levels:** An FPS requires diverse locations. List out the levels your game will have as it will help determine the cost and time to create your game. We will discuss how to create a level later in this book.

■ **Define the camera:** A good camera is important for an FPS. Describe how the game's camera is used in your game, especially specific features such as auto-targeting, quick realignment, or over-the-shoulder perspective.

■ **Guns! Guns! Guns!** Weapons are an important part of an FPS, so list out the weapons in your game. Include their important statistics such as range, capacity, damage, and reload speed. Don't forget about melee weapons and unarmed attacks as well.

■ **User interface:** User Interface (UX) is very important to an FPS. Whether it's health bars, radar maps, experience points or control prompts, you want the UX to be clear to understand and easy to read. We'll talk more about UX later in this book.

Battle Royale

Battle Royale is a subgenre of the FPS genre in which players drop onto a playfield to search for weapons and equipment to help them survive a death match. As the match progresses, the playfield shrinks, forcing the players to confront each other. The last team (or single player) standing wins.

The subgenre first appeared in *Day Z: Battle Royale* (2013), a mod developed by designer Brendan Greene, which later became known as *PlayerUnknown's Battle Royale (2017)*. The format became immensely popular and soon you could play battle royale in *Fortnite* (2017), *Apex Legends* (2019), and *Call of Duty: Warzone* (2020). A battle royale game has unique features that should be addressed in your game design:

■ **Chutes away!** Battle royale games start with the player dropping onto the map. Describe how the player will do this and how it will be unique. What happens when the player lands on the map? Describe the action so the reader understands the order of events.

■ **Weapons:** What weapons can the player find around the map? How many weapons can a player carry at once? What about grenades or health packs? How do they drop and pick these things up?

■ **Scale:** How many players can your game support? 16? 24? 50? 100? Different scales require different levels of balance. You'll need much bigger maps if you have a hundred players.

- **The "ring of death:"** How does the "ring of death" work? What does it look like? How fast does the ring travel? What happens to a player if they get caught outside of the ring?

- **What sets you apart?** Even though it is a new subgenre, you need to do something different to set your game apart from all of the others. *Fortnite* allows players to build structures for defense and objectives.

- **Character elimination:** What happens to the player when their character is eliminated from the game? Do they respawn? Does the player have to wait until the next game to spawn back in? Or does the player have the option to go back to the lobby and jump into another game?

Match Three Games

This popular genre started on computers, moved to internet browsers, and ended up dominating mobile devices. Games like *Bejeweled* (2001), *Candy Crush Saga* (2012) and *Royal Match* (2021) are quick to learn, easy to play and totally addictive. As these games don't have player characters per se, you'll have to focus on the player's interaction and game's feedback in your GDD instead.

- **What kind?** There are four kinds of gameplay in a Match 3 game: swapping, blasting, shooting and linking. Describe how the player uses these to make matches and what happens when a match happens.

- **Positive reinforcement:** Match 3 games depend on positive re-enforcement such as particle effects, congratulatory messages, and animations that describe how the game is going to make the player feel and want to keep playing.

- **Again, level design:** Match 3s are composed of tiles, boards, and specific rules change and create the game's challenge. What sets Match 3 games apart from each other is the level design. We'll talk more about this kind of level design later but remember it's important to describe it in your GDD.

- **What's a Metagame?** In addition to moving or breaking tiles, Match 3 games often have a metagame. Often the "meta" is based around collection (stickers, characters, cards), "base building" or upgrade mechanics. This needs to be described in your GDD.

- **Monetization:** Monetization is the way most Match 3 games make their profit. By offering microtransactions for upgrades and temporary benefits, a developer can make back their cost or even exceed it. Your GDD should discuss what content can be purchased in a game with real money and what can be bought with in-game or "soft currency" that motivates the player to keep playing. We'll talk more about monetization practices in another Level of this book.

Sports Games

Sports inspired the creation of the earliest video games. *Tennis for Two* (1958) and *Pong* (1972) simulated table-tennis, while *Table Tennis* (1972) premiered on the Magnavox Odyssey home system. *Soccer* (1973), *Pro Hockey* (1973), and *TV Basketball* (1974) all premiered in Japanese arcades. Sports were a big part of the Intellivision's lineup, which featured the first licensed sports games including *NFL Football* (1979), *NBA Basketball* (1980), *PGA Golf* (1980) and *PBA Bowling* (1981). At the time of this writing, EA's *Madden NFL* is currently on its 41st version and their *FIFA* soccer is on its 30th title. These two sports series are always top sellers.

Sports games are an interesting design challenge, in that your audience has expectations about how the game is played and how it looks. But just because these games are already established, doesn't mean there isn't room for you to play within the design space. Your sports game GDD should address the following:

- **Rules:** Describe the rules of the sport to the reader. Don't assume that everyone knows how to play the game you are making. Describe how the rules will affect gameplay, where the limits are for the player and where the player can "bend the rules" during play.

- **Realism:** Realism is essential for most sports games. Realistic rules, realistic animations, realistic graphics, and realistic physics. However, you are making a game where you can "fudge" the rules of reality. You will have to balance accuracy against user frustration, which aspects of the game remain in and which are removed because they just aren't fun.

- **AI:** Most sports games have artificial intelligence (AI) for the non-player teammates. You will have to design how these NPC players perform, determining what they do and don't do in different scenarios. Keep in mind that AI characters that are "too smart" or "too accurate"[14] might remove fun from the player's play experience.

- **UX again:** The user interface needs to be designed for the game. It's an important part of a sports game. This includes illustrating plays that the player can select to what happens visually when a goal is scored. We'll discuss UX in a later Level of this book.

- **Animations:** While animating characters is the animator's job, it is design's job to catalog the animations for the game, thus creating a worklist for the animators. Be thorough and creative in listing these character animations. Be sure to describe how interacting character animations work. What happens when two NPC, a player and NPC, or a player and a player interact?

- **Audio:** Audio is a key part of a sports game's design. Are there announcers? How do they work? Are there crowd noises? When do they cheer or boo? What sounds do the

---

[14]Finding out "how much is too much" when it comes to artificial intelligence is something that will happen in-game by having the designer and programmer working together.

players hear that give them cues about gameplay, such as a referee's whistle or the "barks" of a quarterback? You will have to design what sounds are important to your game—again creating a list for the sound designer.

That was a lot of material to cover! If you need a reminder, you'll find an outline of a GDD that you can use for your own designs in Bonus Level 3 of this book!

Now that you know how to construct a proper GDD, you're ready to dig into one of the pillars of game design, something I call the Three Cs. Level 5 will get you started on the first C, Character.

Level 4's Universal Truths and Clever Ideas

- A game is like chili: it needs the right recipe, tools, ingredients, and time to come out right.
- A game design document should be just long enough to describe the action in a game.
- A well-written GDD is like a story that engages the reader's curiosity.
- Know your intended ESRB target rating and design toward it.
- Work your way up from one-sheet to ten-pager to game design document.
- Use tools like beat charts to help find problems early in your game design.
- A GDD is a framework that will help you plan your design…
- …or ditch the GDD. Find an alternative way to communicate your design.
- Everything is liquid; your game design WILL change over the course of production.
- Different game designs require different GDDs.
- Give your players their money's worth.
- Be smart when naming and organizing documents and files.
- Save your documents and game content often and always.
- Different genres of games require their own special GDDs.

Level 5
The Three Cs, Part 1: Character

ALTHOUGH MUCH OF your game design is always changing, you need to establish three fundamentals early in your preproduction. I call them the "**Three Cs**":

1. Character

2. Camera

3. Control

If you change any of these Three Cs during the course of your production, you risk massive problems with your gameplay, which may require extra reworking, and you risk endangering your game. I know this sounds dramatic, but so many game elements hinge on the Three Cs that changing one thing will have a ripple effect throughout your entire game. I have seen teams catastrophically screw up and cancel their games because of their failure to stick to the plans of their Three Cs.

Although you learned about writing a character in Level 2, here I use the term in a different context. In this level, I talk about the way the character is presented to the player and the activities the player does with that character. The **very important rule** about character design is:

FORM FOLLOWS FUNCTION

Let this rule be your motto when designing anything. It will come into play more importantly later in the book, but it should be your guide, especially when designing your game character. You can find several great books on how to design a character visually,[1] so I don't go into great detail about this topic but let me pass on some high-level things to keep in mind.

---

[1] Some of my personal favorites include *Disney Animation: The Illusion of Life* by Frank Thomas and Ollie Johnston (Abbeville Press, 1984), *The Art of Star Wars* (Episodes I - VI) series (Del Rey, 1976 - 2007), and Ben Caldwell's cartooning series *Fantasy! Cartooning* and *Action Cartooning* (Sterling Publishing, 2005).

Who Do You Want to Be Today?

As you are creating your character, you need to think about their personality. What are the three personality traits that you would use to describe your hero?

Mario: Courageous, bouncy, happy

Sonic: Fast, cool, edgy

Kratos: Brutal, vicious, selfish

Apply these traits to your character's physical appearance. Animators have known for decades that the shapes you use for your character's design will help communicate their personality. Circles are used to make a character feel friendly. Squares are often used for strong or dumb characters, depending on just how big the square is. Triangles are interesting. A downward-pointing triangle is often used to give a heroic character a powerful frame. However, if you use that same downward-pointing triangle for the character's head, he seems sinister. Try rotating, mixing, and matching shapes to create compelling characters.

Another old trick that all professional character designers and animators use is the **silhouette.** A strong, clear silhouette of a character is important for many reasons:

- Tells you the character's personality at a glance
- Helps distinguish one character from another
- Identifies "friendly" or "enemy" characters
- Helps the character stand out against background and world elements

For example, look at the silhouettes of the player characters of *Team Fortress 2*.

Due to their unique silhouettes, you can immediately distinguish one character from another. In the preceding image, Heavy is clearly distinguished from Pyro from the Spy. Body language also plays a huge part in creating unique personalities. Each character's silhouette not only gives you a snapshot of their personality, but also indicates differences between characters. This was no happy accident. It was an intentional decision by the game's designers. They knew that making their characters distinct and instantly recognizable was important to gameplay. This way the player would know which enemy was gunning for them—or more importantly, who is in their sight.

If you're designing several characters that appear on-screen at once, as in multiplayer games, design them together. Use their silhouettes to make your characters "fit together" even when they are standing apart. This is an especially useful trick when creating "duo characters" like Jak and Daxter (tall and short) or SpongeBob Squarepants and Patrick Star (square and pointy) or Mario and Luigi (fat and thin).

Other ways to distinguish your characters from each other include using color and texture. Superheroes in early comic books usually wore bright patriotic colors like red and blue, whereas villains were dressed in darker, "opposite colors" like greens and purples. In the original *Star Wars*, the heroes (Luke, Leia, and Han) wore black and white baggy and flowing clothing. Although Darth Vader and the Stormtroopers also wore black and white, their costumes were hard edged and metallic.

Of course, what determines whether your character is good or bad, noble or evil, is personality.

Personality: Do We Really Need Another Kratos?

I have found that there are three types of video game characters. The first two are humorous and heroic. And, of course, you can have a heroic, humorous character. Or a humorous, heroic character. Is there a difference? Either way, here are a couple of tips on creating these types of characters:

Humorous character:

- **Says funny things:** Writing funny dialogue is hard. If you can't write something funny, don't try to do it yourself. Do yourself a favor and hire a professional writer.

- **Does funny things:** Do me a favor and try not to resort to farting or burping. Not only is it puerile, which makes you look as though you couldn't think of anything funny to write, but all that gas flying around impacts your ESRB rating.

- **Looks funny or cute:** Funny characters and cute characters share many traits, including expressive eyes, oversized hands and feet (whether due to anatomy or costuming), and stubby or very lean bodies. Expressive body language used for physical comedy is a must, too. These cute and humorous characters are often known as **mascot characters** not only because they resemble the mascots used by sports teams, entertainment corporations, and small business owners; but also because they often end up being the mascot of the hardware system.

- **Funny doesn't always mean jokes:** If you've watched the *Batman* TV program from the 1960s, Batman was a funny character. Not because actor Adam West played him as a goof, but because he was deadly serious—as if wearing a bat costume and driving around in a bat-shaped car and climbing up a wall on a rope were the most normal things in the world. It was the contrast that made the show so funny.

Heroic character:

- **Does heroic things:** The hero saves the princess or prince, the world, or the day. Whatever your hero does, make sure it matters, but you can also make sure your character is good without becoming sappy.

- **Is always good at something:** Nathan Drake is good at finding treasure. Meatboy is good at jumping. Simon Belmont is an expert with a whip. Make sure your hero has a specialty, whether it's using a weapon or a skill.

- **Can come in all forms:** Look at Octodad, Owlboy, Kirby, or Kratos. No matter how creepy, strange, or brutal these characters look, they still manage to look braver, more heroic, and even friendlier compared to the other inhabitants of their world.

- **However...no one is perfect:** A good hero is relatable, and that means they have problems just like us. Phobias, unrealized ambitions, relationship issues: they all make the character more real. But it's one thing for a character to have these problems, and it's another thing to make it part of your gameplay. Indiana Jones is afraid of snakes. What happens when he comes across a chamber full of them? It can't just be business as usual. Morty Smith of *Rick and Morty Rickstaverse* (2015) lacks self-confidence in his own abilities, which adds more humor to the story. In *Dark Souls: Remastered* (2018), players may choose a super heavy sword which can create disadvantages such as a sluggish swing or slower running speed. I guarantee that these disadvantages will end up inspiring some memorable moments in your game.

Go back to your three character traits. Let them guide your character's creation and everything they do in the game. How do they walk? Fight? Open a door? Celebrate? Do when they lose? How do they act when they are injured? What they do when they're bored and waiting for you to continue playing?

There's another type of popular character archetype and that's the **anti-hero**. This is someone who breaks the rules and is usually violent or cruel. It's someone who we wish we could be but aren't. They're all over the place in video games: Kratos, Wolverine, Dante, Geralt of Rivia, and even Wario. They're just as popular as heroes, if not more so. If you want to create an anti-hero, here are some suggestions:

- **Does hardcore things...with style:** No matter if it's killing enemies or kicking in a door, the anti-hero does it with flair. Make their actions interesting to use and watch. It's good to be bad!

- **Isn't a nice person:** Sure, just about everyone in video games kills and steals (even Link!), but an anti-hero seems to enjoy this behavior a little bit more. He goes out of his way to add insult to injury and then revel in the results.

- **Says cool things but (almost) never shouts:** Because this character is so tough, they never need to shout. Just be careful because a stoic character can be easily mistaken for one without a personality.

- **Dresses like a villain:** Black clothing, leather, chains, spikes, skulls, a deadly arsenal of weapons, a wild haircut, scars—all the things that make a villain look like a villain are true for the anti-hero. The only difference is the anti-hero looks like a villain but acts (mostly) like a hero.

The general public often gives video games a bad rap for teaching kids bad behavior. True, there are some game characters that I don't think are great role models. Unfortunately, beating the audience over the head with morality is generally considered bad form. If you have an issue with this, don't fret; there are subtle (read: sneaky) ways you can steer your character toward being good. Good doesn't always have to equal dumb, sappy, or annoying.

If you are like me and prefer your good guys to be good, here is something I did in *Maximo vs. Army of Zin* to sneak a little morality into the game. In the original game, the main character Maximo was just in the adventure for himself. He wanted to rescue the princess, defeat the bad guy, and collect as much treasure as possible. But to me, he didn't really come off as a heroic character. So, in the sequel, I wanted him to act like a hero and do good things, but I couldn't force the player to do good things if they didn't want to, and I didn't want to be too preachy.

Instead, my team created victims that the players encountered being menaced by the Zin enemies throughout the levels. It was up to the players to rescue the victims or not (sometimes they had to go out of their way to do so). There was no penalty for not saving them, but if the players did save them, they would give Maximo a reward such as a few coins here or an armor power-up there. When play testing the game, players immediately started to become concerned about these villager characters and would feel bad if they didn't rescue them in time. While progression was still the players' primary objective, they would make sure to try to save the villagers. After the session, they mentioned that they liked being a "hero," which is exactly the feeling I wanted them to experience.

Of course, the other side of the coin is presenting players with bad deeds to avoid. In *Baldur's Gate 3* (SCE, 2014), the player doesn't have to be bad, but if the player chooses to do bad things (such as steal from nonplayer characters or kill civilians) and becomes "evil," the locals start to shout abuse or try to arrest you!

Let's Get Personal

Remember when you learned about naming characters back in Level 3? First of all, make sure your character's appearance matches their name. Which of the following characters do you think looks like "Dirk Steele"?

I learned an important lesson about naming characters while playing the classic computer game *X-Com: UFO Defense*. In the game, you command an international military team that battles an invading alien threat. The team members you recruit are given rather non-descript names. I then learned that you could rename them. Suddenly, my team of previously generic soldiers gained personalities. And something funny happened...

I started to care about them. Whereas I previously didn't care whether they died or lived, I now wanted to give them good weapons, heal them, and make sure they returned safely from each mission. What this taught me was the power of **customization**.

Now keep in mind, not all games *need* customizable characters. If your game features a story-based character or a licensed character like Cal Kestis, Batman, or Spongebob Squarebob, then there is no need to let the player rename the character. After all, the player is playing the game to play *that* specific character. However, if your game doesn't feature a licensed character, why not let the players name the character? Heck, Link is one of the most beloved characters in gaming, but the designers of every *Legend of Zelda* game allow you to rename him.

Just remember that if the character's name is mentioned in voice-over or in a cutscene, a changed name might feel jarring. The *Legend of Zelda* games get away with this because all of the dialogue uses text. Regardless, anything you can do to let the players customize their character furthers their feeling of ownership.

Many games now offer players greater and deeper customization tools to allow them to make just about any character they want. *Black Desert Online (2014), Elden Ring (2022),* and *Cyberpunk 2077 (2020)* all offer incredibly deep character customization tools to build very detailed heroes; you can spend hours before you even start "playing" the game. *Grand Theft Auto: San Andreas* (Rockstar Games, 2004) allowed players to customize their character's physique. If your character ate nothing but fast food, eventually he would get fat.

Spore's (EA, 2008) creature creator goes even further: players have used it to build a staggeringly creative array of fantastical creatures from gorgeously detailed dragons to living game controllers! No matter what you build in the editor, the anatomy and physical traits of your character affect the way your creature moves and acts within the game. You don't even need talent to create your hero in the *Drawn to Life* series (THQ, 2007), which allows you to draw your character from scratch even if you can draw only a stick figure.

The level of player customization will only increase as time goes on. *Absolver* (2019) allows players to customize their character's "move sets" by adding and removing cards that are assigned to a specific move and animation. *LittleBigPlanet 3* (SCEE, 2014) even lets you "customize" your character's emotional state! Did you grab the prize bubble before your friend? Make your Sackboy smile? If your friend grabbed it first, you could make your Sackboy frown...or scowl and "reward" your friend with a slap to the head!

Customization doesn't begin and end with the player character; it extends to choosing costumes, picking weapons, and decorating the character's home base. As I say, "Everybody likes to play house."

Give the players options for personalization. Allow the players to customize any of the following:

- **Name:** Not just the character, but also weapons, vehicles

- **Appearance:** Hair/skin/eye color, ethnicity, height, weight

- **Clothing, armor, and gear:** Style, color, texture

- **Vehicles:** Paint job, weapon and tech load outs, decals, hubcaps, even the thing that hangs from the rearview mirror

- **Home base:** Furnishing, lighting, decorations

- **Weapons:** Appearance, decoration, ammo loads, special effects

Traditional role-playing game characters are often "blank slates" defined more by their role (fighter, magic user, thief, soldier, medic, and so on) and gear than their appearance or personality. But that doesn't mean these characters can't have character; you just have to surface it through the play styles. For example, at first glance the wizard character in *Card Hunter* (Blue Manchu, 2013) might only seem to be a template for staffs, robes, and arcane items. The character has no predetermined personality. His name, visual, and gear are all editable, meaning you could change core aspects about him at any time. You could even change his character to female. However, it is the depth of gear selections that helps craft the wizard's character. Because the different spells possess different attributes, a play style emerges that starts to create a character. For example, lightning attacks can be used to hit specific targets at a distance versus fire attacks that work at close range to damage both friends and foes. I found my lightning-throwing wizard became more cautious and more of a team player, whereas my fire-casting wizard was reckless and burned anyone who got in his way. You can see this happening frequently in MMORPGs like *World of Warcraft* and FPSs like *Team Fortress 2* where the play styles of each character and the weapons they use inform the character's personality regardless of who is playing the part.

Speaking of weapons and equipment, you may choose to give your character a signature weapon and gear appearance. In this case, they shouldn't be customizable. These weapons are part of the character's identity. Most licensed characters use signature weapons and gear to keep them unique. Can you imagine Master Chief without his energy sword? Freddy Kruger without his clawed glove? Thor without his hammer? Mario without his cap?

Think about how the players are going to be using these items for gameplay. Make the items appropriate to the action. Although I advocate form following function, sometimes these items can help inspire the design to determine the players' actions.

Sometimes the most important item in a character's design isn't even one that character can use. Because most video game characters are viewed from behind, it's important to have something that creates the feeling of movement. For example, many characters have an object swinging from their back. With Lara Croft, it was her ponytail. With Batman, it was his cape. While these objects added movement and personality, they required both unique and sometimes complex code to create. Talk with your art and programming leads to make sure these visual markers are feasible to have in your game.

nice tail.

While video game character design allows for a wide variety of stylization, the goal of many video game art directors is to create realistic characters. But be aware of the phenomenon called the **"uncanny valley,"** in which a character doesn't look quite right to the viewers. It can be distracting for the players, especially during cutscenes, if this occurs. Here are a few tips to remember when creating realistic-looking characters:

- **Facial proportions:** Realistic human characters look odd if given features are used to enhance personality traits. Watch out for features such as large eyes, exaggerated chins, and wide mouths that can make characters look inhuman.

- **Movement:** The more realistic the model, the worse animation tends to look precisely because of the uncanny valley. Be careful of stiff-limbed movement in the arms and shoulders. Hands can be particularly troublesome because most game art can't support jointed fingers and treats the hands as simple objects, which end up looking like hams. A human is a very flexible being, so make sure your character moves realistically. Put the effort into rigging your character's skeleton to be so.

- **Humanity:** If a character looks extremely human (especially a non-human character, like an alien or robot), people will expect it to do human things and have a human personality. However, you can give humanity to non-human characters. The robot Claptrap from *Borderlands* has enough human features—arms and a "face"—to still make him a relatable character.

Now, for the other side of the coin, here are some tips to remember when creating stylized characters:

- **Facial proportions:** Enlarge facial features such as eyes, chins, and mouths to convey greater expression and range of emotion. You find this all the time in Japanese games and anime.

- **Movement:** If you don't have the time and money to spend on motion capturing, you might be better off using stylized character animations. The more stylized your characters, the more exaggerated the movements can be. Watch and learn from old Tex Avery cartoons (for example) to see just how far you can go with exaggerated character movement.

- **Humanity:** The great thing about stylized characters is that they don't have to be human. Humanized animals have had a long-standing place in video games ever since Donkey Kong captured Pauline. Anthropomorphic characters like Knuckles the Echidna, Fox McCloud, and Tom Nook who can provide just as much emotion and player investment as human ones can.

Realistic or stylized? It's a choice that comes down to what is best for your game. For example, the *Team Fortress 2* team started building their game with realistically designed characters and then did a 180 with character designs inspired by artists J. C. Leyendecker, Dean Cornwell, and Norman Rockwell by way of Pixar. It was a great choice that changed the tone of the entire franchise for the better.

Using All the Parts

As you are designing your characters, try using them to communicate information to the players. Think about it: players spend the majority of their time looking at the characters. What better way to display their in-game status? Personally, I like this method because I find it extremely clear as to what the players' status is at all times. All aspects of the players can be treated visually. Here are some other ways to communicate information through visuals and animation:

- **Movement**
  - Give subtle clues, like a character's head turning to look at interesting and interactive items in the world.
  - Make characters automatically reach for pickups or door handles.
  - Make characters react positively to favorite things, negatively to perilous things. Maybe go as far as to refuse to go into sure-death situations.
  - Adjust the movement of characters' based on their health. In the *Resident Evil* series, wounded characters limp and move at a reduced speed.

- **Appearance**

  - Make characters' health be reflected by their appearance. Many games have the characters' physical appearance become more battered and bruised the more damage they take. In *Batman: Arkham City*, the more often the player "dies," the more tattered Batman's costume becomes. Taking a cue from the *Ghosts N' Goblins* series, we had Maximo lose armor and clothes the closer he reached zero health.

  - Make status part of the character design. Isaac, the main character in the *Dead Space* series, wears a space suit with a glowing spine that doubles as a health meter, as well as readouts that show oxygen and weapon status.

  - Use visual effects to represent state. Have wounded characters bleed out, leak oil, or shoot out sparks.

- **Inventory**

  - Players' gear can be part of the character, rather than hidden within an inventory screen. When designing *Maximo: Ghosts to Glory*, we had inventory items like keys appear on the main character's belt. This allowed players to always know what they had without having to check their inventory system.

  - Any major ability upgrade should have a model and/or animation component to it. Evolving characters keep things interesting for the players, who are looking at the same characters for the entire game. Even better, take a page from *World of Warcraft* and allow players to dress up and customize their characters whenever they gain new gear and abilities.

- **Weapons**

  - Rather than just adding a +3 upgrade to a weapon, give it a physical manifestation of that new power. Have it glow or spit flame; add runes, sights, nozzles, or other "bits" to reflect the weapon's new capabilities. The *Borderland* games do a good job of representing every upgrade with a new part.

  - If you don't want to change the weapon's appearance, consider changing the animation of the player character. A more powerful gun requires a different shooting stance than a lighter one.

In short: Keep it clear, expressive, and visual, and you can't go wrong.

Games Without Characters

Not every game has a main character. Who is the main character of *Tetris*? Or the *Grand Turismo* series? Or *Park Beyond*? The answer, of course, is YOU! However, because the game designers haven't met you (and probably never will), they sadly can't design their games specifically for you. Therefore, they need a proxy, a character to stand in for the game designer. There are a few ways to do this:

- **Introduce a guide character:** This character is the emcee, host, or "figurehead" of the game. They often interact with the player to provide story, help, and challenges but doesn't necessarily have to be the player's friend or guru.

- **Make the story the guide:** Many puzzle games have a loose (or precise) story framing to tie all the levels and experience together. *Star Wars: Hunters* (2024) is based on the *Star Wars Saga* between Episodes VI and VII, whereas *Royal Match* (2020) uses an original storyline to connect the puzzle levels together.

- **Make the world the character:** Some games, particularly social and construction management games, don't have characters in them. So, instead, the world becomes the character. It has a personality all its own that keeps players engaged. The players want to see "what happens" to the world and how it is changed by their play decisions.

Regardless of what genre your game is, remember that players love stories, and a little story can go a long way.

We Are Not Alone

In early video games, players were a single hero battling against computer enemies or a human opponent. Games like *Double Dragon* and *Teenage Mutant Ninja Turtles* allowed a friend to help out, as long as you didn't mind that person bumping into you as you played. While cooperative gameplay with multiple players has advanced greatly in the MMO and FPS space, console games have pushed the envelope in the other direction—the **second character.** When creating gameplay with a second character, you have to decide whether the character is **playable** or a **companion.**

A second playable character (or SPC) lets the player swap or "zap" between controlling multiple characters. When control is relinquished on one character, the second becomes controlled by artificial intelligence. This concept originates from *Ultima III: Exodus* (1983) in which players can "control" each of the party members to battle enemies during the combat sequence. The idea quickly spread across the globe in action games like *The Goonies* (1986) for the Atari XL/XE, *Head over Heels* (1987) for the ZX Spectrum and *Speedball* (1988) on the Amiga. However, control would revert back to a single character for navigation purposes during the rise of consoles like the Famicom (aka the Nintendo Entertainment System), partially due to hardware limitations.

In *Mario & Luigi: Superstar Saga* (2003), players can control either Mario or Luigi for the duration of the game—although there isn't too much difference between them. However, the characters in Lego games like *Lego Batman 2* (2012) have unique abilities used to solve puzzles. Keep the "player zapping"[2] to a single button press to allow players to quickly jump to the other character. If players can swap with more than one SPC, determine the method by which the players will be able to make the choice quickly:

- The player chooses the SPC positioned closest to the player character.
- The player cycles through a preset list of characters.
- A "compass-style" selection window allows the player to select directly rather than in a cyclic order.
- A predetermined location in the level automatically switches characters.

The difference between an SPC and a companion character is that a companion is controlled by the game's AI. In some cases, a companion is the second player character, as in the *Lego Star Wars* games or *Army of Two*.

Originally, AI-controlled characters were a bit of a pain because they were standing right where you wanted to be, and they were being pretty useless in a fight. But thankfully games have evolved. Companions can be useful in combat (Quiet in *Metal Gear Solid V: The Phantom Pain*), provide navigational support and advice (Navi in *The Legend of Zelda: The Ocarina of Time*), aid players in puzzle solving (Elizabeth in *BioShock Infinite*), or even heal or help the players when they are in physical danger (BD-1 in *Star Wars Jedi: Fallen Order*). These characters don't even have to be human, like the canine Shadow in *Dead to Rights 2* (2005), the dog in the *Fable* series (2008), Dogmeat in *Fallout 3* (2008), or the inanimate weighted companion cube in *Portal* (2007).

An interesting phenomenon related to AI characters is the "dadification" of games, particularly in action and adventure games. In these games, the main character is a father figure

---

[2] "Player zapping" was the charming term used for SPC switching in *Resident Evil 0* (Capcom, 2002).

(or an actual father) who feels protective toward a child or female AI character. By playing on traditional gender and paternal roles, designers are able to create a "shorthand" relationship that players quickly understand and (hopefully) will adopt during play. A *Walking Dead Season One (2010)* player might feel protective of Clementine and will often (if not always) skew their choices in favor of protecting her. The companion character can be passive and somewhat helpless, but it helps if they offer something to the relationship in return, such as gathering ammunition, unlocking doors, or healing the player character.

Although companion characters are helpful in gameplay, be aware that creating companion characters is often a significant dedication to game assets because they require complex AI and animations as robust as the main character's. However, the more "intelligent" and helpful these characters are, the more real they will become to the player. And the more real the companions are to the player, the more the players are going to care about them.

When creating these companions, remember that **opposites attract.** Give character abilities, strengths, and limitations that complement and contrast each other. A perfect example can be found in *Resident Evil 2* with Claire Redfield and Sherry Birkin. The two characters couldn't be more different: Claire is a capable fighter, and Sherry is a scared and defenseless little girl. Claire wields two guns to take out zombies, whereas Sherry can crawl into hiding places and access areas to find puzzle pieces and items. Each character couldn't survive without the other, and that's the feeling you must convey with a companion character.

A game's puzzles and progression can be designed around how to utilize the companion to help both characters progress. Heroes of *Dragon's Dogma Dark Arisen (2013)* and *The Outer Worlds (2019) need* their companions' help to complete the game. Because players are going to be spending the entire game with the companion character, you want to create a relationship early in the game, so you don't have to do much AI programming to sell the companion's personalities later. Victor "Sully" Sullivan in *Uncharted: Drake's Fortune* and Captain Price in *Call of Duty: Modern Warfare* are two strong examples of companions with well-written personalities and motivations.

When More Is More

Sometimes two characters aren't enough. *Mortal Kombat: Armageddon* (Midway, 2006) has 63 unique playable characters! Games with large casts can be found in many game genres: fighting, car combat, RPG, RTS, FPS, and survival horror games.

Start your character creation process by creating a stereotype, the old "fighter, magic-user, thief, cleric" class/profession model, for example. Wait a second, what about creating unique, compelling characters? Yeah, yeah, that stuff's all great, but sometimes players will need to judge a book by its cover. At the beginning of many games, players don't have the luxury of a storyline; they're just going to pick a character that looks the coolest or that they identify with the most.

But that doesn't mean your characters have to be stereotypes, particularly in the way they play. Your characters should have something significantly different to offer to gameplay. It helps to build an abilities matrix to compare and contrast your characters so none of them have the same abilities. The characters in *Team Fortress 2* live in one of three classes: offensive, defensive, and support. They have three categories that impact gameplay: health, speed, and attack. Let's see how they stack up:

Offensive Class	Defensive Class		Support Class
Soldier	**DemoMan**		**Medic**
High health	Medium health		Medium health
Mid to strong attack	Slow to mid speed		Medium speed
Medium speed	Strong attack		Medium attack

continued

continued

Offensive Class	Defensive Class	Support Class
Heavy	**Pyro**	**Sniper**
High health	Medium health	Weak health
Slow speed	Medium speed	Medium speed
Strong attack	Strong short-range/weak long-range attack	Medium attack (headshot does instant kill)
Scout	**Engineer**	**Spy**
Weak health	Weak health	Weak health
Very fast speed	Medium speed	Fast speed
Weak to mid attack	Medium attack (gun turret can be improved from weak to very strong attack)	Weak attack (backstab does instant kill)

As you can see, the characters in *TF2* are very finely balanced. No two characters share the same attribute specs, and weaknesses are counterbalanced with strengths. Where the heavy is slow, he has the strongest attack. Where the scout has a weak attack, he is very fast. Even the most statistically average character in the game, the medic, can heal and grant temporary invulnerability to the other players—an ability that is totally unique to this character. This balancing act is like a game of Rock, Paper, Scissors, where each character has a weakness and a strength.

To design a **Rock, Paper, Scissors** (or RPS) system you need clarity. An RPS system gives the player three choices. Those choices need to be simple and clear for the player to understand so they can make the right choice. For example, in a fighting game, there are three types of moves: an attack, a throw, and a reversal. Attacking beats throwing, throwing beats blocking or reversing, and blocking and reversing beat attacking. Making sure the player understands what choices are available and what the possible results of that choice will make for a good RPS system.[3]

These characters also support different types of play. For example, the sniper, heavy, and engineer all work best when they root themselves in place. Notice how one of these types occurs in each class? Your characters will become more balanced the more classifications there are to gauge them against, such as:

- Movement speed
- Movement type
- Attack speed and rate

---

[3] For more on Rock Paper Scissor systems read www.sirlinx.net/articles/rock-paper-scissors-in-strategy-games.html.

- Attack strength

- Attack range and duration

- Armor strength

- Health

- Encumbrance

- Advantages (such as health or puzzle solving)

Be careful to make sure these values and traits are easily editable. If you need to make a global change in your game, you don't want to spend all your time tweaking values.

Who Are the People in Your Neighborhood?

The general. The con-artist. The innkeeper. The service robot. All of these are non-player characters!

Non-player characters (or NPCs, as the kids call them) come from all walks of life: kings who assign quests and award trophies for completing them, blacksmiths who craft new weapons and armor. You know what the great thing is about them? YOU (as the player) are the center of their universe! They solely exist to help (or hinder) you! How's that for stroking your ego? That's why, in some way, every NPC needs to provide the answer to this question:

WHAT DOES THE PLAYER NEED TO SUCCEED?

What **does** the player need to succeed? Good question. I'm glad you asked. Every NPC needs a role. A job. A reason for living. All NPCs should provide one or more of the following:

- Objectives for the player

- Access to new locations where objectives await (anything from keys to maps to pointing in the right direction)

- Methods for the players to travel to said locations

- Rewards for completing objectives (can be economic or pride rewards)

- Tools to defeat enemies

- Gear to protect players from said enemies

- Answers to puzzles and problems

- Backstory about the world and its characters—just don't be too long-winded

- Players' instruction on gameplay (although you should never tell the players something they already know)

- Compliments to your hero on their heroic awesomeness (or to suitably quake in fear if your hero is evil)

- Humor

While your NPCs are waiting to provide help to players, give them something to do. NPCs are the "extras" in the video game universe, and just like extras, they need to be given "business." In movie-making lingo, business is what extras do in the background of a scene to make it look as if life is going on regardless of what the actors are doing: eating, talking, chopping wood, washing the floors. Simple animations are a good start. Complex activities are even better. In some games, NPCs perform different activities depending on the time of day.[4] Just don't make players have to chase the NPCs around to talk to them.

---

[4] In life simulators like *Harvest Moon* and *Animal Crossing*, NPCs will go to bed if it's late enough. That means that many players will not be able to interact with some characters because they're sleeping. Make sure you take this into account, because you don't want to waste production time creating assets that the players will never see!

When putting NPCs into your game worlds and levels, be sure to place them within the eyesight of where players are traveling. Make them easy to find. Place them on the game's mini map if you have one. Don't make players have to hunt them down. Unless your story calls for it, don't put them in strange locations either: an innkeeper should be found in the inn, the police captain in the police station, and so on. Let players know they can interact with them. Don't be afraid to make it obvious. If necessary, put a large arrow over their heads.

Have your NPCs be physically distinct in dress and body language. A soldier is going to look and act very differently than a gang member. Use as many visual cues as possible to help players remember which character has what information or which character is gonna sell them that phase plasma pistol for a good price.

If having lots of unique NPCs in your game isn't possible due to budget or time, you can still distinguish them with different "voices." This can be done through text as well as voice acting. The lead designer of *BioShock* told a story of how players had trouble distinguishing the NPCs from one another until they were written with strong international accents. Giving your NPC's distinguishers like accents, different colored clothing or diverse hairstyles can help your player figure out who is who.

There are plenty of good reasons to use a character. Replacing a gameplay mechanic like a switch or crate with an NPC makes your game feel less contrived and predictable. How about making your NPC the interface for the save system? Or the interface to the game's store? That way you can place the game-saving NPC anywhere a person can stand. For hearing-impaired players (or those who get sick of hearing the same NPC phrase over and over again!), be sure to include a text overlay and character animation to communicate what the NPC is saying.

Interaction with an NPC can also initiate a puzzle, activate a mechanic, or start a countdown clock. Protecting an NPC on escort missions or in battle arenas is another common gameplay mechanic. If you don't want your NPCs to seem so helpless, have them taunt and spur your player into action. In *Darksiders,* a counter pops-up when the smith Ulthane challenges War to see who can kill the most enemies. This not only indicates the start of the contest, but also changes the players' mindset into one of competition.

Study other games and see what they do with their NPCs. Use any good ideas you find and create your own. Making your NPCs less predictable will keep the players on their toes and curious to see who they will meet around the next corner.

Finally, We Talk About Gameplay

Now that we've discussed what the character looks like, let's talk about what they do. All gameplay flows from the main character. You have to think about the character's relationship to the world. How tall is your character? How tall or short are all the other characters and enemies in relationship to the main character? How long is the character's reach? If your character is a quadruped or a vehicle, how long and wide is it? As you create your character, you determine these proportions. These proportions become the basis of the character's **metrics**, which is the cornerstone of your gameplay and design.

But before we dive into metrics, let's talk about fencing.

When you fence, you learn how far you travel when you step forward, how far your weapon goes when you extend your arm. As a fencer, you learn that those distances get greater as you lunge at an opponent. It's important to know these distances to help you gauge how far away you are from your opponent and how close you need to be to score a touch on them. As a fencer, you get accustomed to these distances and adjust your fencing style to compensate for them.

Video game players do the same thing. Metrics are especially important to players because they use them to gauge movement and jump distances "by eye," whether they know it or not. When playing, they get a feel for what is and isn't obtainable, and anything that changes that constant will throw off the players and feel wrong.

Determining metrics starts with the basic height of the character, the speed that character travels, and the height that the character can reach. I always use the hero character as a yardstick for the rest of the world. For example, in *Maximo: Ghost to Glory*, our measurement was called "1 Maximo unit," which was obviously based on the height and width of the main character. All game distances, widths, and heights were expressed in this way.

Use metrics to determine the following:

- **Height:** The height of the player character.
- **Width of passage:** Usually wider than the player character.
- **Walking speed:** How far the character travels per second or unit of time.
- **Running speed:** Same as walking speed, but faster.

- **Jump distance:** The jump takes the player farther in one jump than he would travel while walking, but not while running. Usually based on the character's height and width. The shorter or wider the character, the smaller the jump distance.

- **Jump height:** The metrics for this action are based on the character's height. On average, a jump is half the character's height, and a double jump can be twice as tall as the character. However, this can be greater for bouncier, cartoony characters.

- **Melee attack distance:** Usually not much farther than the length of the character's arm and weapon.

- **Projectile distance:** Can be as short as the character's reach or width to as far as the character can see.

The cliff ledge shown in the following graphic is obviously completely unobtainable with a normal jump/double jump distance. Players will know that they won't ever be able to reach this height and will look for another way to get to their destination.

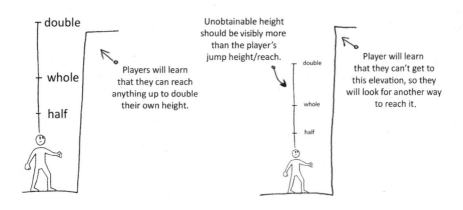

Metrics for Other Player Types

Although the majority of the preceding examples are metrics for human characters, you can still apply these principles for non-character games. Remember, you always want to start with the thing that the player is controlling, be it a puzzle-piece, a car, an airplane, or a stray cat. Your other two C's, camera, and controls should all support the actions of the player.

Abstract games—When determining the metrics for a puzzle game, you will want to think about all of the different shapes that the items that the player interacts with will be. The size of these objects will affect the "rhythm" of the game, that is to say, how the game feels to the player.[5]

Even if your puzzle game isn't a rhythm games per se, they will still create their own special rhythm for the player to follow. For example, Tetris players get used to the time required to rotate a piece into place and the time required for a piece to drop. Or how *Angry Birds* players get used to the "feel" of how far they need to pull back the slingshot to launch a bird. If these metrics were changed mid-game or randomized, they would totally throw off the player's rhythm and ruin their experience.

Why Walk When You Can Run?

Let's talk about walking. Some starting designers believe that walking is a part of gameplay. They have the player walking here. They have the player walking there. All the player does is walk, walk, walk everywhere in the game. The problem is, walking in video games is boring! We're not making boring video games; we're making exciting ones!

WALKING IS NOT GAMEPLAY!

Walking has its place, for example if the character is near a ledge or approaching something interesting, sure. But I often ask developers I work with, "Do you really need a walk?" I have found that players will always choose a faster move over walking, be it jumping, rolling, or dashing. For example, when we were making *God of War*, Kratos could do a tumble/roll move. More often than not, the designers would roll their way around the levels even though doing so looked stupid. We used this move because it felt faster than walking.

While alternating the pace of your action is good, having your player travel for long stretches, no matter how much beautiful art they look at, is just boring. Keep it interesting even if a player is just walking. Why have this:

---

[5] For a great book on this topic, I recommend reading *Game Feel* by Steve Swink (2008, Morgan Kaufmann Game Design Books).

When can you have this?

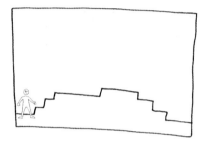

They both do the same thing: get the character from point A to point B. However, the second path is more interesting because it allows the character to use a variety of moves to traverse the terrain rather than just walking.

Walking is useful when navigating edges and ledges. I have found that most players will walk to an edge because they are afraid that they may fall off. There are other tools that you can use in conjunction with the edge—such as a teeter or hoist (more on those in a moment) —but the walk is what the players will use most because it makes them feel safe and in control. There is a trade-off to the teeter. Players can't attack during a teeter state (at least, I've never played a game that has allowed me to), and a teeter reduces the player's movement to zero, which is useful when keeping the player from falling to their death, but not so useful for getting away from that fast-approaching enemy! So maybe having that walk cycle isn't such a bad thing after all.

If your character is a vehicle (as in a driving, flying, or rail shooter) or rides in a vehicle, remember that driving (or flying or jet-skiing or whatever) should always move faster than the character's standard walk. Remember to account for the vehicle's weight, too. If you don't have the vehicle's weight built into your basic movement and metrics, the vehicle will feel "floaty" and not realistic. When dealing with larger-than-normal characters such as cars, hover tanks, and motorbikes, you will be dealing with even more extreme weight differences that can affect the feel of your vehicle.

Weight, in general, makes a character, be it a car or a person, feel as if it is connected to the world. But with weight comes momentum—characters slide and skid to a stop. You need to compensate for these characteristics in the player's metrics. In some games, particularly platformers, the skid is part of the player's movement. In *LittleBigPlanet*, players can very easily skid off a platform or ledge if they don't land in the right place.

I'm torn about the usefulness of the **skid**. When used in the right context, such as skidding down a hill or "grinding" across the asphalt. The character can move faster without expending energy a run might take.

However, in shorter intervals, I find it to be very frustrating, as a character skids on the edge of a floating platform. But without a skid animation, the character movement feels stiff and artificial. Ultimately, you need to choose what is best for your own game.[6]

Whether your game character is a person or a vehicle, you should ask yourself, "What is the speed of my gameplay? Fast or slow?" If your game is fast, the majority of your gameplay should be fast. This includes.

- Running
- Jumping
- Flying
- Driving
- Shooting

- Bouncing
- Fighting
- Spinning
- Falling

Slow-moving moves include:

- Walking
- Ducking
- Crouching
- Sneaking
- Dashing

- Swimming
- Hiding
- Hoisting
- Climbing

---

[6] Which seems to be a running theme in this chapter, doesn't it?

I find it best to alternate between fast experiences and slow ones to keep the game's pacing interesting.

When thinking about **running**, ask what it is being used for. I prefer gameplay in which the run speed is drastically different than the walk. The *Resident Evil* series uses the run action not only as a way to move fast but as a way for the character to push through and escape from slow-moving zombies.

The **dash** is the run's cousin. A dash is usually a faster run that expires after a time limit. It is often used to get through timing puzzles such as closing doorways and fire jets, or as a combat move either to escape an enemy's attack or drive home an extra-powerful blow. To prevent your players from exploiting a dash, give them a **cooldown**: a short period of time (usually a few seconds) before they can use the dash move again.

Let's slow down and talk about "slow walking," aka **stealth.** I admit I have mixed feelings about characters moving stealthily in games. As a general rule, I don't like characters to move slowly, unless the entire game (or a whole experience, like a level) is based on stealth gameplay. Whenever I play games with stealth mixed in (not dedicated), I always end up running around blasting away at the enemies because I get tired with moving so slowly when I could be moving quickly instead. Because this isn't the intention of the game, I usually lose a lot of lives playing like this.[7] But I know my frustration comes from the character moving so slowly.

When you make your characters move stealthily, make a significant difference in speed. It's the same principle as walking versus running. **Creep** is useful if the character is ducking or is behind cover, is getting into position to snipe, or in humorous situations such as when the

---

[7] When you are designing a stealth game, make sure your character looks, or at least acts, stealthy. I once played a really well-made game that featured a burly barbarian hero as the main character. I fully anticipated the game to be a brawler because the hero was armed with several huge weapons that allowed me to cut up the enemies into messy chunks. However, as I played the game, I continually found myself dying in battle after battle. I got so frustrated with the game that I stopped playing it even though I really wanted to like it. I mentioned my regret to a coworker, and he said, "You aren't playing the game correctly." Before I could make him take back such a dire insult, he said "It's not an action game; it's a stealth game." Armed with that information, I replayed the game stealthily and eventually finished it—which I may have never otherwise done due to the mixed signals the game gave the player.

character is trying not to wake a sleeping dragon. The creep move should be a mode that players can activate at any time, but a creep works best when it is given some context.

But creeping aside, the instinct to make stealth gameplay automatically equals a slow-moving character is incorrect. Have you ever seen SWAT team members or ninjas move around? They don't really creep as much as move in short bursts. Stealth comes into play when they have to wait or hide as something happens or some clueless guard with a very slittable neck passes by. This is where the tension that defines good stealth gameplay comes from. The gameplay of waiting.

The Art of Doing Nothing

Even slower than stealth gameplay is no gameplay. However, just because a character is standing still doesn't mean they have to do nothing. An **idle** is an animation that plays while a character isn't moving, triggered after a few seconds of the player being idle.

Did you see that? How the word describing the player's in-action is also the name of the move? Pretty clever, those early video game designers.

The first idle that made an impression on me was in *Sonic the Hedgehog*. When the player stopped running, Sonic would look out at the player with an annoyed look on his face and tap his foot impatiently. That guy wanted to run! Pretty soon humorous idles were a staple of platform games through the 1990s. But they aren't just for laughs. An idle can convey personality and even a little narrative to the player. At the very least, it provides some movement on the screen even when nothing else is going on.

Keep in mind, other than adding character or humor, idles (usually) have no gameplay benefit whatsoever. Some cover shooters like the *Halo* series give the players back health during the idle, but that is meant to be an advantage to keeping in cover. If you add a benefit during an idle, you might end up encouraging the player to do nothing, when you really want them to play the game.

Remember, when creating idles, you don't want to create long and involved animations, because players can press a button at any time and interrupt the idle. In fact, any idle that creates a poor transition into players' moves will cause a problem, no matter what the length. Keep them short and snappy. Don't have any ideas for idles? Here are a few to start with:

- Twirl, reload, or "shoulder" weapon
- Stretch and jog in place

- Glance around or be startled at an imagined noise
- Shiver with cold or wipe sweat from the character's brow
- Knock dirt from the soles of the character's shoes
- Adjust armor or pack
- Crack neck or pop knuckles
- Play air guitar or do a little dance
- Check a map or guide or talk on a cell phone
- Whistle and rock on heels as if waiting
- Eat or drink something
- Scratch self in embarrassing location
- Check watch
- Yawn or fall asleep

Might as Well Jump

Of all the basic moves in video gaming, the **jump** is the most mysterious, the most majestic, and the most misunderstood.

To fully understand the jump, take a look at one with the help of my patented "slo-mo" graphic:

1. The player is at rest. This is when the player is standing or idle. Or even when they are walking, running, and so on.

2. The player presses the action button, so the jump must happen immediately. Many jumps in a game are the player's response to danger or boredom, such as when a player is tired of a slower-moving walk. In some cases, the jump may need a brief animation to sell the anticipation of the leap, but this animation should be kept as short as possible.

3. As the character jumps, they rise to the maximum height quickly.

   - If the player is given the opportunity to do a double jump, allow him to do so before reaching the apex (top height) of the jump. Any time after the apex feels weird.

4. Falling is like jumping in reverse. Don't make the fall last too long, or it will feel "floaty," which is a negative sensation to the player and screws with the player's sense of metrics unless the player has some sort of power-up or ability that allows them to glide or float down to safety.

5. The landing can take a little longer than the jump, but it needs to "stick" to make it feel good and solid. I am not a fan of jumps that end in skids or slides because it is easy for a player to make a jump and still slide off the edge of a platform. This is one instance in which I have found that gamified physics work better than real-world physics.

Let's take a second to talk about physics. Should you model your game physics on the real world or use gamified physics? Or should you abandon the laws of physics entirely? Good questions! And you better know the answer!

Since Sir Isaac Newton did all the hard work back in 1687, one would assume this would be easy, right? Real-world physics is based on the laws of physics we live with every day. But a certain fidelity to real life is necessary to sell real-world physics, and trying to create something that precisely emulates real-world physics usually ends up inferior to something tweaked. For example, gravity in games is not 9.8 m/s² no matter what the real world says. In fact, some games even use different gravitational constants on different objects!

This is where game physics comes into play. Programmers can tweak the real-world values to fit the gameplay needs. Running speeds, jumping heights and distances, and collision bounciness always feel better when adjusted. Most people in the real world can't jump higher than their own waist, but the average platform game character can easily double his own height in a single bound.

What if your game takes place in outer space? Or what if it occurs on a planet with low or high gravity? What if you can do exceptionally powerful jumps like *in Crackdown (2007)* or *Super Mario RPG (2023)*? You need to determine this ahead of time to make sure your metrics match your physics. Tackle this task early and don't change it, or you will cause huge problems.

Okay, let's jump back to jumping. Because platform games were the most popular game genre in the 16-bit days, you can understand how the art of jumping has been taken to its furthest limits—more than any other player character movement. By my count, there are five major ways to jump:

- **Single jump:** The player jumps once, either vertically or horizontally.
- **Double jump:** The player makes a second vertical or horizontal jump that starts while the character is still in mid-air after the initial jump.
- **Triple jump:** The player makes a third jump that can be done after the second jump, usually requiring something for the player to bounce off and most often horizontal.
- **Contextual jump:** This "automatic" jump happens when the player approaches a pre-tagged area such as a ledge.
- **Wall jump:** This special case jump is performed after the player jumps "into" or toward a wall. If the player presses a button while colliding with the wall, they will jump off the wall in the opposite direction. The player can gain altitude by chaining wall jumps, which allows them to "climb walls" by wall jumping between two opposite-facing surfaces. A wall jump can be treated as either a "natural move" that the player has from the beginning of the game (like in *Super Meat Boy*), or it can derive from an earned skill or equipment (as in *Ratchet and Clank*).

Even as the character hurtles through the air, there are design decisions to be made. Some games treat jumping realistically and don't allow the player to change the character's trajectory after jumping, whereas others allow the player to course correct the character. Other games will allow the character to jump higher and further depending on the amount of time the button is pressed.

After years of making "hoppy-skippy" games, I have discovered some curious things about jumping. Players usually do not jump from the edge of a ledge, but from a little way back. Edges make players nervous. They leap from an area I call the **"jump zone,"** which can be up to half a jump's distance to the edge of the platform.

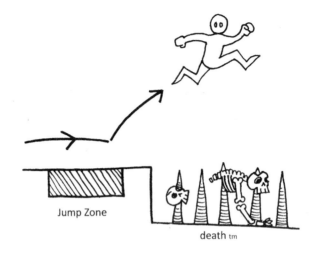

The target the player is trying to hit is a safe spot about half a jump's length away from the edge of the opposite ledge. However, landing right on the edge makes a player nervous! This means that when you create your jump, make sure to add one more jump length to your distances to make the player feel confident and secure when landing.

For smaller and floating platforms, the target should be the dead center of the platform. Make sure there is enough space to land. There's not a lot of room on most floating/single platforms, which is why I don't recommend having a post-landing slide animation to your jump.

When a player gets nervous, they tend to jump again. If the target is too small, they will usually jump their death. Save the really small platforms for expert jumping puzzles. (Usually found late in the game.)

Hoists and Teeters

Hoists and **teeters** are two very useful tools for players to help them get around and avoid dying. A hoist allows players to reach a height slightly higher than their jump allows. The teeter acts as a warning to players that they are too close to an edge and may fall.

Not all games have or need hoists and teeters. However, if you are going to use these moves, make sure to account for them when creating your player metrics. A hoist generally adds up to a full body length of the character to their jump height.

When a player is in a hoist position but hasn't moved back up onto the ledge or dropped down to the ground below, this position is called a **hang**. Some games will bypass this state entirely by having a player automatically hoist themselves back up, whereas other games use the hang for gameplay, allowing the player to hang from objects and surfaces while waiting for timing puzzles and other hazards to pass on by.

I have found that hoists, hangs, and teeters can be really good opportunities to add character to your players. For example, you can have characters react humorously to the fact that they are hanging for their life or about to fall off a cliff! Remember, these animations need to cycle because the players may leave their characters literally in a cliffhanger!

You will have to be careful of what I call the "Wile E. Coyote effect." Remember in those old Chuck Jones[8] cartoons where Wile E. Coyote chases the Road Runner off a cliff? And then he stands on thin air for a beat before he plummets down into a little poof of dust at the bottom of a canyon?

What Goes Up Must Fall Down

Speaking of **falling**, let's talk about it. Using the power of the slo-mo graphic, let's examine a typical fall off a cliff:

1. The player will usually approach an edge with caution. If they plan to jump they will usually do it from the jump zone.

---

[8]Charles "Chuck" Jones (1912 - 2002), director and animator of some of the best cartoons in existence, including *What's Opera, Doc? Duck Amuck,* and *How the Grinch Stole Christmas.* He created the characters of Road Runner and Wile E. Coyote, among others. Do yourself a favor and watch all of these.

2. Does the character teeter? This acts as a warning to the player, but it can also disrupt the player's control.

3. Give the player a chance to jump out of a teeter so they can get to where they want to go. If the result of missing a jump is death, let them see the bottom/death zone as they make the jump. Blind leaps of faith make players very nervous.

4. Does the character have a hoist? If so, the player can use the hoist to abort a jump or as a "last-ditch effort" save option to keep from falling to their death. Because some games use distance to ground as a variable to determine whether the player will take damage upon falling from a great height, a hoist can make the difference between a safe drop and death.

5. When the player is falling, do they have control over the fall? Many games allow for course correction, and some allow for flat-out in-air maneuvering. Make sure the animation of the character falling communicates whether or not the player has control. An out-of-control fall may have the character flailing about or screaming in terror, whereas an in-control fall may reuse the same animation as at the end of a jump.

6. Can the player "air jump" out of a fall? How will this ability be communicated to the player? Make sure there are plenty of gameplay situations that capitalize on this move.

7. What happens to the character when they hit the ground? Do they land on their feet like a cat and take no damage? Do they land hard on the ground and have a longer recovery animation, which would make them vulnerable to approaching enemies? Do they bounce off the ground like a rag doll and die? Make sure the player knows early on in the game whether or not there is any penalty for hitting the ground. And be consistent with this rule. Nothing messes with the player more than inconsistent results.

8. Whether or not your player takes damage from hitting the ground, let them recover quickly so they can get back in control of their character and get moving again. Nothing is worse than waiting for a "get up" animation to finish playing.

Me and My Shadow

As you are building your character in the game, it is important not to forget the player's **shadow.** Having a shadow provides several benefits to the player:

- A shadow acts as a reference point in 3-D space for the player, which is particularly important when gauging jumps.

- A shadow grounds the player in the world; it adds to the illusion that the character has weight and mass.

- A shadow helps players with edge detection. If their shadow doesn't "lie" on the ground, they will get one more hint that it's not meant for them to stand on.

- A shadow conveys lighting and mood. In some survival horror games, the shadow can be a disquieting distraction to the players, literally making them "jump at their own shadow."

- A shadow can be used for gameplay: The Xenomorph in *Alien: Isolation* (Sega, 2014) uses shadow detection as part of the enemy's AI. This can be especially important in stealth or survival horror games.

- If you don't have a shadow, you don't have a soul! (At least according to Egyptian mythology!)

There are many ways to technologically represent a shadow in video games. It can be a complex shape that matches the silhouette and motions of the player character, it can be a rough form that follows the player, or it can be a simple black shadowy spot (or **drop shadow**) on the ground.

While a drop shadow looks less realistic, it is very effective as a device to let players know precisely where they are in the level, particularly while making jumps, where the players can use the drop shadow to determine where they are going to land. However, some gameplay mechanics, like small or moving platforms, can make using the drop shadow as a guide tricky—just one more instance where visual realism can be at odds with gameplay.

No matter what your character's shadow looks like, you should still include it, preferably during the early stage of your production. A few things to keep in mind about shadows:

- Watch out for your character's shadow being in two places at once. While this phenomenon does happen in real life, it will look as if it is a bug in a game.

- Watch out for your shadow "casting" itself through surfaces, especially onto platforms that are above other geometry.

- Shadows react in different ways under different lights and on different surface textures. Although you don't have to adhere to reality, it may seem weird to a player if a shadow shows up underwater.

The Water's Fine...or Is It?

While we're speaking of water, be aware that designing gameplay around swimming can be a difficult task. In the earlier days of game design, video games avoided water traversal altogether, resulting in a long tradition of "water = death" in video games. If you choose to go that route, keep your messaging consistent; otherwise, the players will get confused. Don't expect players to be able to differentiate between water that is safe and water that is deadly. My rule of thumb is that water within a single environment should be one or the other. There is no deep end to the pool. It's either all shallow/safe or deep/deadly. If you must have transitional water, give your players adequate cues and warnings of the danger of swimming too far. One game I worked on had a shark fin appear and swim near players when they strayed out too far. If they ignored the warning and kept going, they got chomped on by a great white shark!

However, water gameplay can be quite interesting because it lends itself to exploration and exotic environments. But you must always consider several gameplay rules when considering swimming:

- How do players enter/exit water? Always make sure water entrances and exits are clearly marked for players. These markings can take the form of clearly marked ledges, sloping ramp geometry, or those little pool ladders just as long as players can tell "this is where I get out."

- Can characters swim under water or just on the surface? Sometimes the ability to dive isn't given to a character until later in the game. Sometimes not at all.

- If characters can swim underwater, can they stay underwater for an extended period of time? Is there some sort of a timer that gauge's air supply or pressure that prevents characters from staying underwater for extended periods of time?

- Does air matter? Can characters die due to lack of air? Do they need to collect power-ups or have some other method to sustain their air supply?

- Can characters attack underwater? Do they carry their weapons and swim at the same time? A typical swim stroke may look strange or cause sorting issues if a player is carrying a weapon at the same time.

- How do characters react when they reach the bottom? Can they glide along the bottom? Or do they bob back up toward the surface?

- Can characters do any actions underwater that they can do on land? Can they pull switches or operate those submarine hatches you always seem to find on underwater levels?

- Do characters travel at a consistent speed or can they "swim faster?"

- Changing directions or elevation underwater can cause problems for the camera as it attempts to match the characters' orientation. Quick underwater moves can cause a camera to struggle to keep up with a character and flip around.

- Don't forget about how sound works when the player is underwater. When underwater, the player can still hear the soundtrack and character's actions, but it's just muffled.

Just remember that swimming is a complicated system to program and design for. That's why so many games just kill players if they are submerged in water!

OK, before we look at the next of the Three Cs—the camera—let's look at the Universal Truths and Clever Ideas!

Level 5's Universal Truths and Clever Ideas

- Form follows function: your characters' actions and personality should determine their appearance.
- Give your characters distinct shapes, silhouettes, colors, and textures.
- Name your hero appropriately.
- Customization will increase player attachment.
- Use the player character to reflect in-game status.
- Companions and SPCs require a fair amount of work to get right. Make them complement the player character.
- Balance multiple player characters to maximize effectiveness.
- Give your NPCs gameplay functions.
- Use the player character to determine game metrics.
- Walking is NOT gameplay.
- Water is complicated, allow lots of time to program and design for it.

Level 6
The Three Cs, Part 2: Camera

DO YOU HEAR that crashing sound? That is the sound of a video game controller being thrown through an 85" QLED screen with a 120Hz refresh rate. Why was this fine piece of technology utterly pulverized? Because your game has a really bad camera.

Did you know that over one billion TVs are destroyed a year because of really bad game cameras?[1] Nothing will cause players to stop playing your game faster than a poor camera. This is why it is so important to get it right.

Get It Right: Camera Views

Choosing the right camera for your game is not only very important for determining how to program the camera, but also impacts how you design your game, map your controls, and create your artwork. It's common for a game to have more than one style of camera, but you should stick with one "main" camera style for the majority of your gameplay and use other camera views only for specific gameplay situations.

---

[1] This is a completely made-up statistic.

A **fixed camera** does not change position, focal distance, or field of view and stays fixed onto a single screen, location, and image. The earliest video games used fixed cameras because (a) the scrolling camera hadn't been invented yet (duh!), and (b) it was easier for players to track all the elements if they were kept to one screen. Early video gamers just weren't that sophisticated. But it didn't take long for them to adapt and evolve...

Even though a fixed camera's roots are old school, this view is still very popular in many games like *Royal Match, Bomberman,* and *Tetris.* A clever use of the fixed camera is to set the mood as found in early survival horror titles like *Alone in the Dark* and *Resident Evil.* These developers not only used the fixed camera shot to represent a single room, but also used it to set up the camera for maximum effectiveness. It maximizes the game's artwork by only requiring art that would be seen only "from certain angles." An item in a game world that is viewed from only one angle doesn't need a backside, which saves production and object rendering time.

Another advantage is that you can easily use a fixed camera to set up story-related events in your game world because you don't run the risk of players looking the other way when it happens. However, you have to be careful with these static screens because they aren't very dynamic. Make sure to compensate for this problem with lots of animation and effects to keep your screen lively.

If you aren't satisfied with a camera that doesn't move, you can always ask your programmer nicely to make it into a **scrolling camera** instead.

Pretend you are looking down at a desktop. Or you can use this picture if you are bad at pretending. On this hypothetical desktop, you can interact with all the elements on the desk, but hey, you just can't find your pen. In the picture, what you can see is represented by the gray box. By moving or "**scrolling**" the camera (in this case your eyes) to another part of the desk—voilà! —you find your missing pen beside a book. Amazing!

A scrollable camera offers all the advantages of a static camera but with the added advantages of (a) movement, which keeps players engaged in the act of moving the camera, and (b) your ability to hide stuff off-screen or reveal it in a big dramatic way. This is why you will find it being used in many old-school adventure games like *Day of the Tentacle* or the *Monkey Island* series. If you use a scrollable camera with a God-mode or isometric view (which I talk about later), you can simulate a tabletop to simulate miniature games. This is why a scrollable camera is used in RTS and dungeon crawl games like *Dawn of War* and *Diablo III*. Make sure your controls for moving your camera are simple and relative to your players' controllers. You don't need anything fancy to move a camera around.

Work with your programmer to **tune the hydraulics** of your camera—the speed at which the camera accelerates and decelerates. The wrong speed can cause the camera to drift past the character or abruptly stop short, which can be very frustrating as the player goes through a process of overshooting back and forth, a condition that eventually leads to insanity and/ or a destroyed monitor. Conversely, don't make your camera scroll too slowly. This can be particularly catastrophic in a game in which your little army's platoons are in danger of being wiped out by enemy tanks and your scrolling camera is too slow to get to them in time. Oh, the humanity!

Why not let the players decide what speed they want the screen to scroll? It's an uncommon option in RTS and strategy games, but it could work for any genre of game with a scrolling camera. I suggest making this option a sliding scale with several speeds to choose from. Just offering "fast" and "slow" won't cut it.

In the beginning, there was a static screen. The static screen was fine for *Invaders from Space* and the *Kongs of Donkey*. And then game players cried out for more. So, in 1982, the great Irem descended from the heavens in *Moon Patrol's* purple moon buggy and introduced **parallax scrolling** to the video games world.

As a parallax scrolling camera moves, the world moves with it. This camera view revolutionized video games, allowing game developers to create longer and deeper game worlds in which

to play. There are two different ways you can treat parallax scrolling. First is plain ol' scrolling. The camera is controlled by a player's movement: the player essentially stays in the center of the screen as the world moves past them just like in those old-fashioned western films. Giddyup!

When using this type of scrolling, be careful to play out how your game level loads because your players may be able to "outrun the load." Always play your game level backward to make sure that your players can't break your game.

Another type of scrolling is the **forced scroll**. Players are forced to "keep up" with a scrolling camera, which is why it was first used on driving and flying games like *Moon Patrol* or *Scramble*. It can be used with 2-D, 2-D parallax, and 3-D scrolling games. It became popular with first person shooters like *Operation Wolf* and third person rail shooters like *Panzer Dragoon* and was later used for "chase" sequences like those found in *Crash Bandicoot*. More often than not, if a player fails to keep up with the camera, something horrible (such as death) happens to them. This makes a forced scroll camera great for gameplay where you really want to put pressure on players, but keep in mind that you don't want to use it consistently in a game—that is, unless your whole game is based on this idea.

Scrolling games dominated home video games throughout the 1990s (really, I was there). There were tons of them! When you have a bunch of people making a genre of game over and over again, innovation eventually sneaks in. And it happened. Twice, in fact.

The first was **Mode 7**, named after the seventh (out of eight) background layer on the Super Nintendo entertainment system.[2] The hardware would convert 2-D art into a 3-D plane which, when scrolled, created the illusion of a background infinitely moving toward or away from the horizon. Add a forward-facing or rear-facing sprite, and you would create the illusion of a car or character traveling toward or away from the screen. Excellent examples of Mode 7 can be seen in *Mario Kart*, *F-Zero*, and *Super Star Wars*. However, designing a level for Mode 7 gameplay can be tricky because

your level has no true back wall, only a horizon the players can never reach. While technology has advanced to allow programmers to easily create 3-D worlds without any special graphic mode, the term still remains in use by some (albeit ancient) game developers.

In addition to scrolling the camera, programmers found inspiration from the **multiplane camera** used in traditional animation. This camera gives the illusion of depth by zooming the camera toward and away from the screen. By having a camera that tracked in and out of the **Z-axis**, developers were able to create level designs with parallel paths. Games like Disney's *Hercules Action Game* (1997) used the multiplane camera to create **bidimensional**

---

[2] The scrolling ground plane actually existed before the SNES's Mode 7. Racing games like *Night Racer* (1977) and *Pole Position* (1982) were some of the first games to feature a scrolling ground plane that gave the illusion of 3-D space.

gameplay, the forerunner to what is known as **two and a half D**. A side effect of the zooming effect in bidimensional games was severe pixilation that occurred when the camera zoomed in on a nonscaling sprite. You can still find this effect being intentionally imitated in "retro"-style games.

First-Person Camera

As gameplay moved into the Z-axis, game creators explored more cinematic camera views. Although a few games in the 1970s featured a **first-person camera**, it wasn't until *Wolfenstein 3D* (1992) and its successor, *Doom* (1993), that the camera view became popularized. The camera is used in a variety of game genres, from racing to platform; it became most associated with the **first-person shooter (FPS).**

Despite the popularity of the first-person camera, it's hard to discern whether it is really the best camera for gameplay. Here's a quick comparison of the pros and cons of the first-person camera:

Advantages	Disadvantages
Aiming weapons is easier.	Gauging jump and movement distance is hard.
Players view their characters as "self," allowing for greater immersion in game world.	Players can't see their characters and can lose emotional connection.
Creating atmospheric situations (like horror) is easier.	Players do not always look where the designer wants them to look.
Players get a close look at weapons, world objects, and puzzle items.	Game objects (like pickups) have to be exaggerated in scale to compensate for distance.

As you can see, the arguments for and against the first-person camera are pretty darn even. But regardless, you can pull off some pretty fun visual effects when using a first-person camera:

- **Blood splatter:** Many FPSs use a blood splatter effect on the screen to show that a player has taken damage. You can also have the screen start to "grow dark" or dim to represent the player dying. Some games use this effect heavily and some games do it light, but I feel it's pretty unfair to punish a dying player with the additional disadvantage of not being able to see the gameplay (or where the damage is coming from!). My advice is to use this effect sparingly.

- **Raindrops/mist/lens flare:** This effect obscures the camera lens with weather effects. Raindrops on the windshield of a car in driving games can increase the feeling of speed. Lens flares in the eyes of a player can increase the realism of a sunset. Mist obscuring the details of a silent and lonely town can make things a little creepier.

- **"Predator vision:"** Based on the thermal camera effect seen in the classic sci-fi movie *Predator*, you can simulate these effects in a first person view to make players actually feel as if they are using high-tech or alien gear, such as night-vision goggles. Just make sure the effect actually gives players a gameplay advantage in addition to looking cool.

- **Blurry/drunken/drugged/poisoned cam:** First person view gives the designer a chance to put a player in the character's shoes. As long as the altered state doesn't interfere too much with the player's control of the game for too long, there's no problem with giving the player a good whack in the head now and then—or at least an awful, simulated hangover.

These effects sound pretty fun, right? Remember, many of these effects can be used with a third person camera too but using them with the first-person camera really makes you feel as though you are "in the action." But wait, before you pass judgment, let's "toss" one more "chunk" of information into the "pot."

DIMS stands for **Doom-induced motion sickness,** and it is a very real thing. It's what happens when your eyes register movement, and your inner ear (responsible for balance) doesn't. Motion sickness is heavily influenced by the field of view of the game's camera. So, the larger the field of view, the more people will feel motion sick.[3] Victims of this form of motion sickness can suffer from clammy skin, sweating, dizziness, headache, and nausea.

To avoid having your players vomit all over your game, try the following remedies:

- Get the game's frame rate as close to 60 frames per second as possible. Avoid bobbing foreground elements, like your player's weapon.

- Keep your floor as level as possible.[4]

- Add large stationary objects to your environment to give the players something to focus on.

- Don't whip the camera around too much.

- Try not to have your players change their elevation view (looking up and down) too quickly or often.

And although I am not a doctor (and don't even play one on television), I recommend getting some fresh air, drinking a glass of water, and taking nondrowsy motion sickness medicine if you end up experiencing any of these symptoms.

Virtual Reality

Let's talk about Virtual Reality for a moment. All of the issues and notes I listed earlier for the FPS camera apply to virtual reality. After all, YOU are the first person in a VR simulation. But there are a few things to think about when designing a camera for VR:

- Don't rotate the camera too quickly. Large swings in the viewer's perspective can cause users to get nauseous. Try to limit the movement to short arcs, gentle motions, or reduce its speed.

- Let the player decide when to rotate the camera. If you move the camera without the player initiating it, it will cause disorientation and sickness. Instead, give the player

---

[3]This is the reason why I never sit closer than the seventh row from the front when I go to the movies.

[4]This is what killed me when I played *Goldeneye* on the N64. Don't get me wrong; this is a brilliant game, but there was one level with an undulating floor that, after I played it for half an hour, made me want to throw up, and I had to stop playing. I haven't finished it since.

control over the camera and when to move it. Or let the player know that the camera is going to move so they can anticipate the movement.

- The player is the camera. Since a VR user can rotate their head and since their head is effectively the camera, treat it as such in your game. All the things a player can do with their head (such as pan, tilt, and such) your VR camera should do as well.

- If your VR experience features a character that isn't the user, then I offer the following advice about third-person cameras....

Third Person Camera

Another good way to avoid turning your game into a puke-a-rama is to pull the view back into the **third person view**. Now remember, this isn't a solve-all solution, but I have found that when players have something to focus on, the effects of DIMS seem to decrease. A third person camera also lets players get a better view of the world, the action, and what's coming up behind them. Watch out, Lara! That mercenary has a machete!

Pulling the camera back behind the player offers many advantages over the first-person view. First off, the player can get a clear view of his character's butt.[5] Well, you can fix that by allowing the character to turn around and run toward the camera. But then you have to make sure the camera can track backward with the player. Does that mean the controls become camera relative or player relative? And how does the player restore the camera back to its original position? Hmmm. This may be more complicated than I first thought.

---

[5]The story goes that Toby Gard, one of the designers of *Tomb Raider* (1996), made his lead character a woman because he didn't want to spend the entire game's production staring at a guy's rear-end.

Getting a third person camera to work correctly may be the biggest challenge a team has to face. Although many things can go wrong with your camera, let's see what you need to be concerned with to get them right:

- **Camera movement:** When I was in high school, I had an after-school job videotaping sporting events. As I concentrated on filming the game, I lost track of everything else that was going on around me. As a result, I tended to back into the coaches and trip over the gear lying on the sidelines, which didn't result in great footage and generally annoyed the coaching staff. To solve this problem, I recruited a friend to act as a spotter as I filmed to make sure the collisions were kept to a minimum.

Having that experience made me realize that every camera needs a spotter, even ones that live within video games. This is why I say, "treat the camera like it's a person." As you program your camera and build your world, give the camera room to maneuver and the player a way to manipulate it. This style of camera is commonly called a **follow cam** because it follows after the player. After my years of working on 3-D follow cams, here's what I've learned to watch out for:

- **Sorting:** Sorting is what happens when a camera moves through a character or geometry with collision. Nothing breaks the illusion of the real world faster than this. It makes the world feel unsubstantial. What's worse, in many cases, the sorting camera will expose the background layer of the world, which in most cases is a sky or flat color layer. It looks bad, and you should take great pains to make sure this doesn't happen in your game.

You can avoid sorting by paying attention to the camera and its relationship to the geometry. One way is to give your camera a detection radius so it can avoid passing through world objects by moving over, under, or around objects. If you don't want your game to process that much collision detection (which causes the game to slow down), have world objects turn translucent. This approach works pretty well with objects within the confines of the walls but shouldn't be used for perimeter walls because they can ruin the entire illusion of your level. Players get disoriented when elements in the level flicker in and out of existence! (And it looks bad.)

- **Controls:** Think about how your camera is going to operate with regard to controls. Many games won't work properly if the player is pointing the camera straight up or straight down. Personally, I dislike "airplane controls." Unless I'm flying an airplane, don't make me push up on the analog stick to make my character go down. It makes no sense to give an FPS character airplane control. However, if you must have this camera-relative control option, at least give the player the option of changing it. Even better, make the character-relative control the default and make the airplane control the option.

- **Camera flipping:** Also called "ping-ponging" or "bouncing," this problem occurs when the camera tries to find a good place to come to rest but ends up bouncing between two or more objects. It's due to a lack of mathematical sophistication, but you'll have to bring that up with your programmer.

The number one cause of camera flipping is **corners**. Instead of trying to come up with an overly complicated camera system to combat flipping (and believe me, it usually ends up being overly complicated), just keep players out of corners in the first place. Rather than creating invisible geometry (oh, how I hate invisible geometry; more ranting on this later), build blocking geometry such as small retaining walls, shrubberies, boulders, or fencing, which tell the players to "stay out!" of corners. Don't invite trouble: keep your collectibles out of corners. Keep your enemy's AI path/detection zones out of corners. Move your gameplay elements to the middle of the room. Stay out of the corners! I mean it!

Okay, so you choose not to listen to me.... If you think you MUST have that one power-up nestled in the corner of that room, then, as your character walks into the corner, make sure your camera goes up the wall. Imagine that the Amazing Spider-Man is your camera man.[6] What does Spidey do when he reaches a wall? He climbs up. Have the camera scoot up along the surface of the wall to look at the player from a bird's-eye view (or would that be spider's-eye view?). But avoid having the camera show the player from a direct top-down view. Not only does the view look bad, but it just invites flipping when the camera tries to decide where to look at the player.

---

[6]Before you laugh, Spider-Man *is* a camera man for a living. He's actually a pretty good choice!

- **Obstruction:** This problem occurs when something in the world gets in between the camera and the player, blocking the player's view. If something gets in the way, I suggest treating like a person...in this case that person is Spider-Man! Make that camera climb up walls, leap over items, or swing up into the air. Anything to quickly get the camera into a location to provide a clear view of the action.

- **Position:** A topic of disagreement among the world's greatest designers is whether the camera should strictly follow the player as if it were attached to a stick that is stuck to the character OR whether the camera should be more laid back and follow the character around freely. Don't stress it, dude; the camera will catch up with the player when it feels like it. (Or when the player chooses to reset it.)

Maybe it's because I grew up in Southern California, but I am definitely in favor of the second, mellower method for the following reasons: there are fewer chances for obstruction, you see the character's face from time to time, you can set up gameplay where players have to deal with enemies that sneak up behind them, and it's easier to orchestrate "chase"-style gameplay. Why this is such a contentious topic is not because the world's greatest designers are against such concepts but because they would have to give up control of the camera.

Giving Up Control

Bad things happen when players are given control of the game camera. They start sticking it in places they shouldn't be sticking it. They find ways to get the camera stuck into the game's level geometry (the model that makes up the game's level).

They generally screw things up. And I can tell you that nothing pisses off a game designer more than watching some idiot screw around with the camera. So, you, the game designer, have three choices to solve this issue. Loosen up your sphincter and let the players take control of the camera or channel the dictator within you and make that camera all yours! *Or* you could decide when they need control and when they don't. You are the designer; you call the shots!

Make your choice, adventurer!

READ THE NEXT SECTION to let players have control of the game camera.

SKIP THE NEXT SECTION AND MOVE AHEAD ONE to take away control of the game camera.

SKIP THE NEXT TWO SECTIONS AND MOVE AHEAD TWO to let players sometimes have control and sometimes not.

So, You've Decided to Let the Player Control the Camera

In the past I've used three methods to give players control over the game camera.

The first method is to **allow players complete control over the follow cam**. By using the analog stick (or a mouse for PC games), players can move the game camera to look around 360 degrees at any time such as while running, standing still, waging combat, or whatever. The disadvantage of this is that players can get quickly disoriented, miss interesting and important level events and clues, or suffer DIMS.

The second method is a **free-look camera**. This camera allows players to stop and look around the world (effectively a first-person view). The free-look camera is usually initiated by pressing a button to activate a mode. The player then can use the analog stick (the one that is usually used to move players) to rotate the camera around 360 degrees. I have seen versions of this camera in which the free-look cam is restricted to a little less than 180 degrees in an attempt to mimic the natural rotation of the human neck. When players press the button to return back to the third person view, they are usually reoriented in the direction that the free-look cam was facing.

Speaking of reorientation, players usually appreciate your giving them the option to reorient the camera to its default position (behind a character in the case of a third person camera). This approach is particularly useful during combat and platform jumping scenarios. Players usually achieve reorientation with a single button press.

Be mindful of the speed of your third person camera as players rotate it around. A good camera feels as if it has hydraulics; it never stops dead, but rather slows down slightly as it decelerates. This will keep players from suffering from DIMS. Because a player character is usually in motion, another trick I learned is to have the camera slightly overshoot its target when players stop and creep back to center on the players if they stay still long enough. Just remember, you NEVER want players to get out of the camera's view.

The third method is to **give players selective control over the camera**. Like with the first person free-look cam. This mode can be activated by pressing a button to bring the camera in for a closer look at an object's detail or into a special mode like a sniper's scope. The difference between selective control and a free-look camera is context.

With the free-look camera, you are simulating the turning of the character's head. With selective control, you are simulating a piece of equipment, such as binoculars or a telescope. Any limitations this selective control camera may have should mirror the limitations of the object the character is using. This realism sells this view, so let reality be your guide.

Some game designers find the transition from third person to first person jarring and feel it risks taking players out of the carefully constructed atmosphere they've created. *Resident Evil 4* created a unique solution for its shooting gameplay. As a player aims his firearm, the camera viewpoint shifts down to hover behind the character's shoulder.

Another infrequently used alternative is to use **second person view**, where the camera mode is given to an entirely different character. In the *Mark of Kri* (2002), players "see" through the eyes of Kuzo, a bird that can be flown on spy missions. In *The Darkness* 2007), players can control a "tentacle cam" to see around corners and farther than the players' point of view (POV). When players see what they want, a button press returns the view back to the third player view.

So, You've Decided Not to Let the Player Have Control over the Camera

Good call. The last thing you need is someone screwing around with the camera making your game look bad. You will realize that there are many benefits to taking away the players' control over the camera:

- Removing camera control gives players one less thing to worry about. If they aren't wrestling with the camera, players are free to concentrate on what's important: playing your game.

- You get more visual bang for your buck. A camera where YOU determine what it's looking at means that game art can be built to maximize polygon and texturing limitations. In *God of War*, the environments were built like theater sets, not in full 3-D. Why build the back of a building if you are never going to see it?

- You can treat your game like a dark ride. Disneyland's *Haunted Mansion* is the perfect real-world example of a designer-controlled camera, as its omni-mover carts[7] always have the guests looking at the most interesting scenes in the ride. You commonly find this kind of **rail camera** in first person shooters like *Time Crisis* (1995), *Sin & Punishment: Star Successor* (2009), and *House of the Dead* (1996).

- Your game world simply looks better. Taking away camera control means you can set up shots. Want a worm's-eye view to make the boss look more menacing? No problem. Want to skew the camera to make the world look demented or creepy? Go right ahead. No one is going to be able to screw it up.

- What did I miss? Have an important clue or event happening in your game world? Want the players to be able to see the Tower of Doom looming in the background or that giant spider that is creeping up on them? No problem. Without camera control, you don't risk players missing anything important in your game.

- Want to have the camera do a barrel roll? Zip in and out between columns? Move around pillars or over or under objects? Match players' movement as they crawl under obstacles and through narrow passages? Go right ahead and go nuts with those complex camera moves. Using a rail camera, you can set up elaborate and cinematic camera angles. You don't have to worry about players wrestling to regain control of the camera. Just make sure your gameplay controls remain consistent during any of these fancy camera moves.

- If you decide to obstruct or let characters get out of the players' view, make sure your character-relative controls let the players guide the characters back into view. For example, if a player moves their character behind a fence, they should be able to keep pushing the control stick in the same direction with the assumption that the character will eventually emerge on the other side. Don't place hazards behind the obstruction or widen the path in these areas, which would allow for movement in the Z-axis: the players could get unjustly hurt or lost when not in view. These situations, however, are great places to hide goodies.

But the most important point to remember when removing the players' control of the camera is to make it clear they don't have control over it. Once they realize this, they can focus on the gameplay and not worry about the camera.

Two-dimensional versus three-dimensional? In the end, all that matters is that you use the camera that is best for your gameplay.

---

[7]Which they call "doom buggies." Heh.

So, You've Decided to Let Players Sometimes Have Control over the Camera

You are a fair and balanced individual who knows the meaning of moderation. Now go back and read about the other two options so you can actually learn something, you know-it-all.

Two and a Half D

Crash Bandicoot (1996) was one of the first games to take two-dimensional platform gameplay and move it into the third dimension. Unlike bidimensional gameplay, which uses sprites for the game world and characters, two and a half D uses three-dimensional character and world models but limits the camera movement in the same manner as a bidimensional game: up, down, and in/out on the Z-axis.

When making your two-and-a-half-dimensional (2.5-D) games, just follow the same rules as with a parallax scrolling camera, with the guidelines of taking control away from the players as listed previously.

Isometric Camera

Introduced with *Zaxxon* (1982), the isometric camera gave players a new way to look at the playing field. Not quite side view and not quite top down, the end result creates a rather toy-like view of the world. This and the smooth scrolling 3-D world on a 2-D display contribute to why the isometric view is popular with building and simulation games.

There are some advantages to an isometric (or iso) camera. Players get a quick snapshot of an environment's layout and the relationship of items within it, which makes it good for environmental puzzle solving. Hordes of enemies seem more impressive when seen from this camera view, as exhibited in games like *Hotline Miami* and *League of Legends*. That said, elevation can cause some problems in iso view. Determining whether something is higher up and closer than something farther away and lower can be difficult, as they both appear to be in the same spot on-screen. Regardless of how small their subjects look compared to their first and third person cousins, iso games can still be quite detailed and beautiful. However, if your gameplay is less concerned about getting a detailed look at the inhabitants of your world, go ahead and step into the sandals of the divine with **God view**.

Because details aren't as important in God view, you will find it in games that are concerned with controlling cities or dominating land masses like *Supreme Commander 2 (2010)* or *Age of*

Empires IV (2021). God view is essentially an isometric camera, but the player is given a wider field of vision over the world, sometimes as high as low orbit.

Here's a pro tip for your artist teammates about creating art for isometric levels: They can draw the game characters from a side view, and they'll still work—as long as your game's art style isn't too realistic. Don't believe me? Take a look at games like *Little Nemo and the Nightmare Fiends* (2023) and *Kingdom Rush 5: Alliance* (2024).

Top-Down Camera

Although it is considered to be an "old-fashioned" camera view, you can still occasionally find action arcade games presented in a **top-down view**. Classic games like *Smash TV* and *Gauntlet* are examples of this camera view. It has some disadvantages, such as not being able to get a good look at the game character or the game world, and concepts like depth should be avoided from this perspective.

An interesting variation on the top-down camera view is the **top-down/side view** camera, also known as "forced-perspective" view. Although some elements in the game level are presented from a top-down view (usually world elements and power-ups), other elements (like characters) are presented from a side view. This view has a certain charm to it, similar to how characters in Egyptian tomb art are always shown from the side view. *Berzerk* (1980) and *Plants vs. Zombies* (2009) use this quirky camera view.

AR Cameras

In **augmented reality** (or **AR** for short) games, the camera is essential to the experience. Players use their camera to "look through the screen" as virtual characters seem to "appear" in the real world. Having gotten their start in camera-based peripherals like the Sony EyeToy and the Microsoft Kinect, AR is more ubiquitous in mobile devices. AR games such as *Star Wars Falcon Arcade Gunner* (2010), *Wonderbook: Book of Spells* (2012), *Pokemon Go* (2016), and *Five Nights at Freddy's: Special Delivery* (2019) blur the line between the game and reality.

There are two styles of AR games. The first requires a printed card (much like a QR code) for the camera to look at. As long as the player keeps the camera trained on or near the patterned image, the game's elements can be displayed. If the player moves the camera, the characters will disappear, and gameplay will suspend.

The other style of AR games displays virtual characters, vehicles, and effects "on top of" the camera's image. For example, *Harry Potter: Wizards Unite* (2019) displayed goblins, trolls and your magic wand over the background of whatever you are, be it a city skyline or inside of your kitchen.

When designing AR games, try not to clutter up the screen with HUD elements or large virtual objects because the main appeal is seeing the virtual characters in the real world. Also make sure your game elements are scalable because players can change their distance from the printed card as easily as taking a few steps backward.

Special Case Cameras

Okay, so you've decided what camera to use for your game. You're ready to go, right? Wrong! What about the camera for special instances? Designing a camera to work underwater or while flying adds another layer of complexity.

Here are a few red flags to be aware of and tricks to keep in mind when adding these extra layers to your own game:

- Make sure your camera is always moving along with the player while flying or swimming. Don't let the player rise or fall off-screen.
- If your player flies or swims straight up or down, make sure your camera doesn't sort through floor geometry.

- While a player is swimming, keep your camera underwater with the player. Don't have it pop out of the water unless the player is swimming on the surface. Try to keep a clear distinction between "in water" and "on land."

- Try to resist the urge to have your camera realistically bob while underwater. Effects like these make players suffer from DIMS.

Tunnel Vision

Another camera problem can occur when the player is moving through tight environments like caves, sewers, or dungeons. Low ceilings, narrow passageways, and doorways can cause all sorts of trouble to the camera.

I find that if you restrict the movement using a rail camera in these troublesome locations, you not only alleviate any camera problems but also help maintain the feeling of claustrophobia. Avoid low angles; instead, keep the camera at the character's shoulder height or slightly above the player—but watch out for low-hanging stalactites that will cause camera sorting issues.

Camera Shot Guide

Now that you've seen all the ways that a camera can present the game, it's time to see all the ways the camera can present the story as well. Let's go to the 5-second film school and find out how to set up your camera to get the best shot—just like those Hollywood professionals!

- **Extreme wide shot (EWS):** This shot shows a character or location from a very far distance. It is perfect for showing castles looming in the distance or a planet-killing space station in orbit.

- **Very wide shot (VWS):** This shot is closer than an extreme wide shot so you can make out some details. It is usually used for establishing shots of buildings or other large things like spaceships or to set the tone that the player is stranded out at sea or in a desert.

- **Wide shot (WS):** The entire subject (be it a car or person) can be seen in frame on a wide shot. It is usually used when first establishing a main character or vehicle so the player can get a good look at it in its entirety.

- **Medium shot (MS):** About half of the figure or the subject can be seen in frame. This is usually your character from the waist up. This means your character can wear pajama pants that day.

- **Medium close-up (MCU):** Also called a "head and shoulders shot," this view is most commonly used when a character is talking. Make sure to animate hands to keep the character on the screen lively.

- **Close-up (CU):** This is also called a "head shot": the camera is tight into a character's face to show expression. When you get this close to a CG character model, you start to see flaws (such as in the interiors of mouths or close views on textures). I recommend using this shot sparingly.

- **Extreme close-up (ECU):** Wham! Right up the nose with this one. This shot is great for focusing on the expression in eyes like in spaghetti westerns and old horror movies. Or you can use it to show details on objects such as puzzle clues or even the puzzles themselves.

- **Cutaway:** You know when the hero says, "I need to get that magic sword" and the next shot is a magic sword? That's a cutaway. A cutaway can be used for a character reaction shot, too.

- **Cut in:** Here, our heroine says, "I need to examine this clue," and then the camera shows a close-up detail of the clue. That's a cut in.

- **Two shot:** This is called a two shot because it features two elements (usually talking characters) shown on-screen at the same time.

- **Over-the-shoulder shot (OSS):** This shot is taken from over the shoulder of a character. It's a good opportunity to show hidden things, too such as characters revealing that they have a gun strapped to their back or are crossing their fingers as they promise not to kill the bad guy.

- **Noddy:** In this shot, a character is reacting to what someone else is saying ("nodding" in response to the speaker). You see this shot a lot with news interviews.

- **Point-of-view shot (POV):** This shot is from the perspective of someone or something. It is usually shown from the eyes of the player but can be from the point of view of a watching enemy, a floating power-up, whatever you want!

Camera Angle Guide

Now that you know what kind of camera you are using and what your shot is going to look like, let's place the camera to make things look as cool as possible:

- **Eye level:** The camera is aiming level at the eyes of your subject.

- **High angle:** The camera is above the subject, looking down on it. This angle can make things look less impressive. A good shot for showing elements in relationship to each other.

- **Low angle:** The camera is below the subject, looking up at it. This makes things look more menacing or impressive. Great for boss fights.

- **Worm's-eye view:** The camera is literally on the floor looking up, as if a worm were watching the action.

- **Bird's-eye view:** This shot is taken from high up in the sky, as if a bird were watching the action.

- **Dutch tilt:** We did this trick in *Maximo: Ghosts to Glory*. We wanted our in-game camera to feel slightly creepy or wacky, like shots you see in a Sam Raimi horror movie or the 1960s *Batman* TV show. Tilt the camera so everything seems to be cockeyed. If you do a Dutch tilt subtly, it has a great effect on

the player, who realizes something is wrong but isn't sure what. If you do it severely, it really makes things feel screwed up.

Camera Movement Guide

Moving the camera is an art all unto itself. Here are the most common ways to move a camera. See whether you can incorporate these moves into your game camera to make it feel more cinematic:

- **Arc:** The camera follows or dollies around a subject in an arc. A common technique is to have the camera arc around the player for 360 degrees if something amazing or wondrous is happening to the character (for example, they just gained a new power).

- **Dolly zoom:** The camera adjusts the focal length but is moved forward or back to keep the subject the same size on camera. You see this shot a lot in Steven Spielberg movies where a character is amazed by something or realizes that something bad is going to happen.

- **Follow:** The camera moves with the subject. Depending on the style of your cutscene, you can try to make your follow a little shaky as if it were taken by a handheld camera.

- **Pedestal:** The camera moves up to match the subject. Like a tracking shot, but vertical. Having the camera pedestal move past objects in the foreground helps add to the illusion of speed, especially if you are trying to show something rise up suddenly or powerfully.

■ **Pan:** The camera moves to the left or the right. Play around with your pans: move them around and past objects. Place items in the foreground to make more interesting shots.

■ **Tilt:** The camera's focus is moved up or down, but the camera's position stays the same. Effects like lens flares can make a tilt more interesting. Just like J.J. Abrams does!

■ **Dolly:** The camera is moved smoothly toward or away from the subject. This is also called a tracking or crab shot. Speed can really make a dolly more interesting. A slow crawl can be used if something is mysterious or suspenseful, or the camera can really rocket forward if something is dangerous or dramatic. Play around with starting and ending your tracking before your subject starts moving to make things feel more dynamic.

■ **Zoom:** The focal length of the lens changes, giving the illusion of the camera moving. Be careful not to zoom in through items (sorting) or zoom too close to characters or world objects that aren't very detailed. Seeing textures go from fine to pixilated breaks reality for the viewer.

Other Camera Notes

Now that you are an expert cinematographer, you can work on your directing skills.

Nothing kills a good shot faster than having an unappealing composition. The most basic guideline for composition is called **the rule of thirds.**

In this image, see how the screen has two horizontal and two vertical imaginary lines running through it? See how it creates three rows of two squares? The rule is that you want your camera's subject to be either a third of the way up or a third of the way to one side or another. Of course, after you have mastered the rule of thirds, you will want to break it. That's okay, too. After all, you are an ar-teest.

Another tried-and-true rule is called **crossing the line.** Just like in the rule of thirds, an imaginary line cuts through the middle of your scene or environment. Let's say you have your hero running away from a deadly trap.

The hero has just crossed the line, which makes it look as though they are running first to the right and then to the left, which just looks weird and doesn't convey that the hero is running in the same direction. Instead, add a shot of the hero from the front to show that this is the same character in the same place.

You also want to apply crossing the line when you have two characters talking to each other; otherwise, they'll look as though they are talking to someone else off-screen.

Always Point the Camera to the Objective

An excellent rule of directing your shot, whether it is in-game or in a cutscene, is that the camera should tell the players what they should be looking at. For example, you enter a mysterious, underground chamber. Players can be told any number of things by the camera's movement: where puzzle elements can be found, the appearance or location of enemies, a dramatic reveal of a beautiful piece of architecture, or where the exit is. Or even better, players can be shown all of the above. Playwright Anton Chekhov said, "If in the first act you have hung a pistol on the wall, then in the following one it should be fired. Otherwise, don't put it there."[8] In other words, show everything that the players need for the entire room or scene. You can spool clues out to them, but don't make them blindly guess.

Even if players can't see the objective, give them tools to find another way to see it. *Batman: Arkham Origins* uses a "detective mode" (literally a pair of X-ray specs) that allows Batman (the player) to see hostiles as well as point the way to secret paths. *Heavenly Sword* (SCEE, 2007) displays a picture-in-picture view to show puzzle clues and "beauty shots" of the enemies during boss fights.

Never Let the Character Get out of the Camera's Sight

Oy. I can hear all the kvetching now. "How can I keep my camera on the character ALL the time? But what if my character goes behind a wall or hides behind a very dense shrub?" Feh. Not a problem. There are several tricks you can do to help players keep track of where they are in the game. Observe:

- Show an arrow, name tag, or "ghost image" outline of a player through geometry.

- Have the screen react as if it were an X-ray or thermal imaging device and show the player's skeleton or heat signature while they are behind the object.

- Make the wall or object turn transparent to show the character behind it.

---

[8]*Anton Chekhov: A Life*, Donald Rayfield (Henry Holt and Company, 1997).

- If your character gets off-screen (this can happen in multiplayer mode[9]), have an arrow or icon point to where they are.

- Zoom into first person mode to show the character's POV.

- Build your geometry to make sure you can always see a little bit of the character. Tinted windows, arrow slits, and grating with gaps all go a long way to show the movement of the player behind it.

While players are in this obscured view, the camera should NOT act any differently. The last thing players need is to have to wrestle with the camera when they can't see their character.

Multiple-Player Cameras

Keeping a camera on a player is tricky enough but what if you have more than one player? I have seen many game designers go mad trying to determine a workable camera scheme for multiple players. Fortunately, I have done all the hard work for you and will save you a trip to a padded cell.

- **Split screen:** *GoldenEye 007* (1997) had a great four-player split screen mode that worked pretty well as long as you didn't expect to make out any detail on the screen. *War of the Monsters* (2003) used a split screen that engaged only when the two combatants were far enough away from each other to trigger it. Now, in the age of giant TV screens, split screens work better because each player can actually see what is going on.

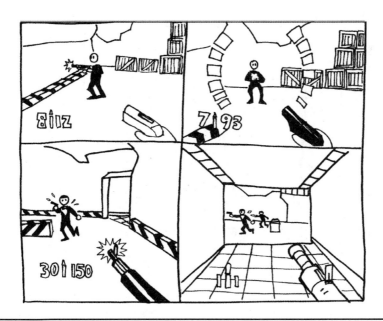

---

[9]But it won't because you aren't going to let your main character get out of the camera's sight, right?

■ **Zooming screen:** *LittleBigPlanet* (2008) zooms out whenever there is more than one character on-screen. If any of the characters get off-screen, they use an arrow to keep track of the player's location. If they stay off-screen for too long, the player is "killed" until the next checkpoint is reached. *Power Stone* (1999) does something similar, but dynamically scales in and out because there can be up to four players on-screen at once. The characters get pretty tiny at times, but coupled with an indicator arrow system, you can keep track of your character pretty well.

■ **Camera in picture:** You can also go with the camera-in-picture route. A main character is represented on the "big screen" with additional characters shown on smaller insert camera views. It's not the best solution for some types of multiplayer games like FPSs, but it works pretty well for sports titles.

Whew. I think we've exhausted the topic of cameras. Time to move on to the last of the Three Cs: Controls.

Level 6's Universal Truths and Clever Ideas

- Choose the right camera for your game.
- Prevent DIMS by minding frame rate, speed of camera movement, and level topography.
- First person camera allows for greater player immersion.
- Third person camera allows players to get a good view of their character and the world.
- Treat the camera like it is a person.
- Remove camera control whenever it becomes a problem.
- When you remove the player's control of the camera, make sure they know it.
- Use Hollywood-style camera angles and shots to heighten game visuals and drama.
- Never let the character out of the camera's sight.
- Accommodate multiple players using the game camera.

Level 7
The Three Cs, Part 3: Controls

WELCOME TO THE last of the "Three Cs"—**controls.** It's worth mentioning that out of all Three Cs, only controls are universally applicable to every style of game. The first C, character, applies only when you have a character. Abstract puzzle games, vehicle simulators, and many sports games don't have a distinct or playable character. The second C, camera, only applies to games that use a game camera: old school, fixed screen cameras don't use any of the fancy camera moves we covered. This makes the third C the most important one of all. Which is why it pains me so much to recount this true story...

Once upon a time, I joined the team of a console game that had been in production for three years. I was asked to look at the current state of the game and report back on any issues I found. Overall, the game was really good, but there was one thing that bothered me. One of the enemies could only be defeated with a quick-timer event (see Level 8 for more details on these events), and even though I'm awesome at playing action games, I just couldn't seem to press the button fast enough to win the contest and kill the monster.

I went to the creative director and told him that I thought the controls for the minigame were too punishing. He asked me, "How did you hold the controller?" This is what I showed him:

He said, "Oh, no wonder. You are holding the controller wrong." Whaaa? As far as I knew, there was only one way to hold the controller. Keeping things respectful, I asked, "How do *you* recommend I hold it?" This is what he showed me:

I wasn't sure whether he was joking. "I don't believe that players would change their hand positions midway through the game. It just doesn't seem very natural."

He became insulted and proceeded to tell me that not only was this the proper way to hold the controller, but that *everyone else* on the team held it that way as well. "Hmm. Did you *tell them* how to hold it that way?" I asked. "Yes," he replied.

I gave his way a try but still didn't win the game. If anything, the new hand position made things worse. I returned to his office and told him, "Sorry, but I think players are going to have difficulty playing this." Pointing his finger at me, he said, "You are 100% WRONG!" and stormed off.

Three months later, after testing revealed that the quick-timer event was too hard to play, the controls were adjusted, and I was proven right. His way was wrong, *nobody* but him held a controller that way. What **very important thing** did I take away from this experience?

ALWAYS REMEMBER THAT HUMANS ARE PLAYING THESE GAMES

It's not six-fingered mutants who play these games. It's *Homo sapiens* who play video games, most of them possessing short if not stubby fingers and mediocre motor skills coordination, which is why it is important to consider ergonomics when you are creating your control schemes.

Control Is in Your Hand

Ergonomics is the study of fitting equipment to the worker. Hardware developers take great pains to see how players hold and use the controller. This is the reason it never made any sense to me that a developer would create a control scheme that forced players to twist up their hands like pretzels. To help with this problem, I created this rule of thumb (BAA DUM! TISH![1]) that I call the **"Gamers' Guide to Flex-O-Fingering."**

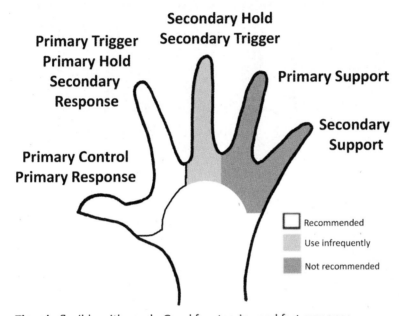

Thumb: flexible with reach. Good for steering and fast response.
Index: strong and fast. Used for response or hold moves.
Middle: weaker but usable for hold moves. Decent reach.
Ring: weak with poor reach. Better for stabilization
Pinkie: poor strength, reach requires hand support.

When you are designing controls, try establishing design rules for your control schemes based on hand placement (for example, in FPS games, it's common to use the keyboard for character movement and the mouse for aiming and shooting). Not only is this approach helpful when determining what controls go where on the controller, but players will begin to associate muscle movement with a certain action even if they don't realize they are doing it.

Speaking of keyboards, just because you have a whole keyboard available for use, doesn't mean you have to use every single key. Keeping your keyboard controls localized around commonly used key groupings like QWERTY or ASWD makes it easier for players to adapt to.

---

[1] Thank you, thank you. I'll be here all week, folks. Try the veal.

Another way to assign controls is thematically. In *Tak and the Guardians of Gross* (THQ, 2008), the motion-controlled Wii Remote was used for all of the player's magic powers while the analog stick/nunchuck controlled all of Tak's real-world capabilities such as interacting with objects and fighting. If players had any question on how to perform a move, they would usually try the thematically related controller first. Just make sure you don't cross signals and start intermingling your themes. That just leads to confusion and sadness.

The preceding suggestions are really no big secret; it boils down to this: you just need to understand the control needs of your audience. Here are a few more tips (exclusive to buyers of this book![2]):

- If you are designing for really young (8 and younger) players, keep the button presses simple. Don't create complex combinations because these younger fingers just can't make them. Or if you are designing a kid's game using the keyboard, try not to spread out your key commands too far because most kids tend to "hunt and peck" the keys, which isn't good if you want them to make quick actions.

- MMO and FPS players often create hotkeys and macros to chain attacks or spell effects. Give your players the option to customize their controls. You never know when you'll need to cast "Combustion," "Icy Veins," and "Fireball" to boost your damage per second. In addition, customizable controls have the benefit of being friendly for disabled gamers.

- Fighting gamers, like fans of Capcom's *Street Fighter* series, pride themselves on mastering ultracomplex control schemes, but remember, not everyone can pull off the dragon punch move in *Street Fighter 6*. If you want to keep your game accessible to other types of players, don't go nuts with the uber-complex controls.

- *Track and Field* (Konami, 1983) was a very popular game that required manic button pressing to make the little athlete character run. However, it was impossible to accurately do this move without the aid of a pencil (see image), resulting in what we kids called the **"pencil trick."** However, the pencil trick destroyed the game controllers.

---

[2] Please do not use these tips if you are just looking at this page in the bookstore. Thanks.

While I'm sure that controller manufacturers loved the pencil trick—because of all the replacement arcade machines they sold—don't make your players resort to a stop-gap measure just so they can succeed at your game. It's unfair.

- Although experimenting with unconventional control schemes is fine, make sure players have the option to revert back to a more traditional one.

- On that note, offer players several control options. Even better, let the players map their own controls in the options screen.

- For Goose's sake, don't reverse your flight controls! Pulling back on the stick should make the plane go up, and pushing forward should make the plane go down. Nobody likes those reversed controls, and

"the pencil trick"

anyone who tells you otherwise should be forced to play the super-awful *Superman 64* and fly through rings for a week straight.

You've Got the Touch

While joysticks are great, we humans come with our own controllers—ten of them in fact! Fingers are great stand-ins for anything a game designer can imagine…a sword, a slingshot, a gun sight, a laser pointer, a joystick, or even a finger! Since the explosion of touchscreen gaming on mobile devices, understanding how to create simple and responsive controls is more important than ever before. But before you start designing your touchscreen game, you really should learn what a finger can do!

- A **tap** is a quick press used to select or make a character perform an action, shoot a weapon, or quickly place an item.

- A **double tap** can be used to verify a selection, open and close selection windows, or indicate a direction for a character to move.

- A **timed tap** requires the player to tap in time with the gameplay, like you would find in a rhythm game.

- **Staccato pokes** are required for more complex or random sequences. Staccato means "short, clipped, and separate." You can use them for moments of intense action such as a finishing move.

- If you are over the age of 30, you probably find two-thumb typing difficult on mobile devices. You will have to **peck** with one finger instead. Unlike timed tapping, actions that can be pecked usually has no time constraint assigned to it.

- **Touch and hold** work well when you need to hold a moving object in place.

- **Hold and drag** is the best move to use when you need to move around inventory items, dressing characters in their finest armor and gear or tossing cards into a play zone.

- A **flick** mimics the action of a character tossing something like a hockey puck, a wadded-up paper ball, or an advancing zombie in a specific direction.

- **Page Up or Page Down** is a flick that works in multiple directions. It's best used to scroll through pages of text or menu options.

- The **pull and release** move is most famously known for launching birds toward pigs, but it can be used for any action that mimics "rubber banding" or springs, such as pinball plungers.

- **Scrubbing** is used to erase or cover something on-screen with a rapid back-and-forth motion.

- A **swipe** is used for indicating directional lines. I find swiping feels better if players associate the motion with using a real-world function such as swinging a sword or drawing a line.

- **Shape drawing** enables players to use a finger as a pen/pencil/crayon. Make sure the players can change the size of their brush. Giving them a little color selection doesn't hurt either.

- **Shape tracing** is often found in games in which spells are cast. Players trace or draw a shape such as a circle, square, triangle, or zigzag on-screen to get the desired effect. Be wary, however, that your game code doesn't mistake similar shapes with each other.

- A **pinch** is used if you want to size something up or down. Since most touchscreens support several fingers, you can do fun things like using four fingers at once.

- A **swirl** is used to draw circles. Remember that your character or object will spin slower or faster depending on how tight the curl is.

Even if you have plenty of touch control schemes to choose from, the secret is to use as few as possible to minimize confusion. *Subway Surfers* (2012), *Angry Birds Journey* (2022), and *Monopoly Go* (2023) all utilize "one-touch" control schemes and still have deep and engaging gameplay.

Another common touchscreen scheme is the **virtual controller.** A virtual controller is exactly that—a digital representation of the game's controller and buttons. Virtual controllers are primarily used when adapting games from other systems (like arcades, for example) to mobile devices. Unfortunately, many virtual controllers have been poorly executed in the past, causing many members of the game development community to view them as an undesirable option. If you must use a virtual controller for your game, I suggest using the following techniques to minimize suckage:

- Clearly delineate the directions players can move their stick. Stick to the eight directions of the compass wherever possible.

- Have your joystick snap back to the center of the controller to prevent drifting. Make the center a dead zone so nothing happens until the stick is pushed in a direction.

- Make the visual of your joystick as big as possible without obscuring gameplay. But don't make it so big that it actually takes time to move it to the extremes.

- Keep your joystick and buttons away from the edges of the screen so players don't miss by sliding off the device! Even better, mark off zones on the screen dedicated to a single action like moving left or right, jumping up, or crouching down.

No matter which control scheme you use for your touchscreen game (or any type of game for that matter), it helps to first consider *how* your game is going to be played.

Dance, Monkey, Dance

A good designer will think about how the game is played in the real world as well as in the game world. Think about how players are going to move those fingers over the controller. Avoid repetition and strive for an uncomplicated control scheme. If you get it right, you create what I call the "dance of the buttons" for players. If your controls get too complex or repetitive, you end up with your players resorting to **button mashing.**

Button mashing is a derogatory term used to describe when players aren't sure how to control the game, resulting in wildly and/or rapidly hitting the buttons randomly to get any sort of positive result. This situation usually happens in action and fighting games when either the control scheme is too complicated, or the players aren't getting satisfactory feedback.

Button mashing contributes to player fatigue and "gamers' thumb" (otherwise known as "occupational overuse syndrome"), characterized by stiffness, burning or cold sensations, numbness, or weakness. The American Physical Therapy Association[3] recommends the following exercises and advice:

- Keep your wrists straight (don't let them droop) as you hold the controller.

- Sit comfortably in a chair with good back support.

- Stretch every 20 minutes to give your head, neck, and shoulder muscles a break.

---

[3] Exercises courtesy of the APTA website (www.apta.org).

- Tap each finger with the thumb of the same hand. Repeat five times.

- Alternate tapping your palm and the back of your hand against your thigh as quickly as you can. Repeat 20 times.

FYI: This is your thigh   This is the same thigh

- Open your hands and spread fingers as far apart as possible. Hold for 10 seconds. Repeat eight times.

- Clasp your hands together, turn your hands away from your body, and extend your arms forward. Hold for 10 seconds and repeat eight times.

- Fold your hands together, turn your palms away from your body, and extend your arms overhead. You should feel the stretch in your upper torso and from your shoulders to your hands. Hold for 10 seconds. Repeat eight times.

However, not all button mashing is bad; you may be able to use it to your advantage. I have observed that the first thing players do when they start a game is to press all the buttons on the controller. This is because (a) players want to see what happens, and (b) no one ever reads the game manual. So how do you get players to learn if their first instinct is to just mash buttons?

Simple. Have the character do something cool whenever players press a button, even if they don't understand how they're doing it. *God of War* does this fantastically well: Kratos pulls off some awesome attack moves even when you just mash buttons, and it's completely intentional. When the players see these moves happen a few times, they will slow down to try to dissect how they pulled them off.

Never have a button do nothing when pressed. Here are some ways to deal with this:

- Play a "negative response" sound effect or animation to make it clear to players that this control isn't available. I always liked that the character in *Dark Castle* shrugged his shoulders if he was out of ammo or missing a key.

- Make it clear during your training mode that a button is inactive. Then make a big deal when it is unlocked. *Brütal Legend* (2009) stops the gameplay to show a full-screen graphic whenever the main character gets a new move. Just remember: (a) Don't teach more than one new move at a time, and (b) don't jam new moves down the players' throats too quickly. Players tune out if they get overloaded with information.

- Assign a redundant but related function. If the triangle button is slated for a projectile attack that players don't have yet, assign the melee attack to the button until they find that kill-o-zap blaster. The players will mentally equate the triangle button with combat until the "true" move is unlocked.

- Go the *Batman: Arkham* series route and don't have the button do anything until it's needed. The triangle button doesn't do anything unless Batman can perform a silent takedown or needs to counter an attack during combat. Then the triangle icon appears, reminding players what button to press. Not only does this technique save players the hassle of memorizing a bat-load of controls, but it also creates a mini-QTE, adding some delicious tension to the gameplay.

Poetry in motion

Motion controllers like the Wii Remote, PlayStation Move, and Xbox 360's Kinect allow designers to re-create real-world controls for moves. But before we get into that, let's talk about how to get the most reality out of traditional controllers.

One of my favorite examples of re-creating real-world moves using an analog stick is found in *Pitfall: The Lost Expedition*. (Activision, 2004). In the game, water is the player's health, and the character carries a canteen to hold water. Whenever the character comes across a cistern, the player pushes the stick forward to fill the canteen. When he pulls back on the stick, the hero, Harry, takes a drink from the canteen to replenish his health. The clever combination of intention and animation makes this feel very satisfying. Mapping the moves to logical control locations helps immerse the player into the game world.

In *Maximo: Ghosts to Glory*, the goal was to create an "out-of-game" correlation between Maximo's moves and the real-world PlayStation 2 controller. Maximo's overhead swing is performed by pressing the triangle, the button at the "top" of the controller, thus echoing the swing from high to low, while the horizontal swing is mapped to the square button on the horizontal plane of the buttons. The jump, which starts on the ground, is mapped to the X button, the lowest button on the pad, while the shield throw is mapped to the circle button where the shape of the button icon matches that of the shield.

Some genres of games like FPS, RTS, and platformers have widely accepted control schemes. For example, the spacebar, X, or A button usually makes the character jump in a platformer. The more your control scheme resembles that of other successful games in the same genre, the more easily new players will be able to quickly master it.

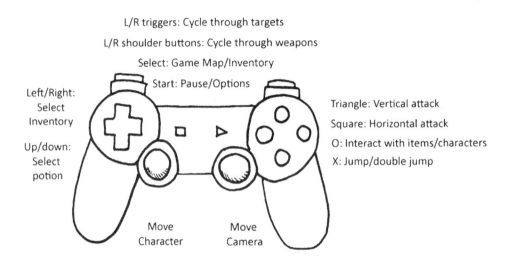

L/R triggers: Cycle through targets

L/R shoulder buttons: Cycle through weapons

Select: Game Map/Inventory

Start: Pause/Options

Left/Right: Select Inventory

Up/down: Select potion

Triangle: Vertical attack

Square: Horizontal attack

O: Interact with items/characters

X: Jump/double jump

Move Character

Move Camera

Shoulder buttons (the long flat button that can be found on the controller's "shoulder") can be found on most modern console controllers, but you should consider the actual button size when mapping controls. For example, on an Xbox One controller, the left and right shoulder buttons are physically smaller than the left and right shoulder triggers. You should assign "quick move" functions to the shoulder triggers, such as shooting, braking, and acceleration or melee attacks. Why? In the heat of combat or when a character skids around a corner, the player will want to quickly respond to the situation. With the smaller shoulder button, there is a risk of the player's finger slipping off. Use these smaller buttons for "slow move" functions, such as precision aiming, looking at a map screen, or swapping inventory.

All the right moves

Speaking of "quick moves," I can't believe I've gone this far into the chapter without mentioning this **very important thing** about controls:

WHEN THE BUTTON IS PRESSED, THE ACTION SHOULD HAPPEN

Don't get me wrong, I love beautiful character animation as much as the next guy, but nothing pisses off a player faster than pressing a button and then having to wait for the gorgeous animation to finish playing. The only thing that happens quickly in these situations is the character dying due to misjudged timing or stray enemy attacks. Save the extended animations for the move's finish.

Long animation and controls do have their place, as long as there is a balance between the risk and reward. Make sure the control represents this, too. Your game can consider a tap to be one action and hold to be something else. For example, in a hockey game, the power of the shot is proportional to the time the button was held before releasing it. A tap will make a quick but less accurate shot while a hold will shoot a more powerful and accurate shot. Have the animation reflect the action. Many action and fighting games use long wind-up animations for the most powerful attacks in the game. When you hit an enemy with one of those suckers, he isn't getting back up again. The risk is the wind-up; the reward is the high damage, powerful shot, or the instant kill.

Character or Camera Relative?

A common snare that game designers can get into is creating controls that alternate between being **character relative** and **camera relative.** Because of the frustration it can cause to players, the designer needs to pick one control scheme or the other for the duration of the game and STICK WITH IT.

With a camera-relative control scheme, the controls change depending on which way the character is facing the camera. Say you are playing the survival horror game *Terror Zombie Death Mansion 3,* and your stalwart hero stands in a hallway.

When you press left on the analog stick, the character walks to the left. The room he enters has the camera pointing at the hero—in the opposite direction from the shot in the hallway.[4]

Now when you press the stick to the left, the character walks to the right because the controls have been mapped to how the game camera sees the character, rather than from the character's orientation. Unfortunately, thanks to the backward controls, the hero has walked right into the arms of a zombie, who proceeds to chew out his brains.

This is why I'm not such a big fan of the camera-relative control scheme. I much prefer a character-relative control scheme. In a character-relative control scheme, the game controls are always relative to the player character. If the control stick is moved to the left, the character will always move to the left no matter where the camera is facing. The game compensates for the player's movement even if the camera turns around 180 degrees.

---

[4] Tsk, tsk! Someone has "crossed the line" with the camera. Didn't you read Level 6?

Shake, Rattle, and Roll

Most modern game controllers and mobile devices are outfitted with **actuators** and **gyroscopes.** They are the devices that make most motion controllers like the ones found on your smart phone or the PS5 possible.

An actuator gives feedback to players in the form of vibrations. As with control schemes, make sure the language of your actuator usage is consistent. Rather than blasting the thing off all the time, limit it to when players take damage or when they earn a reward. You can have a lot of fun with actuators—if you take the time to play with them.

My favorite use of an actuator was in *Silent Hill* (Konami, 1999). The developer figured out how to vibrate the two actuators at different frequencies to simulate a heartbeat. Whenever the character was scared or hurt, the controller's "heart" would vibrate, telling players that they were in trouble. This result was really creepy and effective.

THUMP
THUMP!

A gyroscope allows players to rotate the controller as another way to manipulate an on-screen element. The control applications for gyroscopes can be quite robust. I have played games that allow players to nudge arrows while in flight (*Heavenly Sword*), maneuver falling characters (*Ratchet and Clank: Tools of Destruction*), or even flip over an entire level (*Super Mario Galaxy*).

Gyroscopic controls (also called **tilt controls**) have especially taken hold in mobile games. Some titles like the *Rolando* series, *Doodle Jump,* and *Tilt to Live* use tilt controls exclusively to control gameplay. Because a mobile device fits in one hand, it is easier for players to quickly tilt and shift direction. Tilt controls don't have to be used exclusively to move a player character around. Why not make the player shake the controller or device to roll dice, reload a gun, toss bad guys around, or even jump?

The most important point to remember about having players use gyroscopes is to clearly communicate the direction they have to turn the controller. As the gyroscope is "hidden" within the mechanism of the controller, players can easily forget that this is a control option; make sure to remind players that this function is available.

Whatever the action, I find that players respond best when the moves match a real-world action. If you tell players to swing the controller like a sword (or a tennis racket, a bowling ball, a conductor's baton...), they get it. The trick is to design and tune your in-game sword to *feel* like a sword through animation and physics. Game animations with the right timing, speed, and feel of friction in the world will make them feel less "floaty" and "gamey"—a feeling that is always less desirable to players.

Camera-based motion controllers such as the Microsoft Kinect and the Sony EyeToy use a combination of infrared sensors and computer vision to track players' movements to control gameplay. These controllers allow for a more natural way of interacting with video games. The strength of these motion controls is how they correlate to actual activities. You want your character to punch? Just punch. You need to avoid a swinging hazard? Just duck. You no longer have to mentally convert a button, stick, or even finger move into its real-world analogy. As a result, these controllers have transformed the home console space into a more active place with the players getting up and moving to take part in the action. With that change come a few considerations:

- Many players don't play video games to exercise. Unless the goal of your game is for players to lose weight, don't forget to build in breaks and changes in control motions to keep players from wearing out or suffering repetitive stress injuries.

- Always account for **lag**, the time it takes between performing an action and when it happens on-screen. Lag occurs because it takes time for the console or computer to process the video and figure out what the players are doing. Because most games are based on timing, lag can be extremely frustrating for the player. This is especially true for rhythm games like *Beat Saber (2019)* and fighting games like *Mortal Kombat 1 (2023)*, where lag issues can screw up the player's timing and the game becomes too frustrating to play. The *Guitar Hero* series even allows the player to adjust the lag to match the player's skill level.

- Lag and **latency** are critically important to consider when building online games, especially multiplayer games. There is nothing worse than seeing a player charging at you from across the room and suddenly you are knocked out and they haven't even reached you yet! Latency is a communication delay in the time it takes for game data to be received and decoded. Latency can cause control lock-up, sound distortion or game freeze. Even if care is taken to transmit only the minimal amount of data, it takes time for that data to go cross country. At 60 Hz, it's pretty common to have delays of as much as six frames between when data is sent and received. Sadly, latency is an inescapable fact of life for Internet multiplayer games.

- Keep your players' movements broad. Precise and subtle motions tend not to register on the game cameras.

- Ensure your gestures make sense and match their real-world counterparts. Point to aim, grab to collect, wave to engage, grip to move, type to write.

- Players tend to stick to a single input style or movement unless they have a reason to change. If the input isn't reliable or consistent, players will look for alternative methods of control. If you are going to switch an input style or move, make sure it happens intuitively or at a natural transition point.

- Help guide the players' motions by using on-screen graphics. For example, *Fruit Ninja Kinect* (2011) for the Xbox 360 uses the player silhouettes to help guide where their hands (and their ninja swords) are in relationship to their fruit targets.

- Keep verifying the players' successes. Sometimes motion control players aren't sure whether their moves are being registered. Constant feedback will help reduce their confusion.

- When drawing shapes or glyphs, keep the shapes simple, like circles, triangles, and lines. Even seemingly uncomplicated shapes like figure eights and squares can get misinterpreted by motion-detecting controllers and cameras.

- Don't overdo it. Already many motion-controlled games are getting dinged for being **"waggle-fests,"** where the designers make every game action use the motion control just for the sake of it. Make your game controls a mix of traditional analog stick, button press, and controller motions.

Congratulations! You've mastered the Three Cs! But how are you going to communicate these newly minted design ideas to the player? Come with me to the remarkable Level 8...

Level 7's Universal Truths and Clever Ideas

- Let ergonomics play a role in designing control schemes.
- Consider assigning control functions thematically.
- Consider emulating control schemes of other games in the same genre. Familiarity relieves confusion.
- As the button is pressed, the action should happen.
- Use negative responses as well as positive ones.
- Give your players a break to avoid "gamer's thumb" and other health problems (take a break yourself while you are at it).
- Camera-relative controls or character-relative controls? Pick one and stick with it.
- Avoid creating controls that are contrary to the game's visuals.
- Use the game controller's special features to make your controls more intuitive to the players.
- Be aware of the special needs of touch and motion controls and design to their strengths.
- Players' movement with motion controllers should be broad and mimic reality.

Level 8

Sign Language: UI, HUD, and Icon Design

WELCOME USERS!

User Interface (UI) design (also known as **User Experience** (UX) design) requires both the knowledge of a game designer and the skills of a graphic designer. At first, this might seem like a lot to manage, but if you know the basics of UI design, you'll find that they can apply to every type of game genre.

To begin, a good UI provides **Feedback** to the player. Feedback is, of course, important because if the player doesn't receive feedback, they won't know if their actions have been performed, or what their status is—knowledge that is critical for the player to gauge their success and failure during the game. There are numerous cues that a UI designer can use to provide feedback to the player. Let's look at them!

- **Sound:** Sound is the most common way to indicate an action has been performed. A button clicks when pressed. A control panel beeps when operated. A musical **sting** (a short piece of music) plays when you complete a goal. Just remember that some players play games with the sound off, so you will need cues other than just sound.

- **Animation:** Animation, while more expensive and time consuming to create, is a great way to communicate feedback to a player. It might be a character reloading a gun or applying a bandage to a wound. It might be a door opening when a control panel is pressed. It might be a magical fairy that flies down to create a fireworks display as a player completes a challenge.

- **Color change:** Color is a simple way to show a state change. Whether it is a button that turns red when activated, text that starts "greyed out" and then changes color when the option is available, or a "Christmas Tree" that changes from red to green indicating a drag race has begun.

- **Text change:** Text changes can be used for buttons, status bars, or on diegetic in-game devices. Just remember that if you are translating your game to a different language, you might need more space for your text.

- **Particle effects:** I always say, "You can never have too many particles!" **Particle systems** emit particles (which are actually art files) to create special effects such as bursts of pixie dust or an explosion. Games like *Peggle* (2007), *Monopoly Go* (2023), and *Marvel Snap* (2022) use particle effects during gameplay to indicate an action has happened, an attack has connected, and to celebrate when the player has won.

- **Haptics:** Haptics are created by **actuators** that are in technology like game controllers. Your vibrating cell phone uses haptics to enhance a game experience or let you know that your silenced phone is ringing.

Another decision that you will have to make for your game is whether your UI design is **Skeuomorphic**, **Diegetic**, or **Symbolic.**

Skeuomoprhic design is a graphical user interface that mimics their real-world counterparts in how they appear and/or how the user can interact with them. For example, clickable buttons on an interface are visually given depth, even though they don't need it.

Diegetic interface takes things one step further. It's when a game's interface elements exist in-universe. An example of this can be seen in *Fortnite*. When a player upgrades their rifle, they are standing in front of a worktable and selecting which accessories they are attaching to it.

Symbolic interface exists in some sort of metaphorical space that isn't in-world. It only exists for the player. For example, the skill tree in Spider-Man 2 is symbolic. It exists in some "other" space where you can see and upgrade all of Spider-Man's skills. There's a video clip of how each skill works. There's even a picture of the two Spider-Men on the skill tree screen. How can Spider-Man be in three places at once? It's the magic of video games, baby.

Oh wait, there's one more, and that's **No interface.** As in none, zippo, zilch. Only a handful of games have been ballsy enough to attempt this: *The Getaway* (2002), *Peter Jackson's King Kong the Official Game of the Movie* (2005), and *Hellblade* series (2017, 2024). They have relied on animations, cause-and-effect gameplay, sound effects, and vocal barks to relay information to the player and create a more immersive, cinematic experience.

A good user interface is also **ergonomic,** which means designing things that are efficient and easy to use. There are two types of ergonomics when discussing games: physical and virtual. We touched on **Physical ergonomics** when I talked about using the controller "the right way" (see Chapter 7). You want to think about how the player is using the controls and where their hands and fingers (or other limbs) are when they are playing the game. Don't make a player reach all the way across the keyboard to perform a critical function. Even though it might be inches in the real world, it will be inconvenient during gameplay.

Virtual ergonomics works hand-in-hand with the controls that let the player quickly access information. For example, critical activities like reloading a gun or using a stim pack to regain health should be mapped to button presses or keys that are close to the WASD keys. However, if you want to check your character's game ranking, and it requires accessing a menu dropdown, then it should be placed on the game's start screen, so that way the player can take time to look at the ranking charts, rather than in the middle of the action of the game. Think about how the player uses the function, and that will dictate where and how it should be accessed.

All types of people play games, and this makes **accessibility** more important than ever. This includes allowing the screen settings to be changed to accommodate for color blindness, providing audio descriptions of the action for sight disabled, having the ability to remap interfaces and controls for ease of use and more.[1] *The Last of Us Part II* (2020) was revolutionary in that it had over 60 accessibility features for blind, deaf, and motor function challenged players.[2] Providing accessibility features doesn't just help your players, it shows you care and you want *everyone* to play your game.

Finally, a good UI is **memorable** so it is easy for players to remember the controls and inputs, even if they've left the game for a period of time. Replaying a good game UI should feel like you are "coming home."

How to Create UI

You don't have to be a great graphic designer to design a great user interface. Here are the steps you take to plan and execute user interface.

1. Create **wireframes** first. Wireframes are **storyboards** for how the user interacts with the game. It is a series of drawings that shows what happens when a button is pressed, what happens to the score meter if a coin is collected, or how the player accesses the menu in order to quit the game. Start by drawing an outline of the screen you are representing. Then photocopy or scan and copy that image to draw your next pages. For example, draw a button on a screen. Then, on the next page, draw a finger poking the button. On the third page draw what happens when the button is poked. Does poking the button bring the user to another screen? Does it make text appear on the screen? Does it fire a rocket at an enemy? Illustrate your game—not only does it help to work

---

[1] A full list of accessibility guidelines can be found at https://gameaccessibilityguidelines.com/full-list.

[2] A great article about Naughty Dog's accessibility features can be found at www.naughtydog.com/blog/the_last_of_us_part_ii_accessibility_features_detailed.

things out on paper, but you can pass them along to your programmer teammates who will be implementing your design.

2. Next, **create simple interfaces.** This is usually where "programmer art" comes in (or an actual programmer!). When creating placeholder buttons and interfaces, simple text boxes, circles, squares, rectangles will work as placeholders. All that matters is that these simple forms function in the game.

3. **Playtest the heck out of it!** This is where you get your UI in front of as many people as possible. Their job is to break what you've created. Your job is to be quiet and pay attention as they do it. That way you can find the problems and fix them. Despite all your best efforts, problems can arise when playtesting UI. Here are the steps I like to take when trying to solve them:

   A. **Identify the issue:** Take notes of how the player is not using the interface correctly and why. Ask questions of the player to find out why they are doing things wrong.

   B. **Consider solutions:** Think of several solutions to the problem, not just the first one that pops to mind. There are always several ways to solve a problem.

   C. **Execute the change:** Get that bug fixed!

   D. **Playtest the results:** Test it again! Iteration is the heart of game design.

   E. **Monitor the change:** How did the change affect play? Are players now doing what you want them to do? Are they finding it easier to play your game now that the problem has been fixed? If not, repeat steps A to D. If so, congratulations!

Heads Up!

Named after the **heads-up display** found in modern aircraft, the HUD is the most effective way of communicating with players. The HUD refers to a visual screen overlay that communicates information to the player. The mini-screens and icons found in a HUD are some of the best tools in a video game designer's bag of tricks. They can communicate information, emotion, and even tell players where to go and what to do. Let's look at some of the HUD elements found on a game screen:

1. Health bar/lives

2. Targeting reticule

3. Ammunition gauge

4. Inventory

5. Score/experience

6. Radar/map

7. Context sensitive prompt

There are other HUD elements that aren't represented on the above image including a money counter, timer, player name/portrait and others. Let's look at each of these elements one at a time.

Health Bar

A staple of action, adventure, platform, and shooter games is the **health bar**, which represents how close players are to death, or at least how close they are to restarting the game or a level. Health bars are the most flexible of the HUD elements and come in a variety of forms and imagery depending on the game:

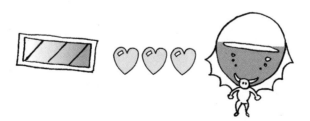

- Many health bars are bars "filled" with color (often red) or icons. As players take damage, they lose a percentage of the bar, or the color empties from the icon. You can even make the color change from green when healthy to red when damaged. When the bar is gone, that player dies.

- Or vice versa; you can have a **damage bar.** When this bar is full, the player dies.

- The health bar may represent the status of some sort of on-board defense system, as seen in the *Metroid* games.

- Both shields and health can be expressed as a numeric percentage (as seen in *Doom*). Health can be represented as shields. When all the shields are gone, the last hit destroys the player, as seen in the space combat game *Star Wars: Squadrons* (2020).

- Health can be represented as a story device. In the *Assassin's Creed* series, the health bar represents the game's narrative. Stray too far from the "correct story," and the narrator says, "That's not the way it happened." The character is then "reset" back to the proper point in the story.

- Just because players lose health, doesn't mean they can't get it back. If *Halo* players find cover and wait, their health bar eventually recharges back to full. This "wait for health" technique is becoming increasingly popular in action games, and it's a good compromise in lieu of a game over/death screen, which pulls players out of the game. On the downside, the pace of the game really slows down as the player waits around to heal.

- Recently, health bars have been replaced by first person-style effects that are also used in third-person view. In *Helldivers 2* (2024), damage is indicated by blood smears or a red blur effect that "points" in the direction of the source of damage. Just don't obscure the players' view so much that they can't see the action.

- In *Metroid Prime* and *Batman: Arkham Origins*, if players are hit by an electrical attack, the screen "fritzes" for a brief moment.

- As players take damage in the *Call of Duty* titles as well as *Uncharted 4: A Thief's End,* the screen darkens, accompanied by heavy breathing and a heartbeat sound effect. In *Silent Hill,* the controller's actuator simulates a heartbeat as the player is dying.

Targeting Reticule

A **targeting reticule** helps players locate and/or lock onto ranged targets. Types of reticules can vary from a simple "dot" of a laser sight to a complex lock-on system that also provides target information such as health and range.

sights can be simple or complex

- A reticule shouldn't dominate the screen, but you should not make it so small that it's hard to see.

- Although I have seen reticules rendered in white, this can make them hard to see on some surfaces and backgrounds.

- Reticules are commonly activated in a zoomed-in mode, such as a sniper's scope. Some reticules change size to allow for more precise targeting when zoomed in, as seen in *Red Faction: Armageddon* (2011).

- Have the reticule change color or "sharpen focus" when over a target. This gives players a clue when to fire.

- Give your reticule some "stickiness," also known as "aim assist." When it is aimed at a target, make the reticule gravitate toward it, allowing for faster targeting. This works great for vehicular weapon targeting.

- Build gameplay into your reticule. *Team Fortress 2*'s zoomed-in sniper's reticule also projects a laser pointer spot. If enemy players see this spot on a wall or object, they can try to avoid being shot.

Ammo Gauge

Whether your **ammunition gauge** displays bullets or a simple number, it will be one of the most watched gauges on-screen. Because some games sparsely distribute ammo (*Resident Evil 2*, I'm looking at you!), placing this gauge in an easy-to-see location is particularly important.

- If you have the screen space, display both clips and individual bullets, like in *Operation Wolf* (1987).

- If the player has to track multiple types of ammo, such as grenades or rockets, make sure they can be brought up with a button press (as they are in *Ratchet & Clank: Tools of Destruction*).

- I know this one seems like a no-brainer, but always display the ammo gauge of the weapon currently armed by the player.

- Even if your player's weapon holds an infinite number of shots, still display it to let the player know what weapon is armed. (The *Metal Slug* and *Fortnite* both do this.) Replace the number with an infinity symbol.

- Many VR games have weapons that appear to have been inspired by the movie *Aliens*. On their side, they display a digital ammunition counter. That way players can tell at a glance how much ammo they have left. It's also a great way to create tension as the counter gets down to zero!

Inventory

A staple in adventure games and RPGs, **inventory** allows players to track and manipulate objects collected during the game. Keys, potions, puzzle items, and weapons are common inventory items.

- Players need quick access to items such as potions and spell components. Hotkey or drag-and-drop systems will help players grab items quickly.

- Allow players a location to see their inventory items in all their glory. *Tomb Raider* (1995) shows the items in Lara's backpack on a larger scale for easier inspection.

- *Diablo* IV (2023) has a limited inventory in which each item has a specific size. Inventory becomes a bit of a puzzle if the player has to fit as many items as possible into a limited space.

- If you have lots of inventory items, let players sort them by type, name, rarity, and so on.

- Inventory items can be represented either realistically or as icons. Whichever graphic style you choose, make sure the items have clear silhouettes and use simple color schemes.

- If you are going to create a restricted inventory system, allow players to expand it later in the game. For example, start with a pouch, expand it to a backpack, and eventually expand it to a magic bag of infinite holding.

- Make sure players have another permanent location in the game (such as their home base) where they can store their items. Players don't like losing their stuff, especially stuff they've bought.

- Why not use a "magic box" or a "bag of holding" for storage, as in *Monster Hunter Rise* or *Baldur's Gate 3*? Whatever items are stored in the box appear in boxes found further in the game. That way, players never have to run back and forth through the game world.

Score/Experience

In the beginning, there was **score.**

SCORE 150

Achievement Unlocked
10G - You have reached Chapter 8

Can you believe the earliest video games had only single-digit scores (*Pong* and *Computer Space*)? I guess no one expected games to last that long! Scoring quickly jumped to four digits (*Space Invaders*), then six (*Galaxian*), and by the time the arcade boom started in the early 1980s, the high score was king. Entering your initials into a game's high score table was the sign of true mastery—provided the arcade owner didn't reset the machine and wipe it out!

As the home market grew, high scores became less important in games (perhaps without networking, there was no one to brag to!) and stat tracking replaced high scores. The percentages of the game completed became more important than a score. Text-based **combo meters** replaced score bars in games like *Devil May Cry* (2001). Players would be congratulated (or judged) on their performance. It's one thing to earn a low score, but another when the game criticizes your performance! And whoever thought up *Resident Evil's* rating system must have been traumatized by grade school. There's nothing more insulting than surviving the zombie apocalypse only to be told you are graded a "C." Sheesh. However, with the increased popularity of online gaming **leaderboards,** scoring has returned to live harmoniously alongside combo meters, stats, and achievements.

Scoring indicators can take a variety of forms. They are still most commonly found in arcade-style games and Japanese RPGs like the *Final Fantasy* series but scoring started to creep back into Western-developed RPGs like *Borderlands* (2009)[3] and *Bulletstorm* (2011).

Positive Messaging

A high score provides validation to the player, but there are other ways to do that as well. *Mortal Kombat's* "Finish Him!" and "Fatality!" text and voice prompts are just as rewarding as seeing high score points flash across the screen. Other games will display "Good job!" and "Awesome!" messages to keep the player excited about their performance. Author Jane McGonigal postulates in her book *Reality is Broken*[4] that one of the reasons video games are so popular is that players are getting the positive re-enforcement for their actions in games that they don't receive for their actions in their everyday lives. I think she makes a valid point. (Good job, Jane!)

Whatever form these positive messages take, make sure that when it happens, it's big and flashy. Video game developers are great at making players feel unskilled and stupid, but bad at making them feel good. There's no such thing as overdoing it when congratulating players. *Zack & Wiki: Quest for Barbaros' Treasure* (2007) does a great job of making even the worst player feel like the smartest, most skilled player in the world. Every little successful action results in a shower of fireworks, congratulatory text, and happy pirate rabbits flipping through the air! And let me tell you, nothing stokes your ego more than back-flipping bunnies!

---

[3] *Borderlands'* developers call it an RPS (a role-playing shooter) but would that qualify as picking nits?

[4] *Reality Is Broken: Why Games Make Us Better and How They Can Change the World*, by Jane McGonigal, Penguin Books, 2011.

Here are a few pointers to make your rewarding feel more rewarding:

- Use voice and sound effects to call attention any time a player gets a reward.

- Match your voice-over talent and music to the tone of your game. *Candy Crush Saga* (2012) has the strangest mix of cheery candy land graphics and depressing funeral parlor music topped off with a dour sounding narrator. It's distracting and downright bizarre.

- Freeze gameplay to allow players to savor the moment of reward or have the hero celebrate along with players with victory animations, sounds, and effects (when appropriate).

- You can never have too many particles, especially when celebrating an achievement or awarding a high score.

- Players need to see a clear "cause and effect" for scoring so they understand how they achieved their score. For example, as a player collects a gold coin in the world, the coin "travels" up to a tally. Don't forget the cool "Las Vegas-style" sound effects. Cha-ching!

- Choose an easy-to-read font. Ornate fonts (like medieval script) with heavy stylization or even serifs can be hard to read. Watch text length because you may run out of screen space!

- Fill up as much of the screen as possible with your celebratory effects, but don't interrupt or cover up gameplay.

Money/Resources

Another important interface tracks the player's currency. If there is a screen where the player gains money, make sure it's there. If there's a screen where the player spends money, make sure it's there. Players like to plan ahead, so it's better to display money on screens, even if the player can't yet spend it. Plan ahead when creating these interfaces. Make sure that the space for your number is larger than the amount of money that the player can earn. Decide how far the counter can go. What happens when it reaches $999.99? Can the player earn any more money after that? These are design decisions you will have to make!

Radar/Map

The first game **radar/map** was found in *Rally-X* (1980), which allowed players to see the location of power-ups without seeing the game map or enemy cars. Since then, map screens have provided much more detail to players, from outlining the playfield to revealing secret clues.

- Make your map large enough to be legible, but not so big that it fills up the whole screen. If you must have the map fill up the whole screen, do your players a favor and pause the gameplay.

- Make it easy for players to move/travel and look at the map at the same time. It's too much of a chore to open a map, memorize the locations, and then close the map to return to the game. Modern sandbox game designers let the players add markers onto the map, which leads players right to the objective!

- Create a legend for your map's icons so players can easily identify and find checkpoints, doorways, quest items, traversal goals, or story points. Also include pop-ups or some other text to remind players what these icons represent.

- Be sure to indicate changes in elevation on your map if you have them in your game world. Players can easily get confused when dealing with levels with multiple elevations. Use a color code or an "onionskin" effect to show what layer players are currently on.

- Show the players' current direction by using an arrow or some other icon. Alternatively, rotate the map to face the direction the players are facing. This way, players won't have to reorient themselves in relation to their goals.

- The **fog of war** occurs when a map is obscured until players actually "clear the fog" from the area by moving through it. You can always give your players ways to expose the whole map. Refogging areas is common in RTS games and is part of the strategy, but I admit, I'm not a fan of this mechanic. I find players can get lost when areas are refogged. If you need it in your game, fine, but don't come crying to me when your players complain.

- Add other information to your map to aid players. *Batman: Arkham Origins* provides a distance-to-goal counter, and the *Metal Gear* series shows the "detection cone" of enemy guards. *Harry Potter and the Order of the Phoenix* (2007) displays the names of NPCs on the "Marauder's Map."

- Incorporate visual themes into your mini map. Fantasy maps look good on parchment, a sci-fi game might use a high-tech holographic display, and so on. Even the map can add to the game's gestalt.[5]

---

[5] *Die Gestalt* is German for "whole." In the context of games, it applies to the overall feel of an experience.

Context-Sensitive Prompts

A **context-sensitive prompt** is an icon or text that appears when players are next to an object or character with which it interacts. The most common context-sensitive prompt displays the icon of the button or control that players must use to make the event happen. For example, in *Helldivers 2* (2024) an icon of the "X" button appears whenever a player stands next to an item they can pick up or a mounted weapon they can use.

Using context-sensitive prompts is a great way to teach players what to do without having them resort to button mashing, memorizing control schemes, or even reading a manual. An added benefit is that using these prompts makes players feel more in character. Because the context-sensitive prompts in the *Batman: Arkham* series let you know when you can carry out an awesome move like a silent takedown or interrogation move, you end up feeling more like Batman.

In the VR game, *Dungeons of Eternity*, a chest displays particles to indicate the lock's hole. This draws the player's attention to the chest and lets them know that they can use the keys they find to open it. These types of prompts don't have to be a letter, word, or arrow. Rather, prompts can be "magic glowing halo" effects.

In *Maximo: Ghosts to Glory*, we created a variation of context-sensitive prompts called **plings**—emoticons that told players when they couldn't do an action as well as when they could. Need ideas to know when to use these guys? Here's a short list of suggested uses for context-sensitive prompts:

- Use prompts to indicate whether doors, gates, and/or hatches can be opened or are locked.

- Use prompts to indicate what controls are required to operate mechanics such as cranks, levers, and pushable objects.

- Use them as NPCs. Because they are not only for talking anymore, you can also use plings and emoticons to show their emotional state. Catch them in a good mood, and you'll get a better response or reward than if they're angry, scared, or sad.

- Use context-sensitive text to see what items and weapons players can collect. Take a page out of the *Uncharted* series to show players where compatible ammo can be collected or from the *Borderland* series to see if an item drop is better than the one you are currently equipped with.

- Use context-sensitive prompts to indicate use of a vehicle or minigame. Numerous games allow players to man a machine gun turret during the middle of regular gameplay.

- It seems a bit strange, but you can use context-sensitive buttons to indicate where players can jump, as in *The Legend of Zelda: The Wind Waker*. Because Link cannot jump on his own, the prompts teach players where they can interact with the world and where they can't.

- Use them as quick-time event prompts, as seen in the *God of War* series: a preset sequence of events that progress if you press the right button (see the quick-time event section later in this chapter).

- Use them as combat notification—icons that show when an enemy is vulnerable to a certain type of attack or even warn when an attack is about to happen so players can perform a blocking or counter move.

- Use them as secret treasure items. Have your icon appear when players are close to a hidden item.

In addition, some HUD elements are self-explanatory, such as fuel gauges, speedometers, and countdown timers. As with the others mentioned previously, keeping it clear, clean, and simple is the winning formula for making a successful HUD system.

Timer

A staple of action and driving games, this shows the player how much time they have left in the game. Make sure that this timer is displayed prominently. Some timers change font size as the timer gets closer to the end of the countdown. Other timers change color (usually red) as the timer reaches zero to emphasize the danger of time running out. Make sure that you accompany your timer with sound and/or voice prompts to help the player know the countdown even if they aren't looking at the timer.

Player Name/Portrait

Some games allow the player to create a **name** or **rename** a character. This means that you will have to provide some sort of keyboard interface that the player will enter the name into. You might have the player select keys with an analog stick or a d-pad. Just with a score interface, you will want to leave room for enough characters—16 characters seems to be the average length for most player name interfaces. Be aware that users might take this opportunity to create a name that is profane or inappropriate. You can ask your programmer for code to identify inappropriate names. An alternative to this is allowing players to select a first and last name from a list of pre-generated names. Or you could have the game provide a randomly generated name. Again, make sure that the names on your list are appropriate for the age range of your game.

A **portrait interface** element shows a picture of the player character. This is used mostly in the FPS, Strategy, VR or the puzzle genre—games where the player character isn't shown on screen. Some games will have the portrait animate to show fear, excitement, pain, or anger. You might want to consider audio barks for the portrait to "say" as they emote. We'll talk more about audio later. Some games will let the player change the portrait according to their mood or taste. Or a portrait might give the player a bonus during gameplay. In *Wordscapes* (2017), depending on the wildlife creature you choose as your avatar, you can earn heart or sun icons at the end of a game or earn bees that help you spell words during the game. (Get it? Spelling bees?)

The Clean Screen

Ah, reality. It's a double-edged sword. You want your game to look like a *cinematic experience*—without that troublesome HUD getting in the way of the action—but you still need to communicate gameplay and controls to your players. What to do, what to do?

Well, the first step in keeping your screen clear is to make your HUD elements move or fade off-screen while they are inactive. Of course, they need to reappear whenever they are valid (such as when players are taking damage or collecting treasure), and you should always make sure that players have a quick and easy way to bring them back up if they need to know the information. A simple shoulder button press usually does the trick.

Some games strive to remove HUD elements altogether. Peter Jackson's *King Kong: The Official Game of the Movie* (2005) utilized a few prompts at the beginning of the game but mostly conveyed game information through sound, animation, and visual effects. The result made for a very cinematic and immersive experience. If you want to go this route, here are some suggestions:

- Have characters react to things in the world to indicate function or interaction. Have them look at collectible items, reach for places they can get to, comment on things in the world that they are supposed to interact with, and so on.

- Opt for full-screen-sized effects over smaller or subtle ones. It never hurts to overemphasize. Use whatever you can to get your point across: sound, voice, visual effects, color, and lighting.

- Use glows or other attention-drawing effects on items to make them stand out. Or use what I call the "Scooby Doo effect."[6]

- Use cinematic characters to lead your players through the world. If you can't afford that much work or it doesn't fit your story or gameplay needs, at least illuminate the path using color or lighting effects. You could even give a subtle clue such as having leaves blow in the direction players need to travel. Something is better than nothing at all.

If you don't completely want to eschew (bless you!) the HUDs, you can at least keep them out of the way. Using a **temporary HUD** is a good way of keeping things clear. I remember *Crash Bandicoot* having one of the first HUDs that "got out of the way" when it wasn't being used. If players collected a mango or an extra life or they took a hit, the HUD would pop onto the screen. If it went a minute or more without any of these events happening, the HUD would slide back off-screen, keeping the screen clear so players could enjoy the pretty game art. The *Infinity Blade* series displays a directional arrow only as players perform a move. This arrow acts more like a guide than a true control path, but it helps eliminate any confusion as to where players need to swipe.

If video game interfaces were a galaxy of planets and on one side of the galaxy was the planet "No Interface," then all the way on the other side of the galaxy would be the planet "Gobs of Interface." I might add that both of these are very dumb names for planets; I mean, what do the inhabitants of these planets call themselves? "No Interfacians" or "Goblings"? But I digress. This is where the RPGs, RTSs, simulations, adventure games, and some slumming shooters all live. Hello there, friendly life forms of planet Gobs of Interface; let's examine your interesting markings and plumage.

Iconography

The first thing you'll notice on many RTS, and adventure games is that there are lots of **icons** on-screen. Icons for tracking stats, icons for weapons, icons for magic spells, icons for the contents of bags of holding and whatnot. I believe part of the allure of these icon-heavy games is that players make lots of choices and have lots of things to build and collect. That's okay; not every game needs to be like one made by Oscar-winner Peter Jackson.[7]

---

[6] The "Scooby Doo effect" is named after a by-product seen in Hanna-Barbera cartoons of the late 1960s and 1970s. While the background image of the cartoon is beautifully painted, the animated elements (such as a character or prop) are more flatly colored (usually lacking shading), making them unintentionally stand out against the more detailed background.

[7] 2004 for *The Lord of the Rings: Return of the King*. He did that HUD-less King Kong game, too. Weren't you paying attention?

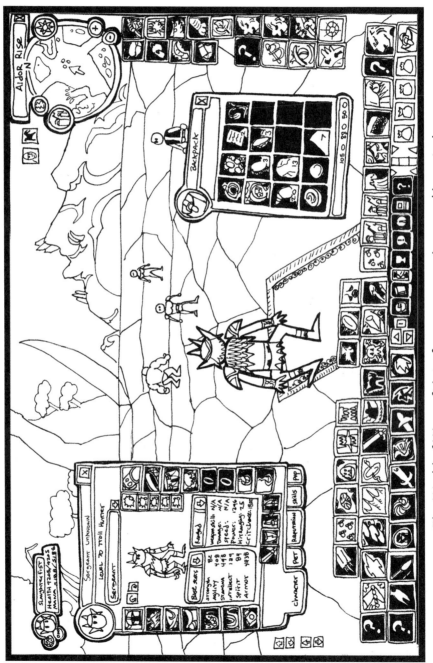

The World of Warcraft interface uses many icons and inventories

So, because you are making icons for your game, here are 157[8] things to think about:

- Pick the right image for your icon. If pressing your icon builds tanks, then guess what picture should be on the icon?[9]

- Make sure the image you use is current and accurate. I was working with a team that had an icon for a stamp function (like an ink stamp) that looked like a postage stamp. Many of the younger testers didn't even know what a postage stamp was! Kids these days!

- Color-code your icons. Fiery punch? Make it red! (Or at least orange.) Chilling hand of frost? I'll give you one guess (blue). You can take color coding one step further and make the image or background of the icon a representative color. For example, all the icons that advance players to the next screen could be green, and your sword combat icons could all have a red background or feature those colors in the artwork (make sure it's a different shade of red than the one you are using for fire attacks!). The goal is for players to understand similarities between icons and be able to choose the correct one at a glance.

- If color isn't enough, use shapes as a differentiator—circles for ammo, squares for health pickups, and so on.

- Try to avoid text in your icons. Not only will you have to change them for localization, but they may be too small to read.

- If you are going to use text (like a word) as an icon, make sure it is legible and looks more like a button than straight text.

- Never, ever combine several visual elements (such as text and a character and a logo) on one icon. Keep them separate graphic files for easier editing, especially when localizing for different languages.

- Surround your icon with a strong black or white outline to make it "pop" off the background or give it a soft surrounding glow or a drop shadow.

- Look at all your icons together to make sure you aren't creating any similar-looking ones. Try to make each one as individual as possible. (but at the same time, they should look like part of a set.[10])

- A good trick is to have text of an item's name ("spell" or whatever) appear if players move their cursor over the icon. Any reminder for the players never hurts!

- Don't forget about icons. There are many great resources online including https:// game-icons.net. Some game creators are relying on AI tools like Midjourney or NightCafe.[11]

---

[8] Give or take 141 or so.

[9] I can't believe you are actually looking down here for an answer!

[10] Games are filled with contradictions! That's why it's hard to make games!

[11] AI art is great for a prototype, but for the final game, you should get human artists to do it. For the record, I'm "Team Human" when it comes to AI art.

- Learn from the experts. Apple, Adobe, and Microsoft have dedicated icon artists who create clear and clever icons for their software and operating systems. Go online and see what icons others have used for their websites. Games that use lots of icons like RTSs and sims are great sources of inspiration. When we were making Maximo's ability icons, we were inspired by the designs on Boy Scout merit badges. You can find icons everywhere. Don't feel you have to reinvent the wheel.

- When players select the icon, make it do SOMETHING. Change color, make a clicky sound effect—anything to register user interaction. I recommend that you avoid using a voice effect, though, because players don't want to hear "Good choice, commander!" every time they press a button. If you need voice, repeat it only once every three or so clicks. And make sure to record a few extra voice cues to avoid repetition. So, to make this point clearer,[12] think of it this way: click no. 1, "Yes, sir!;" click no. 2, "Right away!;" click no. 3, "I'm on it!;" click no. 4, "Yes sir!;" click no. 5, "Right away!"...you get the idea.

- The most important icon on the interface should be the biggest.

- Make the most-used icons easy to reach from the middle of the screen or wherever the players' cursor will spend the most time.

- Make your icons a little "sticky" so the cursor will easily gravitate toward them.

Creating Icons for Mobile Games

In mobile gaming, an icon is used to represent your game in the marketplace. It might just be the most important piece of art you will create for your game. It's like a movie poster or a book cover. Some customers might buy your game just because the icon looks cool, or conversely, choose to skip it because your icon looks lame. When designing your game's icon, strive to give your icon the following traits:

- **Clarity:** Make the images in your icon easy to see. Use silhouettes to create simple, easy-to-understand images. The stronger the silhouette is, the easier it will be to "read."

- **Iconic design:** I often compare a game's icon to the logo on a superhero's chest. It should represent the character in a single image. Make it memorable, cool, or funny—whatever you think will best sum up your game. Because your icon will become your game's identity, make sure it looks great. Try not to use multiple images in one icon. Stick with one image that sums up your game whether it is your main character, a puzzle piece, or an image that captures the game's tone.

- **Color:** Use color to your advantage. There are lots of books on color theory that can help guide you. For example, primary colors like red and yellow always grab the eye more than dark blues, purples, and blacks. Plus, they're easier to see on small screens.

---

[12] Or possibly to make this understandable at all.

Contrasting colors (like blue and orange or black and white) make images pop. Pick a simple color scheme that will visually represent your game.

- **No text or numbers:** If you use raster artwork, text runs the risk of aliasing or blending together to become unreadable, especially when scaled down. Consider skipping text altogether if you want your game to be sold to an international audience.

Ultimately, the rule of thumb when creating icons is:

KYSS = KEEP YOUR SYMBOLS SIMPLE

Today's audiences are familiar with icons, from comics and cartoons[13] to the desktop of their computer, so take advantage of this familiarity. Over the years, video games have developed their own vocabulary of icons. Here are a few classic examples:

- **Red cross:** Designates healing items.[14]

- **1 Up:** Is universal video game-ese for an extra life. Also, the head or little "doll" version of the character works well for this.

- **Heart:** Can be used as a replacement for a red cross or 1 up.

- **Food/soda can/pills:** Means energy or healing, as in "Elf needs food badly."

- **Exclamation point:** Shows surprise when put above enemies' heads. Put one above your hero's head to show he can interact with something.

---

[13] Icons in comics and cartoons? Sure! From stars and tweeting birds over Daffy Duck's head to "Pow!" bursts when Batman throws a punch to scratchy marks over Charlie Brown's head to show that he's mad to those swirly circular "rootbeer-ootles" coming out of Opus, the penguin, to show that he's tanked on A&W, you can find icons all over comics and cartoons.

[14] The Canadian Red Cross has contacted game developers about using the red-colored cross image in "violent video games." The organization interprets the use of the image as a misuse of their trademark. The video game industry as a whole has not officially addressed this complaint.

- **"No" symbol:** Means that players cannot use or do not need this item. Also used for busting ghosts.

- **Skull:** Means poison, death, or danger. And sometimes pirates.

- **Coin:** Represents money, gelt, dough-re-mi. How about a nice big sack o' cash lusted after by bank robbers?

- **Controller icons:** Used as shorthand to prompt players to press a specific control for a specific action. You find this a lot in quick-time events, which I describe next. And here we are!

Don't Get QTE
Quick, press the button!

Now press it again. Too late! You died. Congratulations. You have just lost the first book-based **quick-time event.** Fortunately for you, you have an extra life.

Originally called a "quick-timer event," a quick-time event (or **QTE**) is a prompt that forces players to make a split-second action or suffer usually painful or fatal consequences. Other times it is used to make cutscenes more interactive.

Dragon's Lair (1983) first featured QTE gameplay—heck, the entire game is a quick-time event—but after a brief spurt of similar arcade games (*Cliffhanger, Space Ace, Thayer's Quest*), QTEs almost went the way of the text adventure. *Shenmue* (1999) brought them back and christened them QTEs at the same time. They've become a gameplay staple since *Resident Evil 4* and *God of War* popularized them. In motion-controlled games, you can use player motions to replace the button press of the QTE, but the effect is still the same: the player must quickly react to an on-game action. QTEs are pretty flexible, which is why game designers like them.

Here are just a few things you can use QTEs for:

- Avoiding getting hit by a bolt out of the blue like a falling object, moving car, or soccer ball.

- Fighting off an attack from a biting dog, a hungry hydra, or a killer crocodile man.

- Finishing off a boss with a life-or-death shot or throwing a hail-mary knife at an escaping villain.

- Doing extra damage to an enemy during combat or countering, blocking, or disarming an enemy's attack. You can even throw a grenade back at an enemy!

- Responding to a moral choice such as choosing whom to save from a horde of zombies.

Players either love or hate QTEs, but they are here to stay. There's no need to hate them, though; they're just one more gameplay tool in a designer's toolkit. The trick is to use them responsibly:

- Never use a QTE for something players can do for themselves in the game. I prefer to use them as shortcuts to cinematic sequences. Save QTEs for big, exciting moments and nigh-impossible actions.

- Timing is everything. Give players a "beat" to process the appearance of a QTE icon and another "beat" to press the appropriate button.

- Don't string them out for too long; most QTEs need to be repeated if the player fails the sequence, and there is nothing worse than having to repeat the QTE over and over and over again.

- Wait! There is something worse than repeating a QTE, and that's a QTE that doesn't play fair. While using random QTE icons sounds like a good way to introduce variety, this is the one time you want predictability in your game. Once players memorize the pattern, they can concentrate on watching the cool actions. Now, I know what you're saying. "Wait a second! There are video games with random QTEs in them." And I'd respond, "You are correct." However, I just don't like them. They make players feel as if they won because they were lucky, not by their own skill.

- Keep your QTE controls to a single set of controls. Most games use buttons or sometimes a stick. Try not to use the harder-to-reach shoulder buttons.

- Make sure the QTE icons are big and easy to see. Keep their placement consistent; don't move them around.

- Try not making the QTE mandatory. Both *Uncharted 2* and *Batman: Arkham Asylum* offer QTEs as options for dispatching enemies; however, if players miss that opportunity, they still have plenty of other ways to take out the bad guys.

- A "button mashing" QTE, in which players repeatedly press the button, can heighten an emotional situation, or simulate physical effort.

- You can use QTEs for purely emotional effects such as in *Heavy Rain*'s infamous "Press X to Jason," in which the player must press the X button to call out "Jason" as he's looking for his lost son.

- When using motion controlled QTEs, keep the waggling short. If you are going to make players waggle the controller, don't do it too many times in a row. Gamers want to play your game, not get wrist injuries.

HUDs and Where to Stick 'Em

Now that you have created a whole passel of beautiful icons, what are you going to do with 'em? Why, slap 'em up onto the screen, of course! But before you start displaying them willy-nilly, let's see where they can go. Our zombie friend is going to help us out with this one.

Because the middle of the screen is where the action is, please refrain from putting your HUD there. (Unless it's for targeting or identifying game objects.) If you need to bring up a full-screen display, consider making it translucent like the holographic screen in *Dead Space* (2008). This way, players don't get disjointed from their environment and "lose their place" in the game world.

The upper left side of the screen is traditionally used for the most important information: health, score, and so on. As the (Westerner's[15]) eye travels from left to right when reading information, putting icons to the left so the eye can travel back "into" the game on the right usually feels comfortable to the player.

Displaying icons along the bottom of the screen works well too, as long as you watch out for **clipping** that can occur if a player is using a monitor or TV screen that isn't calibrated for your game. Assume at least 50% of your audience have a crappy television set; heck, even gamers with excellent HD LCD rear-projection sets still can get clipped images on the sides of their screen. Get that information as close to the safe frame as possible (and always offer screen calibration options).

If you are going to use the right, left, and bottom of the screen, be careful of the "bracketing effect" that happens; this will make your game screen seem smaller and claustrophobic. I've seen some RTS screens so filled with HUD elements that it felt as though I was looking out of a mail slot!

If you are going to have lots of icons on screen, why not consider letting players choose which ones they want and prioritize where they should go. This way, the players can

---

[15] Although many Asian and Middle Eastern languages read right to left, I can't think of a single video game that displays information on the screen in this way.

choose what they feel are the most important icons for them. Just make sure you don't give them the option to obstruct the main gameplay field.

Some icons open other screens, like inventory lists. Make sure players have a quick way to get back to the game. You may want to consider allowing players to pause the game, so they don't get bushwhacked by an enemy while they are trying to find their +6 rod of killing. Of course, you could be like the designers of *Dead Space* and intentionally allow enemies to attack while your character is rooting around in his holographic space backpack for another air canister. According to interviews with the team members, this was an intentional choice: they wanted players not to be able to rely on the "gamey" mechanic of the world freezing (as happens in, say, *Resident Evil*) while looking for inventory items. This type of gameplay really conveys the sense of dread as necromorphs are bearing down on you when you realize that you just don't have time for a break.

There Are Other Screens Than the HUD

Oh, video game screens. There are so many of you. Where to start? At the start, of course!

Starting with the Start Screen

The first thing your players see (other than the box cover[16]) is the title/start screen, so it's important to set the right mood. The problem is, there are so many styles to choose from!

There's the **movie poster** title screen that mirrors the cover of the box.

The **heroic pose** title screen where the hero is standing on some high bluff, long hair blowing in the breeze, giant sword and/or gun at the ready.

---

[16] Okay, technically, players also see a warning screen, a publisher logo, a developer logo, and the logos of the companies of any technologies leased by the development team, but starting with those wouldn't make for a very exciting list, would it? Stop making me get ahead of myself!

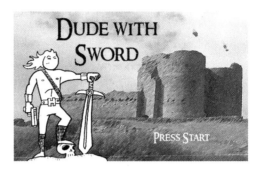

The **enigmatic** image that brings up all sorts of questions: Why am I in a jungle? What is that monkey statue doing there? Is it a relic I will be raiding? The image is something important to the game, but players have no idea because they haven't played the game yet. When they finally learn the significance, their minds will be blown!

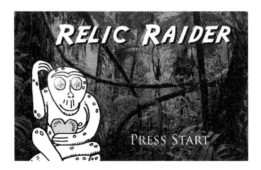

The **logo** screen, where a large image of the game's logo is displayed. Not very exciting but effective. Make it more exciting with strobing colors, rotating effects, bouncing text, anything to get some motion in there.

Title screens often feature menus that offer selections such as save/load, number of players, options, bonus features, and difficulty. How much you include depends on how many button presses you want the players to make before they get into the meat of the game. I find that players just want to get to the good stuff, so you should keep the button pressing to a minimum. Remember, this **very important rule** I never, ever try to break:

YOU SHOULD NEVER HAVE TO PRESS A BUTTON MORE THAN THREE TIMES TO REACH ANY GAME SCREEN

Why? Because players don't want to spend the entire game pressing buttons to reach interface and inventory screens! They want to play the game! Let them play the game!

Sorry. Lost it there for a moment.

Seriously, don't make the players dig to find the options and get to the gameplay. Make everything in the game reachable within a button press or two. Consolidate screens if you have to but keep track of how many button presses it takes to get to that information. I once managed to reduce the "start to play" from 16 button presses to 4 button presses. Not too shabby if I do say so myself.

Let's Pause (Screen) for a Moment....

Every gamer needs a break now and again. That's why we game designers have thoughtfully provided a **pause screen.** This is a screen that the player can bring up that stops the game without leaving the game.

A well-designed pause screen can do more than give players a break. It can be used to save a game; access the options screen, game map, or inventory screen; or even just exist to be enjoyed, as with *Banjo-Kazooie*'s (1998) lovely acoustic version of the theme. Whatever you do, just make sure players don't feel that they are missing any of the game by pausing. Remember, most people use pause screens to take bathroom breaks. Of course, you can always remove the option of a pause screen altogether, like in *Dead Space*, but that could be taxing on your bladder.

When designers create pause screens, they have the bad habit of making the first choice "resume" and the next one down something like "options." Usually, the map and save game options appear a few more choices down in the list. This placement makes no sense to me. Let's say you use the start button to bring up the pause screen. Think of all the times you are going to have to press the start button, then D-pad down the list to the "save game" selection, save the game, and then return back up to the resume button? Why not use the start button to close it again? Why do you even *need* the resume option? If the save button is the most common selection the players will be making, make it the first thing they can select. If it isn't, make it the map or the inventory. Plan out your pause screen as carefully as you do your level! Your players will thank you for it.

Wow! Look at this next graphic. All these options can stem from a pause screen:

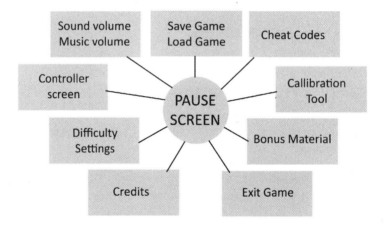

- **Options:** Like the ancient labyrinth, the option screen usually leads to more screens. But don't lose your players in a maze of choices. Think of the option screen as a hub, with the choices of the spokes that radiate from it. Sound and music volume controls, controller settings, difficulty settings, and even bonus and cheat codes can be placed under the options heading.

- **Calibration tool:** If your game is particularly moody and dark in theme and visuals, I suggest having a screen calibration tool. A calibration tool allows players to adjust the screen's contrast on a dark-colored image or set of color bars. While it's fine for this tool to live in the options screen, I prefer to have players adjust it before starting the game, to see the game in the best light...err...darkness possible.

- **Save/load game:** This option is one of the most important aspects of your game, so keep it simple and automate the process whenever possible. Always start a new game with the option to create a new save file. Don't make players hunt around for this option, and make sure they quickly pick up where it is—even in the tutorial if possible.

You'll want to include the following elements on your Save/Load screen. In the figure, (1) is the player's portrait. If a player can change characters, having this is helpful for them to keep track of which save file it is. Plus, it adds some "character" to your screen. (2) The player can name the file. In console and VR games, you will have to have a virtual keyboard appear so the player can type in their file name. (3) is the percentage of how far into the game the player is. Sometimes players like to save onto files that are close to the end in case they want to search levels for secrets or just want to fight a particularly cool boss over again. (5) tells the player what level they are on. You can never have enough redundant information to help the player. (6) is a button press that allows the player to delete a file. This is helpful if the player has screwed up during play and doesn't like the direction the play is going or if they just want to free up space.

I highly recommend that you allow players to have several (at least three) save files. Players often restart new games after completion, want backup files in case they make catastrophic choices during gameplay, or even just want to let someone else play the game concurrently.

Customization goes a long way when creating a save file. Let the players name their own files. Store playtime, titles of game levels or chapters, and even inventory items like lives or gear to help the players remember their progress. Show icons or images to help jog the players' memory further. Everything helps.

Autosave is a useful function that acts as a backup if players are too engrossed in playing. Give players the option to load a game from a saved file or autosave. Make sure you display an icon warning players that the game is autosaving, so they don't shut off the system and lose their file.

When designing the save system, be careful that it doesn't become a "reset system." In many games, it is easier and faster for players to reload the game than to die and start again. Don't let players use the save system as a gameplay mechanic because it breaks the immersion of the play experience.

Let Me Load (Screen) that For You....

Many players consider **loading screens** as a necessary annoyance, but that's just because developers fail to treat these screens as part of the game. Eliminating loading screens can be difficult to implement technically. It may even be impossible to do, given the technical limitations of the game. As a designer, you need to know the limitations of your game code up front.

More recent games strive for a "seamless" loading-screen-free experience by disguising the loading screen with slowly opening doors, long elevator rides, or dissipating fog. Just don't make what happens on the loading screen too complex; loading screens need to be loaded too!

I always recommend that at least one element on your loading screen be animated. This lets the player know that the game hasn't crashed or frozen, which would make the player try to restart the game!

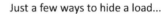
Just a few ways to hide a load...

| abnormally long corridors | very slowly unlocking doors | microwaving popcorn |

If you must have loading screens, here are some ways to spruce them up:

- Show concept art.

- Ask trivia questions.

- Have a playable minigame.[17]

---

[17] Unless you work for Namco, you may want to avoid this one because it owns the U.S. patent (#5,718,632).

- Display the game map.

- Display a character bio.

- Provide tips on gameplay or control (but be careful not to repeat them; even the most useful tip becomes annoying after several viewings, so don't display control tips that players have already seen).

- Fill in gaps in the game story or provide a recap of players' progress and remind them of their goals.

- Play a short video briefing the player on the upcoming mission or location.

- Have players fight endless waves of enemies or destroy a large object.

- Provide "beauty shots" of your character or items in the game.

- Have players manipulate an interactive object such as the game's logo or a significant story item.

Hardware manufacturers require that there be some moving image on a loading screen, so players know that the game hasn't crashed. No matter what your loading screen displays, you should provide a progress bar or percentage loaded indicator, so players know how long they have to wait.

Getting in Control

When showing the **control screen**, first and foremost, you need to display an image of the game controller, as shown in the following image:

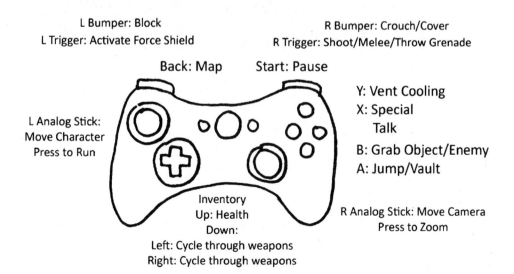

L Bumper: Block
L Trigger: Activate Force Shield

R Bumper: Crouch/Cover
R Trigger: Shoot/Melee/Throw Grenade

Back: Map   Start: Pause

L Analog Stick:
Move Character
Press to Run

Y: Vent Cooling
X: Special
Talk
B: Grab Object/Enemy
A: Jump/Vault

Inventory
Up: Health
Down:
Left: Cycle through weapons
Right: Cycle through weapons

R Analog Stick: Move Camera
Press to Zoom

Some games show the character that performs an action when you press the appropriate button. At the very least, display text explaining the control.

Make sure the control screen is easily accessible from the game for quick player reference. Also, consider allowing players to customize the controls or at least give them several options to remap controls schemes.

What's the Score?

Otherwise known as a "tally screen," the **scoring/stats screen** appears at the end of a level. It displays the players' progress and performance in the game. You can tally just about anything on a tally screen. Here are just a few ideas:

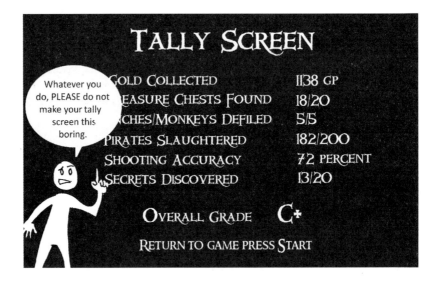

- Score

- Time of completion

- Accuracy of shooting

- Enemies slain

- Money remaining/collected/spent

- Number of lives

- Rating (can be an A-B-C grade or a "word" rating, like "Awesome dude" or "Master of the Universe")

- Objectives reached/completed

- Secrets found (usually expressed as an X/Y value)
- Gallons of blood spilled/distance traveled/chests smashed...you get the idea

The Rest of the Stuff

Legal/copyright screens (there might be more than one) are required by publishers and hardware manufacturers to establish their copyright or give warnings to the player—such as the risk of an epileptic seizure if there are bright, flashing lights or images in the game. They should be used by developers to protect their IP and have disclaimers to avoid legal issues. Make sure that the text on these screens is legible and, more importantly, accurate. Console manufacturers usually require that these screens cannot be skipped.

Credits allow me to pull out my soapbox for a moment. People work very hard on games. Too many people in the video game industry get screwed out of the credit they deserve due to egos, politics, and old-fashioned neglect. I am a firm believer that if you work on a game, you should get credit. That credit should reflect the title on the person's business card. Sadly, it doesn't always happen that way: it's something in the gaming industry that needs to change. I like to follow this simple but **very important thing:**

GIVE CREDIT WHERE CREDIT IS DUE

Credit screens are an important part of the game. They are a celebration of the people who made and contributed to the final game. They deserve to be seen, but these screens should be as entertaining as possible. Some games get it: *LittleBigPlanet,* for example, has an amazingly entertaining and charming opening credit sequence. *Typing of the Dead* (2000) has a playable minigame where the player can type the credits!

If you need more inspiration for great-looking screens or credit sequences, take a look at most movie DVDs. DVD designers do a great job at creating gestalt built around the film. This level of attention to detail takes a lot of time and effort on behalf of the art director and designers, but it's always worthwhile.[18]

A Final Word on Fonts

As you make your HUD and display screens, you need to think about fonts. I find that fonts follow many of the same rules as icons when it comes to legibility and clarity. However, they do present some of their own issues:

- Theme your font to your game, but don't use overly ornate fonts that are hard to read.

---

[18] Some excellent examples of gestalt in games include *Inscryption* (2021), *Hades* (2020), and *What Remains of Edith Finch* (2017).

- In many cases, fonts require a license to use. I know of a game that had to be re-worked at the eleventh hour because the developer didn't have the right to use the font. Fonts are like any other piece of artwork. It's only fair to pay the artist for his work.

- Be mindful of the color of your font and your background. For example, never place red text over a black background, because it usually blurs on many TVs, particularly older ones, or ones where the console is hooked up on composite cables.

- Developers should use higher resolution fonts in general. I have found that any font size under 18 points is very hard to read on a standard definition television. Remember that not every player has a state-of-the-art screen![19]

Game Over

The **game over screen** is often overlooked during the production of a game. Production of this screen is often left to the last minute, resulting in a dull affair such as the words "You're Dead" or "Game Over" simply displayed in some font resembling dripping blood. Maybe there's an enemy cackling off-screen or some dour music that plays after you die. Too boring. Too predictable. Too depressing.

There are some games that go the extra mile. *Dragon's Lair* (1983) has unique death screens depending on the room you died in. The narrators in both *Prince of Persia: The Sands of Time* (2003) and *Bastion* (2011) change the game's narrative to bring the player character back to life. *"That isn't the way it happened,"* they say. The *Batman Arkham* series has the villain who defeated you gloat over your (Batman's) body. It's pretty effective in making you want to get back up and pummel the snot out of the Joker! And who can forget that *Banjo Kazooie* (1998) had an entire cutscene showing what happened to your sister if you didn't save her from the witch?[20] Now those are game over screens!

I have often thought that they should be treated not as an ending point, but as a springboard to launch the player back into the action. If you give the player an opportunity to quit playing, they most likely will. As an alternative to the game over screen, I suggest that we institute what I'd like to call a "Keep Going" screen, where the player gets a little preview of all the in-game content waiting for them if the player keeps playing. Previews of levels, boss fights, weapons, skill upgrades, whatever it takes to entice the player.

---

[19] The text displayed in *Dead Rising* (2006) was so small that players couldn't read mission objectives—rendering the game unplayable to those with standard definition sets.

[20] Spoilers. Your little sister was turned into a Frankenstein monster while the witch transformed into a sexy woman. What can I say? It was the '90s.

Wrapping it up

Remember, the goal of all these screens is to communicate clearly and efficiently to the players. Now let's move on to the good stuff: the game itself! But first, the obligatory Universal Truths and Clever ideas section...

Level 8's Universal Truths and Clever Ideas

- Good UI provides clear feedback to the player.
- Create ergonomic interfaces.
- The HUD communicates game concepts to players.
- Keep HUD elements away from the sides of the screen and closer to the safe frame.
- Design easy-to-see and -read icons.
- Make QTEs fair and easy to perform.
- Players should never have to press a button more than three times to reach anything in the game.
- Don't make players dig through screens for important information.
- Fonts should be easy to read. Don't make them too small or too fancy.
- Give credit where credit is due.
- Even the most "boring" screens can be exciting and interesting.

Level 9
Everything I Learned About Level Design, I Learned from Level 9

YOU CAN'T EXPECT a book called *Level Up!* not to have a chapter on level design. But first, what do I mean by **level**? Much like the word **score**,[1] its definition changes when used in different contexts. Observe:

Level: An environment or location where game play occurs. As in "if you are on the Death Star level, then you are near the end of the game."

and

Level: A term favored by developers that describes how to break up physical space based on a specific gameplay experience. For example, "I must have died a dozen times on the mine cart level."

and

Level: A unit for counting a player's progression, especially when repetitive gameplay is involved. "I'm up to level 20 on *Tetris*."

and

Level: The rank of a player based on earned score, experience, or skills. A term for marking character progression and improvement, as in "I finally leveled up my third *WoW* character to 70." The most common use of "level" in this context can be found in RPGs, although levelling has started to find its way into other genres.

---

[1] Score: (1) To gain something (as in "I scored a battle axe off that weapon drop"), (2) to calculate a total (as when a high score is tallied), (3) to cut without cutting all the way through (like scoring a metal door with a lightsaber slash).

A possible explanation for "level" having so many different definitions in the video game industry is that video game developers have extremely limited vocabularies.

Another reason for the multiple definitions is that developers have used the term "level" in different contexts for so long that it's too late to get everyone in the game industry to agree to call it something else, like a **floobit** or a **placenheimer.**

So, level it is. But why level? Most ancient game designers believe that the term came from *Dungeons and Dragons* when players would travel downward into many dungeon levels (like floors of a building) to reach the dragon. (Hence, the title of the game.) Why no one thought to call it "floors" is beyond me.

In fact, to complicate things further, often a level isn't even called a level. I've played games with **rounds, waves, stages, acts, chapters, maps,** and **worlds**; but even these have their specific definitions. Let's review:

- **Rounds** can be found in games where you play the same action, if not similar gameplay, over and over again. This term can be used for sports games as in a round of golf or boxing where the activity is the same, or there can be variation in the gameplay like rounds of *Fortnite* or *World of Tanks*.

- **Waves** usually refers to combat, as in "wave after wave of enemies assaulted the stalwart heroes!" Pretty exciting stuff! Whole games can be made of waves of enemies as in *Kingdom Rush 5 Alliance* and *Hades*, or waves can be a sequence of play like those found in *The Last of Us 2* or *Marvel Spider-Man 2*.[2] In fact, the SHUMP genre uses almost exclusively waves of enemies to challenge the player.

---

[2] You can find waves in any action game, not just ones with "2" at the end of their names.

- **Stage** is usually interchangeable with the term "wave," but it's often used when describing an experience that has clear separations that relate to the activity much like the separate stages of a rocket.[3] "Stage" is often used when referring to the actions of a boss enemy. For example, the first stage of a robot boss might require the player to attack a specific spot such as a foot or hand. Once the player has conquered that (usually breaking or disabling the enemy's appendage), then the next stage is the robot attacking with heat seeking missiles that the player must avoid. Then the third stage is when the boss exposes the nuclear power core that must be attacked to destroy the enemy. You can have as many of these stages as you like, but just remember that players will get fatigued if there are too many.

- **Acts** and **chapters** are often used when the developer wants players to concentrate on the story of the game. These titles make a game feel classier. They're not fooling anyone; they're really just game levels.

- Levels are often referred to as **maps** or by the location of the environment (like "Power Plant" or "Insane Asylum"). This is most common in FPSs, where players associate the location with a style or method of gameplay.

The term **world** is often confused with level, but I blame this on its origin. "World" was first used in *Super Mario Bros.* with the famous "World 1-1." The game was extremely successful, and the term was immediately embraced by developers. However, by my own definition, World 1-1 should actually be called Level 1-1. **A world** is a video game location that is distinguished primarily by its visual or genre theme and may be composed of multiple locations that share this theme.

world 1-1

In early video games, players referred to the levels as "worlds," as in "Fire World," "Ice World," and so on. However, as the home market demanded longer play experiences and developers wisely learned to create multiple levels using the same texture sets and/or mechanics, worlds gained additional sequences—most famously seen in

---

[3] Remember, these terms were first created and used by early game creators: the same guys who were in your high school rocket club. Sorry, cool kids; the nerds have taken over the world.

Super Mario Bros.'s World 1-1. However, World 1-1 is just the first of four levels of the first world.[4] We needed a term to define these separate sections of play, hence the term "level."

The Top 10 Cliché Video Game Themes

Because so many game worlds have been introduced over the years, some of them have become hoary clichés. Most developers run screaming from these, but they still have their uses. I therefore present them to you:

1. **Outer space:** You can easily see how a black television screen may have served as inspiration to early game developers as the perfect stand-in for outer space. Brightly displayed vector-drawn stars looked great on those early CRT screens. Player-controlled spaceships meant no animations. Spaceships were rendered in simple geometric shapes. Gameplay was based primarily on physics: an important advantage to those early programmers during the days prior to game designers and artists. As the earliest game genre (the shooter) devolved, outer space continued to be a popular locale for video game battles to be waged. Outer space also allows for all the tropes of sci-fi: aliens, spaceships, computers, and futuristic weapons. All things beloved by the geeky game developer community.

2. **Fire/ice:** These levels swiftly became popular for three reasons: first, fire and ice levels created hazards (flames and low-friction surfaces) that were easy to program. These hazardous terrains created perfect timing puzzles causing the players to "break their rhythm," making the level more challenging. Second, fire and ice environments lent themselves to a wide array of deadly inhabitants, from lava men and flame-breathing dragons to snowmen of both the abominable and frosty varieties. And third, fire and ice levels added color (red and blue) to the palette of gameplay worlds,

---

[4] World 1-1 is grassland, 1-2 is an underground cavern, 1-3 is made up of mountain-like platforms, and 1-4 is the interior of a castle. These levels are all part of a world known as the Mushroom Kingdom. And now you know.

especially important to distinguish screenshots on the back of home console boxes in those early 8-bit days. Today, fire and ice levels are camouflaged as snow-bound train wrecks and lava-filled temples, but as long as the color, feel, and mechanics are represented, they'll always be fire and ice levels to me.

3. **Dungeon/cavern/tomb:** The connections between *Dungeons and Dragons* and Tolkien's *Middle Earth* run strong and deep in the DNA of video game developers. Dungeons are laden with traps to avoid, puzzles to solve, and mechanics to circumvent. Dungeons offer up waves of enemies (without a whiff of explanation as to why they live there), and, of course, there was always lots of collectible treasure to be gleaned. Even when the game world isn't themed to medieval fantasy, players still thrill in raiding uncharted dusty tombs. Technically, dungeon locations offer game artists many advantages: great opportunities for dramatic lighting and intricate carvings and statues. Even in the early days of gaming, cave wall textures were made from easily repeatable (or "tiled") art.

4. **Factory:** Factory levels became a staple of platform games, especially as the platform game genre exploded on home gaming systems. Dynamic mechanics offer game developers easily created, combined, and repurposed hazards that can be tuned to a wide variety of difficulty levels. These adaptable factory mechanics quickly spread to other locations too: moving platforms, conveyer belts, and turning gears were present in the tombs, circuses, and space stations of just about every action and platform game.[5]

5. **Jungle:** The jungle theme allows video game designers the flexibility of the dungeon but without the dull colors and right angles. With its exotic traps (like quicksand and pongee-covered knife-lined pits) and exotic creatures (such as crocodiles, snakes, and scorpions) set in a colorful outdoor environment, jungle levels quickly became a prevalent video game level theme as game art became a focus. Jungle levels lend themselves to robust mechanics such as swinging vines, tree branch platforms from which to leap, and rivers with moving logs à la *Frogger*—that keep a player's heart beating like a drum.

---

[5] I consider it a triumph of the video game industry that *Star Wars* creator George Lucas, at the last minute, added a factory level to his 2002 movie *Attack of the Clones*. The movie's heroes ride conveyer belts and make timed jumps through smashing presses worthy of a sequence right out of a Nintendo platformer.

6. **Spooky/haunted house/graveyard:** Spooky environments are great when your game requires mood and story. Players slowly explore creepy environments, punctuated by unsuspected "scares" in the form of play mechanics or enemies that seemingly spring out of nowhere. But scaring people is an art; you must build pacing into your levels. Allow moments of quiet, followed by moments of distraction, before you scare your players. Music and sound design are critical to the spooky theme; it goes hand-in-hand with encounter and puzzle design. But be careful you don't tip your hand too much. You can easily give away your scares if you don't choreograph things correctly. After years of making haunted houses in my garage, I find the best scare is one players, expect but don't know where it's coming from.

The spooky theme is also the most adaptable theme of the video game tropes. There have been spooky adventures, platformers, RPGs, FPSs, and even puzzle games. Everything's more fun when it's scary!

7. **Pirate (ship/town/island):** The spiritual brother to the spooky level is the pirate level.[6] The pirate theme is perfect for high action gameplay, melee combat, and, of course, lots and lots of treasure. Many pirate levels capitalize on the pirate's natural form of transportation: the pirate ship. And then there are the pirate skeletons. Who doesn't love these guys? Like the spooky theme, the pirate theme is treated as a "catch-all" that can be applied to almost any genre of game to increase its sales.

8. **Gritty urban:** No matter whether it's populated by criminals, punks, mutants, or supervillains, the gritty urban theme allows for fantastic action in a realistic and relatable setting. That relatability is part of the genre's appeal. Artistically, it's easier for artists to create the world outside their window. Densely detailed environments just keep looking better and better as system processors and game polygon counts rise. Although it's ironic that players would want to play in a world that mirrors the one right outside, they get a choice that most people never make: to improve it or destroy it.

---

[6] The only reason I can fathom why pirate and spooky levels are often found in the same game is the designer's love for Disneyland. "Pirates of the Caribbean" and "Haunted Mansion" attractions are found in the park's "world" of New Orleans Square. I know that's the reason I put them together in *Pac-Man World*.

9. **Space station:** The space station has become the stand-in for the dungeon in sci-fi games (especially in the FPS and survival horror genres), all strongly influenced by the 1986 film *Aliens*. In video games, most space station halls are infested with horrible aliens and malfunctioning robots. The space station theme lends itself to a variety of tech-based mechanics including laser-based force fields and factory-style moving platforms. Space stations allow the art team to show off when creating spectacular visual effects, whether it is holographic computer displays or stunning starscapes.

10. **Sewer:** While you could eat off the floor of *Mario Bros.*'s sewer, video game sewers got more disgusting as game graphics improved. This modern analog for the fantasy dungeon[7] grew more complex and deadly with hazards ranging from giant rats and albino alligators to fetid water that caused instant death upon immersion. You can also

---

[7] Didja know that early D&D players would play live-action sessions in sewer and drainage systems? The forerunner to today's live-action role playing (or LARPing).

find the harmonious addition of factory-level mechanics in sewers, such as whirling ventilation fans and sinking platforms to challenge players. Just be glad that smell-o-vision never caught on.[8]

Just because the preceding themes are considered clichés doesn't mean they are unusable. To give them a twist, just apply the **Mexican pizza** technique.

You might be familiar with Taco Bell's "Mexican pizza:" a pizza-shaped snack made with Mexican food fixings. When it first came out in the 1980s, I was intrigued. Growing up in an Italian household, I knew what pizza was. Growing up in San Diego, I knew what Mexican food was. Curiosity got the better of me and I tried it. It wasn't bad. But what I learned was that you can combine two things you wouldn't think go together to get something surprisingly good and, more importantly, completely original.

While designing *Maximo: Ghosts to Glory*, we applied the Mexican pizza technique. Instead of just a regular graveyard, our graveyard was cracked apart by volcanic eruptions that blasted out flashes of fire. A fire graveyard if you will. We also made a pirate level enshrouded in ice. You get the idea. We took hoary level themes and breathed new life into them simply by combining them with each other.

The Name Game

Now that you have your level's theme, you must give it a name. However, keep in mind that a level always has two names: one for the development team and one for the players. The level name is a file name, created to be referenced with the game's code. Remember these tips when creating file names:

- Keep the name to eight characters max (not including the extension) because (a) a short file name is easy for team members to remember, and (b) it takes up less space

---

[8] There have been several attempts to bring smell hardware into gaming. The most recent device, GameScent, blasted player's noses with the smells of a pine forest, a briny ocean, and shotgun fire.

in the code. Traditionally, this was necessary because of technical limitations in DOS filenames. That restriction is no longer relevant. Note also that short file names are not always easier to remember as names might need to be truncated in weird ways; for example, frstclea.lvl might be the Forest Clearing level or something having to do with cleaning the Frost world.

■ Players don't see the file names, so you don't have to be witty. For example, "Castle01" succinctly lets your team members know the most important info: location and order.

■ For more complex titles, use abbreviated text: for example, "fac01s01" might stand for "factory 1, section 01."

■ Make sure your naming conventions don't overlap. If "sec" stands for "section" in one area, don't use it for "secret" in another.

■ Organize your levels. Keep files in folders where it is easy for other team members to find them. Use file-sharing software to make sure changes aren't made without the other team members knowing about them.

In the context of the game, the level's name is a different matter. Just as with naming characters, you need to give your level the right name—one that fits its feel. There are a few schools of thought to naming levels:

■ **Functional:** A straight-up number system is a hallmark of retro gaming. It cuts to the chase and gives players an idea of progress. However, because most players aren't exposed to the highest number in advance, they have no way to accurately track overall progress. Another disadvantage to functional naming is that it lacks personality.

■ **Location:** Police station. Sewer. Science lab. What's good about using the location names is that you immediately get an idea of what players will be seeing and/or encountering. However, these expectations are based on the players' knowledge, which is something that might not match what you are going for. Using the right words is important when naming a location.

■ **Descriptive:** "A nasty surprise." "On the road again." "Death from above." Descriptive level names read more like chapters of a book. This type of naming is great for providing foreshadowing or tone. Be careful not to tip your hand too much and ruin any surprises your plot or level may hold. Or you can be tricky like the *Dead Space* designers and have the first word in every level spell out a secret message!

■ **Punny:** If you are feeling particularly creative, try writing a punny title for your game level. Punny titles were all the rage in the late 1990s, starting with *Crash Bandicoot*. Usually, you want to reserve this type of naming for games that are meant to be funny.

Remember, level names provide the first impression of your level, so put your best foot forward!

Everything I Learned About Level Design, I Learned from Disneyland

The world is the best narrator.

Ken Levine[9]

I believe it is within a game's level where the story should actually be told. Using space to tell a story isn't a new concept; this approach has been used in architectural design for centuries. When I first started designing game levels, I found that theme parks held the answers to many of my questions on how to tell a story as well as inform players. I pored over theme park maps[10] and studied how they were laid out. Theme parks are designed to move guests from one adventure to the next in the most effective way possible, much like a well-designed game level.

Disneyland, in particular, proved to be a source of great inspiration. I read about Walt Disney's imagineers and how they went about designing their own world. Walt Disney had a deep love of miniature railroads, and Disneyland was structured around a train track. The imagineers needed something to fill in the middle of the track, so five "lands" were created, each inspired by Disney's passions: history, progress, nature, his animated movies, and nostalgia for his childhood hometown. These became Frontierland, Tomorrowland, Adventureland, Fantasyland, and Main Street.

The imagineers filled these lands with attractions, themed adventures that allowed guests to "ride the Disney movies." These attractions were built as storytelling experiences within a physical space, and detailed attention was given to each scene as guests passed through it.

I noticed that the creation and structure of Disneyland bore a strong resemblance to creating and structuring a video game world. The basic progression of creation is this:

- **Disneyland:** *World* to *land* to *attraction* to *scene*.
- **Video game:** World to level to experience to moment-to-moment gameplay.

The world of Disneyland contains **lands**. Within each themed land are attractions, each with its own story. The "story" of the attraction is composed of scenes.

The world of the video game contains **levels**, each with its own part of the story. Within each themed level are encounters, challenges, and story points that move players through the level. Connecting these experiences is the moment-to-moment gameplay that keeps players engaged.

---

[9] Ken Levine is the creative director of the *BioShock* series, a highly rated FPS whose fully realized worlds have become the gold standard for level design.

[10] I used to love to collect theme park brochures during family road trips to other, more educational destinations. These were souvenirs of places I never actually visited. Who knew they'd come in so useful in the future!

Mapping the World

This notion of working from the "top down" helped me approach a game world and determine what the confines are and what lives within it; to determine that, you need to make a **game world map.**

Early game designers really got into creating their world map and loved to share it with players. Common pack-ins with early computer games were lovingly rendered maps printed on parchment, cloth, and even faux leather. But you don't need to create anything so fancy. Your world map can be something as simple as a flow chart created in Microsoft Visio. It only needs to chart out where the players are going and what they'll find there. A map can also define the spatial relationships of locations in the world; this can help the designer determine how players are going to get around and in what order.

The game world map is important not only to help your team understand the connection of all the levels to one another but also to offer players some advantages.

One of the earliest arcade games to expose players to a map of sorts was *Donkey Kong*. It was a simple graphic of several Donkey Kongs stacked on top of one another with the challenge "how high can you get?" There was room for four Donkey Kongs on the screen. With each progressive level, the game added a Donkey Kong. The player could figure out by the space on the screen how many Donkey Kongs could fit on the stack and therefore realize there were four distinct environments in the game.

The next great advance in mapping came with the arcade game *Ghosts 'n' Goblins*. Before gameplay started, a map was displayed with a little icon of the player at his current location: "You are here." The camera then panned over the entire world, teasing the player with everything that was to come. I remember seeing this and thinking, "I wonder what's in that ice level at the far end of the map?"

Even if your characters don't physically travel anywhere in your game, you can still use a map to show progression. The fighting game *Mortal Kombat* displays a screen full of characters' headshots, with the majority of them "locked up" at the beginning of the game. But by showing all the locked windows, the game's map of opponents provides foreshadowing that players will eventually fight several characters. As more opponents are unlocked, players are then compelled to "collect them all."

Foreshadowing

Foreshadowing is a powerful tool to get players excited about the activities and dangers found in a level. Building anticipation is just as important as delivering on it. In all my years of making haunted houses, I've found that a scare is bigger and better if the victims know it's coming. It's waiting for the scare to happen that drives them nuts.

You can use lighting, sound effects, and geometry to make a level look foreboding. And remember, nothing says "beware" like a pile of skulls.

Another lesson I learned from Disneyland is to provide foreshadowing with **posters.** Guests pass by posters advertising attractions as they enter the park. While the guests don't understand the significance of the images they're seeing, the posters provide foreshadowing for future adventures. In games, one of the best uses of posters is in *BioShock* when the player, first entering Rapture, sees posters advertising the superpower-giving plasmids. Only when the player learns about plasmids and what they can do is their significance understood.

Goal Setting

Much like a game map, the level itself should help transport players through the level from story point to story point. The always eloquent imagineers of Disneyland describe it this way:

> *When we began designing Disneyland, we looked at it just as we do a motion picture. We had to tell a story, or in this case, a series of stories. In filmmaking, we develop a logical flow of events or scenes that will take our audience from point to point through a story. If I were to 'leapfrog' from Scene One to Scene Three, leaving out Scene Two, it would be like sending the entire audience out to the lobby for popcorn in the middle of the film.[11]*

Disneyland's attractions tell four different stories to their guests. I have found these stories have parallels with the players' goals within a video game level:

- Escape/survive

- Explore

- Educate

- Provide a moral

With the **escape/survive** goal, players have to survive being in a place they have no business being in—whether it's a ghost-infested manor or a crazy factory where one misstep means being ground up into cat food. Storytelling is shown through **action** and **location,** which move the player along quickly, using gameplay centered on movement and combat.

[11] *Disneyland The First Quarter Century,* Walt Disney Productions, 1979.

The **explore** goal allows players to discover the story at their own pace. The wilds of Hyrule in *The Legend of Zelda: The Breath of the Wild* and city of Baldur's Gate in *Baldur's Gate 3* let players explore the environment and create the story in their own order. **Freedom of mobility** and **conversation** are important storytelling tools when exploring is the players' goal.

Although there are many educational games, the **educate** goal has yet to make the full transition into entertainment games. Educational games carry a stigma that they are only for younger or "non-gamer" audiences. There are exceptions. The *Assassin's Creed* series exposes players to historical characters and events. *Rock Band* focuses on teaching players the same skills needed to actually play music (at least in the case of vocals and drums). Emphasize **observation** and **imitation** when determining the players' goals and gameplay.

Examples of the goal of learning a **moral** can be found in many of Disneyland's attractions. Mr. Toad's Wild Ride's moral message is: "Drive recklessly and you'll crash and burn." Quite a statement for the happiest place on Earth! But we're talking about video games. Morals and consequences have been in games since early adventure games. Games like *Dishonored 2* and *Cyberpunk 2077* allow players to experience "good" or "bad" endings based on choices made during the game. In some games, players are being morally tested beyond "good and evil" with themes such as morality during wartime (*Spec Ops: The Line*), loyalty to individuals versus groups (*The Walking Dead: Season One*), and even whether or not to perform torture (*Call of Duty: Black Ops*). These games use choice and consequence to deliver the level's moral goal and then make those choices impact gameplay.

In addition to these goals, you need to ask, "What is the players' objective in this level?" Some levels exist to teach a specific gameplay move such as jumping, engaging in combat, driving, or simply how to play the game. Answering this question will guide and focus on how you design the players' moment-to-moment gameplay within the level and even how you construct and pace the level. Make sure players stay focused on the specific level-oriented goal because it's easy to get distracted, especially when you have many choices. Use NPCs, story, quest goals, and even powers and gear to guide the players toward the goal you want them to reach.

Now that we've got our world figured out, the game's theme selected, and goals for the player planned out, we have one more important choice to make.

Following Procedure

The most common way to build a level during production is by using a **scripting tool** or **scripting editor**. A scripting tool is the program you use to create and place scripts. A script tells the game engine what to do and when to do it. Scripts control mechanics, enemies, cameras, and other in-level elements. Scripting is done by the designer during the game's production—so why are we talking about it here? Because there are two ways to build a game level, and the method the dev team uses will impact how you design your game during pre-production.

An alternative method is to create your levels *procedurally*. A **procedural game** has levels that are generated using an algorithm rather than using levels that are created in an editor. The advantage of procedural games is that they create unique environments so that every game level is different.

Procedurally generated content can vary depending on the game. *Candy Crush Saga* (2012) (2011) procedurally generates how gems populate the game board. *Dorf Romantik* (2021) procedurally generates puzzles with each new game. *The Binding of Isaac* (2011), *Spelunky 2* (2020), and *Hades* (2020) have procedurally generated levels and encounters. You can even procedurally generate entire worlds as seen in *Slaves to Armok: Gold of Blood Chapter II: Dwarf Fortress* (2006), *Minecraft* (2009), and *No Man's Sky* (2018). Using procedurally generated content is a powerful tool for both the development team and the player, but it's not without its problems. Here are a few tricks to help you make the most of your procedural levels:

- **Know your metrics.** Even though procedural content is generated randomly, it still needs to follow the rules of your game. Knowing the distances your player can move and act will determine the parameters of your design. That way, the game isn't generating an invalid situation such as one where the player can never hope to win.

- **Provide structure.** Even though the appeal of procedural levels for designers is randomness, players still need something to latch on to. Procedural levels tend to feel too random, too empty, or too unstructured. Create a standard for your level and use it as a top-down approach to how a level should be generated. As you generate new levels, pay attention to which elements repeat and how often, and adjust your values to provide maximum content without making the level too difficult.

- **Symmetry helps.** Symmetry helps players navigate the game as they look for patterns in the environment, the mechanics, and encounters. Build in instances of symmetry to function as guides for your player and to keep environments from getting too disorientating.

- **Use just a little randomness**. Just because your game uses procedural design doesn't mean everything in the game has to be generated procedurally. *Left 4 Dead* (2008) uses an artificial intelligence called "The Director" to create procedural encounters and music cues as the players fight their way through pre-designed levels.

- **Mix in predesigned elements.** Just because a game is procedural doesn't mean the entire game has to be. Mix in pre-designed gameplay to offset the randomness. The challenge is to make procedural gameplay feel designed and designed gameplay feel procedural. Why not have the best of both worlds?

The irony about procedurally generated gameplay is that when it's good, players won't notice it. You'll have to weigh the benefits and costs to your development team to see if procedural design is worth using.

You've Got the Beat

Look at all the useful tools you have available to help you: character, character actions, story, level themes, a world map. These tools are all you need to build an entire universe! To help organize my thoughts, I like to create a **beat chart** (remember these from Level 4?). A beat chart is a tool Hollywood writers and directors often use to help them organize and plan their movie's production. Creating a beat chart helps the designer determine gaps and clumping in your game. You can reorganize the game elements to spread things out and make the game feel more organic.

Pretend you are making a game called *Relic Raider*. Your hero, Jake Hunter, travels the globe looking for lost treasure. You've developed the story and have brainstormed the gameplay and the game's environments and enemies. Take a look at this sample beat chart for *Relic Raider* and see if you spot any problems:

Relic Raider beat chart

| Game Element | Level Name/File Name | | | | |
	Shanghai/ Roof01	Jungle 01/ Jung01	Jungle 02/ Jung02	Temple of the Hidden Skulls/ Jung03	Mountain Escape!/ Road01
Location	Shanghai rooftops	Jungle	Jungle	Ancient temple (int)	Mountain pass
Gameplay	Stealth, shooting, jumping	Shooting	Fighting	Platform, jumping	Driving
Objective	Find crime boss Wu-Fan	Jungle part 1	Jungle part 2	Reach chamber of skulls	Car chase
Story beat	Jake steals medallion, is caught by Wu-Fan	Jake explores jungle	Jake finds temple of skulls	Jake places medallion in statue; General Hauser shows up	Jake steals truck, flees Hauser
New weapon	.45, machine gun	Machete	No	No	No
Enemies	Enemy thug, Enemy axe man, Enemy machine gunner	Jaguar, native (spear)	Jaguar	Jaguar, Enemy soldier	Enemy truck, Enemy Jeep w/machine gun
Mechanics	Swinging rope, zip line	Swinging rope, zip line	Zip line	Spiked pits, blow darts, crushing walls, fall-away floor	Falling rocks
NPC	Wu-Fan	Guide	None	Hauser	None
Bonus materials	Art gallery 1	Art gallery 2	Art gallery 3	Alt. costume	Art gallery 4
Time of day	Night	Night	Night	Day	Day
Color mapping	Blue/red	Green/brown	Green/brown	Green/gray	Tan/sky blue

Did you spot all the issues the beat chart exposed?

- Level naming is inconsistent. Rather than have generic titles like "jungle 01," find a way to give them more descriptive names like "temple of the hidden skulls."

- Roof01 and Road01 could be mistaken for each other. Name the Shanghai level "Shang01;" the more distinctive, the better.

- Since "Jung03" doesn't seem to share too many assets, I recommend calling it "temp01" to show that it's a different place than the other jungle levels.

- Do you need two jungle levels back-to-back? The activities in "Jung01" and "Jung02" would be better combined to make one improved jungle level.

- Driving is introduced a little late in the game. There seems to be four "on-foot" levels before that point. Find a way to bring the driving in sooner or lose a walking level.

- Although the other levels are extremely specific, the jungle objectives seem unfocused. Give the players more of a purpose.

- The introduction of weapons seems to ramp up quickly and then dry out just as fast. That's a warning sign that you need more interesting things for players to do and toys for the players to use.

- The enemies are clumped up at the beginning of the game. Enemy AI could be repurposed for more effective use.

- Jungle 02, while listed as a fighting level, doesn't seem to have any enemies that would work well with fighting.

- Those jungle levels are re-using enemies too much. How about adding another type of enemy like a deadly python, piranhas, or a pack of vicious apes?

- Repurpose mechanics like you would enemies. The temple has too many unique mechanics that will take time and effort to create. Can any of them be re-used in other ways?

- Art galleries are a pretty basic reward. What other bonuses can you give players rather than just the same thing over and over again?

- There are three-night levels in a row. Break this up with morning, evening, atmospheric effects like rain or snow, and so on. And because the interior of a temple is going to be dark, it won't matter whether it's day or night.

- The color map has a lot of green in it. Make sure that the visuals offer a more diverse palette; otherwise, all the levels are going to feel the same.

Just by creating and observing the patterns created by a beat chart, you are able to make significant improvements to production, gameplay, and art before you build a single asset!

Re-using Re-use

While looking at the preceding beat chart, I noticed different gameplay systems: platforming, shooting, driving, and stealth. These different systems add diversity to a game, but when it comes to creating them, they have nothing to do with each other. One of the most important design decisions you can make is how and when to re-use gameplay systems over the course of the game.

If you use a game system fewer than three times over the course of a game, it's not worth having. This doesn't mean that you need to have the same gameplay section over and over again. Instead, you can be smart with your art assets and repurpose them.

For example, a vehicle system can support a jeep, a hatchback, and a sedan. Creating the vehicle system costs more time and money than building the three different cars does. But remember, you can stretch your recycling only so far; the same system you use for your cars can't support a hovercraft or motorcycle. Although they are both ground vehicles, they behave quite differently.

There is always a trade-off between design and programming. Learn the limitations of the game system and craft your game accordingly. Create a few gameplay systems that you can re-use over and over again throughout your game. This way, you maximize your game as well as your schedule and budget. Use the limitations to your advantage. Study any game created by Japanese developer Treasure Co. Ltd. (*Gunstar Heroes, Dynamite Heady, Ikaruga*), they really knew how to milk a small palette of mechanics. When you are creating your beat chart, make sure you don't use the same gameplay systems back-to-back. Unless your game is specifically a driving game, don't follow a driving level with more driving.

You also can collaborate with your artists on how to best re-use art assets. Simply recoloring and retexturing game items will make them look different from level to level. **TIP**

The Gary Gygax[12] Memorial Mapping Section

There are several ways to start building level maps. The designers of the original *Metal Gear* built their levels out of LEGO blocks. Some developers do rapid-level prototyping in 3D tools like Maya or 3D Studio Max. One designer I know liked to model his levels in clay. I like to start with a ream of blank paper, a very sharp #2 pencil, and an eraser. I like making maps on paper because it reminds me of the good old days of creating *Dungeons and Dragon* levels.

One of the easiest ways to start a game design is with **alleys** and **islands.** I have found that there are primarily two types of spaces in three-dimensional video game level design: a long

---

[12] Ernest Gary Gygax (1938 - 2008) was the co-creator of the first role-playing fantasy game, *Dungeons and Dragons.* Creating dungeons and adventures for D&D served as the springboard for many a young game designer's career, including myself!

hallway (an alley) and a wide arena (the island). Alleys create a directed gameplay experience: players have a goal to reach, and the level is built to help them reach it. Your alley can be narrow to create a sense of claustrophobia and tension, or it can be wider to give the feeling of sprawl and space, but it achieves the same goal; to funnel a player toward the other side.

An example of "alley" level design

Alleys offer the following advantages to designers:

- Placing camera trigger zones is easier when you know where and how players will be entering and moving through the level.

- You can get dramatic with your camera movements to inform players or enhance the action and drama.

- You can remove the camera controls from the game, allowing players to concentrate on gameplay.

- You can create scripted, triggered gameplay events because you know where players are looking.

- It is easier to choreograph combat and traps since there is only one way for the player to go.

- Bottlenecks can be used to prevent backtracking.

- You can use illusional narrative (more on this in a moment) to tell the level's story.

An island is a bit more challenging to design and build. Your game camera has to be flexible enough to accommodate a wide variety of widths and elevations. Scripted events are tough to execute because there's no guarantee that players will be looking in the right direction. Players can completely circumnavigate combat encounters. Even stagecraft-style tricks like façades are useless because players can view and interact with level geometry from all directions.

Despite these limitations, island level design offers expansive space that allows players the freedom to choose the order in which they want to experience the gameplay. *Mario 64* is one of the earliest examples of island level design in which players could choose to climb mountains, explore hills, or swim into underwater grottos in any order they liked. Islands allow players unparalleled freedom. In fact, an entire genre (the **sandbox**) has emerged as island level designs have grown bigger and bigger. *Just Cause 2*, *LEGO Batman 2*, and *Red Dead Redemption 2* are just huge island playgrounds.

An example of "Island" level design

Sandbox Play

When creating these sandbox worlds, you should divide them up into distinct areas to aid the players' navigation and orientation, like the "lands" of Disneyland. Disneyland goes through great pains to make each land visually distinct. Take Frontierland: it has everything you would expect in the Old West: watering troughs, wooden cigar-store Indians, wagons, cactus, and even those old video game standbys, crates, and barrels. (Frontierland's main thoroughfare was originally a dirt road until guests complained about dusty pants and shoes.) Disneyland even themes the trash cans! For example, Frontierland's trash cans are painted to look like wood, while Tomorrowland's are futuristic silver. You always know where you are even when throwing out the trash.

The game *Crackdown* uses this technique throughout its sandbox world of Pacific City. Not only is each zone themed to aid navigation, but the themes match the criminal gang that players have to overthrow. The Shai-Gen Corporation runs Chinatown while the tech-using Volk inhabits gleaming skyscrapers. To draw your viewers' attention, you should use as many cues as possible, such as color, sound, lighting, even weather, but first, I like to use weenies.

Disneyland's imagineers pioneered the use of architectural landmarks like Sleeping Beauty's castle, the Matterhorn, and Space Mountain, which they call **weenies.**[13] Weenies are used to get the interest of guests and draw them in their direction. Weenies don't have to be giant castles or mountains. They can be interesting architectural elements like statues, bridges, and buildings, or even natural elements like a distinct tree or rock.

---

[13] Walt Disney himself coined the term after the frankfurter that off-screen animal trainers would wave at their dog actors to get them to walk past the camera to where they wanted them to go.

Theoretically, you want to string your weenies along your path to keep players moving from one to the next. When creating 3D maps, make sure the path is clearly marked with weenies. I once created a map that looked like this:

Top View

When I playtested this part of the level, players would travel down the road, see the path leading behind the house, and walk around the back of the house looking for treasure. When they emerged onto the road, they turned around and walked back down the way they came!

Top View

I realized that the area needed a landmark (marked on the map) so that when players came out, they were able to re-orient themselves.

This brings up an important truth about designing games: players will ALWAYS find a way to break your game, whether or not they are doing it intentionally. Tackle this issue head-on by making players play the game the way YOU want it to be played but provide help to show them the way.

Top View

Islands work particularly well for multiplayer games because you can accommodate many assorted styles of playing. Do you like to sneak around the back of the map? Islands provide a back to sneak around. You can still charge up the front if you want, or you can camp over on that hill and snipe to your heart's content.[14]

That doesn't mean alleys and islands can't live together in perfect harmony. Islands can still have alley-like sections. *Red Faction Guerrilla* and *Overwatch 2* use interior spaces that feel like alley level designs, but their freedom of approach and wide perimeter edges mark them as islands. The *Uncharted* series alternates between using alleys and islands frequently. The *Dark Souls* games use alleys for their dungeon levels and islands for their hubs and battle arenas. Whether to use island or alley all depends on the gameplay.

Islands have the following advantages:

- They give an extraordinary feeling of space and scale. It's quite an experience the first time you realize a level goes on and on.
- Islands promote exploration and encourage designers to fill in "in-between spaces" with secrets, additional missions, and objectives.
- Gameplay options are laid out in front of players like a smorgasbord.
- Vehicle gameplay (like racing and car combat) feels better in wide-open spaces than in tight alleys.

[14] Not that anyone reading this book would stoop so low as to be a camper. And remember, there is a special place in hell for spawn campers.

Sandboxes are tricky things because I have found that no matter what players tell you, a world where players can choose to do anything at any time can be intimidating and confusing. Despite the freedom that the sandbox world promises players, they should still get some prompting on what to do next even if they don't want to do it. There's a reason your annoying cousin is always calling to tell you about your next mission in *Grand Theft Auto 5*.

Illusional Narrative

Another challenge for designers that a sandbox (or even a plain old level) provides is how to use the world to tell a story. **Illusional narrative** is a storytelling trick I first observed when riding the Peter Pan's Flight attraction at Disneyland. Having flown over London and to Never-Land, we have reached the part where Peter Pan and Captain Hook are engaged in a pitched sword duel on the deck of the pirate ship. The Darling children have been captured by the pirate crew and watch the battle.

The guest's ship flies around a corner (cleverly disguised as the sail of the pirate ship). Now Peter Pan is victorious, the Darlings are freed, and Captain Hook is keeping himself from being eaten by the crocodile.

Illusional narrative is the video game equivalent of what happens in the gutter of comic book panels or between edits in a movie: players fill in story when given two or more images or environments. With the proper transition and presentation, you could convince players that a train has crashed, a world has become overrun by aliens, or a character has crossed a room without animating a single element. The savings to production is significant. Real-time animations take time to produce and have to be ripped up and redone if the designer decides to change something in the level.

Here's a good example. In *Medal of Honor Allied Assault* (2002), your commanding officer meets you at the outskirts of a village with orders to attack a Nazi command post. He says that he'll meet you at the far end of the village. Now, the game could have had you follow the commander all the way through the command post, fighting side by side—the series had done this before—but instead, after you cut your way through the base, you reach the exit of the compound to find your commander, who congratulates you for a good job. If you viewed the level map from above, you'd see two commander models, and the illusion would be broken. But because you never see the two versions of the character together, in your (the player's) mind, it's the same character just at a different time.

Make sure you use gating mechanisms in your level design such as bottlenecks, camera views, checkpoints, elements that turn on and off, or even plain ol' doors to keep players from breaking the illusion.

The Dave Arneson[15] Memorial Mapping Section

It's time to get cracking and get your game design down on paper with a map.

When creating a map, you first must determine a scale. When drawing a **top-down view map** on graph paper, the size of the player usually equals one square. All other elements, such as treasure, mechanics, enemies, or objects, are drawn in relation to the size of the player—much like how you determine player metrics. Represent these elements as icons on your map. Create a legend for the icons on your map so readers can determine what they are looking at. You should include:

- Player's starting point
- Enemy starting locations
- Doors, teleporters, gates
- Puzzle mechanics (like levers and switches)
- Treasure chests and power-ups
- Traps and their areas of effect
- Significant landmarks (like statues, pools, pits, and so on)

I start my level map creation process by roughing out the major locations where I want big events to happen: a treasure chamber, a battle arena, a puzzle room, a mechanic that I want the player to learn, a spectacular view, and so on. Then I start to consider what I can use to connect those rooms: hallways, mazes, chasms, or passages. Then I usually move on to graph paper, which helps me communicate the scale of the level to the level artist. I often draw in elements such as tombstones, crypts, mechanics, and enemies.

---

[15] David "Dave" Arneson (1947 - 2009) was the co-creator of *Dungeons and Dragons*. Arneson's pre-D&D campaign *Blackmoor* introduced the concept of hit points, armor class and the term "dungeon crawl" to gaming. We owe him much.

a (very rough) level outline

Level Map from Pac-Man World

When you are creating passages for a top-down view map for a 3-D level, I recommend making it five squares wide: that's the width of the player plus two more widths on each side. It provides enough room for the player to navigate, for combat to occur, and the camera to have some room to maneuver. However, I can guarantee that your first few efforts at level design will usually end up too small and too cramped, so don't be afraid to be generous with your proportions.

Use geometry and lighting to help move the player down the path. Players are drawn toward light, but they tend to avoid or overlook dark places. You can use shapes like diagonal lines to draw the player's eye in a specific direction. I learned my favorite trick from the designers at Naughty Dog, the creators of the *Crash Bandicoot* and *Uncharted* games. They use a trick they call the **squint test.** Look at the following image and squint your eyes until they are almost closed:

What's the brightest thing on the screen? The main path. You can do the same thing in your game using color and lighting. Even if players don't consciously notice this, they will still be able to see which way to go. If players have someplace to go, don't waste their time with needless wandering. Never intentionally try to get players lost. Instead, find ways for them to get quickly to the main objective.

A good trick is to talk your way through a level design. For example, "The player is Astronaut Baker, who is finishing up testing the ODIN weapon platform. He and astronaut Mosely spacewalk back to the station, as a shuttle docks. As the astronauts enter, the new arrivals start killing the station's crew, forcing Baker and Mosely to flee. Baker is ambushed by an enemy and takes his gun in the fight. Baker and Mosley continue to battle their way through the station as they receive messages that ODIN is locking onto targets all around the U.S. The astronauts watch helplessly as ODIN fires on Los Angeles, San Diego, Phoenix, Houston, Miami.... Mission control detonates the station, and the two astronauts are sucked into space. Dodging debris, the two fight their way to ODIN. Opening ODIN's control panel, Baker blasts away at the fuel lines, making the weapon platform alter its trajectory. As the player's faceplate fills with fire, the last view is of ODIN burning up as it re-enters the Earth's atmosphere." Whew. That's the way to do a level!

This example not only tells an exciting story but also gives the audience an idea of the actions the players will be performing (spacewalking, fighting, opening the control panel, and shooting fuel lines) as well as how they will receive information (watching ODIN fire, hearing mission control give instructions, listening to astronaut Mosley). Just like the beat chart, this exercise will help you find lulls in the level design. If you ever find yourself saying, "Then the player walks over to here," cut that section out of your game. Because a **very important thing** is:

WALKING IS NEVER, EVER GAMEPLAY!

Only **lazy designers** consider walking to be gameplay. You're not a lazy designer, are you? Of course, you aren't. You are an **active designer.** An active designer who creates active things for your active character to do. Actively. This is why you should think about your game in terms of what I call the **primary action.** The best game concepts can be described with *one action verb* (although sometimes it takes more). You remember what a verb is, right? It's a word that shows action or a state of being. All levels should support the primary action. *Valorant* is all about shooting. *Hole.io* is all about dropping things in a hole. *Rhythm Doctor* is about keeping the beat. *Flight Control Rocket* is about directing rockets. *Pony Island* is about solving puzzles. Some games have more than primary action. *Elite Dangerous* focuses on shooting and flying. *Dishonored* splits the players' focus between sneaking and fighting.

Here are just a few more primary actions you can have your players perform:

- Jumping
- Collecting
- Climbing
- Swinging
- Breaking
- Adding
- Creating
- Flinging
- Drawing
- Exploring

Speaking of exploring, let's talk about multiple paths. Which one to take? The one that leads to the harem of 1,000 delights or the one that leads to the lava pits of Overfiend? Decisions, decisions.

I equate creating multiple paths in a level to a good action scene in a movie: you don't always see (or do) everything the first time around. The fact is players want **variety.** It's what keeps most players playing games. They want to find out what's around the next corner, who the next enemy is, what the next power-up or weapon will be. The minute a game gets predictable, players get bored. Keep in mind, this is a different type of predictability than I mentioned earlier. I guess a better word would be "sameness." If things start to feel the same level after level, encounter after encounter, the player is going to get bored.

Players also want **discovery** and **surprise,** but surprise is just discovery that they don't expect. Of course, you can have both good and bad surprises, but if you don't play fair with your players, they will get frustrated and stop playing.

Getting back to giving players variety, you will need multiple paths, multiple things to interact with, multiple enemies, randomized AI behavior, randomized treasure drops, multiple storylines, and endings. No matter which multiple choice you provide, creating this alternative content can be a tricky thing to deal with, especially with level design.

Creating multiple paths raises multiple questions that need to be addressed: Which path will players choose? What can you do to entice players to go down one path over another? What can the designer do to promote players to use that alternative path? Hidden power-ups or cash prizes? Provide an achievement for all secrets discovered? Will the game change depending on which path you choose? You can design an entire game around the concept of choice—the *Stanley Parable* (2013) did.

I've worked with producers who balked at the idea of designing and building a level that players may never see. They feel the effort from the team doesn't justify the experience the players have. In some cases, those producers were right. In others, that variety has made a level design shine. Levels with multiple paths work better in some genres than others. For example, the wide-open worlds found in FPSs, RPGs, and driving games require multiple paths just to prevent regular traversal from getting boring and to create the feeling of a real world.

Whatever answer you decide on, make sure your effort provides something significant to your level.

Some designers don't like **backtracking**, that is, when players have to go back to a part of the level they've already been to. I don't mind it. I think it's a good way to get the most out of a level. I like to use backtracking for puzzles. I always say, "show players the door first and then let them find the key." Just don't make players go back and forth too many times or travel too far away from the door (chest, whatever). If you need to make players go to a location more than twice, do something to make that experience different: add gameplay like (new) combat or collectibles, change the topography by having an earthquake change a flat spot into jump-able hills. A nice natural (or unnatural) disaster can work wonders.

Another lesson I learned from Disneyland is that there are three ways for players to get around the world. The first is the main path—using weenies and the tricks described earlier in this chapter—that helps guide players around the level. The second is to use secret paths and shortcuts; these are sneaky and tricky ways players learn as they explore and get more familiar with the level. Using these shortcuts makes players feel smarter. They can also be used for gameplay, such as time trials were getting from point A to point B as quickly as possible is the goal. The third way is to use circuit transportation. Like the train that circles Disneyland, players need a fast way to get around the level but one that provides a handful of stops. It has to be faster than traveling on foot. It doesn't have to be a train. It can be a car or a horse, or a mythical mount like a griffin or dragon. Let them catch a lift in a zeppelin or on a spaceship, or, if your fiction supports it, there's always the ever-popular teleporter.

Just be aware that traveling in vehicles can really chew up real estate. You'll need to build that space into your levels. But it's a double-edged sword. Don't make the experience last too long, especially if it's something you will be doing often. Just remember this **very important thing** when it comes to traveling through levels:

IF IT EVER FEELS TOO LONG OR TOO BORING, THEN IT IS

Avoid boring levels! But how? Variety is one way. **Fingers** are another way of making a world feel deeper and fuller without having to build lots of complex geometry and multiple paths that players may never take. Picture a linear path:

Top View

Not too exciting, huh? You can place all type of hazards and enemies along the way to make things challenging for players, but it's just going to feel like a straight path even if you crinkle it up and bend it around.

However, if you start to add fingers off your path, little dead ends for players to explore and go down, it makes the players feel as if they are exploring the level and not just promenading down it. These fingers expand the life of your level, and you can promote the players exploring them. Take a look at the level now that a few fingers have been added off the main path:

Top View

Now you have interesting places for players to explore as they work their way through a level. Although I wouldn't suggest putting something that is important to the critical path down a finger, you can place whatever you want along a finger: combat, treasure, bonus materials, or just something visual or fun. Remember this simple yet **very important thing:**

EVERY FINGER SHOULD HAVE A REWARD AT THE END, EVEN IF IT'S JUST A TRASH CAN[16]

The point of this? Variety. Avoiding boredom. Boredom in a game is worse than death. I can't count the number of times I've been bored with a video game. Video games should never be boring. They should be awesome! But coming up with ways to keep players entertained can be hard. Fortunately, I have done the hard work for you. Here are just a few ways to prevent players from getting bored:

- **Change modes.** Spice things up with a shooting level, a puzzle, a minigame.

- **Add beauty shots.** These moments of wonder help tell the story and make for a cool screenshot.

- **Make the familiar unfamiliar.** As in the *Poseidon Adventure*, turn the commonplace on its head to get double duty from something you've already created. Turn the location of a boss fight into an arena battle against an army of foes.

---

[16] Whether that trash can have trash or treasure in it is up to you.

- **Change the direction that players move.** Left to right, straight or spiral, take them up or drop them down. Changing elevation can work wonders.

- **Use texturing and color.** Change the time of day, the weather, anything to make your level feel different.

Time of day and weather can be used to emphasize events and elements in your level. How would players traverse the level if it were covered in snow or took place during a blizzard? How would a fairy village look differently if it were set at night? Make sure that any weather effects extend to the player character, the mechanics, the enemies, and other elements in the level. If one element isn't affected by the weather, it will ruin the entire effect. Give your game levels a variety of atmospheric effects and times of day to keep things interesting.

Variety should be applied to the level geometry as well as to gameplay. Alternating interior and exterior spaces keep your level from feeling too much of the same physical space. You don't have to alternate the spaces in between every room but break it up according to what feels natural. Players usually feel safer in large spaces. Tighter spaces feel more mysterious and dangerous. Be mindful of your camera placement throughout your level design. Allow enough room in tight spaces for the players and camera to move around, or just resort to a fixed or rail camera. When you are staging combat, larger spaces allow you to throw in bigger and larger groups of bad guys, whereas narrower spaces work better for one-on-one battles.

Verticality is very important when designing levels. Alternating elevation makes an environment feel natural, provides much-needed variety, and allows designers to set up "Kodak moments" of any impressive visuals like statues, vistas, and horizons. As players walk or climb up, they feel as though they are making progress and heading toward a goal.

However, as players travel downward, they may try to skip elevations by jumping downward. If players can be killed by very long drops, make sure they have a way to look down to gauge the metrics of the drop. There's nothing more annoying than falling to your death if it looks as though you can safely make the drop. If you don't want players to drop down, corral them in the direction you want them to travel with switchbacks, ladders, or other climbable surfaces.

My golden rule of level design is this **very important thing:**

IF IT LOOKS AS IF PLAYERS CAN GO THERE, THEY SHOULD BE ABLE TO

Establish a visual language within your level to clarify where players can and cannot go. Use low walls, shrubbery, or rock walls to indicate impassable areas in the level to players. They will learn that these visual cues mean "you can't go there." Whatever you do, please don't be a lazy designer and use **invisible walls.**

Nothing breaks immersion faster and makes a level feel less like a real place than smacking headlong into a big fat wall of nothing.

Want to screw with your players' heads? Have your character travel from right to left, particularly if you are making a 2-D game. Western audiences are used to reading and viewing information in a left-to-right orientation. Making a character walk from right to left can make players feel uneasy, even if they can't articulate why. I find this works best when the character is entering the boss's lair at the end of the game.

Another fun way to torture your players using level geometry is to force them to walk across very thin platforms over great heights, boiling lava, or swirling whirlpools. Increase the danger by using a bird's-eye view camera to view the action. I call these perilous situations "sphincter twitchers" and use them in all my level designs. Even if players are never in danger of dying, they sure will feel as if they are!

When collaborating with your artist, unless the surface is specifically designed like a ramp, stairs, or natural incline, make sure any geometry that players can stand on (like platforms) is relatively flat. Most characters are not programmed to adjust their body to uneven surfaces and, even if they are, they can "stutter" or misstep as they are playing their walking animations. Try to have smooth transitions between even small elevations to avoid this problem.

While making a level feel like a real place helps the designer create the level, remember that you shouldn't be bound by realism: this is a game after all, and you are limited only by how real you want to make it.

However, here is a cautionary tale about realism. A friend of mine was a designer on the team of an action shooter. The levels had already been created by the artists, who were extremely proud that they had created architecturally accurate buildings. These buildings had realistic nooks, stairwells, in-scale hallways, and even bathrooms on each level. The buildings were completely unusable in the game because the spaces didn't allow for gameplay or work well with the game camera. Think of it this way: in the movie *Star Wars,* we never saw the toilets on the Death Star. I am sure they were there just off-camera, but because we didn't need to see them, we didn't have to see them. Omit any parts of your building, temple, city, and so on that don't help support telling the story that you want to tell.

Wrapping Up Mapping

Now that we've covered these topics, how do you communicate them to your team members? For example, designing elevations for a top-down view map can be a bit tricky, but here are a few tricks that might help:

- You can draw levels in different colors, but I find that approach gets visually crowded.

- Use tracing paper or paper and a light board to layer the elevations of your level and break them up by the height of the players.

- Be sure to clearly mark what each elevation is so that viewers can read them in the correct order.

- While you are at it, number the consecutive map pages or tape them together into one huge map so they are easier to read.

- Just because a sheet of paper is square doesn't mean you have to design a square shape. Cut, fold, extend, or do whatever you have to do to make your map accurately represent your design.

- If you are drawing your map from the side view, determine the height of your character first and then draw the map to scale.

- It's a lot easier to show vertical gameplay from a side view. Sometimes you are going to need a combination of side and top view maps.

You don't need to be working on a game with an isometric camera to use an isometric map. This type of map is a little trickier to draw, and it requires some artistic skill to create, but it works great for showing things like elevation.

Side view level design

Isometric maps work best when representing games using a two and a half D camera. If you need to show depth or a part of the level that is obscured by geometry on your map, you can show the missing information using a cutaway or X-ray view. Or you can create a flap that the viewer can lift to see what lies underneath. Make as many layers as you need to convey your idea for your level. Some of my levels have had so many panels that they started to look like an advent calendar!

Here's some other information to include on your level design maps:

- Enemy spawn locations and detection/aggro radius
- "Bread crumb" collectibles (like coins or *Pac-Man* dots) that lead players through the level
- Secret entrances/breakable walls or other concealed locations

- Obstacles and barriers like walls, trees, tombstones, and so on
- Clearly marked terrain like cursed earth, swampy water, slippery ice, and hot lava

Gray Matters

Armed with your level maps, you are now ready to start building (or have an artist start building) your game levels. But hold on there, tiger! Before you even start thinking about enemies, mechanics, or even detailed geometry, you will have to flesh out your level in **gray box** form.

A **gray box level** is created within an art tool (Maya and 3D Studio Max are the two most common industry art tools, although others exist, like the open-source tool Blender). The gray box level shows the scale, size, and relationship of basic elements pertaining to camera and character metrics. It is pivotal in determining scale, camera, and pacing. Spend time running your game character around the gray box level. Have others play the level to find confusing areas and trouble spots. Iterate on your level while it's still easy to make big sweeping changes. You may find that a level works better if you rip out an entire section and stitch the remaining pieces together. A straight hallway may be more thrilling with plenty of twists and turns to transform "boring old" enemies, mechanics, and treasure into unexpected surprises.

As you are building your level, you might be wondering how long a level should be. Early in the production process, you should **pace out** a level to determine its overall length. Start your character at the beginning of your gray box level, and then start walking. Don't worry about hazards or combat or collecting every musical note in the level. Just walk from the start to the finish. Whatever time it took for you to get from point A to point B is roughly half the time it will take you in the final game. So, if you need your levels to average a half-hour each, it should take 15 minutes to pace out the level. While it seems weird to do this, remember that many publishers and reviewers are concerned with the overall length of a game. I tell developers that a single-player action game should last at least eight to ten hours. Going longer than that is great; just make sure your production schedule and team plan for it.

Conversely, VR and mobile games require shorter pacing because their play sessions are meant to be short. You don't want to wear out a VR player with a long play session. With mobile games, sometimes the sessions are as short as a few minutes, depending on the game!

Another pacing technique is to change the player's emotion every 15 to 20 minutes. Sadly, the gamut of emotions experienced in most video games is pretty limited,[17] but you can make a player go from mystery to wonder to fear to panic using geometry alone.

Divide your gameplay between "big moments" and "small moments." Don't stack too many big moments next to each other; you'll wear out your players. Conversely, small moments of calm and quiet will only feel boring if there are too many of them in a row. *Shadow of the Colossus* successfully balances the big moments of battling giant monsters and quiet moments of traveling through the expansive game world.

Stop! Wait! You haven't built your gray box levels yet, have you?

Good, because you will want to create a **playground** first. A playground is a gray box level not intended to be used in the game. It is a separate testing ground for game mechanics and hazards. All mechanics and hazards should be tested and tweaked in the playground until they feel right; then you can use them in your levels. Here are a few things to test in your own playground:

- Create ground angles to test basic walking, running, inverse kinematics (IK), and other technology to make sure the player looks good while moving even when not on level ground.

- Build several simple boxes at a variety of elevations to test the player's metrics with jumping, hoisting, teeter, and so on. You should create any specific length and height geometry to test double and wall jumps.

- Test mechanics and hazards to determine distance, timing, and lethality.

- Test powerups that grant the player new powers such as hover, jumping or speed bursts.

---

[17] I think it's fair to say that most video games let players experience only eight emotions: anger, panic, dread, surprise, wonder, satisfaction, joy, and disappointment. And some games only disappoint.

Let's Get Fighty

The sister to the playground is the **combat arena.** This is just like a playground but used by the dev team to test combat systems, cover systems, and enemies. Have a way to quickly spawn and test combinations of enemies to create the best combat experiences. I'd rather hold off on talking about this topic because—SPOILER ALERT—the next two chapters are all about combat and enemies!

Leave the Training Level for Last

The **training level** is the place where players learn all the basics of gameplay. It teaches players the game's basics. It provides players with their first impression of gameplay. It stokes their enthusiasm[18] for the rest of the game. You'd think that this is the most important level of the game.

You'd think!

Unfortunately, the training level is often left until the end of the game's production. Now, I know why this is done. Developers will argue that you won't know the most important lessons of gameplay until everything is in the game. They will insist that because gameplay elements are often added during development, they should build the training level last after all the elements are set.

They state that by the end of the game's production, the art team is capable of creating the best-looking art and effects for the training level in order to give the first level of the game the biggest bang for the buck. Sometimes they claim the players will learn the basics over the course of the game. The reality is, production schedules get tight and priorities shift, resulting in the training level usually not getting the love and attention it deserves.

You may want to consider creating the training level first. Sure, it may not look as pretty, but your team can always go back and polish up the art. The advantage is that you, along with players, will be learning the basics and can accurately determine what the players should learn before the designer blinders kick in. A training level always benefits from a pair of fresh eyes.

---

[18] Hey, I think I found a ninth emotion!

Even better, don't have a training level at all. A player should learn as they play. Rather than having one level dedicated to learning moves that you'll just forget five minutes into the game, why not make the whole game a learning experience. I have found that in the best games, players are always learning new moves, gaining new gear, experiencing new gameplay, and constantly learning. Your **entire game** should be a training level!

Levels without Characters

Now that I've spent an entire chapter explaining how to make levels for primarily character-based games, what do you do if your level has no character? What if it's a puzzle game or a driving game or a flying game? Well, much of the advice from this chapter still applies, but here are a few more tips for these types of games:

- Make levels dependent on new mechanics. If you can now purchase nitro for their car, make sure there is a ramp that requires a nitro-powered jump to cross or a close race that can be won with the judicious application of a nitro-boost. If you just unlocked a new cluster bomb that activates when you connect five or more gems, then you should use it!

- Just because it's not an environment doesn't mean it can't have a theme. Many people don't realize even an abstract game like *Tetris* had a theme: each board was based on a cultural or architectural achievement of Soviet-era Russia.

- Even if you are designing a purely abstract game like *Super Hexagon*, *Hundreds*, or *Impossible Road*, changing the color of your level every so often helps indicate progress.

- If you are playing as a vehicle, the environment in which the action takes place can be a different biome or season for each level. Or if gameplay happens in an "empty" environment like an open sky or outer space, put a different colored planet or nebula in the background.

Now that you've started to create your levels, what are you going to fill them with? I have a sneaking suspicion you'll find out in the next chapter.

Level 9's Universal Truths and Clever Ideas

- Even a cliché can be made compelling.
- Use the "Mexican pizza" technique to make level themes unique.
- Level names can help convey mood and info to your players.
- Design from the top down: world, level, experience, to moment-to-moment gameplay.
- Use level maps and posters to give information and build anticipation.
- Determine the theme of your levels: escape/survive, explore, educate, or learn a moral.
- Decide early whether to use scripted or procedural gameplay.
- Use the beat chart to point out weaknesses in your game's overall design.
- Design your games using a tight set of gameplay systems and mechanics: maximize play through re-use.
- Players will always find a way to break your game.
- Is your level an alley or island? Design to each style's strength.
- Map and gray box your levels to plan camera placement and prevent architectural issues and gameplay problems.
- Walking is never, ever gameplay.
- Every finger on the level map should have a reward at the end, even if it's just a trash can. (or a cat hiding in the trash can!)
- Players need variety and discovery, and surprise is just discovery that players don't expect.
- If it looks like players can go there, they should be able to go there.
- Use playgrounds and combat arenas to test metrics and systems.
- The entire game should train players.
- Even games without a story can have a theme.

Level 10
The Elements of Combat

Every action is seen to fall into one of three main categories, guarding, hitting, or moving. Here, then, are the elements of combat, whether in war or pugilism.

B.H. Liddell Hart

BRITISH MILITARY THEORIST Sir Basil Liddell Hart may have died before video games became popular, but his quote neatly covers the basics of video game combat. Combat is a popular and major component of a video game player's moves and activities. A good combat system requires much thought and work from the development team to get it right. But before diving into combat, we need to open the can of worms and look at the messy topic of **violence.**

The simple truth is this: many video games are *violent.*

Let me amend that.

Video games are about **action.** Some of those actions, like hitting, shooting, stabbing, and killing, are *violent.*

However, anyone who assumes that all video games are violent obviously knows nothing about video games. A large number of video games don't rely on violence. This is true from the first video game, *Tennis for Two,* all the way to the latest mobile match three puzzle game. I could fill this entire book with a catalog of non-violent games. But somehow, it's always the *Dooms, Mortal Kombats,* and *Call of Duty's* that get all of the attention. Why? Because:

1. Violence in video games is graphic, dramatic, and visceral.

2. As a result of the above, it offers a player the quickest positive response feedback loop.

The player does an action (hitting, shooting) and sees the immediate result (enemy is killed by attack), which grants a reward (experience, money, power-up). This elegant feedback loop allows for quick and frequent player-to-world interaction. It's Freud's pleasure principle in practice.[1] Ring the bell, a reward is gained. Why stop ringing the bell?

Another reason violence is common in video games is that other human interactions such as conversation, romance, humor, and manipulation are often hard to re-create in games! The results are (a) development teams do not explore alternate methods of gameplay as often as they do violent ones. (b) Because game players tend to buy the same types of games over and over, (c) publishers find that newer styles of play are harder to sell.[2] (d) Parents and other social groups who mean well don't always find out all the facts before leaping to the assumption that all video games are violent.

Let's avoid all this stress by doing our part as responsible members of society and keeping mature games out of the hands of younger gamers. Plenty of alternative games are available out there. You wouldn't take little kids to an R-rated movie, so why would you let them play an M-rated video game? Okay, I'll get off of my soapbox now.

As mentioned back in Level 4, the ESRB reviews and provides ratings for game content. At its website,[3] you can find the board's descriptors of violence and violence references found in games:

- **Comic mischief:** Depictions or dialogue involving slapstick or suggestive humor.

- **Cartoon violence:** Violent actions involving cartoon-like situations and characters. May include violence where a character is unharmed after the action has been inflicted.

- **Fantasy violence:** Violent actions of a fantasy nature, involving human or non-human characters in situations easily distinguishable from real life.

---

[1] The fact that a developer called "id" created the FPS, a genre that directly adheres to Freud's pleasure principle, is almost too delicious to ignore.

[2] EA's marketing team tried to cancel the company's bestselling game, *The Sims*, during its entire development; they thought no one would buy it!

[3] www.esrb.org/ratings/ratings_guide.jsp

- **Violence:** Scenes involving aggressive conflict. May contain bloodless dismemberment.

- **Intense violence:** Graphic and realistic-looking depictions of physical conflict. May involve extreme and/or realistic blood, gore, weapons, and depictions of human injury and death.

When designing violence in games, you should realize that it's all about context. The more violent activities the player does himself, the higher the rating. Ask yourself the following questions to help determine the proper rating for your game:

- Does the player do the violence themselve? Do they use realistic weapons?

- How frequently does the player perform violent acts?

- Does the game reward the player for performing violent acts? Does the game show in any way that violence is "not appropriate?"

- How graphic is the violence? Is there dismemberment? Do the game visuals linger on the violence?

- Is there leftover residue like bloodstains or gibs? Better graphics equal more realistic graphics equal more realistic violence.

- Is the violence against "bad guys" or non-humans like bug aliens or robots?

- Do the enemies suffer as they are being killed or defeated?

Now that you know how violent your gameplay will be, you can start to design how it is going to happen.

400 Quatloos on the Newcomer!

When designing combat moves for your character, first consider your character's personality. Is your character acrobatic like Lara Croft? Is your character jumpy like Mario? Stealthy like Agent 47? Brutal like Kratos? Each of these characters has a unique combat style because each has a unique personality.

So... you guys wanna fight?

* smoking kills

What genre is your game? What kinds of gameplay experiences do you want the players to have? These questions will help determine what weapons your character will use. Maybe you just want to have your hero carry a circuit sword *and* a neurolizer pistol for no other reason than it looks awesome. You'll still want to consider the ramifications of them carrying both because it impacts your games and everything the player does in it.

In combat, the attack used totally depends on the player's distance from the target. Check out the different ranges of combat including close range, medium range, long range, and area effect.

- **Close-range combat** consists of grapples, punches, strikes, sweeps, tickle fights, and quick burst moves like head butts and upper cuts.

- **Medium-range combat** consists of weapon swings, flying kicks, and dash attacks.

- **Long-range combat** consists of shooting or throwing projectiles or spells at enemies.

- **Area effects** will affect enemies within a radius or cone of effect.

- **Distance effects** can strike enemies even further than the range of the player's influence. These include missile strikes and orbital weapon platform strikes. These usually do a lot of damage, sometimes even to the player characters if they are caught within its range.

Knowing what your character's combat range (or ranges) is going to be makes a huge difference in how the player approaches combat during gameplay. A *Sonic* game is almost exclusively close/medium-range combat, whereas *Call of Duty* is a long-range combat game. As a result, Sonic must come into close contact with enemies to be able to defeat them, whereas in *Call of Duty*, the player's goal is to keep away from enemies and keep them from ever getting close by shooting them from a distance. In the VR game *Dungeons of Eternity* (2023), you need to select weapons for your character that take into consideration both distance and close-range melee attacks. If you choose only one of the two types, you'll likely die a gruesome death. Weapon choice is as much a part of the game play as the fighting itself.

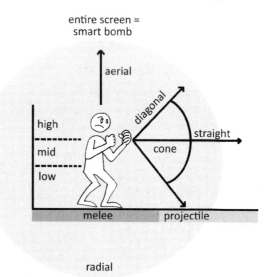

Attacks can be delivered from four different elevations to give combat variety: standing, low, high, and aerial. Although you don't have to use all four of these elevations in your game, you will have to make each of these elevations have its own set of attacks because they make the player deal with combat in very different ways:

- **Standing position** is the basic shoulder height of the player. Human-sized and larger opponents can be struck at this elevation.

- **Low position** strikes are at the waist height (or lower) of the enemy and delivered from a crouched or kneeling position.

- **High position** attacks are delivered over the head of an average height enemy. They can be done only by jumping and then attacking. High attacks are used against flying or large enemies like bosses.

- **Aerial position** is achieved when a player jumps or flies into the air to attack. Aerial attacks can be extended jumps like those found in *Super Smash Bros. Ultimate* and *Jo Jo's Bizarre Adventures: Eyes of Heaven*, or they can be true flying like in *Dragon Ball Sparking! Zero* or *Gravity Rush Remastered*.

Attacks from any elevation and range can be delivered both **vertically** and **horizontally.** In *Maximo: Ghosts to Glory*, we designed enemies that could be defeated by only one of the two attacks.

A skeleton guard wore an armored helmet that deflected Maximo's overhead vertical attack. Another skeleton warrior used a shield that blocked Maximo's horizontal attacks. The solution was to use the opposite direction attacks to smash the skeletons.

An **attack matrix** is useful to track important information about combat moves. An attack matrix should include the following data:

- Attack name

- Control scheme

- Range of attack

- Speed of attack

- Direction of attack

- Damage—in terms of strength as well as numeric damage (usually expressed as a value or percentage)

- Special—anything that distinguishes the attack from other attack moves

Here's a nice example of an attack matrix:

Attack	Control	Range	Speed	Direction	Damage	Special
Slash	Square	Close	Med	Horizontal	Medium (10 hps)	Can be blocked by shield
Over-head strike	Triangle	Close	Med	Vertical	Medium (10 hps)	Can be thwarted by helmet
Thrust	Forward on stick, Triangle	Close	Fast	Forward	Strong (25 hps)	Knockback to target
Jump strike	X, down on stick, Triangle	Close/medium	Slow	Downward	Strong (25 hps)	Stun to any target in two-unit radius

Feel free to add as many columns as you need to your attack matrix to accommodate degrees of severity, defensive items/moves, and so on.

You can use an attack matrix to track combat moves and compare and contrast values for maximum variety. Each attack should be distinct and usable in a specific combat situation.

Before you start whacking away with swords and blasting everything in sight with your guns, look first at the most dangerous weapon...the hand.

Put 'Em Up!

Hand-to-hand combat has been a staple of video games ever since early brawlers and fighters. How your character fights depend on who your character is. You won't find a better case study than the *Street Fighter* characters. Each one is a personification of a different martial arts style. Even if your character lives in a crazy fantasy world, you should study real-world fighting styles to make your character's attacks feel more realistic and distinct. Let's look at some different hand-to-hand fighting moves:

- **Strong and weak attacks:** Attacks in action and fighting games are often broken up into two categories: strong and weak (also called **heavy** and **light attacks**). Both types of attacks can be composed of punches or kicks or other moves, but what matters is the damage they do and the opponent's reaction to the attack when struck. Strong attacks do more damage than weak attacks. Strong attacks often have a longer animation. The time it takes for the attack to connect is the risk the player takes for the reward of the higher damage. Weak attacks are quick but do very little damage. However, weak attacks often act as the opening move for a chain of attacks leading up to a super-move. Weak attacks are often blockable, whereas strong attacks may not be. Strong attacks might act as shield breakers or cause stuns or knockbacks to the enemy as an added benefit.

- **Punch:** A punch should happen quickly. When the player taps the button (or screen), the character should immediately throw a punch. The animation of the punch shouldn't have too long of a wind-up unless it is for some spectacular finishing super-move. When animating a punch attack, be mindful of the distance between the character and where the punch lands. The distance can't be so short that the player doesn't see it happening thanks to poor camera placement or an enemy getting in the way. By throwing a fast punch, the player can **chain** punches, which means to throw several punches within a short period of time. But speed isn't the only thing important to a punch. A punch feels powerful when the enemy reacts to it. Stronger punches, such as an **upper cut,** should really rock the enemy's world. A good reaction animation, sound effect, and special effect really help sell a punch. I will talk more about how to do this correctly later.

- **Kick:** While you have to be flexible to do a kick, kicks are more flexible than punches. They can be a quick snap kick at an enemy's torso, a **sweep** at the legs to cause the enemy to lose balance and fall, or a **flying kick** attack—a dramatic mid-air cartwheel attack or a flurry of kicks like Chun-Li's famous *Hyakuretsu Kyaku* attack. Kicks provide a little more distance between the player and the enemy than a punch and often cause knockback. Because kicking offers so many variations in fighting games, entire games like *DiveKick* (2013) have been built around it.

- **Knock-up** and **juggling:** An especially powerful attack, known as a **launcher,** can hit an enemy so hard he goes flying up into the air. Depending on the time it takes the enemy to come back down, the player can jump into the air, intercepting him, and repeatedly attack to keep the enemy suspended in air, helpless to defend himself. The *Devil May Cry* series allows player character Dante to use his pistols and swords in several combinations to perform a spectacular array of juggling moves.

- **Stealth kill:** This quick attack is used to kill or disable an enemy in one move without alerting other enemies nearby. These moves are usually performed from a crouch or cover position or by positioning the player behind their target. They often use quick timer event-style prompts to activate and reward players with dramatic enemy kills. Make sure that stealth kills can be done only under certain conditions (in the right position, while under cover, while in shadow); otherwise, players will constantly use them over regular attacks as an exploit. Don't let a cool move become stale to the players.

- **Grapple:** This move is similar to a stealth kill in that a player can activate it under specific circumstances. A grapple is achieved when the character grabs another character to detain him and execute an additional attack. Grappling used to be rare early on in games because it was hard to program the collision needed to make a grapple look convincing. However, many wrestling games have perfected the grapple, and the move has found its way into more fighting and action games. Just as with grabbing items, you should make it easy for players to grab and release their opponents. Many games make this a context-sensitive move, as in Batman's interrogation move, which grabs an enemy and transitions into cutscenes of Batman demanding information from the enemy. The grapple is also the basis for a **piledriver attack,** in which the enemy is grabbed upside-down and driven head-first into the ground. Ow! That's gotta hurt!

- **Throw:** Throws are used to toss an enemy away from the player. The player grabs the enemy and then tosses him away in a desired direction. A throw can be used defensively, giving the player a little more time to prepare for the next attack, to clear some space when surrounded by foes, or as a way to set up another attack while the enemy is stunned on the ground. Throws can be used to toss ene- mies off ledges or platforms, often to their death, and some games like *Marvel's Midnight Suns* (2022) where players can use throws to toss enemies into traps.

- **Slap:** A slap is used to stun rather than do damage. Slap fights aren't very common in gaming, but *Rose & Camellia* (2007) features Victorian-era ladies slapping the heck out of each other. As in *Rose & Camellia,* an especially good slap reaction should really extend the enemy's neck and head to make the player really feel the sting. If your slap stuns an enemy, don't forget the stunned woozy stance, dancing stars, or tweeting birds flitting around the enemy's head. Slapping the ground is known as a **ground pound.** In this move, the player smashes his fists into the ground Hulk-style, causing all standing enemies to lose their balance and fall to the ground. Ground pounds have big wind-ups and dramatic reactions, sending people, vehicles, and even stationary objects flying.

- **Block** and **Cancel:** Are you just going to take all those punches, kicks, and slaps? Of course not! Blocks and cancels allow the player (or the enemy) to keep from taking damage. Whereas a block stops an enemy's attack (sometimes at the risk of being thrown), a cancel (also known as an **interrupt**) actually interrupts the animation of an attack, allowing the opponent to make an attack of their own. Cancel systems are often used in conjunction with the blocking system, allowing the player to cancel out their own block move to perform a quick attack or one that takes advantage of an opening in the enemy's attack animation.

■ **Parry** and **Counter:** While blocks prevent damage, parries allow the player to stop the attack, often stunning, disabling, or even disarming the enemy. Counters allow the player to not only stop the attack, but also strike back with an attack of their own! Action games like the *Batman: Arkham* series and *Marvel's Spider-Man* series warn the player of an incoming attack so the player can perform a counter move.

■ **Focus attack:** Introduced in *Street Fighter IV,* focus moves allow the player to "charge up" an attack, which does major damage to the enemy upon release. There are often multiple stages to a focus attack, each level doing progressively more damage and allowing the player to follow up the attack with more attacks. However, focus attacks aren't always invincible; they can be "broken" by special **armor break** moves.

■ **Taunt:** When your opponent won't fight you like a man (using a strategy known as **"turtling"**), you have no choice but to taunt him. Most taunts just mock your opponent, trying to make him angry enough to attack. Sometimes taunts can increase the player's health, decrease an opponent's power meter, or even cause damage like Pyro's Hadouken taunt in *Team Fortress 2.*

And a One and a Two...

Timing is one of the major keys to great combat. When the player presses a button, the character should immediately perform the attack. If you want your combat animations to feel smooth, you must strive to have your game run at 60 frames per second (fps). While many games run satisfactorily at 30 fps, lagging, and stuttering that can happen at these lower frame rates will really impact your player's combat experience. Don't waste time with long and elaborate wind-up animations. If you do this, it will throw off the player's timing and they may end up missing or striking when they don't want to. Quick moves can be rapidly done in succession, but they tend to lead to button mashing.

When designing combat for touchscreens or motion controls, keep the moves localized. Don't expect the player to stretch all the way across the screen or room. Give the player lots of opportunities to stretch and take a break.

Lunges are more fluid thrusts that return the character back to their original standing position. By combining quick strikes and lunges, you can create a **combat chain** that will keep the player's basic attack from feeling boring.

To create a combat chain, create three or more attack moves that will run one after another. If the player presses the attack move once, play the first animation. If the player presses the button again within a short (usually within a second) time period, the player character goes into a second attack move. Usually, this second attack move deals more damage, so there is an advantage for the player to "chain" these attacks together. A third attack will do even more damage, and so on.

first button press   second button press   third button press

If the player is allowed to land multiple hits in a row, make sure your animation (or game code) also moves the player character forward; otherwise, when the enemy is knocked back, the player won't be able to land the next attack in the chain. The hero in the following image misses because he doesn't translate forward. His attack succeeds only when he shifts forward.

Okay, remember a few paragraphs ago when I said that you shouldn't do elaborate wind-up animations? I meant it, but only then. Elaborate wind-ups are awesome because they lead to powerful attacks that can knock a player into the air or chop an enemy in two! These moves work great when the player is wielding an oversized or heavy weapon. Because of the long wind-up, the player is forced to risk the wait for the reward of landing a more powerful attack! Risk versus reward. Remember it. It's gonna be big.

Speaking of rewards, use particle and visual effects to make attacks feel more dynamic and rewarding. Use "slice streaks" on sword attacks and speed lines for dash moves like those seen in the *Onimusha* games. Or resort to those old standbys, the fire trails and blood splatters. If an attack is going to hurt, you can make the character's hands or weapon burst into flame, arc with lightning, or shine with mystical rays of light. Be big, be dynamic, and be dramatic! Give big action moves like ground pounds and smashing uppercuts big screen effects that fill the screen with debris, dust, screen flashes, and other eye-catchers. The more spectacular, the better!

The Big Finish

The most spectacular move in video games is the **super move.** These spectacular show-stopping attacks are often performed at the end of a combo chain or are the super moves originally found in fighters and JPRGs. They have blasted into other genres, making the final move as awesome as possible. Here are a few things you need to perform a super move:

- Super moves almost always require a charge to activate. The player must work up to earning the right to execute a super move.

- Super moves require a specific chain of controls. The moves are so awesome that the player shouldn't be able to press one button to perform it. They're going to have to earn it by completing a series of moves leading up to the super move.

- When the player finally performs the super move, stop the action, and focus the player's attention on what's going on: dim the screen, drop out the background, bring in other characters. Games like *Guilty Gear, Super Smash Bros.*, the *Marvel vs. Capcom* series, and the *Final Fantasy* series have particularly cool super moves that you can look to for inspiration.

- Super moves require super visual effects. The screen should light up when the player is executing a super move, so much so that even the receiver of the beatdown should be able to appreciate the spectacle.

- Super moves do lots of damage or finish off the opponent. They're not called **"finishing moves"** for nothing!

- Super moves should award extra points or a bonus of some sort on execution. They're a great way to reward a player an achievement.

- Super moves (almost) never miss. In fighting games, the opposing player should have an opportunity to counter a super move. There's nothing more satisfying than turning the tables on someone who thinks they have you dead to rights.

- If you use a super move in a multiplayer game, make sure there is a pause afterward, so the other players aren't unfairly penalized by the delay.

So, what happens when that super move or any attack actually connects? Well, as I mentioned earlier, a strike without a reaction animation from the enemy doesn't feel as though the player has hit anything. It's as if the attack is merely skipping off the surface of the enemy. If you don't have enemy reaction animations, at least have visual effects and sound effects that indicate a successful hit has landed. Powerful sound effects make attacks feel more rewarding. Vocal reactions such as a big "Oof!" from enemies are always satisfying!

Exaggerate the impact of a powerful hit to heighten the feeling of strength of the attack and increase drama. The enemy should react to wherever they've been hit. Got cracked in the coconut? The enemy's head (and some teeth) should fly. Kick out their leg and a bone should splinter, or the enemy should at least topple to the ground. This kind of animation is getting easier to do within the game code using rag doll physics systems like Havok and PhysX, but sometimes nothing beats good old-fashioned key frame animation.

If conflict is drama, then combat should be a freakin' opera complete with flying, spear-carrying Valkyries and a glass-shattering fat lady! Hype up that drama! A particularly powerful strike should be accompanied with a camera shake, a rumble from the controller's actuator, or combat slowing down to show off the power of the hit. Many games, from *Call of Duty* to *Peggle*, use slow motion to indicate that the player has defeated the last of the enemies in a combat encounter.

Before I forget, here's a pearl of wisdom: close battles are more exciting. Don't get me wrong, kicking hordes of enemies' butts can be quite satisfying, but just make sure that your player is evenly matched to their skill level for the majority of the game.

You can really pull out all the stops if you use a **cinematic finishing move** such that the action slows or freezes and the camera pans around the action. These finishes are frequently seen in fighting games like the *Guilty Gear* and *Mortal Kombat* titles, but they've crept into other action games because they just look so darn cool! This happened because of this **very important thing:**

PEOPLE WANT TO PLAY GAMES THAT MAKE THEM LOOK COOL

And nothing makes a player look cooler than a combo chain and a finishing move. Just look at the Mighty Bedbug in action here. You have to admit that pressing button prompts to create a choreographed combat sequence makes the battle look spectacular.

Case in point: Batman's combat in *Batman: Arkham Asylum* relies on QTEs to choreograph combat moves rather than leaving the player to flounder around on their own. Why? Because Batman would never miss a punch. Why should the player? The result? When the player successfully does the correct combat sequence, the player feels like an expert of combat—just like Batman.

Live by the Sword...

There has been a long history of heroes with signature weapons such as King Arthur wielded Excalibur, the Monkey King fought with Ruyi Jingu Bang, Thor clobbered trolls with Mjolnir, and Honjo Shigenaga defeated armies with the Honjo Masamune.

Video game characters are no different. These new heroes have their own signature weapons. For example, Link wields the Master Sword, Kratos thrashes monsters with his Leviathan Axe, An Infinity Spartan-IV brandishes their plasma sword against the Covenant, and The Chosen Undead uses Murakumo against Lothric Knights.

No matter what the weapon—swords, axes, daggers, hammers, clubs, chain-blades, staffs, boomerang, nunchucks—you want to give your own hero a signature weapon. The weapon and how they fight with it becomes an extension of the character's personality. Your character's weapon is going to dictate how they fight. Rygar's throwable shield creates a different combat experience than Big Daddy's melee drill. Even if your hero uses an unconventional weapon like a giant spatula or bubble wand, you should have a variety of attacks and moves that the player can perform with them. The more original and memorable, the better!

Often in games, the camera is farther back so the player doesn't get a good look at their weapon. Give them an opportunity to see it up close. This can be done when the weapon is first awarded to the player or through an inventory screen where the player can rotate and examine the weapon.

When designing how a weapon is used, think about its speed, range, the damage it does, and what other effects it may have, such as fire or poison. If a weapon is upgradable, make sure the effects are seen on the weapon. Merely adding a +3 to the stats doesn't provide the player with the gameplay information and visual rewards that they deserve.

While the player is swinging a weapon around, be mind-ful of it penetrating through objects. That just looks bad. Instead, have weapons respond to the world, such as rebounding off stone or metal surfaces or blades sinking into wooden ones. Be aware of the flipside of this: that the player's weapon will rebound off any non-breakable item in the world. Carefully design your combat environments to use this to the player's advantage and disadvantage. For example, a hero would learn they can't swing their giant axe around in an arena filled with unbreakable stone pil-lars lest they risk rebounding off them, which would give the skeletons a chance to attack.

Don't forget the player character can use impromptu weapons as well, including props or objects such as lead pipes, chairs, or even cars! Make it easy for players to find and pick up these items; provide on-screen prompts if you have to.

What's another way to make the player look like an expert? Use a **lock-on system.** *Mark of Kri* (2002) had an innovative lock-on system that had players use the DuelShock controller's analog stick to do a "radar-style" sweep to target a sequence of enemies that the players could program. This technique was patented by the game's creators.

The *Legend of Zelda* games have a particularly good lock-on system in which players can lock on to the enemy closest/in front of them with a button press and flick the analog stick to select the next one over to the right or left. The characters can still perform sidestep and backup while locked on. As long as the button remains pressed, the player is locked on to an enemy. As each enemy is dispatched, the targeting system latches on to the next available enemy. Lock-on systems require HUD visuals to help players track their targets. Here are some examples:

floor marker   pointer arrow   glowing aura   health bar

Even easier to operate than lock-on systems are **auto-targeting weapons.** These can be "fire and forget" missiles or projectiles like those seen in SHUMPs or they can be AI driven weapons like War-Machine's auto-turret in *Fortnite* or *Helldiver II's* AC8 Autocannon. With auto-targeting, the player doesn't have to think about where to aim or be pointed in the same direction as the target. The gun automatically targets an enemy and blasts away. While powerful, this kind of AI driven weapon can be foiled by fast moving enemies or obstacles in the environment that block its line of sight.

Auto-targeting can also be used as a handicap for, shall we say, less skillful gamers. This type of auto-targeting automatically nudges the aim of the weapon toward the enemy. In extreme cases, the weapon actually "snaps" to aim directly at the enemy. All the player has to do is pull the trigger. They literally can't miss.

Now You Have to Kiss Me

Letting the player miss isn't such a bad thing. The player will be forced to become more skilled with their attacks, which will make them feel like more of a cool dude as he masters combat timing. If the player just doesn't get it, you can always increase an enemy's collision dynamically if the player misses or dies too many times in a row. Another option is that you can offer to drop the game down to a lower difficulty setting. Do whatever you can to keep your players playing.

Let's Get Defensive

If you learn any martial art, you quickly are taught that defensive moves are just as important as attacking. The goal in a real-life fight[4] is to NOT get hit. Why should video games be any different? Allow your players moves that give them options for retreating or avoiding damage, and ones that can be combined with combat moves for quicker or more powerful attacks.

---

[4] Not that I'm advocating fighting in the real world: remember, the first rule of fight club is...oops, I've already said too much.

Dodges and **rolls** allow players to get the heck out of dodge and quickly move out of the way of attacks. They should be quick and easy to perform too: a button presses and single control stick move. Mind your metrics and keep an eye on your movement lengths, so the player doesn't roll off a platform or the edge of the world or fighting arena. A dodge move is done as a reflex to another danger. Don't turn a defensive maneuver into a disadvantage. Make sure your dodge lets the player get completely clear of wide-range attacks and longer-reaching weapons like halberds and huge swords, or radius-based attacks like explosions and magic spells; otherwise, you might be doing what, in *WOW*, they call "the graveyard hustle."

After the player does a dodge, there should be a beat to allow them to get back on their feet. Not only does this beat give the player a chance to reorient themselves, but it keeps them from using the dodge as a movement exploit.

Allow players to use dodges and rolls to get past hazards. These movements add a nice moment of tension when the player character is dashing through a closing door or rolling under a swinging blade. But be careful. During a roll or dash, the camera tends to collide with whatever the player is trying to avoid. I don't suggest having the camera pass through the hazard (that looks sloppy) or having the camera dip down with the player (because that gets disorienting). Consider the camera locking in place as the player dodges and then have it "catch up" with the player when they've cleared the obstacle.

Dashes are forward moves that can be used for defense or attack. Like dodges, dashes should be very quick to perform. Many action games like *Hades* (2020) and *Ghostrunner* (2020) have dash moves that can be upgraded with more powerful sword or punch moves. Even your basic dash move should do something besides moving the player. You want a dash to feel quick and powerful. And fast. And dare I say, dashing?

The player should be able to use the dash to ram into enemies or smash breakable objects. Even though a dash targets one enemy, you can have the player's momentum continue to have them hit several enemies at once or create a "sonic boom" to send bad guys flying! Whee!

While generally used for traversal, **jump** moves can be combat moves, too. Where would Mario be without his famous **"butt bounce"** attack? The collision zone should be like a good pair of pants: there should be plenty of room in the butt. Don't make these pixel-perfect attacks. After the attack hits, apply **recoil bounce** to move the player a short distance away so the player doesn't land on or next to the enemy and take damage. If the enemy hasn't been killed by the butt bounce, minimize risk to the player by putting the enemy in a stunned state.

Many games allow the player to maneuver during this recoil bounce to let them chain bounce attacks off the heads of multiple enemies! Make sure you award an escalating bonus for each additional bad guy bounced. Make it a big moment for the player: they've just done something cool!

You don't have to be a short Italian plumber to do jump attacks. Weapon-wielding tough guys can do these moves, too. Just make sure you follow these guidelines:

- Make sure the player's maximum jump is taller than the tallest enemy you can jump attack. Otherwise, you'll be colliding with the enemy's head or shoulders, which will look strange.

- When the player lands, apply the same rules as an attack impact: stop the action for a beat by freezing the enemy or world's action, generate explosive effects, rumble the controller—do anything to make the attack feel more powerful.

- Even if the player misses, the strike could generate some radial effect such as a stun or knockback for nearby enemies.

- Allow the player a quick recovery; they'll want to get back into action immediately.

- Then again, you could give the player a delay as part of the risk/reward of performing the attack. For example, Mario firmly plants his butt into the ground after a butt bounce. If he misses an enemy, he's vulnerable for a beat to getting hurt by an enemy.

If jumping is a little too frivolous for your big bad space marine or soldier, you can have them **vault** over obstacles to add variety to battlefield movement. Vaulting works well with cover systems (see following sections) and ducking. *Gears of War 2* (Microsoft Games Studio, 2008) provides players with a prompt to notify them when they can vault over a low wall.

Dodging the Bullet

Combining a dodge with an attack, **bullet time** was first introduced in the 1999 movie *The Matrix*. Video game developers immediately fell in love with the visual of the player character leaping through the air, avoiding bad guys' bullets while blasting away with his own slow-motion projectiles. *Max Payne* (2001) was the first game to use bullet time, and it's been a staple of 3D person action games ever since. It doesn't matter if you call it Reaction Time (*Mirror's Edge*), Reflex (*FEAR*), DeadEye (*Red Dead Redemption*), or Tequila Time (*John Woo's Stranglehold*); here are a few tips when designing bullet time for your games:

- **Let the player know it's started.** Flash the screen with an effect, dial down the color saturation, play a distinctive "activation" sound effect—any clue to let the player know they've entered this hyper-reality state.

- **Outnumber the player.** Bullet time works best when the odds are against the player, and all seems lost. Being able to take out individual foes amid the chaos of a large gun or fistfight makes the player feel unstoppable—at least until their meter runs out.

- **The player should still move faster than everyone else.** Let the player perform actions before any of the other characters can. You want the player to feel as if they've got the upper hand on the bad guys.

- **Give opportunities for precision shooting.** *Max Payne 3*'s bullet time increases Max's move set with each accurate shot the player makes. *Red Dead Revolver* lets the player shoot hats off heads and guns out of hands as well as precisely target lethal shots during DeadEye mode.

- **Make the soundtrack match the action.** Slow down the music or make the sound muffled as if it were running in slow motion.

- **You can never have too many effects.** Bullet casings, blooming muzzle flashes, exploding heads, or shattering glass, the star of bullet time is all the debris and flash that come with seeing the world in slow motion.

- **Make bullet time a "sometimes" mechanic or save it for special occasions.** If the player can use bullet time everywhere, they will abuse it. Limit its use by requiring the player to build up a charge or collect a power-up.

- **Save it for "super dramatic" moments.** The villain has a gun to the president's head, and you have only seconds to make the shot. High noon has struck, and you're surrounded by banditos. You and your partner have accidentally stumbled onto a gangland crime scene. Is your superhero punching out the last baddie during a combat arena round? That's when you want to break out the bullet time.

On Guarding

WATCH OUT!

*That's how fast you have to **be** to respond to an attack, so **you better** make sure your block **can be executed quickly**!* Blocks can be either general or positional.

General blocks are found in action games and are generally a single button press to cross weapons, cross arms, or lift a shield to block an incoming attack. These all-purpose blocks can be used for any situation or enemy. It doesn't matter whether your shield is a one-handed buckler or tall Roman Scuta; the function is still the same: the player blocks an attack with the press of a button, holding it aside during the rest of combat.

Don't underestimate the use of sound effects in conjunction with a block. A nice loud "CLANG!" lets the player know they've successfully executed a block. Sound cues provide important information to the player and help to differentiate between a miss and a block. Have the blocked hit create some sparks or some other effect (as long as it's not blood; you'll want to save that for when the character is hit) visually clue in the player. Some blocks displace the player backwards a little bit to make them need to move in again to hold their ground. Giving a successful block a disadvantage is a bit of a jerk move, but if you want to, then go ahead—it's your game.

Positional blocks correlate with a particular elevation and require a stick move and/or button press to block at the appropriate height, whether it's high or low. You find these blocks most often in fighting games. You'll have to decide whether or not a player can hold a block. Arm blocks are usually quick and drop down after a second or so. Other fighting and action games allow the player to hold the block indefinitely, or at least until an enemy performs an attack that breaks the player's block or knocks them off their feet. Shield blocks can last longer, allowing the player to "hide" behind the shield for an extended period of time. Some designers don't like letting the player camp a block, but that can be circumnavigated by using breakable shields, unblockable attacks or giving enemies knockback attacks. Oh, and don't let your shield sort through[5] the ground when the player crouches to block low attacks.

---

[5] "Sorting" is the phenomenon when one piece of game geometry passes through another, giving the appearing of the item being "half-stuck" through or into a wall or another object. Think of Kitty Pryde's phasing power in the X-Men, and you'll get the idea. I'm sure that the term "sorting" has to do with something programmer related.

As a designer, you need to decide whether or not your shield is breakable. This decision will make a big difference in how the player uses it. In the first *Maximo* game, we had a breakable shield. The player was able to upgrade it to a stronger shield through the course of the game. However, because it was still a limited resource, we found that players were reluctant to use it, preferring to jump and dodge out of the way of attacks instead. In the sequel, we wanted to promote shield usage, so we made the shield unbreakable. Players were much happier to block because the worry of breakage was taken away. But shields aren't just for blocking anymore. You can use a shield to

- Clear obstacles when combined with a dash move

- Smash enemies at close range

- Throw as a short-range projectile

- Sled down steep inclines

- Protect from falling debris or lava when placed overhead

- Act as a crowbar to move large objects

- Protect from back-stabbing enemies when placed on the player's back

Heck, attach a shield to a chain like in *Rygar*, and it becomes a whole new weapon!

If a shield isn't enough protection, then **armor** will do the trick. There are several things to consider when giving the player armor. **Encumbrance** is one. The more armor the player wears, the slower (and noisier) they become. You usually find encumbrance in RPGs, not often in action games. It's fine if you are trying to be "realistic," but if your game's emphasis is on action and combat, not using it may be a better choice.

Perhaps your game makes a distinction between different parts of the body in combat. If so, you can use the "paper doll" approach to armor. The player has to armor their head, torso, arms, hands, legs, and feet. This feels more realistic and gives your player more items to buy and collect. However, it does require an interface—usually quite large, because it has to show the entire body. Make sure players can easily find, select, and change their armor. Also allow players to discard or sell unwanted armor as well.

Your hero has finally defeated the first boss and won their prize: a new suit of armor. Don't cop out and just give the player a +2-chainmail shirt. Whenever the player earns an armor upgrade, make it look dramatically different. For example, full plate looks substantially different (and cooler) than a leather jerkin. When you visually improve the player's armor, the player can tell their "rank" at a glance.

Give it a unique name, too, like the "Holy Armor of Protection" or "Dragon Scale Armor." This will make the player feel as if they've won something important and worth having.

But armor is not just for protection. Isaac's spacesuit in *Dead Space* has a health meter right down the spine. Players can check their status at a glance without the need for a HUD. *Ghosts 'N Goblins* also shows health status...but in reverse: as the armor pops off, the player gets closer to death. This is a good trick for enemies too because it lets the player know how many hits are left to defeat a foe.

Armor upgrades are a great way to give a player a new ability. Can't move that heavy block? This hydraulically powered armor can help them move it. It doesn't even have to be a "suit of armor." Mario's Tanooki[6] suit not only added protection, but also let him fly, grow, and turn into an invincible statue.

---

[6] Tanuki are Japanese raccoon dogs. Mario wears Tanuki footie pajamas with raccoon ears. It's adorable. Really.

What's great about armor is that it's an easy way for players to customize their character without changing the base model—depending on the armor, of course. Chain mail wouldn't change the model, but plate mail armor or a full-head helmet would. The advantage to armor upgrades is that when another player sees your cool new helmet, they're gonna want one too. It's a great way to motivate players to spend more time seeking out cool loot in your game. It doesn't have to be armor; it can be hats, unique weapons, or mounts. The more unique gear you allow players to earn, find, and buy, the better.

State of the Art Bang Bang

Ooooh! Guns, guns, guns!
        —Clarence Boddicker (RoboCop)

Shooting is simple. Aim the gun, pull the trigger. Right? But let's look at some of the most popular multiplayer shooters and see how wide they vary from each other:

- **Quake** has maps that promote linear action and predictable looping movement patterns. Weapon and armor pickups can change the dynamics of the action in a heartbeat.

- **Halo** is played more like a sport with game-like modes of play. The rhythm of the action is slower than many shooters, partially due to the player's regenerating health, and promotes "attack then retreat" strategies. Vehicles play a big part in the gameplay as well.

- The **Call of Duty** series has a multiplayer mode that concentrates on short-range combat with intense action. Players can concentrate on upgrading their weapons and characters like in an RPG.

- ***Team Fortress 2*** resembles an RPG, but the players assume widely varying skill-based roles. The game modes promote teamwork over single player actions. The turnover time from "play to death" is very quick compared to the preceding games because players can be killed with a single shot.

- The ***Left4Dead*** series is also all about teamwork; in fact, you can't win without it. While most multiplayer shooters match opponents one-to-one, *Left4Dead* pits a handful of players against an endless horde of zombies. Game modes resemble stories more than in other shooters.

Even in games where shooting isn't the main focus of play, **ranged combat** can immediately change the dynamic of the game. This is why I recommend that if a game isn't a shooter, guns should be saved until later in the game. Let players get used to their moves and attacks without a gun first. When you feel that they've learned all they can, go ahead and arm them.

Creative Director Hardy LeBel, who has designed many successful shooters like *Halo: Combat Evolved* and *SOCOM 3,* says that ranged combat is about building a distinctive rhythm. Several factors influence that rhythm, such as targeting methods, reload times, weapon fire rate, weapon accuracy, rate of fire and lethality, the availability of ammunition, the availability of area-of-effect weapons like grenades, player health mechanics, and so on. Even level design, AI behavior, and mechanics contribute to that rhythm. Whew! That's a lot to digest at once, so let's start with the **three A's**: action, aiming, and ammo.

Action is the loading, firing, and unloading of a gun. Here are some questions you need to ask about a weapon's action:

- How quickly can the player reload his gun?

- Does the player need to reload with a button press, or does it occur automatically? Does reloading in VR mimic real world loading a bullet or shell with a hand gesture or by cocking a shotgun? You can create some great risk/reward gameplay around reloading a gun because the player is vulnerable during loading (such as in *Gears of War*, where a properly executed manual reload is faster, but a botched one is even slower and leaves the player defenseless for longer).

- Is there a limit to the ammo? Does the player even need to reload the gun at all?

- What is the gun's rate of fire? A faster firing gun is going to use ammo quicker than a single shot weapon. Can the weapon be fired one shot at a time or in bursts?

- Does the firing bloom obscure the player's view?

- Can a shot take out more than one target at a time?

- Does an attack cause ongoing damage like fire or poison?

Aiming is how the player sights a target. Aiming is a huge issue in games. It can make or break a shooter. Early shooters relied on the players' reflexes and skill in positioning the cursor over the target and pulling the trigger at the right time. Until *Halo: Combat Evolved* (Microsoft, 2001), the most successful first-person shooters were played on PCs. This was partially because of the ease of aiming with a mouse. To help players manage the tricky task of aiming with the Xbox's analog sticks, the game used aim assist such that the cursor became "sticky" when it was moved over a target. This made it easier for the players to lock on to a target. Since *Halo*, other aim assists have been developed, such as **reticule snapping**, in which the reticule immediately snaps to a target if it gets near, and **free aiming,** in which players can shoot different parts of the target to gain different effects.

No matter what type of aiming method you use (aim assist, auto-aim, free aiming, and so on), you need to design and implement targeting mechanics for the tastes of your target audience:

- How does the player aim? Is there a scope? How much of the player's view does the scope obstruct?

- How does depth of field affect aiming? An effective visual trick is to have far-away objects that are blurry suddenly become clear when viewed through a long-range sight.

- Is aiming manual? Does the gun have drift? Can the player steady their shot? Some games allow the snipers to "hold their breath" to prevent drifting. From how far away can a player make a shot?

- Is aiming automatic? Is there a quick-fire mode? Is there an auto-aiming/lock-on system?

- When you fire the gun, does it kick, throwing off the player's aim? Does it rise like a Thompson submachine gun?

- Are there systems to improve the player's aiming such as laser pointers, bullet time, or heat-seeking ammo?

- Can the player move while aiming? Are there limitations to where the player can aim, like diagonally or overhead?

- Does the scope detect other ways of seeing the target such as IR, motion detection, or heartbeat? Can the gun be modified in any way to become silenced or have additional add-on weapons like grenade launchers or bayonets?

- Can the player use shooting for puzzle solving or trick shooting? Shoot targets? Shoot locks off doors? Shoot the gun out of the hands of enemies? Ricochet a bullet into an enemy?

- Can the player disable the targeting mechanism or replace it with another style?

The targeting reticule and/or the iron sights on your weapons should be among the most sophisticated feedback mechanisms in your game. They will likely need to communicate aim, bullet spread, recoil, jamming, overheat, ammo, successful hits versus near misses, friend or foe, and the list goes on and on. And they will need to accomplish that while remaining useful and unobtrusive to the player.

Ammo is what the player shoots. Ammo raises its own questions:

- Where and how is ammo carried? Is there a limit to the amount of ammo carried by a player? Do you need the right ammo for the right gun?

- Does ammo have any special effects like incendiary, poisonous, heat-seeking, or armor-piercing properties?

- What happens when a shot misses a target? Does it impact something in the environment? Does it affect that item? Break glass? Chip plaster? Ricochet off metal?

Put that thing away!
You're gonna get us killed!

Here are a few more tricks to make your gunplay more effective:

- Accentuate the excitement and danger of a gunfight with sound: weapon firing, bullet impacts, enemy gunfire, whizzing bullets, and so on.

- Play the SFX of the gunshot and bullet impact at full volume regardless of the target's distance to the player. This will let the player know whether they scored a successful shot. Let the player hear their target reacting to being shot. In multiplayer games, this should be localized to the player who shot only. Otherwise, you will be aurally bombarded by every other player's sound effects!

- Don't forget the weapon visual effects. A weapon's muzzle flash. Spent shells kicking out. Smoke from the barrel. These all make the experience more realistic.

- In general, players like gunfights at shorter ranges because they are more exciting. Closer range not only makes it easier for players to aim but allows them to see if they have successfully hit their target.

- Regardless of how graphic your weapon hits are, show some sort of impact effect when a bullet hits its target—from sparks to explosions to spraying gore.

- Needless to say, level design IS game design when it comes to building the rhythm of ranged combat. If you design spaces that are long, open corridors and you have a high-lethality combat model, players will play cautiously. If you have lots of cover and break line of sight frequently PLUS use a regenerating health model, gunfights will feel like swirling dogfights as players engage and disengage to heal.

A great deal of time and writing could be dedicated to designing the targeting reticules for shooting, but suffice it to say this **very important thing** applies:

PLAY THE BEST SHOOTERS AND STUDY THEIR SOLUTIONS

Taking some time to deconstruct the mechanics and behaviors of the best-in-breed games will add immeasurably to your own gameplay.

Mr. LeBel leaves us with this important thought: "In general, players expect ranged combat to feel powerful and satisfying. It's an easy mistake to try and make ranged weapons weak to help offset the perception of too much power in the hands of the player; fight that impulse and try to remember to be 'generous' to the player[s], and they will thank you for it."

The Best Gun for You

When you're designing guns, even if you are creating made-up weapons, it's helpful to start with their real-life counterparts; after all, weapons are built for particular roles that can directly apply to their use in your game. But that will get you only halfway there. You should consider thinking about them in terms of effectiveness.

zap pistol = good

zap rifle = better

blazer cannon = best

kill-o-zap = freakin' awesome

Balancing weapons can be tricky, especially if you're basing them on real-world equivalents. There are gun-nut players who have their own opinions about which gun is better and how they should perform. You could go crazy trying to please everyone, so base your weapons on what fits the needs of your game first. Here are some guidelines to get you started:

- **Pistols** fire in a straight line (unless you are Wesley Gibson from *Wanted*), which will dictate where you can shoot and whom you can shoot. A pistol shoots one enemy at a time unless your ammo pierces several enemies at once! That's going to keep the pace of shooting slow. Pistols usually require frequent reloading, too because their magazines carry from 6 to 15 rounds.

- **Rifles,** especially sniper rifles, mean the player has to aim and shoot. You usually can't fire from the hip with a rifle. That means the player is going to be vulnerable and usually looking down at a scope, which means tunnel blindness. Sounds like a good opportunity for an enemy to sneak up. Many rifles carry large quantities of ammo: some have drum magazines that hold up to 100 rounds.

- **Shotguns** and **flamethrowers** fire in a cone, rather than a straight line. The cone is shorter range than a pistol or rifle but can hit several targets at once. Both weapons do high damage to targets when hit at close range. Shotguns carry less ammo and have a slower rate of fire than guns or rifles, and flamethrowers go through propellant at a fast rate. A flamethrower's blast can be maintained for an extended time and does residual burning damage to an enemy.

- **Automatic weapons** allow you to fire quickly, but accuracy goes out the window. This high rate of fire also uses up ammo fast, regardless of larger magazine sizes. Designing your machine gun to have a little kick, drift, or spray will not only make it feel real, but push the player to master using the weapon accurately. Are your automatic weapons one handed or two? Can the player use two at the same time? This will determine what other actions the player can do while shooting.

- **Heavy weapons** pack a big punch, but usually take a while to warm up or cool down. The Heavy's **minigun** in *Team Fortress 2* takes a few beats to start spinning, but the player has a way to keep the gun spinning even when he isn't shooting with it. The disadvantage is that enemies hear you coming a mile away. **Grenade launchers** are also harder to aim but do big damage to an enemy when they explode. They also let you shoot at enemies that might be hiding around a corner or a shield! There is an element of risk in using a grenade launcher as the projectile bounces around after shooting, which can make things dangerous for the player as well as his target. Magazine sizes vary from a dozen grenades to hundreds of rounds for fast-shooting miniguns. **Rocket launchers** (and their sci-fi cousin, the laser ray) allow the player to make a one-hit kill at the cost of a longer reload or recharge time. They often have limited ammo but work as effectively against troops and armored vehicles. In VR games and some combat simulations, these heavier weapons cause recoil or are a little harder to aim unless you take a moment to steady it.

No matter what the weapon is, think about its range, speed, and strength. You can use an attack matrix like the following one to track these values and compare and contrast your weapons for maximum variety.

| Weapon | Range | | |
	Short	Medium	Long
Dual pistols	Strong	Weak	N/A
Assault rifle	Strong but slow	Very strong	Weak
Shotgun	Very strong	N/A	N/A
Sniper rifle	N/A	Medium	Very strong

Notice how there is very little overlap in weapon attributes, and any overlap that does exist has a disadvantage like shooting/reloading speed. Keeping the weapons distinct will help in making the game feel well-rounded.

Ranged combat weapons aren't always guns. Fantasy games, for example, have a wide variety of projectiles, from arrows to magic missiles to cones of cold. In the case of things like **bows**, gravity should be considered. Bows tend to shoot arrows in an arc rather than in a straight line.

Regardless of the genre or the type of weapon, as long as you design your ranged combat with the guidelines set down for guns—range, damage, and the three A's—you should be fine.

One last question to ask in a multiplayer game is whether or not you should allow **friendly fire.** Your choice totally depends on the gameplay mode. Having friendly fire in a player versus player mode seems much more logical than in a cooperative mode. Whatever your choice, allow the player to turn it on or off.

Oh, no. You've just run out of bullets. Now what?

Players feel incredibly powerless when they're playing a shooter and have nothing to shoot with! So, give your player a melee weapon that is always available. It can be a knife, fists, or even a pistol whip or clubbing attack with a rifle butt. Giving the player this option to bash the baddie allows things to feel fair and realistic. The *Gears of War* games don't mess around in this department: they have a chainsaw mounted onto their gun!

They say you can never have enough guns, but you don't want your player to be carrying around a golf bag full of firearms. Many games limit weapons to a main gun and a side arm. But if you do that, you'll need to be able to switch between them quickly, preferably with a single button press. *Call of Duty: Modern Warfare 2* allows you to draw your side arm faster than you can raise your rifle, which is helpful for those situations requiring a quick shot.

Since *Gears of War* came out, many action games have incorporated a **cover system.** This allows the player a way not only to take cover against a surface or barricade to avoid being shot, but also to fire "blindly" or in a limited manner at the enemy. The player is often penalized for avoiding risk by not being able to aim while under cover. Cover systems usually require the player to press a button or issue a command to move in and out of this mode. Be careful that your cover system doesn't become too "sticky" so that it takes time and effort for the player to disengage from cover; otherwise, the player may be going into cover when they don't want to.

"I was going to wait for him to empty it before I said anything."

Run and Gun

There are many, many ways to shoot at things in video games: from a plane, from a train, out of a box, at a fox—you name it! Take a look at this image of a shooting gallery gameplay and notice all the elements in it:

1. Turret showing weapon and player

2. Shootable object containing reward or power-up

3. Ground-based target

4. Visual element that indicates why the player can't shoot "past the screen"

5. Aerial target (note the clear indication to the player that the target has been hit)

6. Smaller aerial target (generally worth more points)

7. Smaller ground target (also worth more points)

One of the main styles of shooting gameplay is the **shooting gallery.** In some shooting gallery type games, the player is locked to a single screen and lots and lots of enemies and targets come in and out of the screen, as in *Duck Hunt* and *Spooky Spirit Shooting Gallery.* **Mounted ranged combat** is this kind of shooting gallery-style gameplay, in which the players defend against waves of incoming enemies. Mounted ranged combat can take place in the middle of anywhere; it offers a change in gameplay styles and lets players shoot up lots and lots of things. Players will tend to fire constantly if the weapon has unlimited ammo or in short bursts if it doesn't. You can also get the players to fire in bursts if the weapon needs a cool-down time. To help players aim, add tracer bullets. Not only do these bullets look cool, but they will help players get "leads" on fast-moving enemies or ones with erratic movement patterns. Let players know the range of the weapon. If they can't reach a target, create a good visual justification as to why there are areas of the screen they can't hit.

Because both the target and the weapon move during **aerial combat** and **vehicular combat,** give the players opportunities to line up the target in their sights. If they have a chance to see the target coming, line up the target, and fire at it, they will feel in control. If too many targets are whipped by the players without giving them a chance to react, they will resort to firing blindly, which will make the experience seem mindless and frustrating. Adjust the speed of the targets or the craft either naturally or artificially to give the players ample shooting opportunities.

Another type of shooting gallery game is the **rail shooter,** in which the player is locked into a scrolling environment where lots and lots of enemies and targets pop up for the player to shoot. Rail shooters take movement (other than aiming and shooting) and camera control out of the player's hands so they can just concentrate on the action—as if the player were moving on a rail, hence the name. Clever, right? Games like *House of the Dead: Remake* (2022) and *Attack of the Movies 3D* (2010) are rail shooters.

A unique advantage of rail shooters is that the game developer has complete control over the game camera and the sequence of events. This allows the developer to create scripted action sequences and scares they know the player will experience, without worrying about the player moving the camera and missing the cool event.

In fact, some rail shooters bear more resemblance to a theme park **dark ride** like Disneyland's *Haunted Mansion*[7] than a video game. Now, interactive dark rides have started to appear in theme parks around the world,[8] completing the circle of inspiration from dark ride to video game to dark ride.

Speaking of haunted places—mansions or otherwise—if you want to scare players during a rail shooter, or any other type of game for that matter, here are a few tricks you can use:

1. **Let players know they're going to be scared.** Nothing builds fear like anticipation. If they know the game is going to scare them, they will be much more susceptible to being scared.

2. **Don't be afraid to use "cheap scares."** These are things like a banging shutter, a blast of steam, or a jumping cat. A fast-moving distraction will make players jump.

3. **Don't rely solely on darkness.** Players can turn up the contrast. Or they can play the game in a lit room. There are too many ways players can make your game not-so-scary, so don't rely on just one trick to create mood.

---

[7] This reminds me of the time Disneyland's *Haunted Mansion* literally became a shooter. In the summer of 1974, a Disneyland guest wielding a .22 pistol took a shot at one of the duelist ghosts in the Ballroom scene. The bullet made a hole in the giant pane of glass used to create the scene's pepper ghost illusion. The management was frantic. Originally, a helicopter had been needed to install the giant sheet of glass, and they'd have to rip the ceiling off the ride to replace it. However, a clever imagineer took one look at the spider-web cracks in the glass and slapped a rubber spider over the bullet hole. Voilà, problem solved! The spider is there to this day.

[8] On your next vacation, why not travel the world playing interactive dark rides? *Buzz Lightyear's Space Ranger Spin* (Walt Disney World, Florida), *Men in Black: Alien Attack* (Universal Studios, Florida), *Laser Raiders* (Legoland Windsor, UK), *Challenge of Tutankhamen* (Six Flags, Belgium), *Labyrinth of the Minotaur* (Terra Mitica Theme Park, Spain), and *Toy Story Midway Mania* (Disney's California Adventure) —all dark ride rail shooters.

4. **Sound is the scariest thing there is.** A player's mind is your most powerful weapon against them. Use sound to make players think there are things that aren't there, and soon enough they'll be jumping at any stray noise. It's even worse when they have to rely on sound to tell if something is coming, like the radio in *Silent Hill*.

5. **Don't stack scares.** If you constantly try to scare players, they aren't going to have time to relax. Only when they've relaxed between scares are they ready to be scared again. It's like a roller coaster: the lows are just as important as the highs.

6. **You can be gross, but don't be too gross.** Dead bodies and bloody or dirty environments in video games are missing two of the most important things that make them gross: touch and smell. If you rely too much on vile environments, players are going to get used to them. A small splash of blood in the middle of an otherwise clean room has far more impact than a room decorated with bodies that are strung up like Christmas ornaments.

7. **Boo!** (Did I scare you?) Nothing gets the blood going like something unexpectedly rushing in or leaping out at the players. If you really want to mess with the players' minds, let them hear a distinctive sound first before the scare happens. They'll get used to hearing that sound and start to panic when they hear it. Panicking almost certainly leads to player death.

8. **Surprise!** A surprise is like a scare but without shock or gruesome visuals. Sometimes a surprise can be that a single target explodes into three! Or a target that appears right in front of the player! A target can surprise a player by suddenly springing in the air or moving back and forth. Make the player look for targets in unexpected places (like the top and edges of the screen) to find the big point values.

When designing shooting gallery gameplay, give players time to recognize the target or threat, aim at it, and shoot at it. Enemies and targets can appear at close range, which surprises players, or long range, which gives players a chance to anticipate and aim at a target. Alternating between these two distances will make a shooting gallery more robust.

Not Just Shooting

You don't really need a gun or melee weapon to defeat enemies. There are so many ways; one hardly knows what to choose! The more variety you introduce into your combat, the more fun the players will have.

When players are throwing **grenades,** allow them to predict the arc. *Gears of War* and the *Uncharted* series use "throw path" targeting aids to assist players. In VR games, the speed at which the player moves their arm and the arc they move their hand should determine the distance and velocity of where the grenade goes. Don't neglect the effects when those suckers blow. When you blow up anything in a game, kick up dust and debris and blow props sky high to really sell the explosion.

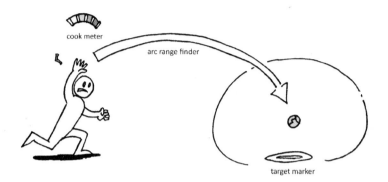

Throwing a grenade should always carry the risk or reward of having it accidentally go off if held for too long or even bounce back at the player. Soldiers "cook" their grenades by holding on to them after pulling the pin to make sure they go off where they land. *Helldivers 2* not only uses a HUD element to warn players of an incoming grenade but allows players to pick it up and throw it back! Remember that grenades can also be shot from rifles and launchers for greater accuracy and range.

Because many players duck back under cover after throwing a grenade, make sure you provide enough sound, visual, and controller rumble cues to inform players when a grenade detonates, even if they aren't looking at the place where it landed. If players get too close to an exploding grenade, don't hesitate to blow them up as well.

Sometimes you just need to blow up everything. It doesn't matter whether you're calling it carpet bombing or a magical meteor storm; **smart bombs** are great one-shot solutions to keep the baddies off your back, if only for a few seconds. Show players the controls for a smart bomb so they don't confuse it with a regular attack. When activated, smart bombs should destroy everything on-screen save the player. If there are destructible items, they should blow up, too.

You have a few options for ways players can activate a smart bomb, depending on how much tension you want to create. In *Defender*, the smart bomb is immediate, whereas in *R-Type*, players have to charge up the smart bomb before firing it. Let players know what they are working toward so they can make an accurate decision as to when to use it. Be careful that you don't let the bomb charge up too fast or used too frequently; otherwise, all the bad guys in your carefully designed combat encounters will be wiped out in the blink of an eye!

Wherever there are explosions, there is **fire.** Sometimes there's fire even without explosions—things just need to be burned. Fire creates great-looking visuals and lingering damage to enemies and environments. But fire takes no sides: players should get hurt by fire if they stray into it. The fire should eventually burn out so that players don't paint themselves into a napalm-colored corner.

Fire also means flamethrowers. The closer players are to the enemy, the more damage a flamethrower should do. Flamethrowers are the weapon of choice for players who don't like to aim. Allow them to "fire and forget" or "hose down" enemies with flame. Burning damage allows players an opportunity to turn away from one threat and address another. That doesn't mean they can't be attacked by a flaming enemy, however.

Don't forget to use fire-based weapons as a gameplay mechanic, too. Flaming swords and other weapons don't just do extra damage to ice-themed enemies; they can ignite braziers, detonate explosives, burn through rope, illuminate dark areas, or cauterize wounds. The gameplay possibilities are nearly endless.

Another lingering indirect attack is **poison.** Make sure you have an associated visual for poisoned items. A green gassy effect, a dripping blade, a hovering "death's head" effect—all are traditional video game indicators of poison. Players should be able to tell when they are wielding a poisoned item or have poisoned an enemy: make the visual unique and distinct. As a poisoned character loses health, make sure each increment that the poison takes has a clear sound effect and visual effect associated with it. You are creating a timer in which the players' focus will shift from regular gameplay to "find and administer the antidote." If the antidote is an inventory-based item, don't make it too hard for players to retrieve it. Even if poison is uncommon, make the antidote more common. There is no worse feeling in a video game than making players feel like death is inevitable. Always give them a fighting chance.

Another horrible feeling for players is to take away their control. While **stunning, knock-back, transformation, loss of balance,** and **sliding** are worthwhile tools to use in lieu of taking damage, the designer should use them judiciously.

- **Stun:** When hit by a stun, the player loses all control of the character for a short period of time, usually leaving the character in danger of being hit by an enemy attack or finishing move. Stuns are usually accompanied by visual (like cartoon stars or "tweeting birds") and sound effects.

- **Knockback:** The player is knocked back through the air a short distance and then falls to the ground. A knockback (or KB) can be lethal if a player is on a platform or next to a ledge. Be careful not to put the player into a situation in which they can be "double bolted"[9] by KBs.

- **Knockdown:** The player is knocked to the ground, which requires a second or two to get back up. While on the ground, the player is vulnerable to additional attacks. In some games, getting back up is automatic; in others it requires button mashing, stick waggling, or a QTE.

- **Latching on:** An enemy grabs or latches on to the player, pinning his arms and restricting his movement. Enemies can cause damage every second they are latched on. Enemies can be shaken off the player by waggling the controls or performing jump or spin moves.

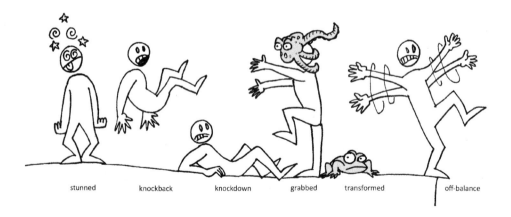

stunned   knockback   knockdown   grabbed   transformed   off-balance

---

[9] The term "double bolting" comes from the LEGO video games when a player is hit by an enemy and loses bolts, the game's unit of currency. The bolts disappear if not collected after a period of time. However, in some situations, the player is knocked by an enemy into another hazard or enemy, which causes more bolts to fly out of the player. The player is stunned by the attack and cannot regain control fast enough to collect any of the first bolts before they disappear, let alone the ones that were just knocked out of him. Thus, the player loses double the bolts from the initial attack.

- **Transformation:** The player has been hit by a magic spell that transforms the character into some other form. In *Ghosts 'N Goblins*, Arthur turned into a frog. In *Maximo: Ghosts to Glory*, the hero could be transformed into a hopping old man and a tottering baby. In all cases, the player's move set becomes limited; he cannot attack or jump and, in some cases, loses almost all control. During a transformation, game controls can be reversed to sow player confusion (for example, push controls left and the character moves right). While players might find this funny or surprising, I recommend ending the transformation quickly as the novelty wears off after the player loses control. Reserve transformations for special occasions because the players will tire of them if used too often.

- **Loss of balance:** This animation is used as a teeter move. The player briefly loses complete control as the character reacts to losing their balance. This works well as an indicator rather than a disabling move.

- **Sliding/skidding:** After a run, dash, or jump move, the character slides to regain their balance. While this animation adds quite a bit of personality to the character, it can be annoying, especially when it happens several times in a row as the player struggles to bring the character to a stop. Like a KB, a skid can slide a character right off the edge of a narrow platform.

Don't let enemies have all the fun! Design enemy-disabling attacks to give your players the advantage in combat. Use caution when creating attacks with these types of results, however. Consider what they add to the gameplay. Tell yourself this **very important thing:**

ALWAYS STRIVE TO ENABLE THE PLAYERS, EVEN WHEN YOU'RE DISABLING THEM

Remember, don't let enemies have all the fun! Design enemy-disabling attacks to give your players the advantage in combat. They'll thank you for it.

Dang it, Jones! Where *Doesn't* It Hurt?

For all this combat to mean anything, the player must have something to lose. That means **health** and **lives.**

To calculate the player's starting health, I suggest calculating in terms of the maximum damage the player can take. For example, at the beginning of the game, your hero can take 20 hits from enemies before losing a life and without replenishing health. Next, determine how much damage an average enemy's attack does. In this example, a normal hit will cause 10 **hit points** of damage. That means the player's starting health should be 10 times 20 hit points, which equals 200 health.

There are many ways to represent losing that health to the player. **Numbers** are simple and transparent but boring. They stand out against cluttered HUDs, like those found in MMOs and RPGs. Just keep the font legible.

A **health bar** doesn't take up much space running along the top or side of the screen. It can be framed with themed artwork to make it look more interesting and part of the HUD. However, telling when small amounts of damage have been taken can be difficult. A health bar can be segmented for readability.

If you're feeling artistic, **icons** can represent the player's health with simple visuals: human outlines that go from green to red (*WWE Smackdown*), crystal globes of blood (*Diablo*), or hearts (*Legend of Zelda*).

Some platform games use a **companion character** as the player's health meter. For example, *Crash Bandicoot* is followed by a tiki head that loses feathers with each hit the player takes. The problem with this type system is that it cannot support a large amount of health.

Things are more direct with **character-based health** systems. *Ghosts 'N Goblins* represents health with armor that pops off the player. *Dead Space* and *Ghostbusters* have status meters as part of the character's armor or equipment. The characters of *Resident Evil* clutch their midsections and limp when they've taken damage. Many car combat and driving games show visible damage to the vehicle. You know your car is close to exploding in *Grand Theft Auto* when you are dragging a bumper, and your engine is smoking! Whatever method you use, you need to have some sort of feedback: players can't always keep their eyes on the health bar, so these character-based feedback mechanisms make it possible for players to gauge how close to death or restart they are. They can then adjust their strategy (retreat, heal themselves, and so on) based on this knowledge. Just make sure these systems don't interfere with the character's movement or attacks.

(That Elf needs food badly!)

Many modern games have moved toward a **HUD-less health system.** As the player takes damage, the screen becomes splattered with blood, which gets thicker as more damage is taken. More dramatic effects, like turning the whole screen blood red, monochromatic, or blurry, can be used too. Sound and music can drop off and be replaced by heavy breathing and a heartbeat.

Other systems that defy classification have shown up over the years. In *Sonic the Hedgehog*, as long as the player held one collectable ring, he could not be killed. Or at the other end of the scale, *Bushido Blade 2* featured one-hit kill attacks, so the health bar was completely dropped.

Players can regain health with the aid of power-ups, increases in level or experience, and even time. *Halo: Combat Evolved* pioneered the concept of regenerating health in first person shooters. As long as the player wasn't taking damage, the health meter would refill at a slow but steady rate. The *Ratchet and Clank* games ditched health altogether because the developer wanted the player to reach the end of the game, not constantly see a Game Over screen.

Whatever method of displaying health is used, players should clearly know when they are getting hurt and losing health. Don't skimp on the dramatic animations and particle effects. Both a **hit sound effect** and a **vocal reaction** ("ow!" "oomph!" and so on) should play. Health should deplete in a very obvious manner because all hit players are closer to losing their lives.

Death: What Is It Good For?

Some game designers think that **lives** and the **Game Over screen** are outmoded concepts.

When video games first arrived, their goal was to suck quarters as fast as possible out of players' pockets. The best way to achieve that was to make players want to keep playing despite being killed as often as possible. Additional lives became a good short-term goal for players to keep in the game. When game characters became little people in lieu of blips and spaceships, the concept of dying came with them. (After all, a spaceship doesn't die, does it?) The emotional impact of the finality of dying (Unless...Quick! Get that next quarter into the slot!) was too good to pass up. When games moved to home systems, lives followed—but the players had paid for their game, and there were no more quarters to gain. So why kill players?

Another problem with killing off players often is that it discourages players from continuing the game fairly. If players are threatened with the loss of equipment, skills, or money by dying, they will just revert back to an earlier save point. For example, players of *Doom* (1993) found that it was easier to restart the game from a saved file than it was from an in-game checkpoint. By using this exploit, players ceased to worry about death and never even saw the game over screen.

Many developers have caught on to this workaround and abandoned the concept of player lives. Instead of killing players and ending the game, players are reset to checkpoints within the level, where they can keep trying over and over until they succeed. In *Prince of Persia: The Sands of Time*, players can "rewind time" to a point where the character is safe. This type of mechanic has to be carefully implemented, though; it is possible for players to get into a situation in which they can't rewind far enough to avoid death and would die all over again. A narrator tells players "That's not how the story happened" before the character restarts from a checkpoint. In *Batman: Arkham Asylum*, players are given a chance to save the caped crusader from a fall to death by pressing a QTE button. If they are successful, Batman climbs back up to safety.

Lives and **Game Over screens** are necessary for many genres such as survival horror and first-person shooters. If you *have* to kill your character, remember the following:

- Let players know they have lives and they will be lost. Players become protective of their character and will fear for their safety.

- Display lives clearly in the HUD. Make it clear when the character is losing a life.

- Allow players plenty of opportunities to regain their lives. These opportunities can happen during level-ups or be power-ups or rewards for collecting objects.

- When killing a player character, do it quickly. Don't create a long, drawn-out death animation that players have to watch over and over again when things get hard in the game.

- The same goes for Game Over screens. Don't make players sit through long death sequence cutscenes. Make the path to restarting gameplay after death as quick as possible.

- When killing a character, make it as violent as your rating allows. Let players really feel some pain when it happens. Empathy toward the game character will motivate players toward self-preservation.

- If players earn something during one life, don't double punish them by taking it away from them when they lose that life.

- If killing the character during a boss round, don't make players have to play the whole sequence all over again. Why not let them continue on with the fight as if nothing ever happened, or only punish them with a little bit of boss health regained?

- That said, the threat of death is a great motivator for players to do better and learn that skill or control. Just use this power judiciously, okay? I trust you.

- If using alternative death systems, such as the player dying if their NPC partner dies, make it clear that (a) players need to protect the partner character with their lives, and (b) they will die if they don't.

Think very carefully about using lives in your game. If you don't think killing players will make the game experience better or more exciting, or you think it will actually be more frustrating, don't do it. Because this **very important thing** applies:

YOU WANT TO KEEP THEM PLAYING

Never give players a good reason to stop playing. Once you've lost them, you may never get them back. Instead of a Game Over screen, why not create a **"keep going" screen**? When a player dies or leaves the game, show a preview of the next level; the next story point; or the next treasure item, weapon, or power-up? Give players a sneak peek to get them so excited they won't want to stop playing!

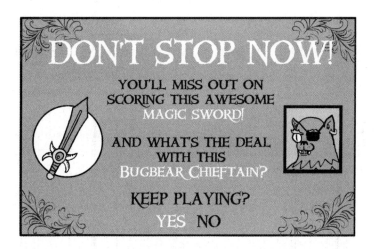

Conflict Without Combat

Although many critics of video games claim all games all super-violent, nothing could be further from the truth. For every *Bulletstorm*, there is a *Braid*. For every *Call of Duty*, there is a *Journey*. For every *Mortal Kombat*, there is a *Katamari Damancy Reroll.* In truth, the super-violent games are the exception, not the rule. And that's not counting the hundreds of thousands of puzzle games, music games, sports games, adventure games, farming games...to name just a few. However, these games do need conflict. Programmer John Rose states that the cornerstone of conflict is tension...and release.[10] Here are a few ways to interject some conflict into a game without a trigger being pulled or a punch being thrown:

- **Timer:** Whether you have to race against time to find a hidden object, assemble a puzzle, or drive a lap around a track, nothing gets the heart beating like a ticking clock. Make sure your clock allows players just enough time to get the task done. Don't force your players to be perfect to the second because, odds are, they won't be. I have quit playing many games because of a timer that didn't give me a fair amount of time.

- **Speed:** If you want to make things tense, just make the game go faster. *Tetris* is the king of racking up tension using speed. The further the player progresses, the faster the pieces drop. This was a common trick back in the days of arcade games when the code could make moves faster than the human player ever could. Go too fast, and it feels unfair to players.

- **Limited options:** Limit the number of moves players can make or allow them to move their pieces only in a limited capacity like in *Chess*. Limited options will force players to start thinking strategically because every move counts.

- **Limited space:** If players can move only within a limited area, they will have to be extra careful with their movements, making the tension rise. However, you must make sure there is a little room for mistakes, even if players don't realize it's there.

- **Precision:** Precision can create tension, and often players will mess up if they have to be too precise. Rhythm games often use precision as a way to make players sweat.

- **Moral dilemmas:** We talked about this issue in Level 9. Making players choose between right and wrong or even two different options when both paths are clear to the players will really drive up the tension. They spend the rest of the game wondering what would have happened if they had taken the "other path."

- **Cost:** When players have to start thinking about what things cost, they feel pressure to spend their money wisely. Make sure players have lots of choices and limited finances so the decision becomes even more excruciating. Of course, every choice should have its pros and cons.

Now that I've covered all types of fighting and conflict, it's time to look at who is causing all this trouble: enemies!

---

[10] John Rose, "Addressing Conflict: Tension and Release in Games," 2010, www.starming.com/index.php?action=plugin&v=wave&tpl=union&ac=viewgrouppost&gid=56&tid=8033

Level 10's Universal Truths and Clever Ideas

- Violence is all about context: a violent act is going to feel more violent if it is the player who does it.
- Give your character a signature attack or weapon.
- Create an attack matrix to track your combat moves and reactions.
- People want to play games that make them look cool.
- Use a lock-on system to enable players during combat.
- Close battles are more exciting.
- Use QTEs to heighten combat drama, but don't overdo them because they get old.
- Fighting enemies is supposed to be fun.
- Be aware of the three A's (Action, Aiming and Ammo) when designing projectile combat.
- Use attacks to hamper and incapacitate players rather than kill.
- Make it clear to players that they have taken damage.
- Always strive to enable players even when disabling them.
- Keep the players playing.
- You can add conflict without having combat.

Level 11
They All Want You Dead

Video games are populated with a plethora of beings that want to kill you: aliens and androids, pirates and parasites, mercenaries, and mushroom people. However, I realize not every video game features slobbering, sword-wielding enemies—often they use guns, too!

Yes, yes. I realize that plenty of other video games use other forms of conflict, such as time, human competitors, or even the player's' own skills to challenge the players. But I'm not talking about those types of games.[1] As I flip back to Level 3, I am reminded of three types of conflict found in stories: **man versus nature** (like a hurricane or a giant white whale); **man versus self** (where the hero is struggling with an internal issue such as "where to go for lunch"[2]); and **man versus man**, or in the case of video games, man versus zombie, man

---

[1] At least, not yet.

[2] I have seen large groups of full-grown people completely paralyzed by this internal conflict.

versus ninja pirate, or man versus hideous-alien-creature-made-from-the-skins-of-your-dead-crewmates.

Those are the types of enemies I talk about here. While zombies and ninja pirates and alien-crew-skin thingee enemies are great fun to design, you first need to follow this **very important** golden rule:

FORM FOLLOWS FUNCTION

Hey! I saw you trying to design that winged skeleton enemy without thinking about how he's going to attack.[3] Put down the pencil as I repeat myself because **THIS REALLY IS VERY IMPORTANT:**

FORM FOLLOWS FUNCTION!

You *need* to determine the function of your enemies first. So many things rest on the decisions in your design: how the programmer will code it, how the animator will build the rigging model, how the artist will texture it. These important enemy attributes are:

- Size
- Behavior
- Speed
- Movement
- Attacks
- Aggression[4]
- Health

All these attributes, along with your level's theme, will guide you determine what those enemies do, what they look like, and how those different enemies will work together when placed in your game. Having to redo an enemy character again and again and again is a big morale killer for your team and a huge waste of time and money.[5]

---

[3] He does look pretty awesome though.

[4] I realize that aggression is considered part of behavior, but because designers often treat combat as its own system, I felt it deserved its own heading.

[5] And it is irresponsible. Please do not be an irresponsible designer. I've worked with them. They suck.

Sizing Up the Enemy

Speaking of huge, enemies come in a wide range of **sizes:**

Short enemies are no taller than the player character's waist.

Average enemies are roughly the same height as the player character.

Large enemies are several heads taller than the player character.[6]

Huge enemies are at least twice the player character's own size.

Gigantic enemies are so large that they can be completely seen only from a distance.

short   average   large   huge

The size of the enemy will determine how the player will fight it. For example, a short enemy can be fought only by crouching or with a low attack like an upward sweep or radial spin attack. On the other end of the scale, a huge enemy with a vulnerable head can be reached only with a jump attack. Design your combat so the player character "fights their way up" the enemy: the player character should be able to hit an average enemy using a low or medium attack; the player character should be able to hit a huge enemy using a low, medium, or high attack; and so on.

Hey! Quit it, you big bully!

Size also influences health. Larger enemies traditionally have more health (are harder to kill) than smaller ones. This might account for why many bosses are so darn big. Size will also dictate the enemies' reaction

---

[6] Artists measure characters in terms of "heads," which is literally the height of one average human head. For example, an average six-foot human is seven heads tall, whereas a heroic character is eight-and-a-half heads tall.

to attacks. Hit a short enemy with a knockback attack, and they should go flying. Hit a large enemy with the same attack, and they may not even budge. You'd be lucky if a gigantic enemy even notices your attack, let alone reacts to it.

They say variety is the spice of life. I don't know about spice, but I do know it is variety that keeps a player from getting bored. Size can influence a player's emotions, too. Defeating a huge enemy can make a player feel heroic, whereas defeating a short one can make him feel like a bully.

Bad Behavior

Now that you've determined size, ask yourself, what is the enemy's **behavior?**

- How does the enemy move?

- What does the enemy do when in combat?

- What does the enemy do when hurt?

Answer these questions, and you will have the foundation to build robust enemies. When you are designing enemy behavior, the goal is not to have different enemy characters repeat the same behaviors. Even better, design your enemies' behaviors to complement each other.

A **patroller** moves back and forth or up and down in a mechanical fashion. The path of movement can be more involved than this, but the movement is always predictable.

A **chaser** pursues a player if approached or some other condition is met. In many games, patrollers can turn into chasers when they see the player, or when the player attacks them. Often, these enemies will do **melee attacks**, attacks with fists or a sword or club or some other hand-held weapon. They might try to run over you with a vehicle! Often, these attacks can be dodged or blocked by the player.

A **shooter** is an enemy that fires a projectile. Shooting patrollers and chasers will fire at the player once they've been spotted. Due to the nature of the attack, this enemy will try to keep distance between them and the player rather than engage him.

A **guard** is an enemy whose AI priority is to guard an item or location (like a doorway) rather than actively pursue the player. Guard behavior can be easily combined with chasing or shooting if the player manages to steal the item or get past the guard.

A **flyer** is an enemy that, well…flies. Flyers are aerial patrollers, but because flying adds another dimension (literally) to the movement, these characters deserve their own classification. Flyers can swoop down to attack players, or they might fire projectiles from a safe distance. Flyers are more advanced enemies for the player to deal with because their movement and attack patterns can be difficult to predict. Players trying to attack flyers usually stop to target or make a jump attack.

A **bomber** is a flyer that attacks from above. Give the player warning that a bomber is above to drop down (or drop its payload) so it doesn't come as a nasty surprise. In a game that uses a third-person camera, bombers can be difficult for a player to see as they fly above the player to attack.

A **burrower** is an enemy with an invulnerable state that allows them to get into an advantageous position to attack the player. The player must wait for the enemy to emerge before they can attack.

A **teleporter** is an enemy that can change position around the playfield. The player must attack quickly lest the enemy teleport out of harm's way. Some teleporters vanish after they are hit and change their location, forcing the player to have to search for them. Many times they teleport behind you for a cheap shot! The teleporter enemy varies from the burrower enemy in that the teleportation is instantaneous, giving the player no time to attack. Give your player a way to disrupt the enemy's teleportation, such as a stun or another disruptive attack.

A **blocker** is an enemy that defends themself against the player's attack with a shield or other defensive device. The shield can either be circumnavigated with an attack from another direction or elevation (such as from down low or from behind), or the player can disarm the enemy with a specific move or attack. Shields can make the enemy temporarily invulnerable, requiring the player to break the shield with a specific move or action or wait around until the invulnerable state passes.

A **doppelganger** is an enemy that looks like the player; they move, attack, and use AI that mimics the player's own. Doppelganger enemies force players to use moves or weapons in an unusual manner in order to defeat "themselves."

The goal of having all these different behavior types is to have enemies that complement each other. Enemies should "live harmoniously" with each other, creating interesting combat challenges for the players to solve. Once you create enemy behaviors that work well together, it will create gameplay. In dealing with these enemy combinations, players will learn how to perform **threat analysis.** They'll find that sometimes it's easy to take out the weak enemies first, and other times it will be better to tackle the deadlier foe and ignore the little guys. As a designer, you can force the player to make these kinds of interesting decisions during combat.

Here are a few interesting enemy combinations that I've found work well together:

- A blocker with a shooter positioned behind him. As the player tries to whittle down the blocker, the shooter is taking pot-shots at the player.

- A big chaser and a group of smaller flyers. While the player goes after the big guy, the little guys attack. However, if the player leaves the big guy alone and goes after the flyers, he's gonna get thumped by the big guy.

- A teleporter and a chaser. As the player tries to catch the teleporter, they leaves themselves open to the chaser's attacks.

- A guard and a bomber. While the player is tied up with the guard, the bomber attacks from above.

How Rapid is Rapid?

Depending on **speed** and **movement,** an enemy can be more dangerous, harder to target, and more frightening. Use the different speeds **stationery, slow, medium, fast,** and **quick** for your enemies.

The difference between a hazard and an enemy is mobility and AI, but every rule has its exceptions. Just because an enemy is **non-mobile** doesn't mean they can't move.

Movement = character and life.

A humongous Cthulhu-esque creature may be too big to walk or fly around, but players would still consider them an enemy. Even an "inanimate object" like a turret can be smart enough to make life difficult for players. Design ways to keep players engaged as they attack non-mobile enemies, whether it's a timing puzzle that stands between the enemy and the players, or even a puzzle that's part of the enemy itself.

TK-42I
Don't just stand
there, get him!

The speed, size, and strength[7] of an enemy are inversely proportional: small enemies are fast but not strong, big enemies are strong but not fast. Medium-sized enemies can be either strong or fast, but if you give them both attributes, they end up feeling **"cheap"** because they've been given an advantage that the player cannot match. Whenever an enemy is extremely overpowered or too perfect at making attacks, it feels as though the player is fighting artificial intelligence rather than an actual living creature.

But I digress.

Slow enemies work best when there are lots of them. One zombie isn't very threatening, but a dozen of the slow-moving undead can make even the most stalwart hero a little nervous. Often, a slow enemy packs a big wallop: if players get hit, it's their own darn fault. Or you can give a slow-moving enemy a fast attack to keep players on their toes. Slow enemies often have built-in defenses, allowing them to brace themselves against a player's attack or casually swat them aside. If you want your enemies to feel powerful, have them move slowly like Orogman from *Resident Evil*, *Yhorm the Giant* from Dark Souls 3, or Titan Lume from *Sanctum 2*. A big bad guy advancing on the hero can make the player panic and make fatal mistakes.

any day now...

---

[7] Hey! It's the three Ss!

Medium speed is just what it sounds like: the speed of the enemy's movement and attacks will likely match the player's own speed. Medium speed may be a little predictable, but it's useful for most situations. I've found it's helpful to make medium-speed enemies run slightly slower than the player character, especially when chasing him. This allows the player to retreat at running speed, if necessary, without fear of getting cut down from behind. The player can then reorient themself and face the enemy in time to deliver an attack or effectively defend. It's OK to tweak speed values here and there to get the effect you want. There's no hard and fast rule when it comes to this; you've just got to do what feels right and fair.

Fast enemies either dart forward to quickly strike and back away, or they move quickly around and then jump in to do multiple attacks. Fast enemies work great in horror and action games. Players will have less time to react to an incoming enemy and may panic and make dumb mistakes—until they learn to keep their cool. However, don't make fast enemies constantly attack the players because they get frustrated by getting hit by something they can't hit back—unless this is the strategy you want. The smaller the enemies, the quicker they are. Give fast-moving enemies an erratic movement pattern to give your players a real challenge.

Quick enemies move in bursts. They can move blindingly fast or even teleport around the battlefield. That may seem unfair to players, but you can balance that by limiting their damage, attacks, health, or number of moves they can make. Help players see quick moves coming by playing a warning animation. This will allow players to dodge, block, or strike before an enemy completes its quick move.

Movement Style

What is your enemy's **movement style?** Does your enemy charge the player like an angry bull? Do they zigzag erratically to avoid taking fire? Do they make a beeline and then retreat? Do they jump from cover to cover? Do they crawl on the walls to ambush the player from above? Do they run away and never fight at all?[8] Knowing your enemy's movement styles will not only determine their attacks but also their personality.

Determine whether your enemy moves randomly or predictably. Avoid extremes and insert variety. Too random and the player might feel the enemy moves too arbitrarily. Too predictable and an enemy feels too "game-y."

The best solution doesn't include unpredictability. For *Crash Bandicoot 2*, Naughty Dog tried creating more behavioral AI with fewer simple patterns. Focus groups found them inferior. The players liked the challenge of figuring out the enemy's patterns. On the flipside, players like unpredictability in sports games. Predictable patterns become "holes" for players to exploit, which ruins the realism of the experience.

Coordinating several enemies' movements adds complexity. Consider how your enemies behave and group together during a fight. Some enemies can use flocking behavior to create realistic group movement.

---

[8] Personally, I think enemies are more fun when they put up a fight.

Look at the movement behaviors of different animals, birds, and insects for inspiration. Humans usually move in straight lines. Predatory mammals like wolves and tigers move in looping arcs as they circle their prey. Crabs move sideways rather than straight ahead. Birds fly in swooping patterns as they catch updrafts to aid their flight. Insects zigzag as they course-correct during flight. Giving your enemies different movement patterns will make them feel more realistic.

Let's consider how the bad guys in a Bruce Lee movie fight scene behave. Bruce Lee is surrounded by dozens of karate experts, but they never attack him in more than groups of ones and twos. They are very polite, those kung fu villains. This strategy works well in games, too. It allows you to create the illusion of a group without overtaxing your game or the players.

This might go better if we all went at once...

Work with your programmer to create **pathing AI.** Determine the needs of your enemies to figure out how they are going to move around. Here are some questions that you should address when creating pathing and behavior AI:

- **How mobile are your enemies?** Do they have more than one movement speed? Can they break into a run or slide to a stop? Do they leap over obstacles or use doors?

- **How aggressive are your enemies?** Fast-moving frothing berserkers or slowly advancing stone-cold killers? Enemies can even be cautious or cowardly, afraid to get hurt or die. Giving enemies a sense of self-preservation makes them feel like real people.

- **How much like team players are your enemies?** Do your enemies raise the alarm and alert other enemies to assist them? Will they try to keep a player pinned down while others close in for a melee attack or better shot? Will they try to flush a player into the open where another enemy will have the advantage? Will one grab and grapple the player while another attacks? Do they have a "partner," like a guard dog or attack drone?

- **How defensive are your enemies?** Do they crouch or duck behind objects? Do they use cover or hold the line? Do they act stealthily when they spot a player? Do they try to attack from behind and sneak up on a player? Do they have defensive items like shields or defense systems?

- **How versatile are your enemies?** Can they pick up and use dropped weapons or health? Do they drive vehicles or man weapon emplacements? Can they take over functions for other enemies if they are killed? Can they fly or use non-ground-based movement?

Most AI characters use a **waypoint navigation system** to move around. The designer lays out a grid or path that determines where the AI moves. As the AI moves, the programmer can determine what movement and animations are played to create specific AI behavior. Areas can be designated as "go" or "no-go" areas based on world geometry or to achieve a specific AI behavior.

All this means is that your bad guys either travel along a preplanned network of paths or wander around within the confines of an invisible box (or sphere).

Using such a system allows the designer to choreograph a world event with an enemy—like crashing through a wall or reaching a specific spot at a particular time. However, placing waypoints can be time-consuming, and they don't always meet all the AI needs.

Because most waypoint-guided enemies are programmed to determine the shortest and quickest path to the player, be careful of enemies clipping corners and objects. You can fix this issue by tweaking your waypoint paths. Pull the waypoints in a bit at corners or near objects to compensate for this movement.

Bring on the Bad Guys

The player is walking through a graveyard winding his way through the tombstones when he sees a skeleton blocking his path, ready to fight.

Wait a second. Rewind. There's a much more dramatic way to introduce this bad guy into your world.

The player is walking through a graveyard, winding his way through the tombstones. One of them shakes as he passes by. Suddenly, the camera zooms in on the player's face as the screen shakes and the controller rumbles. The camera whip-pans around to a grave as a bony hand thrusts out of the ground! The tombstone shatters into a million shards as a skeleton warrior bursts from the grave, its eyes glowing evilly and bony fingers clenched, ready to fight!

Now that's exciting!

Enemy introductions are a really effective way to tell players that they've encountered something new, exciting, and dangerous:

- Freeze the camera or zoom in on the creature: let players get a good look at what's about to kick their butt!

- Display the name of the enemy on-screen. You could freeze the action to show the enemy in some cool action shot, display its name for a second or two, and then start the gameplay again. I like it when I can put a name to an enemy.

- Foreshadow what will happen. *Resident Evil 2* provides a great "what the heck was that?" moment when a Licker enemy runs past a window right before the player encounters him. The foreshadowing builds up suspense for the moment when the Licker bursts through the ceiling in front of the player.

- Introduce your enemies in a very dramatic way. Have them smash through a window, kick down a door, blast into the world in an explosion of special effects—anything to let your bad guys make a good first impression! Make the first appearance of your enemies an event! Your players will remember them!

Keep in mind, not all games warrant an enemy introduction. Players of multiplayer games wouldn't want their own game play stopped while the introduction occurs. (Maybe they would if they could attack the player who is watching the introduction!)

Spawning enemies into the world is just as important as removing them. You want to make sure that players aren't able to slaughter the enemies before they get a chance to arrive on the scene. Some games make enemies invulnerable upon spawning or have them spawn from off-screen where players can't reach them. You may consider creating a hazard or mechanic that allows enemies to spawn on the playfield without getting killed.

In *Maximo: Ghosts to Glory,* we designed coffins that burst up through the ground to deliver enemies into the world. If you collided with them, you would be knocked backwards. If you swung at them, you would shatter the coffin, but the enemy inside wouldn't be hurt, which was important because the enemy needed to survive entering the world long enough to fight against you—otherwise there'd be no combat in the game!

Why go through all this trouble? Because of this **very important thing:**

FIGHTING ENEMIES IS SUPPOSED TO BE FUN!

Before I forget, here's another **very important thing:**

ENEMIES SHOULD BE FOUGHT, NOT AVOIDED

I'm not talking about enemies that you have to dodge before they hit you during a fight. No. I'm talking about the "this enemy is too hard, too cheap, too much of a hassle to fight, so I don't want to fight them" type of enemy. And yet, I always see the following type of enemy in a game:

Some days you can't get rid of a bomb!

This enemy has a bomb or some other explosive device. The enemy runs toward the player. If the player doesn't explode, they will run away. Although this might sound exciting, in my experience this type of enemy always causes problems.

When the player runs, if the game is in third person, the camera tends to flip around to show the back of the player. In first-person, the player can't even see the enemy following them. In either case, the player can't see the enemy at all. When the enemy explodes, it comes as a nasty surprise. Sure, you can give the player a warning with a HUD or in-game warning indicator, but in the end, you are going to design all kinds of stop-gap measures to help the player spot the enemy—but then that kind of defeats the purpose of the enemy, doesn't it? Ultimately, this kind of explodey enemy just isn't very good design.

In an action game, you are going to be fighting a lot of enemies, so do whatever you can to make the action **awesome**! Explosive effects, funny or dramatic hit reaction animations, cool and/or gory kills and, of course, lots of feedback and rewards.[9] Why fight enemies?

- **They have the loot.** Gold, items, bolts, experience points, health—it doesn't matter what it is as long as they have it and you want it.

---

[9] I talk about how to make the most of rewards in Level 13.

- **They block the path.** You can block the player artificially to force a fight, like a battle arena.

- **They have the something you want.** And that something is a key. And you need that key to get through the gate that leads to the next room, section, or level. I've always wondered: why is it the last enemy you fight is always the one who is holding the key?

- **You need to take their power.** Tired of getting shot at? Defeat those enemies and take their bigger, better guns! Want to upgrade your +1 mace to a +2? You're going to have to fight that orc to get it!

- **They're making fun of you.** Taunts are a great way to motivate players into fighting. Having enemies taunt or challenge players if they're standing still for too long not only can force a player into attacking, but also is a great way to get some character into the enemies. Taunts work great in multiplayer fighting games like

Street Fighter where the player takes a risk by taking a break from combat or defense to mock his opponent.

- **It's fun to fight.** Nothing will keep a player fighting more than having a solid combat system. To achieve that, see Level 10.

Don't forget to let enemies have a chance to be bad, too! Give your enemies some sweet attacks like these:

- **Melee attacks:** Do they use hands, claws, tentacles, or feet? Do they have raking attacks or punches? Do they know martial arts? Can they grab or ensnare? Can they perform throws? Can they "ground pound" or cause earthquake attacks?

- **Weapon combat:** Do they use weapons? One-handed or two-handed weapons? Are they barbaric or skilled fighters? Can they disarm or be disarmed by the players? Can their weapon be used by the players? Can the weapon extend, be thrown, or boomerang?

- **Projectile combat:** Do they use guns/magic spells/ranged weapons? How accurate are they with their attacks? Will they blindly fire or wait for the perfect shot? Do they track movement or lead when aiming? Do they need to reload? Are there projectile explosives? Can they be disarmed? Do they have a close-range melee attack if engaged or disarmed?

- **Persistent damage:** Does your enemies' attack have a side effect like acid, poison, fire, or bleeding that does lingering damage to the player? Is it an effect that can't be healed by a player without a special item? Does it wear off over time?

Telegraphing attacks is important for effective enemy combat. An enemy should have a "tell" animation that informs observant players that the enemy is about to go all stabby, shooty, or clawey. Tells include:

- Cocking a fist back to punch
- Growling or yelling before swinging a weapon or charging
- Moving part of the anatomy (like a twitching tail or reptilian fins) before attacking
- The weapon's laser sight acquiring a target before firing
- A weapon or spell "charging up" before firing

Not every attack needs to do damage to the player. There are plenty of ways to give the player grief without doing permanent harm:

- **Block/parry:** The enemy can block or parry the player's attack, causing a stagger in the player's combat flow. This can break combat chains, reset combo meters, and cause the player's weapon to rebound or ricochet. Whatever the source of the block, be it a force field, an actual shield, or a defensive grab, don't ever make the player wonder why it happened.

- **Knockback:** Rather than taking damage, the player is knocked backward when hit. Putting distance between the enemy and player can upset any combat chain or disrupt any activity the player was engaged in, like spell casting or operating a mechanic. It is particularly effective when the player is hit while standing on a narrow platform, knocking them off or to their death.

- **Stun:** The player is stunned into a defenseless state. The player should lose momentary control—just as long as it doesn't last too long, which can be very frustrating for the player. Circling stars and tweeting birds effects are optional.

- **Freeze/paralyze/capture:** This is when the player is entombed with a freeze attack, or snared by a spider's web, or caught in some sort of netting. This type of attack acts like a stun, but the player can break out of it by button mashing or furiously waggling the control stick. You will have to decide if the player may or may not take damage during this attack. Make sure you have a cool "breaking free" animation and sound effects when the player finally regains control.

- **Repair/heal:** The enemy regains health. I suggest using this behavior infrequently because it can feel unfair to the player. It works best if the enemy has a healing animation as well as a health bar to show that they've **returned** to their fully (or partially) healed state. Consider allowing the player to attack the enemy to disrupt their healing.

- **Buff:** This effect works like healing, but the enemy gains power to charge an attack. Usually, this effect can be found when charging magical attacks. You also find it in shooters when the bad guy is charging up his weapon to unleash his wrath on the player. The enemy can be in either an invulnerable state while buffing up or the reverse, which would cause the enemy to lose the advantage he sought.

- **Steal:** The enemy steals money or equipment from the player, causing the gameplay dynamic to shift from "fight the enemy" to "get that creep who just stole my chainmail!" Make sure the player has a fair opportunity to get back what's been stolen. Never steal anything the player has bought or won as part of progression; make it something that is (somewhat) easily replaceable.

- **Leech:** The enemy drains the player's "charged up" resources. This can be super meter power, mana, shield power, or even fuel. Usually, the player doesn't have an opportunity to regain the resource from the enemy that attacked it. Once it's gone, it's **gone.** Players will soon pick up that leeching enemies should be dispatched as soon as possible.

- **Perform unexpected behaviors:** If the player is anticipating the enemy's movement pattern or attack, giving the enemy another unexpected action or attack adds a nice bit of variety to the encounter. For example, an enemy gets hit a couple of times by the player and then they use their sword for a parry move if the player tries to do the same attack again. The variety adds to the illusion that the enemy is learning to react and defend against the player. The player will have to adjust their battle plan as they goes rather than falling into the same old routine.

- **Show vulnerabilities** or **resist-
  ances:** Make sure they're clear to the
  player and follow logic. Of course,
  that murderous snow angel is going
  to be vulnerable to fire, just like that
  flaming pyre corpse is just going to
  laugh in your face when you wave
  that burning torch in front of them.
  Let the player make logical connections; don't ever let them wonder why something doesn't work.

  Enemy taunts are great for conveying that information. The smugger or cutting the
  enemy's taunt, the better. Just don't overdo it; even the funniest or best-delivered line
  gets boring after the third time.

Even if an enemy has fierce attacks, nimble defenses, and cool behaviors, there still has to
be a way to kill them. You determine an enemy's health the same way you would for player
characters. Balance your enemy's health in relationship to the player's attack. Start with how
many hits you want your enemy to take before they die. Consider all the different attacks
your hero has when determining this. Your goblin enemy may be able to withstand three
normal hits, but a flaming sword may be able to kill them in one stroke.

All the notes about displaying player health apply to the enemy's health as well. Refer to
Level 10 rather than make me retype it all here.

I Love Designing Enemies

Enemies offer you a chance to really flex your creative muscles as a designer. It's fun to come
up with horrible monsters and evil villains. Personally, I find adversaries to be the most
interesting characters in a story—and not just the "big bad" bosses. Look at all the great
cannon fodder found in books, movies, and comics: Imperial Stormtroopers, Orcs, Cobra
troopers, Death Eaters, AIM scientists, whatever those henchmen in James Bond films that
flip through the air whenever a grenade explodes.

I'm proud to report that no one comes up with more creative cannon fodder than video game
designers. In games, **anything** can be an enemy! An angry pickle! An irate toaster! Whatever
the heck a Goomba is! A whole glorious world of sociopathic possibilities is yours for the
choosing! Here are things to consider when designing your own enemies:

- **Start with your theme.** Brainstorm the types of enemies based on your game's environment. For example, an ice world can have killer snowmen, yetis, disgruntled skaters, snowball-throwing wizards, and penguins with rocket launchers.

- **...or start with your story.** Who is the main enemy in your story? For example, in an original trilogy *Star Wars* game, I would expect to be fighting stormtroopers no matter what planet I am on. Other enemies such as bounty hunters, irate aliens, or Black Sun pirates can appear, but players should be constantly reminded of their arch-nemesis whether it's Darth Vader or Jabba the Hutt.

- **Tie the game's antagonist and their minion together.** In *Star Wars*, the Stormtroopers were armored just like Darth Vader. What's a visual cue or behavior that will make them feel part of the same team or universe? Then find something that will differentiate your enemy from the others in your game. In *Star Wars* Darth Vader wore black armor, and the stormtroopers wore white. Within your game, you can create enemies based on shapes, color, physical attributes, weapons, or uniforms.

- **Be smart with re-use of enemies and textures.** Re-use models, animations, and textures wherever possible to get the most bang for your production buck. When creating similar enemies with different behaviors and attacks, make them look different at a glance. I call this design mentality **"Red Ninja/Blue Ninja"** because a red ninja enemy may be set to hop and throw shuriken, whereas a blue ninja may use dash attacks with Sai. Sub-Zero and Scorpion, two of the most famous characters from the *Mortal Kombat* series, were originally just reskinned versions of each other.[10]

- **Decide whether the enemy belongs in your world.** You wouldn't expect to find a cybernetic death-mecha in a *Super Mario* game; that world is too whimsical for such "serious" enemies. Conversely, a Goomba would be seriously out of place in a realistic *Tom Clancy's Ghost Protocol* style title.

- **Make your enemy look like an enemy.** Glowing red eyes, demonic horns, fangs, clawed hands, spikes, skull ornamentation, ragged capes, fearsome masks, and helmets that obscure faces. Sure, this is stereotypical imagery, but if your players see characters in the world with any of these visual traits, they're going to shoot first and ask questions later. Stereotypes are stereotypes for a reason: they're easy for viewers to understand. Don't be afraid to use them to your advantage.

- **...or go against expectation and character type.** You can go against type and juxtapose your enemies' visual with their behavior. How about a cute bunny that turns into a slavering killer? Or a hulking troll that will burst into tears when attacked? The more personality you can add to make your enemies feel and look unique, the better.[11]

---

[10] Of course, in the case of Sub-Zero and Scorpion, it would be "blue ninja, yellow ninja," which doesn't quite have the same zing.

[11] Just remember not to violate the triangle of weirdness.

I Hate You to Pieces

When introducing your boss character to players, do it in a memorable fashion. Who can forget Darth Vader's entrance in *Star Wars*? Make sure players get a good look at the villain, that they understand "this is the bad guy" they will eventually fight. You always want to give your main villain[12] a "Joker moment," when the bad guy kills one of their own henchmen or some other NPC to show what a truly bad guy (or girl or he-she-demon) they are. Have other characters talk about how bad the boss is before you introduce him. You can also give the players information in collectible form like audio clips or data files or letters to warn them about the enemy. This works when dropping hints to players on how to defeat the enemy or boss. Arm them with knowledge along with the firepower. Anticipation of fighting the boss will be greater if players know the fight is coming.

When I was working on a game based on the movie *Demolition Man,* the designers were presented with an interesting challenge. Simon, the movie's bad guy, didn't fight the hero until the very end of the game. But the designers knew that Simon had to be a recurring villain in the game, so they came up with a clever solution. At the start of every level, Simon would run out onto the screen, shake his fist at players, and then run off. The effect on players was electric. They'd shake their fists back and say, "Oooh! That darn Simon! I'm a-gonna git him!" and then proceed to blast their way through a half hour of gameplay. By the time these players reached the next level, they were probably so heady from all the killin', they forgot why they were there until Simon would run out again, shake his fist, and re-energize the players. This taught me a **very important thing:**

---

[12] If you have the bandwidth in your game schedule, it's great to have all the enemies in the game get a "being bad" moment.

MAKE THE PLAYERS HATE THEIR ENEMY

How? Simple. Make sure your boss does bad things! This is why villains are always killing off their own henchmen—so that they have someone to kill if they can't kill the main characters! Have the enemy take something the player needs or cares about. Kill the hero's aunt and uncle, kidnap the princess girlfriend, kick the dog, burn down their quaint village. You get the idea. Whatever your enemy does, make sure it impacts the gameplay as well as the story. Make the parent the blacksmith that gives the hero that magic sword. Does the girlfriend heal the hero whenever he visits her hut? Not anymore! The enemy just kidnapped her! And now that the village has burned to the ground, where is the player going to store all the collectibles he's found? Japanese RPGs do this right: they kill off the player's girlfriend, who happens to be your best party member. Are those tears I see? Are they being shed for a lost love or because you can no longer heal every other turn?

When it comes time to design your boss fights, you don't have to kill the boss at the end of each battle. In fact, it's better if you don't. This way, you give the player someone to fight with later in the game. Because your player will have "history" with this bad guy, they will hate them even more! If you kill off your enemy in the first act, who is left for the player to fight? Unmotivated, your hero loses the will to live, starts drinking, and moves in with their parents.[13]

Pathetic. And more importantly, not fun.

Taunts are a great way to get the player mad at an enemy, but you need to be careful not to overuse them. To paraphrase Spider-Man, "With great power comes

---

[13] Oh right, his parents are dead! Now you've turned your hero into a homeless person. Are you happy with yourself?

dialogue-the-player-is-going-to-tire-of-hearing-over-and-over-again." Taunt the player physically as well as verbally. You can even build these taunts into your enemy's attack moves. For example, in *Maximo: Ghosts to Glory,* there is a sword-wielding skeleton that every time he successfully hits the player, he does a little flourish with his sword like a gunslinger spinning his guns before he holsters them. This flourish was created to give the player an opportunity to strike back and wipe the grin off that cocky little so-and-so's face.

Simple animations like idles and taunts go a long way toward making an enemy feel smarter than they actually are and provide lots of character. Has the player retreated too far for the enemy to attack? Have the enemy berate the player or make "come here" gestures. Did the player successfully elude the enemy with stealth? The player should shrug their shoulders and mutter that they must have been seeing things. Some games have guard enemies taking smoking breaks or falling asleep at their post to make them easier pickings for the hero. But keep in mind you don't want every one of your enemies to act this way; otherwise, you've just thwarted the uniqueness you were trying to achieve.

One last thing about enemies: sometimes you should let the bad guys win.

I don't mean killing off players to give your enemies a victory, but you shouldn't baby your players either.[14] Let the enemy get in a hit (or a cheap shot) once in a while. Give the enemy a temporary invulnerable attack state. Force the player to run away or at least block an attack. Have your enemies outnumber the player several times over. Let them sweat it out as to whether they'll survive the encounter. The player should feel as though they are actually in danger from enemies. Bad guys aren't going to feel very threatening if the player doesn't have to struggle to defeat them. And the players' victory is going to feel hollow if the enemies don't provide a challenge.

Non-Enemy Enemies

As mentioned at the start of this chapter, not every game has physical enemies that are to be overcome with hot lead and cold steel. There are plenty of ways to push and punish your players without resorting to fighting sentient beings:

- **Gremlin:** This character looks like an enemy but doesn't directly engage the player. Instead, a gremlin will disrupt the game by undoing the player's progress. For example, *SimCity* features an unkillable Godzilla-like monster that stomps through the player's city, leaving destruction in his wake.

---

[14] I talk more about difficulty in Level 13, so hold your horses.

- **Tormentor:** This type of enemy challenges and taunts the player throughout the course of the game but never directly confronts or attacks them. *Portal's* sentient computer GLaDOS is a great example of tormentor enemy. It makes it much more satisfying to tear her apart at the end of the game.

- **Time:** "Time pressure makes people think something is a lot more complicated than it really is."[15] Found primarily in skill-based games like driving/racing and puzzle games, a ticking clock is a great way to unnerve the player, creating pressure without using an enemy. Some games will allow the player to extend or slow the clock for temporary relief. If the player doesn't achieve the objective or finish the task within the allotted time, the player either loses a life or the scenario is reset. Time can also be used as an endgame, where the player must escape a base before it blows up.

- **Human competitor:** Player versus player, competitive or cooperative—regardless of the gameplay mode, I find the best and worst thing about multiplayer games is...the other players.[16] Your friends (and complete strangers) will always find new ways to torture, torment, and humiliate you during a game. As a designer, never underestimate the power of one-upmanship and revenge. Just give the players the tools they need to act on these and sit back and watch the fun unfold. As the old saying goes, keep your friends close and your enemies closer because sometimes they are the same person.

How to Create the World's Greatest Boss Battle

Video game BOSS (n): a large and/or challenging enemy that blocks a player's progression and acts as the climax/ending to the game's environment, level, or world.

At first glance, a **boss battle** may appear to be an encounter with a very, very, very large enemy with too much health. But this is an underestimation. Bosses are very complex creatures with many separate working parts that should be thoughtfully designed.

Just as with other enemies, boss characters are fun to create. But before you start designing your boss in any way, you must first make sure that you have completely defined the player's actions. Once that's been determined, you can design a boss fight in three different ways:

- **Learned moves:** The boss encounter is designed around the players' existing set of moves. You don't have to teach the players anything new, and they feel as though they've mastered those skills when they defeat the boss. The *Mario* games design their bosses this way.

---

[15] A succinct quote from Portal designer Kim Swift from GDC 08: Portal Creators on Writing, Multiplayer and Government Interrogation Techniques, Chris Faylor, Shacknews.com (www.shacknews.com/featuredarticle.x?id=784).

[16] I am reminded of Jean-Paul Sartre's famous quote: "Hell is other people." Because Sartre died in 1980, we'll never know whether he would have appreciated a good death match.

- **New abilities:** The boss encounter is designed around players gaining a new weapon or new move. The players' learning curve is part of the boss round's difficulty. You find this in many of the bosses in the *Legend of Zelda* series.

- **Combination:** You can try to use both methods in one boss fight, but why complicate things for players? Don't be so mean.

Who's the Boss?

Boss design is just like other enemy design: form should follow function. Knowing the boss's movement and attacks will determine the boss's appearance: if they can shoot, give your boss a gun (or a magic spell or a rocket launcher or a large nose to sneeze out nose goblins); and if they can defend themselves, give them a shield (or a force field or protective cowling or a missile-deflecting karate move). In a nutshell, if the boss can use it, they should have it.

Next, consider how the boss relates to the hero. No, I don't mean in a "Darth Vader is your father" way, but rather what the boss represents. The James Bond movies of the 1960s and 1970s had a really good formula for bad guys. There were technically three "boss types" that Bond had to defeat.

physical   mental   global

The first villain was the arch henchman: the **physical adversary.** A muscle-bound goon would beat the tar out of Bond until he turned the tables with one of his spy gadgets or a deftly executed judo move to throw the goon into a pool of piranhas. Physical adversaries in the Bond films are the classic henchmen like Jaws, Tee Hee, and OddJob. In video games, these characters are monstrously large, freakishly hideous, and very heavily armed.

The second villain type is the mastermind: the **mental adversary.** Bond fought these villains at the film's climax. Usually, mastermind intelligence leaves the hero at a disadvantage and against overwhelming odds. In video games, this is when the boss gets into their robotic suit to blast away at the hero or forces the player to solve an environmental puzzle that, when solved, brings the cackling villain to their knees.

Even though the mastermind has been defeated, there is still one more "villain" to defeat: the **global threat.** This isn't a person so much as a threat to the hero's world. This can be the timer on Goldfinger's nuclear bomb, Hugo Drax's deadly spore bombs, or SPECTRE's space-capsule-eating rocket.

Here are some questions to consider when designing bosses:

- **What makes the boss a worthy adversary?** Most bosses have the upper hand on players in size, strength, firepower, and defenses. Make sure players know they are in trouble even before the fight begins.

- **What does the boss represent to the hero?** In many games and movies, the villain is merely an obstacle to the hero gaining true love (rescuing the princess) or a threat to peace. But don't be content with those tropes. Villains can represent the inner demons of the hero. In *Return of the Jedi*, Luke Skywalker must reject the dark side and become like his father in order to defeat the Emperor (or at least motivate his daddy to toss Palps down a shaft).

- **What does the hero gain by defeating the villain?** It shouldn't be treasure, weapons, or power. In most movies and games, the hero is content to merely save the world and restore the status quo. But in the classic "Hero's Journey" story structure, the hero returns from his adventure with knowledge. For example, in *Indiana Jones and the Temple of Doom,* Indy finds out that fortune and glory aren't the only important things in life.

- **What is the boss's motivation and goal?** Give your boss a more compelling motivation than "he's evil." I find "the seven deadly sins of man" (lust, gluttony, greed, sloth, wrath, envy, and pride) to be a great starting point for villainous motivations. The Riddler wants to prove that he's smarter than everyone. Voldemort wanted to regain his corporeal form and power. Galactus is just hungry. Whatever the villain's motivations and goals, they have to come in conflict with the hero's own. The boss is the primary obstacle to the hero's success. Only after the villain is defeated can the hero truly achieve his goal.

- **What's the boss's job?** In video games, most bosses are guardians: the guardian of a magic weapon, of a captured princess, of progression. But by keeping it at just this, you are doing a disservice to your villain. Give your boss some kind of motivation for doing what they do.

- **Is your game based on a licensed property?** Remember that these boss fights are the highlight of the fans' play experience. If you aren't a fan of the property yourself, research it enough to find out what the players would want to do. It's safe to say that *Star Wars* fans will find a lightsaber fight against Darth Vader a lot more thrilling than shooting him down in his advanced TIE fighter.

Congratulations! You've done a great job giving your boss a believable motivation, clear goals, and an intriguing backstory. He looks menacing and has awesome attacks and behaviors. But the most common way to make a boss look bad and dangerous is to make him **huge**.

Size Matters

A bigger boss means a badder boss...and bigger camera problems. You can start to solve this issue by always focusing the camera on the boss.

Because the boss should completely command the player's attention, you should try to keep the boss within camera view (unless the player does something stupid like turn his back on the boss). Avoid placing your camera:

- **Too high:** The high angle de-emphasizes drama and the scale of the boss.
- **Too low:** The foreshortening that happens makes it hard to gauge the distance to the boss and see incoming attacks. It can also cause clipping issues if the camera drops through level geometry.

Use elevation in the level and with the boss to help
rectify some of this issue. Allow the player to reach
the boss by climbing geometry to higher elevations.
Or you can bring the boss down to the player's level
just in time for the player to give the enemy a good
smack to the face. One thing you want to avoid is
crotch whacking. This is when the player is just tall
enough to reach the crotch of the huge boss.

A big boss means big attacks. Why be content
with the boss throwing rocks when you can have
him throw cars? Why not buildings? Or entire city
blocks? The more dramatic your attacks, the more
memorable they are. Take inspiration from games with bombastic bosses like *Contra* and *God
of War 3*. Regardless of how spectacular the attacks are, you will need to give the player an
opportunity to fight back. The player needs to work out when it is safe to attack. The player
needs to memorize the boss **attack patterns.** Patterns are at the heart of every traditional
boss fight and are created when several attacks and behaviors are strung together into a predictable sequence. Here's a simple example to show how patterns can be created:

fig. 1.   fig. 2   fig. 3.   fig. 4.

Let's say the player is fighting a giant mech armed with a laser cannon. The cannon's laser
sight sweeps the arena three times (fig. 1). Once the sight has acquired a target (the player),
the cannon will fire a stream of laser blasts going first to the right, then to the left and then
in the middle of the arena. The mech's cannon then transforms into a larger weapon. This
new form charges up for a second (fig. 2) and then fires a single thick beam that sweeps the
ground of the arena and can be avoided only by jumping or ducking behind cover (fig. 3).
When the attack is over, the mech's chest cowling pops open and vents steam (fig. 4). After
a couple of seconds, the cowling snaps back closed in a burst of electricity, and the mech
retransforms its cannon into its original configuration. The attacks cycle until there is a break
in the pattern initiated by the player, such as the player taking damage, dying, or successfully
attacking the boss.

This example shows the components of a boss fight: the primary attack, the invulnerable attack, the vulnerable state, and opportunities.

The **primary attack,** the laser blasts, create **movement patterns** for the player to memorize and follow (left, right, center). As long as the player knows that sequence, they'll be able to avoid taking damage.

Movement patterns should be easy to remember, but you should feel free to change the order of events to add some variety. Random movement patterns can be used, but I have found that many players find them difficult to determine and get frustrated if they don't "luck" into a favorable pattern.

The **invulnerable attack,** the charged cannon shot, is a dramatic, large-scale attack that forces the player to take avoiding action. As the player cannot hurt the boss during this attack, the player must act defensively, breaking up the play pattern.

The **vulnerable state,** the mech's chest cowling opening up, reveals the boss's weak spot to the player and is vulnerable to the player's attacks. This should be the chance the player has to inflict the most damage on the boss. The boss's weak spot should be visually designed to be obvious to the player: make it flash or glow or highlight it in some manner. It should stick out like a sore thumb. You can prolong a vulnerable state by stunning or incapacitating the boss. It becomes very clear to the player that they have a chance to attack without the fear of being attacked in return. Make sure you end the vulnerable state with an attack/event of some sort (in this case the electric burst), which pushes the player away from the boss and informs the player that their chance to attack the boss is over.

Opportunities, like the cannon changing form, are chances the player has to attack. The window of opportunity is usually shorter than the one given by the vulnerable state. Taunts work well for this, too. Just don't overuse any vocal cues or the player will get tired of hearing them over and over again.

I like to think of boss battles as a dance between the enemy and the player. Alternate between offensive and defensive moves for both the boss and player. Get more mileage out of your boss attacks and moves by changing the timing, speed, and range; just make sure these changes escalate. Most bosses start out pretty easily and get harder as they go. This is why many bosses have several rounds of patterns: the boss gets madder, and the threats ramp up until the ultimate climax when the boss is defeated.

Even as your boss is trying to kill the player, make sure to do all you can to keep the fight going. Provide plenty of opportunities for the player to regain health or power during the fight. Tools like **dynamic difficulty** will programmatically determine what the player needs to succeed. You can apply dynamic difficulty to enemy AI, reaction times, and, in fact, to just about anything. Delivering the right power-up exactly when the player needs it makes the boss fight feel exciting and dramatic. I also think the last boss battle of the game should be the easiest. Why? Because I want the player to end the game on a high note and feel like a triumphant hero. They've already done the hard part—playing through the entire game.

When the player gives the boss his comeuppance, use animations, sound cues, and visual effects to show that the player is damaging him. A robotic enemy can shoot off sparks; a fleshy foe can spray out spurts of blood or ichor. Other bosses will limp or crawl as they are close to death. Work with your artist to build your boss to have parts get chopped off or use several models that show increasingly damaged states. No matter how your boss goes, remember this **very important thing**:

LET THE PLAYER ADMINISTER THE COUP DE GRÂCE

The last strike of the fight *needs* to be delivered by the player. It's very important psychologically for the player to feel that they have won. This is the climax of the encounter. Don't rob your player of their victory with a cutscene or a canned animation. Once the boss is dead, let the player savor the moment with celebratory text, music, or effects.

Sometimes, due to story or licensing needs, your enemy will escape at the end of a boss fight. As the enemy escapes, do it with style. Having an enemy escape to fight another day shows the player that they are a worthy adversary, and another encounter is coming. But even if the boss escapes, you still need to make the end of the fight satisfying. You need the **false kill.** You must first knock the boss on his knees before he gets up and runs away. Hold the camera on that defeated boss for a moment. Let him curse the player's good luck (because it's never skill that defeats a bad guy, right?). Make sure it's clear to the player that they've won the fight.

When the enemy is defeated or killed, what happens to the enemy? Does he vanish in a puff of smoke or pop like soap bubbles? Does he dramatically clutch his heart and die an agonizing death? Does he explode? How is treasure delivered to the player after the enemy is defeated?[17]

Determine how the enemy model is removed from the world. Does he fade away, leaving only weapon pickups where his body once was? Does he dissolve into a pile of goo that then melts away? Or does the body stay on-screen as a gory reminder of your combat? Remember, what happens to your enemy affects your ESRB rating.

One more thing: sometimes a player is going to die. When they do, make sure they return to a safe respawn point. The boss shouldn't attack until the player is ready to fight. Consider keeping the boss's game state upon the player respawn. This means picking up the fight where the player left it rather than restarting the entire boss fight sequence from the beginning.

Location, Location, Location

Where a boss fight takes place is just as important as the design of the fight itself. The level is an extension of the boss fight...and sometimes, the level IS the boss fight.

The basic boss fight takes place either in a circular arena or a linear screen-wide walkway. This allows the camera to stay focused on the boss, who generally inhabits the center or back of the room with occasional trips to the side and outer edges. For more dynamic boss fights, add elevation to the arena. *Devil May Cry* had an interesting fight in which the player kept alternating between fighting the boss high up on the walls of a castle and down low in the castle's courtyard.

---

[17] Looks like Level 13 has its work cut out for it!

Think about the boss in relationship to the environment. How will a boss use the level for movement or attacks? Having dynamic elements like collapsing statues or walls or break-away floors can keep things exciting and surprising as the environment gets wrecked by the boss (and the player) over the course of the battle. Bust that joint up! Just be aware that if the player has to replay the boss fight, seeing the event happen again and again may get a little stale.

Designing boss arenas with dynamic level elements is the best of both worlds. The arena contains dynamic objects and elements that will react to a certain boss attack or action. These can be breakable windows, smashable floorboards, crushable computer consoles, and so on. This way, no matter what order the boss interacts with these elements during the battle, interesting things will happen. It creates a different experience every time.

A **scrolling battle,** where the player and boss fight their way through several locations, makes for a dynamic boss fight. First determine the method of player locomotion during the fight. Are the player and boss fighting on foot (chasing each other?), on top of vehicles (like the moving train in *Uncharted 2: Among Thieves* or hopping from car to car as in *Wet*), or while piloting vehicles? (Maybe they *are* vehicles!) Just be careful because scrolling boss fights require as much work if not more than a full level.

Another variation is the **puzzle boss:** a boss that is actually invulnerable and cannot be defeated by a direct assault by the player. Instead of fighting, the player has to survive the boss's attacks long enough to use objects in the level that will defeat it. Spidey can't actually hurt the Rhino boss in *Spider-Man 2* (2004), but if Spidey can trick the Rhino into smashing into electrified machinery, he can defeat him. The most obvious (and hilarious) example of a puzzle boss is in *You Have To Burn The Rope* (www.youhavetoburntherope.net) where the Grinning Colossus can only be defeated by...well, I'll let you guess how to beat this one.[18]

---

[18] Spoiler alert: you have to burn the rope.

Why Not to Create the World's Greatest Boss Battle

Some designers believe that boss fights are too "old school"—that they grind game progression to a halt. They believe that the time and effort to create bosses with their non-reusable artwork, hard-coded behaviors, and unique animations just isn't worth the production cost. Boss fights create a skill gateway; whenever someone has told me that they quit playing a game, the reason was usually that a boss was too hard.

An alternative to these problems can be found in turning the boss fight on its head. Instead of making it about a big *creature*, make it about big *drama*. Make the fight personal to the player and more about pivotal moments in the story.

My friend, designer Paul Guirao (*Dead to Rights*, *Afro Samurai*), created what I thought was the best boss fight design I had ever heard. Early in the game, the player learns an arm-wrestling mechanics. At the climax of the game, the hero is knocked to the ground by the villain, who attempts to plunge a dagger into the hero's eye! The player has to use that arm-wrestling mechanic to force the dagger away and eventually turn it on the villain himself.

Paul's design really opened my eyes (groan) to what a boss fight could be. It sounded awesome and dramatic and very different from anything else I had seen in games. It wasn't just another big stompy boss. What I really liked about it was that it:

- **Emphasized drama over scale:** It didn't need a rocket-firing colossus rampaging through a city to be exciting.

- **Used intimacy to create urgency:** Because the camera view was to be very tight (only the faces of the two characters, their hands, and the dagger were to be shown), the impending danger was heightened to a degree not seen in most video games.

- **Better utilized existing assets:** All the assets for the fight (the hero, the villain, the dagger, the arm-wrestling HUD meter) were used in other parts of the game. Nothing new had to be created to make this boss fight playable.

- **Told the story with a boss fight, not cutscenes:** Video games are **interactive** entertainment, so playing the story is always better than watching it.

Years later, as I played the ending of *Call of Duty: Modern Warfare 2*, I was reminded of Paul's knife-fight design. In *CoD:MW2*, the player character is stabbed by the game's villain. As the bad guy attempts to murder your partner, the player has to (painfully) pull the knife from his own chest and hurl it into the bad guy's eye (all occurring in very dramatic slow-motion).

Had the designers at Infinity Ward read my book? Had they heard of Paul's knife-fight design idea? Or was it just a good design for a boss fights whose time had finally come? All I know is that boss fight was as awesome and dramatic as Paul's idea had sounded to me all those years ago.

Level 11's Universal Truths and Clever Ideas

- Form follows function.
- Design your enemies to complement and contrast with each other.
- Carefully balance the enemies' strength, speed, and size.
- Fighting enemies is supposed to be fun.
- Enemies are meant to be fought, not avoided.
- Not every enemy attack has to do damage.
- You always want the player to hate the enemy.
- Use dynamic difficulty to give the player some help.
- Watch out for camera issues when creating a large-scale boss.
- Where the boss fight takes place is just as important as who the player is fighting.
- The player has to give the boss the killing blow.
- There are other types of enemies besides big stompy monsters.
- Emphasize drama over scale.

Level 12
The Nuts and Bolts of Mechanics

If you find a path with no obstacles, it probably doesn't lead anywhere.

—Author unknown

THERE'S NOTHING WORSE than an empty level that you *just walk through*.[1] Obstacles equal gameplay. Tension and drama equal gameplay. Discovery and variety and surprise equals gameplay. You need to start throwing things in the player's way: good things, bad things, things that make the player cry with pleasure and weep with sadness. You need **mechanics.** In first- and third-person action games, there are four types: **mechanics, hazards, props,** and **puzzles.**

The Mechanics of Mechanics

Before you dig in, be aware that "mechanics" is another term that suffers from *MDS*: multiple definition syndrome. In board game design, mechanics are also called *mechanisms* and are the systems that are combined to create gameplay. These are actions like drawing cards, resource management, competitive bidding, and even rolling the die.

Video game mechanics are *objects* that, when combined, create gameplay. The player *must interact* with them during the game. In many games, these mechanics are very literal. They can be jumped on, activated with a button press, or pushed around. Combine them with interesting level layouts and enemies. Some of the more common video game mechanics found in first- and third-person games include:

- Moving platforms
- Opening/closing doors
- Pushable blocks
- Switches and levers
- Cranks
- Slippery floors
- Conveyor belts

---

[1] Because WALKING IS NOT GAMEPLAY! Sorry *Journey*, *Death Stranding*, and all of you "walking simulators."

PLATFORM PRIMER

floating

moving (horizontal)

moving (verticle)

flips to create stairs

flips to reveal hazard

expanding/ shrinking

tilting

exploding

3..2..1

ferris wheel pattern

bouncy

tipping

collasping

scrolling hazard

rolling

"chasing" hazard

moves into hazard

pendulum

extending/ retracting

weight balance

swinging

rope bridge

smashable

growing

sinking

switch activated

returns when stepped off

Platforms are a beloved mechanic of action game designers. They come in a wide variety of styles and flavors that can be used to bedevil and delight players. Here's a suitable-for-framing chart I've devised to help you identify platforms in the wild. Be careful; some of them bite!

You would think that something like a **door** would be easy to design; after all, everyone has used doors in the real world, right? But doors open their own set of issues. Think about how the player is meant to open a door. Normally? Carefully? Aggressively? Remember, the character's personality comes into play when you're thinking about this. Kratos kicks open doors. "Soap" MacTavish uses explosives to blow open doors. Jill Valentine opens doors very slowly and carefully. Does a player have to pick the lock before entering? After all, they are masters of unlocking.

Be mindful of which way your door opens. Does it open in? Does it rise like a portcullis? Does it lower down? Does it swing out? All these opening actions can lead to different gameplay scenarios. You can turn opening a door into gameplay. Some multiplayer games have players work together to crank open a door simultaneously. *Mappy* (1983) used doors to whack and temporally stun enemies. A portcullis in an action game might lower back down after raised, requiring the player to dash under it before it drops down. Even a simple door in a survival horror game can be closed in the face of an enemy to buy the player time to reload or escape.

Despite their benefits, doors can bring their own problems. Quickly opening doors can clip into the player or cause the player to get knocked back. Make sure your player doesn't get caught on doors and doorway geometry. This problem may seem insignificant, but after getting caught up in hundreds of doorways, your player will get mad. That's the reason so many games make opening doors a canned animation sequence. The early *Resident Evil* games designed their level loading to correspond with the player opening a door. This design not only masked the loading of the level section, but also built tension as the door slowly swung open.

Make sure you know the answers to these questions and then keep the method of entry consistent throughout your entire game.

You can use doors as level gating mechanisms. You might not be ready to let the player enter the next room or level. They might have to find the right key, solve the right puzzle, complete the right quest, or earn more XP. A closed door doesn't need to look like a door. It can be a magic mirror, a mystic portal, a pool of water, a wall of vines, a force field, debris, or a guard blocking the player's way.

Some doors are just not meant to be opened. Locked doors are perfect for getting players to find another route through a level, but just make sure it's super clear why they can't get through. Your locked door can look as if it's made of unbreakable metal, it can have a huge lock on it that the player doesn't have the key for, or it can be blocked with debris that the player can't move. Whatever the choice, the appearance needs to be obvious to avoid frustrating the players. Locked doors are often (some say too often) used to introduce this common gameplay scenario: the quest to find the key.[2]

Switches and **levers** are more old standbys in video games. Some designers love using them; others avoid them like the plague. I admit that nothing makes my eyes roll faster than seeing a lever sitting in the middle of a room. It's something that screams "video game" to me. However, a lever can be a very useful gameplay mechanic. If you do use switches and levers, keep them visually simple. Now I know that one of the great pleasures in designing video games is creating fantastical things, but if you want your players to be able to identify these items in your world it helps to keep things grounded in reality.

Whatever you end up doing with your switches and levers, make sure:

- You include a visual clue. Consider placing a visual effect like a glow or an icon on your switch or lever. Since levers are often shown as slender poles, the player might have a hard time seeing them.

---

[2] I talk more about keys in Level 13.

- The player sees the effect of activating the switch or pulling the lever. That means using a camera cut, a voice, or sound effect to indicate what has happened.

- The switch or button changes appearance to show that it is in a new state. Have it change color, position, or shape. If you use a one-way switch (one that operates only once), play a nice meaty sound effect to indicate that it's permanently changed its state. If it's a resetting switch, play a "timer" sound effect to indicate that that switch is going to revert to its original state. You can even display a timer graphic, so players know how much time they have left.

Cranks are like levers and switches that take time for the player to activate. Some cranks are operated by pressing a button and holding it, whereas others require furious button mashing to open. In VR, a player might have to actually rotate their hand to simulate turning a crank.

One common gameplay scenario is to have the player operate a crank to open a door and then run back to the door before it closes. Some games turn rotating a crank into a rhythm game where the player has to sync button presses with the animation of the character on-screen. You can even turn a crank into a combat puzzle like the ones in *Devil May Cry*. If turning a crank takes X seconds to activate, spawn enemies to attack the player as they are turning it. If the enemies hit the player, they'll be knocked off the crank, which will unwind the crank's progress. The player will have to alternate between fighting enemies and turning the crank.

Other Types of Mechanics

There are a couple of other types of mechanisms you should know about as well. Let's look at match-three and racing game mechanisms.

Match Three Mechanics

In **match-three games** like the *Royal Match* or *Fishdom*, players match three or more icons (or jewels or pirate skulls or quilted teddy bears) for points, coins, or to complete objectives. Match three expert Jasper Juul splits these "breaker" games into four design foundations: manipulation, match criteria, obligatory matches, and time. Each of these factors can greatly impact how the game is played and affect the game's difficulty. Match-three games offer short play sessions, which has made them popular on mobile devices. This extremely flexible genre is a good match (ugh) with other game genres such as RPGs, word games, and even horror.

Most match-three games don't have characters that run, jump, or pull levers. Instead, they have mechanics that are triggered by the actions (swiping or tapping) of the player. A piece that can be moved is commonly called an **element**. The space that an element is in is called a **cell.** A group of cells is known as a **grid**. Here are some other terms related to match-three game mechanics:

- **Matching:** When three or more elements are next to each other in a predetermined configuration (such as a straight line or a block), a match is made. In most match-three games, when a match is made, the elements **break**.

- **Dropping:** Elements need to drop in order for the grid to be filled. Dropping can be used strategically to trigger chains.

- **Chaining:** When matching elements connect, they create a chain. A chain usually scores and breaks, clearing the cells and allowing new elements to drop in their place.

- **Blocks:** Elements that can't be moved by the player. They cannot be broken by chains. Sometimes they can be destroyed by exploding elements.

- **Exploding:** When a player makes a match next to an exploding element or if an exploding element is matched by a player, it will blow up, destroying all of the element in a radius, line, or some other predetermined configuration. It is optimal for the player to create a chain of explosions, resulting in an exciting display of exploding particle effects and elements dropping into the vacant cells.

- **Expansion:** This is where the grid expands in some way, either predetermined by the design or due to an element being removed, allowing more elements to drop into the new cells.

- **Conveyer belt:** A section of the grid where the cells move over time, requiring the player to strategically make matches as the elements move into position.

- **Objective:** These are conditions that the player must achieve to finish the level. For example, "freeing" 12 bird elements by dropping them "out" of the level.

- **Clearing:** Cells are "covered" or "painted" with a texture that needs to be removed by making a match on or near it. Clearing these cells might be an objective for the player to achieve.

- **Transformation:** When a special match is made (usually a configuration), the elements transform into a "better" element such as a bomb or a special element that yields a higher score or more expansive effect when matched.

- **Walls:** Walls of the level keep cells contained within the grid. Sometimes they are used to form paths, creating channels for the elements to flow into as they drop. Sometimes walls separate the cells from the elements dropping into them, requiring special elements (like element seeking bombs) to clear the cells to allow new elements to flow into them. The bottom of the level is usually considered "out"—an area where some special elements escape the grid and help complete an objective.

- **Crafted element:** A special element that can only exist if the player creates a series of matches. For example, a cheese element can only be created after cow elements are matched, resulting in milk elements, and when those milk elements are then matched to make the cheese element. These matches clear grids as new elements are formed, resulting in exciting chains as well as the newly crafted element.

There are always new mechanics being added to this genre. The best way to keep up with what's going on is to play the games. Fortunately, most match three games on mobile are inexpensive and play quick enough for you to grasp what the new mechanics are. The takeaway: PLAY ALL THE GAMES!

Racing Game Mechanics

At first glance racing games might seem simple: a car, a track—what more is there to it? Turns out there's a lot! First of all, you could be racing in a truck! On a hovercraft! A boat! A camel! A dragon!

For now, let's concentrate on racing games like *Forza Motorsport* (2023) and *MotoGP 24* (2024), which offer more to the player both on and off the track.

- **Speed:** Players need to feel the speed! Giving players a way to accelerate makes racing feel fast! Does the player start to lose control of the vehicle if they go too fast? Does a player lose speed if they take damage? Consider creating tracks with downhill slopes and jumps to really get the player's heart jumping!

- **Handling:** Control is the most important aspect of a racing game. If driving doesn't "feel" good, then the player can't maneuver around the track and concentrate on the race. You want the car to accelerate quickly when the gas is pressed, no sluggishness or lagging. You want the car to be able to take turns sharply.

- **Upgrades:** These are things like better engines, superior tires, and sleeker car frames. Upgrades should feel significantly different. They should affect handling, speed, performance, etc., in a dramatic way so the player feels like they got something for their money.

- **Customization:** Skins, sprays, stickers, tail fins, or anything that you can put onto your vehicle that says, "this is MY vehicle!"

- **Boosts:** Nitro and boost pads on the track create small adrenaline rushes for the player as the vehicle speeds up. There's nothing better than activating an explosive boost of nitro to shoot a player forward. Sometimes the player is in control of this boost, which is activated with the press of a button. Sometimes you start to lose control during the speed boost, making it challenging to maneuver your vehicle!

- **Powerups:** We talk more about powerups in a moment, but there are several games, such as *Mario Kart 8 Deluxe* (2020) and *Lego 2K Drive* (2023), that make powerups key to their gameplay. The famous spiny blue shell in Mario Kart comes to mind—a projectile that targets the player in first place. If they fail to avoid it, it explodes, and the kart is knocked for a literal loop, giving the other players an opportunity to catch up or pass by the loopy leader of the pack.

- **Progression:** Whether it's getting a new driver, a new car, or unlocking a new track, racing games thrive on progression. How about unlocking new race tournaments that take place in different countries or even unlocking music tracks. As long as the player feels like they are progressing in the game, it's worthwhile!

Holy Death Trap!

A **hazard** is a mechanic's nasty little brother who will slip an M-80 into your underpants when you aren't looking. Hazards look like mechanics, often act like mechanics, but will kill a player without hesitation. Hazards may also resemble enemies, but the key difference is intelligence and/or mobility. All hazards have predictable patterns and limited movement and usually aren't very smart. They are things like

- Spiky pits

- Smashing blocks

- Blasting flames

- Exploding barrels

- Laser-guided missile launching turrets

When you are designing hazards, the first rule is to make sure that they look dangerous. That means spiky, flamey, frosty, sparky, poison-y. Slap a big death's head on it if you must.

When creating your mechanics, take inspiration from the theme of your level. Create things that look as though they belong in the level. For example, in the dungeon level of *Maximo: Ghosts to Glory*, we had

- Grabbing prisoner hands that pop out from grates

- A suit of armor wielding a chopping axe

- Spinning, spiked iron maidens

- A toxic sewer filled with floating coffin platforms

Get inspiration from dangerous-looking things in the real world: from spiny cacti to razor wire. Use shape, color, sound effects, and particle effects. Use anything to make it clear to players that they WILL get hurt if they touch or collide with this hazard. Don't make the player have to play a guessing game to what your intention is. Use visual shortcuts and stereotypes because they are great shorthand tips to the player. To demonstrate this point, here is a great example of what I DON'T mean.

I was designing a hazard and took the design to the artist who was going to be modeling it. I suggested that the hazard be colored red, as many cultures associate the color red with danger. The artist said, "That's too predictable. I think it should have yellow and black stripes." I was intrigued (I was thinking of the yellow and black hazard edging found on loading docks), so I asked her why. They replied, "Because bees have black and yellow stripes, and everyone knows that bees are dangerous."

Epilogue no. 1: The hazard ended up red and not looking like a bee.

That story reminds of another story. A designer and I were reviewing level designs. A particular level featured a ship that would sail away as the player started the level. The player had to run to catch up with the ship; otherwise, they would literally miss the boat. I told the designer that I thought that the player would stop and look around to get their bearings when they started a level. If the player took the time to do that, they would literally miss the boat. What would happen to the player if that happened? The designer said, "Oh, we can just drop a big rock on the player's head, so they'll die and have to start the level over again."

Epilogue no. 2: We didn't make that level. Because it was uncool to drop a rock on the player's head. Since then, I made this **very important thing** my motto:

NO DROPPING ROCKS ON THE PLAYER'S HEAD[3]

Instant death hazards just suck. They are cheap and mean-spirited. If the player dies because of a hazard, it should be because they didn't pay attention or get the timing right. Make the player realize it was their fault they died, not because the designer decided they needed to die. Death is never a good way to educate the player. It just makes the player frustrated and sad.

What I Learned from Making Kids Cry

Whenever I meet gamers who played *Maximo: Ghosts to Glory,* they will often tell me that they never finished the game because it was just too hard. And you know what? It is. It demanded players make pixel-perfect jumps and be combat-ready the minute they landed in front of an enemy. It has a needlessly cruel save system. It's been called one of the most difficult games of all time.[4] It *is* a difficult game. And after making that game and reading the reviews, I learned my most important lesson as a game designer: The difference between difficulty and challenge.

Difficulty = Promotes pain and loss

Challenge = Promotes skill and improvement

A difficult game does whatever it can to punish the player. A challenging game confronts the player with obstacles that can be overcome with skill and knowledge. I believe a challenging game is much more rewarding than a difficult one.

Some gamers absolutely love difficult games. The list of ridiculously difficult games could fill this entire chapter: *Dark Souls/Demon's Souls* series, the *Ninja Gaiden* series, *Contra, Ikaruga, Shinobi, Devil May Cry 3,* the *Ghosts 'N Goblins* series, *Super Meat Boy, Battletoads.* The list goes on and on.

Some people find that it is quite an accomplishment to finish a difficult game, but those who do are in the minority because most players quit before then. If you want players to play your game to completion, your game needs to be challenging, not difficult.

When I first started designing video games, I would refer to the balance between challenge and difficulty as the **"fun curve."** There is a point in the game at which things have ceased to

---

[3]I mean that figuratively as well as literally.

[4]www.ign.com/articles/2005/04/27/the-top-10-most-challenging-ps2-games-of-all-time

be challenging and drop straight into difficult and frustrating. The goal was to never "go over the fun curve." Years later, I learned there was an actual psychological theory about the fun curve called **"flow."** I will get to flow in a moment.

My key to keep players from "going over the fun curve" is to create **ramping gameplay.** A designer must build one gameplay system upon the last, teaching players a new move and how to master it against mechanics and enemies. These gameplay elements are combined and gently intensify as the game progresses. But I'm getting ahead of myself. If we are going to talk about the timepiece, we are going to have to examine the clockworks first.

Time to Die

When I think of clocks, I think of time. When I think of time, I think of **timing puzzles.** Timing puzzles are mechanics that move. They are perfect for creating tense moments when a player has to wait for the right time to dash through whirling blades or to smash through pylons.[5] They cause anticipation for the player as they wait for the right moment to jump to a moving platform. A timing puzzle should have the following:

1. A discernible movement pattern for the hazard. The pattern can be back and forth, up and down, zigzag, circular, or figure eight: just as long as players can track the hazard's movement and determine when to act.

2. Predictable timing for the hazard. Random timing is unfair to players who need to understand the pattern to be successful.

3. A tight window of opportunity, but not impossible. Allow leeway for players at the start and close of the window's opening.

4. "Tells" in the world to give players clues to where it is safe to stand and where they will be hurt or killed. Bloodstains, grooves in the floor, lighting and shadows, sound effects, particle effects, geometry, and decorative elements are things a player will notice and learn to use as markers for success.

wait for it...   wait for it...   ...go for it!

---

[5] To this day, I still get tense thinking about those spinning paddles in the Specter chamber of *Dragon's Lair*, a scenario that may be the first video game timing puzzle.

Props are mechanics that have eaten a big Thanksgiving dinner; they don't move unless someone asks them to get off the couch and do the dishes. Designers and artists can place these items into the level to make it feel more like a real place. Sometimes props act as barricades or obstacles for the player to avoid, jump over, or take cover behind:

- Desks and chairs
- Parked cars
- Barricades
- Statues and gravestones
- Refrigerators
- Fences and walls
- Coffins and alters

- Fire hydrants
- Mailboxes
- Filing cabinets and toolboxes
- Computer consoles
- Tables, wardrobes, and dressers
- Crates
- Potted plants and water coolers

Thinking up props can be an entertaining exercise in free association and brainstorming. Start with the predictable items that you would find in your level and go from there. Here's an exercise: come up with as many items and props as you can for the following level themes:

- **Easy:** A Wild West town
- **Medium:** A supervillain's lair
- **Hard:** A Chinese factory that makes industrial parts

Pro tip: If you find your brainstorming ideas getting silly or obnoxious, you know you've reached a good place to stop. Let your ideas settle overnight or for a day or two before starting again. Or take a research break and look for more inspiration in books, games, movies, or the interwebs.

Don't be satisfied with merely thinking up items to decorate your world; allow your players to interact with them. Start with natural reactions. If you shoot a water cooler, it should explode in a watery splash. Let players knock over light items or shove around heavy ones. Let players closely examine interesting statues, objects on bookshelves, or paintings.

You can shoot or smash props to access new areas or yield treasure. In the LEGO games (like *LEGO Star Wars* and *LEGO Batman*), you can pretty much destroy anything—all yielding studs, the game's version of money. Nothing is more satisfying than busting up a bunch of junk to get tons of treasure. Try not to overdo it because it can turn your carefully designed level into an empty room full of rubble.

Crates are breakable items that yield goodies and double as platforms, but they're also overused clichés that have become a joke within the gaming industry. They are visually boring and, frankly, a lazy fallback for designers and artists who don't want to burn the brainpower to think up more interesting breakable objects.

Gaming website *Old Man Murray*[6] created a review system called **start to crate** that gauges the time it takes a player to encounter a crate in a game. While the article is meant to be satire, I find it to be a good gauge to determine just how creative your game is. Rather than reinvent the wheel...er, crate, you can use this list of 50 breakable objects other than a crate to populate your game:

Barrel, treasure chest, vase, urn, trash can, mailbox, newspaper stand, baby carriage, metal drum, cargo container, cardboard box, cage, lantern, lamp post, filing cabinet, fish tank, toy box, keg, hay bale, pile of skulls, dog house, bird house, Tiki idol, statue, fortune-telling machine, church donation box, suggestion box, ATM, hollow tree stump, attaché case, safe, suitcase, TV monitor, fuel tank, refrigerator, oven, breadbox, bureau, wardrobe, parked car, coffin, arcade machine, soda machine, fire hydrant, vending machine, oxygen canister, filled shopping cart, one-armed bandit, copy machine, and toilet.

There. You never have to have a crate in your game again.

There is one more type of mechanic, which is the rarest one of all. It's the mechanic that's "just for fun." This can be the player piano that plinks out a tune as you approach it or the toilet that flushes if you interact with it. Don't be afraid to include these just-for-fun props in your own game.

---

[6] www.oldmanmurray.com/features/39.html

The Music of Mechanics

The goal of good level design is to help players achieve what psychologist Mihály Csíkszentmihályi[7] calls **flow.** (I told you we'd get back to it.) Csíkszentmihályi's theory proposes that there is a point between boredom and difficulty. A place where players become so engrossed that they become energized, focused, and unaware of time. But in order to create flow, you need to know how to orchestrate these elements together.

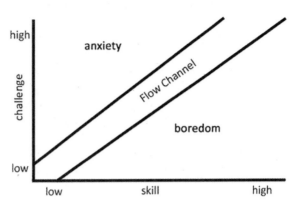

Reaching the state of flow feels like making music; it's the rhythm of a great level. A natural rhythm of the player's movement and actions—or flow—starts to emerge as they traverse the level.[8]

To me, placement of elements in a game is orchestrated like the instruments in Sergei Prokofiev's *Peter and the Wolf*. In this famous musical piece, each character (Peter, a duck, a cat, a bird, and the wolf) is represented by a different musical instrument. The piece starts out with Peter (represented by strings) walking through the forest. This musical theme gives the impression of movement, just as the player is learning how to do the basics in a game: walking, driving, or manipulating the game character.

Then Peter is joined by the bird, which adds a higher register flute to the music. The two themes intertwine, adding excitement to the music, just as treasure and collectibles keep the player

---

[7] Pronounced "cheek sent me high-ee."

[8] The ancient Greeks proved there was a correlation between music and mathematics; that each higher octave is twice the frequency of the one below it. The same concept can be applied from a mathematical perspective where the gameplay elements and mechanics are combined to create a formula of successful gameplay.

excited and motivated to continue playing. The duck (represented by an oboe) joins in, and the music speeds up and gets more complex, similar to the addition of complex player actions and level mechanics to your design. When the lower register cat (a clarinet) comes in, the music picks up as the cat chases the bird, adding a little conflict to the piece, much like hazards in a level.

After all the characters are together, the wolf's dangerous-sounding theme comes in; this echoes the arrival of enemy characters in a game. The music in *Peter and the Wolf* intensifies as the wolf eats the duck, is attacked by the bird, and threatens and battles the heroes until they are rescued by the crashing arrival of hunters. (Represented by drums.)

Let's take a look at how to introduce and orchestrate gameplay elements the same way that *Peter and the Wolf* add instruments.

1. Start your player character moving through the world with simple movement challenges: walking, jumping, and collecting goodies.

2. Start with one mechanic. Repeat it a couple of times so the player understands how it works.

3. Add a second mechanic, and let the player learn that one, too. Then combine the first one with the second.

4. Make things exciting with a hazard. Let the player get used to doing the things they would normally do in the game (traversal, collection, interaction with mechanics) but now with the hazard being part of the equation.

5. Now come the enemies! Give the player a chance to learn how to fight them.

6. Combine the enemies with the hazards for more excitement.

7. Finally, just as the player is getting used to all these game elements, toss one of them on its head just to keep the player on their toes!

If you create enemies and hazards to complement each other,[9] they'll end up being versatile tools when populating your level. Think about what order you want players to do the activities and set up the scenario for the players to figure out. Here are a few examples of how to combine enemies and hazards to make life more difficult for your players.

---

[9] This is easy because form always follows function, right?

- The player has to jump over the hazardous pit with an enemy waiting on the other side. Place the enemy far enough away so they don't engage the player until they safely land after the jump. To make this scenario more intense, make sure the pit has a timing element: the pit opens and closes, a pendulum blade swings back and forth, fire shoots up, a stone block slides down, and so on.

- Here's an enemy that throws or shoots a projectile through the path of a moving hazard. Design the timing so that it passes through when the opening appears. The solution is for the player to dispatch the enemy (with their own projectile) before running through the moving hazard. Or the player can use the moving obstacle as cover to get in closer to the enemy.

- The whirling saw blade in this chamber will cut the player in half if they collide with it, which makes fighting these multiple enemies a challenge; the player must dance between combat and avoiding the hazard. However, the blade should also kill the enemies, which makes the player feel clever when they lure them to their death by saw blade. Give the player plenty of opportunities to turn the death traps against their makers. It's all about the villains getting their comeuppance!

Fire pit, moving obstacle, and whirling blade—there are many more combinations you can do with just these three mechanics. As these examples show, you really need only a few mechanics and enemy types to make a rich play experience. A well-designed game uses a handful of mechanics. The key is how you combine them. Play any game by developers Treasure (*Gunstar Heroes*, *Dynamite Heady*, *Ikaruga*) or Naughty Dog (*Crash Bandicoot*, *Uncharted*) to see some great examples. Or you can just read the next section.

Chip Off the Old Block

I believe that the best mechanics are also the ones that are the most flexible. By changing a mechanic's context and use you can create an entirely new challenge. Let's look at a mechanic that can be found in many action and adventure games—the pushable block. While this mechanic is often maligned for being slow, unrealistic, or boring, the pushable block mechanic continues to be used by designers because it's flexible. Let's follow our hero through the dungeon to see different ways we can use a pushable block for gameplay.

Welcome to the dungeon! Unfortunately, our hero's path is blocked by a large stone block. But if we push it aside, we can enter.

Now our hero has to get up to that ledge. No problem. We just push a block to create a platform that he can jump up onto.

Ah, the old switch gate. If our hero stands on the switch, the gate will open, but when he steps off, the gate closes. What to do? I know! Let's drag that block on top of the switch, its weight will keep the gate open!

What's this? A vent shooting a jet of fire? Let's have our hero push the block over it. Now the fire is blocked, and our hero can progress without getting roasted.

Curious. These pushable blocks have letters on them. It must be a puzzle! Nobody said we would have to think in this game! By pushing these blocks into the proper sequence our hero can E-X-I-T the room!

Who put a pit of acid in our way? That's a dirty trick! Fortunately, our hero can push a block into the pit and use it as a steppingstone.

This monster is looking for us! But the monster can't see our hero when he's standing behind the block. Maybe if he alternates between pushing and hiding, he can escape being captured!

That skeleton archer is making life difficult for our hero. But if he pushes the block and uses it for cover, he can survive to reach the far end of the room.

Oh no! How is our hero going to get past that Cyclops sentry? Pushing that block off the ledge onto to his head ought to do the trick!

That's a lot of flexibility for just one pushable block! And we haven't even explored pulling the block! Be mindful that it is possible for players to get bored with mechanics if they are repeated too often, so think about the context in which they are used. A good mechanic is like a baseball pitcher. You need to rotate them in and out of your game to keep them fresh and effective.

A Nice Little Calm Spot

Now that you've gotten past the hazards with your life, it's time to talk about a friendlier mechanic: **checkpoints.** Checkpoints are predesignated locations within the level where players can save their progress; take a break; or reassess their choices of equipment, route, and so on. Checkpoints can be visible or invisible to the players. You will want to determine which method is better for your own game.

On one hand, visible checkpoints offer players a target in the level, provide a sense of security when they are activated, and can be an opportunity for an exciting or fun animation. The players feel a sense of accomplishment every time they reach and activate one.

On the other hand, visible checkpoints can look "gamey" and sometimes require explanation on how they can be activated.

Invisible checkpoints don't break the players' immersion while playing the game. However, because they are invisible, players may not be sure when they are activating a checkpoint or where they will respawn upon death. This can be frustrating for players as they wonder how far back in the level they will end up.

No matter which style checkpoint you use, here are a few rules of thumb to remember:

- Always face the checkpoint in the direction you want players to travel. Otherwise, they'll get turned around or need to reorient themselves or the camera upon respawn.

- Never place a checkpoint next to a hazard or in the detection zone of an enemy. It's totally cheap to take damage when you (re)appear in a level.

- Players should respawn on the ground, not in mid-air. Don't make the player wait for the character to land from a drop. Also, avoid long respawn animations for the same reason.

- Place the checkpoint on flat, even ground to avoid any collision problems upon respawn.

- Make sure your game's saved data is retained whenever a checkpoint is activated. Don't make players go into another menu just to save the game.

Riddle Me This

Puzzle mechanics can be tricky; not just because they can be difficult to design or because they often require unique assets to create. It's just that puzzles are tricky to classify. Here's one definition I've found:

A puzzle is fun and has a right answer.
—Scott Kim

While Mr. Kim has designed waaaay more puzzles than I ever will,[10] this definition doesn't feel quite right to me. What bothers me is the use of the word "fun." Fun is completely subjective, like the words "funny" and "sexy." What I think is fun may not be fun for you. And frankly, I don't find many puzzles in video games to be fun. For me, there's nothing worse than a puzzle whose solution I just can't fathom. At least with a difficult boss monster, you can brute force your way through to victory. You just can't do that with a puzzle. So, with apologies to Mr. Kim, I have created my own definition:

A puzzle is a challenge that has a right answer.
—Scott Rogers

[10] Go to www.scottkim.com for loads of "puzzley" goodness, including free games!

The difference is the word "challenge." That's a puzzle's job (and the entire game's job for that matter!): to challenge players. The challenge the puzzle offers players is "solve me."

Players first need to know what reward is offered for solving the puzzle. It can be to open a door, create a picture, or translate a message. Just make sure players know what they need to do first. I always think this **very important thing** applies:

SHOW 'EM THE DOOR AND *THEN* SEND 'EM AFTER THE KEY[11]

When creating the puzzle, keep the puzzle's pieces simple and modular. You need only a few pieces to create many combinations. Work with as few pieces as possible to prevent players getting confused. Make it simple for players to manipulate the puzzle pieces when rotating or flipping them. Make sure that when a puzzle piece is adjusted or changed, players can see that it's been adjusted and there is a clear way to return it to its original position. Many times it's easy to lose track of any progress. Keep the pieces uniform unless irregularity is part of the puzzle. Uniformity and consistency will make it easy for players to understand how the elements fit together. Let them concentrate on the puzzle, not the manipulation of the pieces. When players interact with a puzzle piece, a simple button press should show a result. It may not automatically lead to the solution, but they should get the idea that doing the action in a different way will eventually get them there.

When I'm confronted with a puzzle in a game, I "check the puzzle" against every ability I have, every item I'm carrying, and every object in the room. This is the biggest pitfall of puzzle games; they end up being boring permutation fests. Think about what the piece *is* and its relationship to the other pieces as well as to the entire puzzle. If the relationship of the puzzle pieces isn't clear, it's easy to get stumped. And another thing, don't use cultural references (which could be confusing to a foreign audience) or make the player need to use the piece in a bizarre or absurd way to solve the puzzle.

---

[11] It doesn't have to be a door. And it doesn't have to be a key. I'm speaking metaphorically here.

For example, *Resident Evil 2* had a puzzle in which the player needed to open a door in a police station. The puzzle required placing chess pieces into a control panel. Whaaaat? First of all, when do you find chess pieces in a police station, let alone ones that operate a control panel? Now if it had been…I don't know…the ID cards of dead police officers found throughout the station, then the puzzle would have made more sense. What I'm getting at is that you need to tie the puzzle into the game's story or setting, so it doesn't seem so senseless or random to the players.

Players should have all the tools nearby that they need to solve the puzzle. I like to place puzzle pieces no farther than two rooms away from the puzzle's solution. It's not fair to make players run all over the level, let alone the game world, wondering what does or doesn't works to solve the puzzle.

The layout of the puzzle is as much a clue as the pieces. For example, if you present a chess board-style layout, players can visualize movement and patterns using the board as a guide before they tackle the problem. If the puzzle pieces are moved in a certain way, players should be able to visualize the consequences of moving the pieces. Just like with timing puzzles, movement and layout will help players see patterns that will help them reach their goal.

Puzzles in video games are essentially gating mechanisms. If you have lots of puzzles, make sure there are multiple paths of progression. Eventually, players will have to come back to the puzzle that stumped them to solve it. Give the players time to figure out the solution of a stumper while giving them another puzzle to solve in the meantime.

Tell players whether they are close to finding the solution…or not. Remember that kid's game where you are searching for a hidden item and another player says "you're hot" or "you're cold" based on how close you are? Essentially, that's what the game designer needs to do for the players. Make your hints relevant to the puzzle. Ask yourself, "What would I want to know at this point?" Remind players what their goal is. Use camera cuts to show causes and effects that happen during the puzzle. Use voice and sound effects to give positive reinforcement.

There are really only four ways to solve a puzzle: reason, knowledge, skill, or plain ol' dumb luck. The best puzzles allow players to use all four of these ways in some capacity to solve a puzzle. Granted, you don't want players to stumble onto the solution, but if that's what it takes, then stumped players should at least be able to do that.

You need to give players the "Ah-ha!" moment. It's the moment when they realize how the puzzle fits together and what the solution is. They may still need to complete the puzzle, but that part should happen quickly; by that point, it's just a matter of getting the grunt work done.

However, if players don't get that "Ah-ha!" moment and fail to solve the puzzle, don't make it a big deal. Find a way for the puzzle to be solved regardless of the players. Give them hints or even the answer if you have to. Of course, getting the solution without solving the puzzle should cost players something—be it points or cash. If players need a hint, just charge them a fine and then let them skip ahead. Don't make them keep guessing wrong answers and then punish them for their mistake. And don't make the punishment something so severe as losing a life. Progression is a right, not a reward.

While I have found that players are generally smarter than you might think when it comes to solving puzzles, you should not give your puzzles cryptic or nonsensical solutions. The most infamous adventure game puzzle was in *Gabriel Knight 3: Blood of the Sacred, Blood of the Damned*. The player had to disguise himself as a non-player character to enter a location. To create his disguise, the player had to stick tape over a hole in a fence that a black cat passed through. The cat's back would rub against the tape and hair would stick to the tape, which the player would then use to create a mustache for his disguise. However, the character the player was disguising himself as DIDN'T EVEN HAVE A MUSTACHE! My **very important motto** for creating puzzles has since become:

NO CAT MUSTACHES

In other words, don't be so darn clever that players never figure out the puzzle. If you have created a Rube Goldberg-style[12] solution to your puzzle, you've overthought things and you need to simplify your puzzle. The conflict for players shouldn't be "game designer versus

---

[12] Rube Goldberg was a newspaper cartoonist who drew very complex and amusing contraptions to do very simple things. The famous board game *Mouse Trap* is unofficially based on his cartoons.

player" but "player versus puzzle." So, check your ego at the door and do what's right for the players and the game.

Puzzle Me That

Of course, up to now, I've been talking about the kinds of puzzles that you find in story-based games, but there are so many more types of puzzles. The puzzle genre is the broadest in video games, and these games vary widely in content and gameplay. Let's look at some of the different types of puzzle games:

- **Logic puzzles** are often found in adventure games like the classic games from Lucas-Arts and Sierra. They rely on players finding inventory items and then combining them to solve the puzzle. Make sure the relationship between the items and the solution makes sense (no cat mustaches!) and make it easy for players to combine and test items as they seek the solution.

- **Math puzzles** challenge players with arithmetic, subtraction, multiplication, division, spatial geometry, and number ordering. If you are going to have math puzzles in your game, it doesn't hurt to disguise them. You can put learning into a game, but the minute players catch on that they're learning, they won't want to play anymore. Give them something else (that would be gameplay!) to concentrate on as they learn.

- **Rigid body physics puzzles** like *Angry Birds 2* or *ADR1FT* simulate real-world interactions between objects and environments to create challenges for players. Weight, density, momentum, force, velocity, and kinetic energy become design tools to create challenges. They can be based on balancing stacks of items, engineering stable structures, launching aerodynamic craft, and just smashing up stuff!

- **Liquid physics puzzles** like *Where's My Water* or *Hydrophobia* simulate fluid dynamics from streams of water to giant waves. Don't forget water has momentum, viscosity, force, drag, and buoyancy that affect your sea-worthy game elements.

- When creating **trivia** and **knowledge puzzles,** don't assume everyone knows what you do. Keep your questions short and clear. Do your research and determine what kinds of questions your audience would have fun answering. Players should feel smart for knowing the answers. Make sure you have a wide range of difficulty from simple to obscure, but mostly simple. Write **lots** of questions. Knowledge games cease to be fun the minute you have answered all the questions. There are many different ways players can answer a question. Which one is right for your game?

    - **Multiple choice:** Give players a range of choices, but always include at least three. Create "close answers" that are similar to the answer but could be easily confused with the real answer. Change things up occasionally by asking "Which of these is not true?" style questions.

- **Find the object/image:** Players must hunt for the answer among a variety of images or objects. Don't make the hunt be pixel perfect. Instead, allow a little space around the item so players can eventually spot and select the answer. Play with image orientation, color, and size to keep your players hunting.

- **Fill in the blank:** This type of response requires keyboard or writing tablet input. Make sure your word parser is flexible enough to allow for misspellings, synonyms, colloquialisms, and regional terms. *Scribblenauts* has 22,802 words in its vocabulary! If your puzzle's vocabulary is smaller than that, consider letting players learn what words are available so they don't waste time guessing ones that aren't available.

- **Traditional puzzle** games like *Sudoku* and crossword puzzles offers simple challenges. Simplicity is the key here. Make sure your puzzle has only one solution. Allow players to make notes or try out different solutions before committing to the final answer. Add prompts and helpful hints to players. It's better to help players along than let them get frustrated and quit playing the game. Create multiple challenge levels for all levels of players.

- **Visual puzzles,** especially hidden object games like the *Hidden Objects Superthief* or *Zoo Detective,* rely on the players' observation skills. Unlike fill-in-the-blank puzzles, you'll find that visual puzzle games come in a variety of genres, including mystery, horror, and romance. This may be thanks to the popularity of hidden object games with female gamers. Here are a few pointers for designing hidden object games:

  - People search for visual patterns like shapes, sizes, and colors. By adjusting these, you can hide your objects easily.

  - Fool around with player expectations by using non-stereotypical visuals for your items.

  - Hide objects in plain sight. The most overlooked image is the one right in front of the players.

  - Direction and rotation make a big difference in how an object is recognized. Turn an object 45 or 180 degrees to throw off your players.

- **Word puzzles** like *Scrabble, Words with Friends,* and *Wordle* focus on spelling. When creating word puzzles, be careful about using slang and colloquialisms. Word games should be visually uncomplicated. Design your interface with clarity in mind. Be careful not to use an illegible font for your letters (see Chapter 8).

Overall, I think that most word games are sort of boarding. Think about how you can present your word game in a more unique and interesting way like *Typing of the Dead* did. A typing game where you are killing zombies by making words? Incredible.

Whew! I've just barely scratched the surface on puzzle games. It doesn't matter which puzzle genre you design. Just make sure you keep the gameplay fair, the objectives simple, and the puzzle's logic sound.

Minigames and Microgames

A **minigame** is a simple game created to provide variety, represent activities, and add value to a product. Many minigames are based on or are variations of classic arcade and classic home console games.

A **microgame** is a minigame that takes only seconds to play. Half of the challenge of microgames is learning how to play them within the short time allotted. The *WarioWare* titles are compilations of microgames.

Minigames offer many advantages to game developers. They are quick to create and test, they are easy to play, and they can be used as metaphors for complex player activities. I truly believe ANY activity can be represented by a minigame. Observe:

- Lockpicking - *The Elder Scrolls Online* (2014)
- Hacking electronics - *Batman: Arkham Knight* (2015)
- Portrait painting - *SpongeBob Atlantis SquarePantis* (2008)
- Tagging walls - *Mark Echo's Getting Up: Contents Under Pressure* (2006)
- Cooking dinner - *Good Pizza, Great Pizza* (2014)
- Serving dinner - *Order Up* (2008)
- Picking a nose - *WarioWare* (2004)

Any activity.

When designing a minigame, make sure to:

- Keep the controls simple. Minigames, by their nature, imply easy-to-learn gameplay.
- Keep the gameplay sessions short—no longer than 2 to 3 minutes. Some microgames can last only a few seconds.
- Ramp the difficulty gently. Minigames are meant to provide variety, not torture players.
- Add something new with each level. Even a different piece of background art, sound effect, or song keeps the game from getting stale or repetitive.

- Design the minigame's controls using one button, touch control, or a very simple control scheme.

- Allow for player customization if possible. The web-based minigame *Upgrade Complete* (2009) allows players to upgrade EVERYTHING, including the player's ship, the background graphics, and even the copyright screen!

- Make the victory condition clear to players. How does your minigame end? Does it have an end? Some games can be played "forever"—or at least until the kill screen appears.

Minigames don't even need to be segregated from the core game. The platformer/puzzle game *Henry Hatsworth in the Puzzling Adventure* (2009) and the RPG/puzzle game *Puzzle Quest* (2007) combine two styles of gameplay: platforming and puzzle. If you do this in your own game, just make sure you allow time for players to make a "brain shift" between the two gaming styles. Give them a second to reorient themselves with a "ready" screen or pause in the action.

And finally, when you've run out of all other creative ideas for minigames and puzzles, you can always resort to Whack-A-Mole.

Seriously, please don't. I consider Whack-A-Mole the last stop on the designer's creativity train. And here's why:

Really?
This is the best
you can do?

- It relies solely on the player's reaction time, which requires no thought or decision making from the player.

- It's random, which doesn't let the player utilize strategy.

- It's very repetitive. There's no variety to the gameplay other than possibly the speed of the popping moles.

- It requires almost no input from the player other than a single motion, button press, or click.

- It is an "endless game"—there is no end unless the designer dictates it. Usually, the player stops because they're tired of playing it.

I know you can design something more engaging than that! Let's move on to something more exciting: power-ups!

Level 12's Universal Truths and Clever Ideas

- Design mechanics, hazards, and props that work with enemies and complement each other.

- Good game design is like music: it has a rhythm that players can feel.

- Reuse mechanics to create new challenges.

- Games should be challenging, not overly difficult.

- No rocks on the head - be fair when punishing your player.

- Be creative: don't resort to worn-out clichés like crates and Whack-A-Mole unless you have to.

- No cat mustaches: don't make puzzles so cryptic that players can't use logic, knowledge, or skill to solve them.

- A puzzle is a challenge that has a right answer.

- Show them the door and *then* send them after the key.

- Give players opportunities to catch their breath by providing plenty of checkpoints.

- Keep puzzle games simple and fair.

- Keep minigames and microgames simple and short.

Level 13
Now You're Playing with Power

POWER-UPS can be found in every genre of gaming, from driving to puzzle games to action-adventure games to shooters. They are dropped by defeated enemies, hidden in treasure chests, and sometimes just lying all over the place in the middle of the road.

A well-designed power-up is concentrated action. A player only has to touch it to become energized to move at lightning speeds, blow up the world, or return from the dead! The great thing about a power-up is its effects are **immediate**: who wouldn't want to immediately gain awesome power?! The only downside is that its effects are usually **temporary,** so use that power wisely.

Powering Up

A designer should be wise when creating power-ups and should ask the following questions:

- What does the power-up do?

- What does it look like? How will it (or its effects) visually stand out in the world? Does it glow or strobe? Does it rotate or bounce?

- Can power-ups be combined, or can the player have only one active at a time? Can the player retrieve power-ups that are unused or discarded?

- How does it affect the player's movement, rate of speed, number or type of attacks, Health, or status?

- How are its effects communicated to the player visually? Aurally?

- What is the player's trade-off for using the power-up? Some reduce speed or mobility or the types of moves the player can do while under the influence of the power-up.

- If the power-up ability is temporary, what cues will let the player know it is about to expire? Is there a HUD element, a visual cue, a sound cue, or a music cue? Does it last until the player loses a life?

Consider how the player will be collecting the collectible or power-up:

- Does the player have to walk over it to collect it?

- Does the player have to reach out and actively choose to pick it up?

- Some power-ups are automatically drawn toward the player when they get a certain distance from them. If so, how close does the player have to be, how quickly does this happen, and so on?

- Is the power-up or collectible activated when the player gets into its proximity?

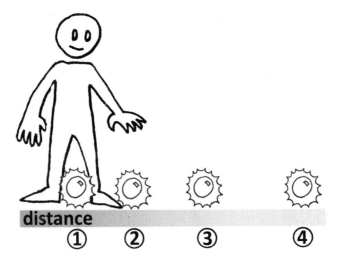

Knowing how close the player needs to get will help you determine the effects of the power-up after it's collected.

Power-ups can be divided into four categories: **defensive, offensive, movement,** and **game changers.**

Defensive power-ups help boost the player's ability to survive damage and continue progress in the game. The most common defensive power-ups include:

- **Health-up:** This power-up refills the player's health meter. It can be a partial or full refill. If you have different power-ups that heal different amounts, make sure the power-ups look different from one another.

- **Ability recharge:** This power-up is like a health-up, but it recharges an ability meter rather than the player's health.

- **Extra life:** When the player collects this power-up, she gains one more life/restart that will allow her to continue the game after she loses all her health.

- **Invulnerability:** This power-up makes the player resistant to all damage from an enemy's attack. An invulnerable player might be open to effects from hazards that use physics and geometry (for example, falling off a cliff edge); otherwise, problems can arise with collision detection.

- **Invincibility:** With this power-up, as with invulnerability, the player cannot be hurt when hit by an enemy or his attack, but she can also automatically destroy most enemies by colliding with them as seen in *Metroid*'s screw attack and *Mario Kart*'s super star. Many games don't allow this kind of ability to work on bosses, or if they do, they cause only minor damage.

- **Protective:** This type of power-up includes temporary forcefields, physical shields, or auras that protect the player from enemy projectiles, fire, or poisonous floors. Protective power-ups may or may not have their own "health meter" or timer to show how much protection remains. Protective defenses are different from invulnerability and invincibility because the player usually can improve, modify, and extend them.

- **Indirect attack:** Commonly found in fast-moving car combat and kart-racing games, this power-up lets the player "fire and forget" smokescreens, oil slicks, and black bombs with fuses on top, causing havoc to those unlucky enemies and players behind them.

- **Smart bomb:** This power-up provides a clear-the-game screen when things get too tough, or the player needs a moment to breathe during all the action.

Offensive power-ups improve or modify attacks, allowing players to defeat enemies faster, more efficiently, or more spectacularly.

- **Ammo boost:** This power-up fully restocks the player's ammunition. Most ammo boosts pertain to a specific weapon in the player's inventory.

- **Buffs:** These power-ups increase the player's skills and abilities for a short period of time. Awesome flame effects that surround the player are optional.

we're boned.

- **Multi-weapon:** This power-up improves the player's current weapon without fundamentally changing it. For example, *Contra's* spread attack fires five projectiles in a fan-shaped configuration, while heat-seeking rockets will home in on enemies.

- **Weapon upgrade/swap:** This power-up increases the strength, speed, and damage of the player's attack or can change their weapon to an entirely new one (sometimes more powerful, sometimes as powerful but with differing capabilities that may be more suitable—and hence more useful—in a particular situation). New visuals usually accompany the change. For example, *Ghosts 'N Goblins* lets the player change from lance to dagger to torch. The size and effect should at least change if not improve in spectacular-ness as the weapon upgrades.

- **Damage modifiers:** Flame! Poison! Ice! Electricity! These power-ups improve the player's base damage, usually accompanied by dynamic visual. By creating enemies that have vulnerabilities and immunity to these different factors, allows for the player to discover strategies to defeat them.

- **Direction:** This power-up allows the player to change or augment the direction of their attack. It is most commonly found in shooters, allowing the player to shoot behind as well as above and below them. The change in direction can also be applied to the projectile, as in the case of enemy-seeking missiles.

- **Companion:** When the player picks up this power-up, a small object appears next to the character that can provide an additional attack or shielding function. The companion may or may not have hit points. Many last until the character is destroyed or for a specific duration of time. *Galaga* (1981) added the novel twist that a captured ship became your companion. You lost a life, but you gained double shot ability.

Movement power-ups allow the player to improve an existing movement or add some new ones. For example, in *New Super Mario Bros. Wii (2009)*, the players may fly through large parts of the level using the propeller helmet. This power-up allows players to fly through levels and over hazards as well as avoid bad guys altogether. Be particularly careful to account for these power-ups when designing player metrics:

- **Speed change:** Nitro boosts and other power-ups allow the player to move at incredible speeds. As a trade-off, the player usually has less control of the vehicle or character because of the faster reaction time needed.

told ya.

- **Access:** The player gains access to locations normally unreachable via an ability bestowed by this power-up. The access methods are as varied as flying, helicoptering, gliding, and swimming. For example, Mario's bee suit in *Super Mario Galaxy* allows the player to fly for a short period of time, which can be extended by collecting coins.

- **Size change:** Depending on the game, changing size can allow a whole suite of abilities, the least of which is being able to get into tiny holes. In *Super Mario Bros.,* the super mushroom not only increases the player's size, but also allows the player to take one extra hit and to break bricks to access new locations. The mini mushroom in *New Super Mario Bros.* causes Mario to shrink, allowing the player to leap great distances.

Game changers alter the dynamics of the gameplay and the player's interaction with the game in a significant manner:

- **Change state:** This power-up changes the play dynamics in the game. For example, in *Pac-Man*, the player normally flees from the enemy ghosts. However, when you eat a power pellet, the ghosts become vulnerable, and you become the aggressor.

- **Score/treasure modifier:** Whether it's a *Crazy Taxi* fare multiplier or *Rock Band's* star power, the value of any points/treasure you collect is increased for a short period of time when using this power-up. Be sure to accompany this modifier with a timer, effects and even music or sound effects to let the player know when it's active or about to end.

- **Magnetic:** This power-up draws treasure items toward the player, relieving them of the risk of entering dangerous territory or having to "clean up" treasure and collectibles after combat. Work with your programmer to determine pathing for this power. Do items collide with other objects in the world as they are drawn toward the player?

Do they ignore collision and zip right up? Do they follow a path? Or are they smart enough to avoid objects all together?

- **Invisibility/disguise:** When using this power-up, the player is rendered temporarily undetectable by enemies and hazards, allowing them to safely avoid potentially deadly combat and enter locations barred by annoyingly alert guards. Work with your artist on how this is represented visually. Even though you are invisible, you still need to see your character to control them. Invisibility has been presented in many ways in games, and it is most commonly presented in the "Predator sheen" where you often see the outline of the figure, which is occasionally highlighted with a shimmer.

- **Comedy power-up:** This power-up exists solely to surprise and amuse the player. For example, *MDK*'s "Earthworm Jim" power-up drops a cow onto enemies' heads.

Most power-ups are content to sit still and wait patiently to be consumed by the player, whereas others have a keen sense of self-preservation. Power-ups have been known to move upon spawning out of their hiding place, like the super mushrooms in *Super Mario Bros*. Still others will run and hide when they spot the player, like the "cowardly power-up" in *MDK*. Give your player a chance to catch these **mobile power-ups.** Do not make them move faster than the player or make them resistant to the lure of a magnetic power-up.

Power-ups can be designed to work conditionally. In *Maximo: Ghosts to Glory*, we had an armor power-up that worked only when the player had collected the full set of armor. Another one required a special ability to activate. As long as the conditions for gaining these special powers are clear to the player, there's no reason why you can't add this technique to your design arsenal.

Not all power-ups are delicious and useful. Very evil game designers in their secret lair high in the Alps have created **anti-power-ups.** Like a chocolate truffle stuffed with dog poo, these sinister collectibles look like regular, nice power-ups, but they hold a deadly surprise. Poisonous power-ups can sap health, slow movement, drain experience, or even turn the player into a zombie, complete with backward control schemes. While they are fun, they are fun only once or twice. I suggest using anti-power-ups judiciously and with caution.

"Love Thy Player"

Pureiya aishi nasai

Once upon a time, a Japanese game director[1] told me this should be the motto of all game designers. I agree with him, although I have a different way of saying it:

The game designer should be the gentle hand on the rear of the player, pushing them ever upward.[2]

The designer can use many systems to enable players during the game, and we've already talked about some of them in other levels: checkpoints, hoists, and teeters, aim assist, ramping difficulty. But there are others that are worth discussing: dynamic difficulty balancing, difficulty level adjustment, rubber banding, game length, and autosave.

Thanks!

- **Dynamic difficulty balancing** (or **DDB**) is a way to adjust the challenge and rewards based on performance. For example, if the player dies too often fighting an enemy, the enemy's health is reduced slightly, or the enemy doesn't attack as often. If the player is low on health and opens a treasure chest, a health-up will pop out. But if the player isn't low

---

[1]A different Japanese game director from the "fisherman" from Level 4, btw.

[2]*Not as concise, but much more pronounceable.*

on health when opening the chest, they will be rewarded with treasure instead. The goal of DDB is to give players what they need when they need it to propel them along to success.

- **Difficulty level adjustment** gives a player the option to shift the game down to a lower difficulty setting if too many parameters, such as multiple player deaths, are detected. The player can be given the option to decline, or the adjustment may happen automatically. Personally, I don't recommend the latter because some players find it insulting.

- **Rubber banding** is primarily found in racing games, but it can be used any time the player who is behind needs to be given an advantage to level the playing field. That advantage should be proportional to how far behind the player is. Rubber banding does not need to be limited to physical distance. Both *NBA Jam* and *NFL Blitz* provide advantages to the player by tweaking the opponent's AI or speed. Rubber banding is a great solution to help the player when they most need it.

- The **game's length** is actually a good tool for adjusting difficulty. Take, for example, a battle arena. If the player fights bad guys for about three to five minutes, with sufficient health and a modicum of skill, they should be able to survive just fine. However, make that player fight for a half hour, and player fatigue and attrition start to set in. Odds are the player won't survive the encounter because they'll get exhausted...or at least bored.

Trust your feelings, Luke. After you play a level a thousand times,[3] you will know when your level gets boring. That said, you must be very, very careful because you can develop what I call **designer blinders.** Designer blinders occur when you've played your game so many times that you will require a much more difficult level to feel challenged than the consumers, who will play it only a few times. It is a very common problem within game development, which I have seen happen many, many times. Consolidate your level. Kill the boring parts. Death to boring! Don't be afraid to cut elements if it will make your game better.

---

[3]Honestly, you will play a level a thousand times (at least) between setting it up; populating it; testing the mechanics, hazards, and combat; placing the collectibles and readjusting them; and then finally officially play testing it.

- **Autosaving** occurs when the game periodically records and saves game data automatically. This way, the player can concentrate on playing the game rather than micromanaging the game's save files. Autosave is helpful when the game crashes[4] or if the player forgets to save the game at a critical part and then dies. Many games autosave whenever loading a new area.

Seriously. "Love Thy Player"

For every positive example of player difficulty, there is at least one negative one. Here's a story illustrating what I **don't** mean about how to design player difficulty: I was reviewing an enemy encounter with a creative director. I told him that I thought the encounter wasn't bad, but it could stand to be a little more challenging. He agreed and his instructions to me were, "The player has to die six times before he can progress." I thought, "I'm sorry, Mr. Creative Director, I know you are my boss and all, but you are an idiot." But I didn't say it because I wanted to keep my job.

What I *did do* was not design the encounter so that the player had to die six times to progress. And neither should you. Player death should **never** be a yardstick for game design. "Rewarding" the player with damage or death is negative reinforcement.

In *Maximo*, one of the enemies was a treasure chest mimic—a fun enemy that, when "opened" up, snapped, and attacked the player like a dog. But it had an unfortunate side effect. I saw players actually cringe before opening a chest because they expected it to be a mimic.

While it was fun for this designer to watch the player get tricked, it was not fun for the player. This defeats the point of the game: to have fun. Your players will hate you for it and stop playing the game. This is bad because the ultimate goal of any game designer should be to keep the player playing. If I ever create this kind of enemy again, I will give some clues to the players so they can spot this enemy and prepare for it. A clue can be as simple as a color change or wobbling pots with an enemy inside like in *Legend of Zelda: Spirit Tracks*.

---

[4]But your game isn't going to crash, is it?

The way I see it, if a player plays and finishes the entire game, they will be happy. They will be happy enough to tell others how much they liked your game, and they will be happy enough to buy your next game. Then you stay employed as a game designer. It's a win-win for all parties involved.

More Wealth Than You Can Imagine!

I don't know, I can imagine quite a bit.
            —Han Solo.

Game designers have many very powerful tools to keep players playing. Mystery, delight, pride, and power we've already talked about, but now we come to the three most powerful of these tools: greed, hope, and reward.

Greed will get players to do interesting things. They will grind their way through the grindiest MMOs to get that stronger sword, that unique hat, gain that next level. They will jump onto the smallest platform festooned with the deadliest traps just to grab that one additional coin. They will fight the biggest, meanest enemies just to find out what comes next in the story. Or to score that achievement. The following **very important thing** rings true:

NEVER UNDERESTIMATE THE GREED OF THE PLAYERS

But...instead of using the players' greed for evil such as luring players to their death to prove that you, the game designer, are cleverer than the players, you can use their greed for good instead:

- Use the promise of treasure and items to motivate players to fight enemies.

- Give the players a personal and customizable space to show off their trophies and rewards. When they start seeing some of the "shelves" filling up, they'll want to "catch them all."

- Exploit the "me too" factor. Keeping up with the Joneses is a powerful urge for players, especially in the multiplayer space. I was once playing *World of Warcraft* and minding my own business when I saw another player ride by on a mechanical chicken mount. All of a sudden, my player agenda went from "get to the next level" to "MUST OWN THAT ROBOT CHICKEN!"

- Create "guidelines" when placing treasure and hidden objects. Sharp players will pick up on these guidelines, and their observations will be rewarded. For example, in *Maximo: Ghosts to Glory*, buried treasure chests were placed next to trees. If there weren't trees in the level, they would be hidden next to similar vertical architectural elements like pillars or gravestones.

- Like the dots in *Pac-Man World* or rings in any *Sonic the Hedgehog* game, you can string collectibles through the level to guide players where to go next.

■ The designers of *Half-Life* (1998) have an interesting method of introducing a new weapon or item to players. First, players hear about the new item from another character. Second, the players see the item in the possession of another character. Third, the players see the item being used by another character, and finally, the players obtain and use the new item for themselves. By the time the new item is in the players' hands, not only have they learned what it looks like, what it is, and what it does, but they want it for themselves.

The second tool we have to work with is **hope**. This is what keeps a player coming back to a game. I hope I will do better than the last time. I hope I can win enough rounds to earn that special reward. I hope that this time I won't die right away on the mission. I hope that I can make that jump this time. By giving the player hope, we give them the confidence that they can win the game.

Hope is a powerful motivator and we game designers can use it to manipulate players. But not always in a bad way. Manipulation is a tool that can be used for good as well. By making a player do something a certain way in a game, we help them achieve success. Missions in many MMOs ask the player to do something out of their way or a certain number of times in order to gain an objective. I have never liked pulling weeds in real life, but I will happily do it in *Stardew Valley* to keep my farm looking nice!

Like greed, **rewards** are a powerful player motivator. A reward is what players are ultimately working toward. After all, you can't have a game without a victory condition, and you should never have a victory without a reward:

- Expose players to what rewards are available early in the game. This way, they have a laundry list of things "to do" throughout the game and what they will get for achieving them.

- In the earlier stages of the game, players increase levels pretty fast at the beginning. This makes the player feel more invested in the game. As they get to higher levels, however, it requires more points to progress.

- Reward players as soon as possible, reward often, and provide some variety and surprise to the rewards. For example, In *Maximo vs. Army of Zin*, sometimes players would get money as a reward for defeating an enemy, but other times they would get a power-up. Players were never quite sure what they would get, which kept things interesting.

- A win condition needs to show evidence of success. There's no such thing as enough fanfare. Be dramatic, exciting, and even a little goofy. Or a lot goofy! Set off fireworks, do exciting camera pans around the player, have the player character jump in the air excitedly, play cheering crowds and slot-machine sound effects. Use visual effects and particles, lots, and lots of particles! The more, the better! You want players to feel as though they are the victors of World War III, the scorer of the winning run at a baseball game, and a lottery winner all at the same time.

- Whatever the reward is, make it matter to the players. Award players something that gives them the edge on the next level and is the solution to a problem that plagued them on the last. The best reward is the one player doesn't realize they need until they get it.

In video games, rewards come in many shapes and sizes: scoring, achievements, treasure, loot, power-ups, souvenirs, bonus materials, praise, surprise, and progression.

High Score

Back in the prehistoric era of video games,[5] the players' only reward was a **high score.** Scoring is a useful system to showcase the players' success in a very simple way: a number and three little letters. It's a little hard to describe to someone these days why seeing your three initials displayed on an arcade game screen was so exciting, but it was a little like writing your name in wet cement: something the whole world can see to show that YOU were the master of the game—at least until the game's power was turned off for the night and the scoreboard reset.[6] Many gamers thrive on competition, even when it's against themselves, and love having the bragging rights that come with getting a high score. But is scoring in gaming still relevant?

---

[5]Back in those days, the only video games we had to play with were two rocks connected by vines to one bigger rock. Now get off my lawn, you darned kids!

[6]This is why it was always better when you got the high score at a 7-11 store. Those places NEVER closed!

That was the question many game developers asked themselves in the late 1990s. As the arcade scene was dying and most gaming had moved to PCs and home consoles, scoring represented the old school. Scoring was regarded as a remnant of game designs whose sole intent was to keep players dropping quarters into the slot. Scoring soon became regarded as a meaningless number compared to collecting 100% of the game's secrets and finishing the game's story. A simple numeric score just wasn't as sexy or cinematic as a full-blown ending cutscene. Scoring in gaming was almost as dead as the dodo.

Almost.

In the early 2000s, scoring started to matter again with the rising popularity of browser games like *Bejeweled* (2001) and *Feeding Frenzy* (2004). When **leaderboards** were introduced to Xbox Live (and later to the PlayStation Network), scoring was back up and running. Thanks to connectivity, achievements and scores could be used as bragging rights with the rest of the world! Players can share their scores and stats on the PlayStation Network, Game Center, Steam, Google Play, and Window's Game Explorer. Developers have even created their own tracking programs such as UbiSoft's Uplay, EA's Origin and Apple Arcade.

Achievements

Achievements are high scores with personality. Debuting with *Halo 2* on the Xbox 360, achievements motivate players to show off their in-game skills and brag about their accomplishments. Doing a task *X* number of times, completing game goals like defeating bosses, collecting one specific item (or all of them), or just finishing the game are all valid achievements.

Achievements are great fun for the developer to create—as much as they are for players to collect. You can give your achievements clever names and fun icons. Usually published before the game's release, achievement lists act as a play "to-do" list. Achievements are a great way for the designer to point out to players the gameplay concepts that they otherwise may not think of attempting. Achievements can be awarded for anything the developer desires. Here are a few of my favorites:

- **Easiest achievement ever:** Press Start to play (*The Simpsons*).

- **Not bulletproof:** Die on an easy level (*50 Cent: Bulletproof*).

- **Street cleaner:** Hide five dead bodies in bales of hay (*Assassin's Creed 2*).

- **Be polite:** Provide an enemy with a freezecam shot of you doffing your hat (*Team Fortress 2*).

- **Six degrees of Schafer:** Play with or against any player who has this achievement (which means that at least one player in the chain has played the game with creator Tim Schafer; *Brütal Legend*).

- **You've wasted your life:** Be idle for 5 minutes (*Saw*).

- **Losing his mind:** Decapitate a captain with a shield (*Conan*).

- **Wheeeeeee!**: Slide 330 feet continuously through blood (*Fairy Tale Fights*).

- **Skidmark:** Give 50 wedgies (*Bully: Scholarship edition*).

- **I feel so funky:** Get slimed by a charging ghost (*Ghostbusters*).

- **Jawa juicer:** Crush five Jawas by using the grinder in the garbage processing room (*The Force Unleashed: Ultimate Sith Edition*).

- **The cake:** You found the cake, yummy! (*X-Men Origins: Wolverine*).

Money! Money! Money!

Who doesn't love getting **treasure?** The way the coins jingle merrily when they pop out of a treasure chest. The way they glitter and sparkle on the ground after spilling out of a headless enemy. The way they spin in place, luring you to jump through a flaming hoop of death and over a pit of punji sticks...

Yeah, collecting treasure is great and all, but what are you going to spend it on? To make treasure mean anything, you need an **economic system.** When designing treasure items for your game, create them in escalating values: 1, 5, 10, 50, 100.... You get the idea. But don't spread your values too far apart either. The last thing you want is the virtual equivalent of pennies—treasure that no one wants to pick up.

One of the things I love about video games is that I am far richer than I am in real life. Players feel great when they are flushed with cash. The benefit of having wads of dough is that players have lots of choices when shopping—but to do that, you must make sure there are plenty of items for the players to buy. It's always fun to give players choices between two really good things. Not only do they have the delicious agony over what to buy, but it gives them something to look forward to buying the next time they go shopping. Stock your stores with a variety of things and find ways to rotate the stock to keep the selection from getting stale. Next, determine the price your items will be. Start by classifying your treasure, loot, and other buyable items by their rarity: common, uncommon, rare, and unique. Then apply a price to each of the items. Think about what items you want available to the players from the beginning of the game. Always have some items that can be bought quickly and others that lie tantalizingly out of reach. If I only had a few more coins!

Once you've created a preliminary economy (don't worry about setting it in stone, prices will change over the course of production as you figure out what players will want or need), think about placing treasure in the world. If you want players to be able to afford $300 worth of items, make sure there is at least $300 worth of treasure in the level. You will have to answer the question, "Does treasure regenerate?" If it does, be aware that players can "mine" levels for treasure, which can completely screw up your economy. On the other hand, replaying a level without any treasure to act as a motivator isn't as much fun for players. You may want the players to replay a level multiple times so they can collect enough money to buy what they need. A shortage of funds encourages replay…or exploration off the beaten path. If you expose players to all the items they could buy at the beginning of the game (via a "skill tree" like in *Marvel Spider-Man 2*), the players can start to plan how they are going to spend their money once they earn it. Sometimes players might have to buy cheaper and necessary gear like ammo or health-ups to be able to progress. Give them options as to how and what they upgrade.

Use color to clarify your treasure's value like the old standbys copper, silver, and gold. Or use different shapes like coins, bags, and gems. Don't get too diverse or crazy; otherwise, players will mistake treasure items for power-ups.

Does your treasure have encumbrance, meaning there is a limit to what players can carry? If so, then how are they going to carry it? Many RPGs and MMOs have a limit to encumbrance, forcing players to find other storage solutions such as magical holding bags or a bank. Whatever the solution, make sure that players don't have to shuttle cash from their storage to the store. Just have it come out of the players' accounts to avoid all the hassle.

Your treasure doesn't even have to be money. Treasure can be bolts as in *Ratchet and Clank*, studs as in the *LEGO* games, souls as in the *God of War* series, even trash, such as the bottle caps in *Fallout*. It doesn't matter what it looks like, as long as it's sparkly and makes a satisfying cha-ching! sound effect when you collect it!

Speaking of all that treasure, where are your players going to spend it? Most RPGs have friendly (and not so friendly) stores that sell all manner of adventuring goods. *Borderlands* and *BioShock* use vending machines. Make your store specific to the game you're making. A racing game could have a garage where players can buy car upgrades and customizations. A sports game could have a sporting goods shop. Adding a store is just one more way to add character and theme to your game.

Hey, maybe that slightly creepy guy in the trench coat over there in the alley has the magic sword we're looking for? Let's go talk to him.

Who's there? Come in, come in. I have everything the daring hero needs to survive. Take a look around and don't be afraid to ask for help:

- **Offense:** Need a new sword? Lusting after that more powerful gun? How about a nice magic missile spell? It was owned by a little old witch who only used it on Sundays.

- **Defense:** Armor, shields, helmets, forcefield generators: I've got everything that can repel a blade or deflect a laser beam.

- **Repairs:** Swung that sword a little too hard, did ya? Well, it will only cost you a few coins to get it swing-worthy again.

- **Replenishable resources:** Ammunition, health potions, batteries, gasoline; we'll get you back up and running again!

- **Skills:** Want to learn a whirlwind sword attack? Or how to add +2 to your accuracy skill? How about a nice set that grants a lock-picking ability? All ya need is some cash...

- **Access:** I've got keys, treasure maps, and even a statue that looks like it may fit into a hole. I'll bet it opens a secret door somewhere.

- **Vanity:** That hat looks very stylish on ya. So is that a new costume? It looks much better than your old one, if I do say so myself.

- **Whimsy:** Oh, I absolutely think your hair would look better pink, sir. And yes, Ma'am, a mustache is just the thing ya need.

- **Information:** For just a few coins, I can tell you where the King is handing out jobs for adventurers such as yourself.

- **Saves:** Only the cruelest of designers would charge someone to keep playing.... That will be $100 gold, good sir. Thanks, and come again!

Let's get out of this place; it's horribly overpriced, especially because you can find most of this stuff lying around the levels.

Loot is all the great stuff you can buy, but it's FREE! Well, if you consider navigating through the temple of eternal pain and defeating the goblin army free. The difference between loot you buy and loot you find is you should always find much better loot on your adventure. Loot can be part of an upgrade system. Make it part of your story like *The Legend of Zelda's* famous "It's dangerous to go alone, take this..." moment. Progression in the game can be marked by getting a new weapon or piece of equipment. Save the best weapons, the strongest armor, and the "shootiest" guns for loot. Let players earn their keep by solving puzzles, surviving hazards, and defeating bosses. And remember this **very important thing**:

THE BEST REWARDS ARE HARD WON

Souvenirs

Souvenirs are physical (well, virtual) reminders of the players' adventures during the game. Souvenirs can be displayed back at the players' base or castle or spaceship or condo.

Give players a special place to show them off, like Lara Croft's trophy room in *Tomb Raider Anniversary* (2006) or a nice shelf with proper lighting. They can be animated interactive exhibits like those found in *LEGO Indiana Jones: The Original Adventures* (2008) or virtual museums like the one in *Uncharted 2: Among Thieves*. No matter which style you choose, use a tight camera or viewer to let players get a good look at 'em and a label to remind them where they found the souvenir.

Not all souvenirs should be kept on a shelf, however. Turning souvenirs into useful game items gives those items more meaning. Defeat the Lich King in *World of Warcraft* and take his sword. *Mega Man* takes the powers of the Robot Masters as he defeats them. Instead of awarding a dragon skin rug, why not give the player a pair of dragon skin boots? That way, as long as the player wears the boots, everyone will know who slew the red dragon. Make sure to give the souvenir items special proper-

ties, too. Those red dragon boots may allow players resistance to fire attacks or let them walk over hot coals or on lava. It may even give them a special flaming kick attack. Make it special and the players will want to get to the next encounter to see what they can win.

Bonus Section about Bonus Features

The biggest problem with **bonus features** is the production team usually creates them at the last minute. Design them early, but they should be one of the last things you create. This way, you can judge just what constitutes a "bonus" to the players by comparing it to the rest of the game's content. Bonus materials may include:

- **Skins:** Skins, aka costume changes help add a little variety (and humor) to your bonus features. The Starkiller from *Star Wars: The Force Unleashed* can wear costumes from the game's other levels. Kratos in the original *God of War* could unlock a business suit or chef's costume. Why? Because it was funny.

- **Alternative models:** Create a new look for your hero or villains! In *Uncharted 2: Among Thieves*, players can unlock a fat version of the hero, while in *Batman: Arkham Asylum*, players can turn all the enemies into skeletons.

- **Alternative modes:** Ah, big head mode. You are so easy to code and yet you get so many laughs. Is it any wonder why we love you? Silly modes run the gamut from changing an enemy's exploding body parts into birthday presents to turning all the cars in a game pink. You are limited only by your imagination and how much time you have left in your production schedule.

- **New levels:** The most time-consuming of all bonus materials to make, new levels (and game content) have become a popular type of DLC. Many console games have introduced "season passes:" the customers buy the pass when the game is released so they can gain access to new levels that are released later. *BioShock Infinite, Assassin's Creed III,* and *Batman: Arkham Origins* are just a few of the games that offer season passes to expand the play experience with new levels and stories. By scheduling these passes as additional material that is released after the game has shipped, the development team can put more time, effort, and polish into the levels, thus keeping up the quality of the material.

I'm not sure why this is hilarious.

- **Music:** Want to listen to the game's music without playing the game? Simple. Create an audio player to allow players to hear the music. Or you can just let them insert the game disc into a CD player.

- **Commentary:** An audio track of the team may talk about the game's development. Starting with *Half-Life 2: Lost Coast,* developer Valve has made interactive in-game commentary one of its standard bonus features.

- **"Making of" video:** Another bonus feature is a documentary-style featurette (or feature) that explores the game's creation. These videos are very time-consuming to make; however, they can be a great way to spotlight your hard-working team.

- **Model viewers:** Players can view the 3-D models and assets in the game. Allow the player's camera control to pan around, rotate, and zoom in and out on your models to show them off in the best possible light. This feature is particularly good in games like RTSs, where the characters are normally viewed from a more distant camera angle.

- **Art viewers:** These viewers are the most common bonus features: just scan your pre-production art and voilà! You're done! Okay, lazy, you can do better than that. Don't be content to just show a slideshow of your team's art. Set the images to music or commentary from the artists. Show off environments, props, maps, and design materials that will make the players appreciate all the hard work you've put into your games. Make sure the players have control over the pace of the presentation. Don't make them wait around for the next piece of art to appear. How about a magnifier so they can zoom in closely to examine the art? (You can even hide a reward within the art for the players to find!)

- **Promotional materials:** Promo materials are more commonly found in sequels because the assets are usually created late in the game's production process. If included with long-standing franchises, they can be particularly interesting for nostalgia purposes.

- **Trailers:** Movie trailers (especially relevant if the game is a movie tie-in), previews of other games, a sneak peek at a sequel. Just don't make watching them mandatory: allow players the option to skip them.

- **Minigames:** Although some whole games are collections of minigames,[7] don't forget to include them in bigger games, too. They provide players a chance to take a break from the protracted grind of a longer adventure without ever having to "leave the disc." Give your minigame a place to live, such as an arcade. Minigames are moderately easy to make, just identify some of your game's most fun gameplay and recontextualize it. In *God of War*, we did just that—everything in the "Challenge of the Gods" was already in the game code; it just gave players a different set of victory conditions. Some minigames give rewards that can be used back in the main game's economy system. Sometimes they are promotional tools, as seen in the case of the iPhone game *Mass Effect Galaxy*, which gives players a reward in *Mass Effect 2* for completing it.

- **Multiplayer modes:** While describing multiplayer gameplay could take up an entire chapter,[8] there are still other modes that aren't directly related to gameplay. Asset trading, chat functions, spectator modes, friends, and rival rosters that allow you to check your friends' game stats—these additional modes will give your game value. Remember to keep their interfaces intuitive and user-friendly.

- **Alternative endings:** Will the player turn out good or evil? Save the world or get blown up? Get the love interest? Many RPG, adventure, action, and survival horror games offer multiple endings to their stories. For example, the *Mass Effect* series offers different endings depending on the sex of the player character and the relationships built with the other NPCs over the course of the game. Multiple endings are a great way to get players to replay the game, as long as they know there are multiple endings to be seen. I've found that it's no longer enough to just have a few different endings based on the decisions made at a few key moments in the game. The struggle between good and evil is much more interesting if they are evenly matched. Build systems and opportunities for the players to "course correct" toward one outcome or another. Make the outcome be the players' choice, rather than one decided by the game.

- **Cheats:** Cheats are usually reserved for use by the development team during production. Cheat modes can be enabled to give players unlimited resources like health, ammo, lives, or just plain ol' invulnerability. I suggest that you don't enable cheating until players have played through the game once; otherwise, they are CHEATING!!!... themselves out of experiencing the game the way it was meant to be played. Some games go as far as to encourage "proper" play: cheats might not get the "good" ending of a game, or they might be marked out as a cheater, as in *GTA*. In *Team Fortress 2*, anyone who didn't use a cheat received a special wearable angel's halo called "the cheater's lament."

---

[7]For examples, just check out most of the games on the Wii.
[8]It does, in Level 14, which is coming up next!

- **User created content:** Some games such as *Team Fortress 2*, *Dota 2*, *The Sims* and *Gun Raiders* allow players to create and submit custom skins or models for characters, weapons and even levels! If the content is good enough, they will put them into the store in the game so other players can buy (with game currency) the content. Approved item creators for *Team Fortress 2 and Dota 2* earned (on average) $15,000 in one year![9]

How to Win at Losing

As an industry, we are really, really good at making players feel really, really bad. We kill player characters at the drop of a hat, force them into near impossible situations, and then mock them when they fail. We steal from them in a heartbeat, and we mess with their minds any chance we can get. What we're not very good at doing is offering **praise.** And as an industry, we wonder why players complain about games. What we need to do is make players feel like the best people in the world instead. The best example I've seen of giving players praise is in *Zak and Wiki: The Quest for Barbaros'*

Treasure (2007). Whenever players do something correctly, the following happens:

- A "success" musical sting plays.

- The hero does a funny reaction or victory animation.

- There is a particle effect coming off the hero.

- Wiki, the player's monkey sidekick, congratulates players (in text form) on how good they just did; Wiki also has his own musical sting and particle effect.

Not only does all the preceding happen whenever players complete a puzzle, but also:

- A burst of special effects tints the screen yellow with streaking stars.

- A "success" musical tune plays, longer than the sting.

- A "look at me!" animation from the hero displays the puzzle piece or item they've just won.

- The name of the item the players have just won is shown.

---

[9] https://np.reddit.com/r/DotA2/comments/1ve4dm/on_average_team_fortress_2_and_dota_2_item

Eight things to support praising players in the form of character animation, visual effects, music, and text for solving one puzzle! Fantastic! This game made me feel as if I was the smartest player in the world, and as a result, I wanted to keep playing! Just remember that you can have too much of a good thing. Praise ceases to be meaningful if you receive it for doing nothing or performing insignificant acts.

See how often you can stroke players' egos during the course of the game. NPCs in *Fable* either recoil in horror or compliment the hero, depending on what alignment he is, which is exactly what players want to hear, especially because they've spent so much time cultivating their goodness or evil.

There are other rewards than just treasure. I'm talking about **surprises** and fun. At Disneyland, Pirate's Lair is a pirate-themed playground. Guests at Pirate's Lair can interact with several items, including a bilge pump and a turn wheel.

As you turn the wheel, a rope on a pulley starts to pull up a treasure chest from underwater. In a video game, once the treasure chest is revealed, players would get their treasure and go on their way.

However, if you keep cranking the wheel and raising the chest, you reveal a clinging skeleton who is trying to keep the chest for himself. The skeleton serves no purpose other than to get a laugh out of viewers. There's no reason why video games can't have little moments like this. Some game developers do similar things, such as Marvel Comics creator Stan Lee appearing in *Marvel Ultimate Alliance 2*, *Ape Escape*'s monkeys in *Metal Gear Solid 3*'s jungle level, or *Braid*'s homage to Mario's World 1-1.

Some will argue that **progression** isn't much of a reward and that players shouldn't be rewarded for merely finishing the game. After all, isn't the point to finish it? There are a lot of things competing for your players' free time. What can be done to keep them engaged? You only need a great story, intriguing level design, ridiculously cool boss battles, and awesome upgrades. Easy, right? But what if more than one player at a time wants to play? Well, that's why we're moving on to Level 14!

Level 13's Universal Truths and Clever Ideas

- Create power-ups that are compatible and complementary to the players' actions and attacks.
- Love thy players! Give them the tools to succeed like DDB and rubber banding.
- If you think something in your game is too difficult or boring, it is. Get rid of it.
- Never underestimate the greed of the players and use it to prompt interesting scenarios and challenges.
- Plan out your economy for the entire game. Price items according to when you want the players to earn them.
- Provide enough money for the players so they have choices when shopping.
- Have a variety of cool things to buy. Make the players choose between (at least) two really good things so they come back for more.
- Determine whether scoring is right for your game; then reward players when high scores or achievements are obtained.
- Don't forget bonus materials and DLC. Remember that it takes time to make this content, so don't leave it until the end of your production.
- Some rewards are just for fun.

Level 14
Multiplayer—The More the Merrier

THE FIRST TRUE multiplayer game I remember playing was *Gauntlet* (1985); up to four people were able to play together. Because of the arcade cabinet's configuration, what I remember most from playing *Gauntlet* (other than "elf needs food badly") is that my friends and I would push and jostle each other as we played the game. Even though *Gauntlet* is a cooperative game, we sure didn't play it that way. We were always trying to grab the health or be the first to activate the "smart bomb" potion.

The jostling continued through the years with *Teenage Mutant Ninja Turtles* (1989) and *Captain America and the Avengers* (Data East, 1991). When *Doom* (1993) reared its ugly demon head, the jostling became virtual via our local area network (LAN) connection. And by jostling, I mean blasting each other with plasma rifles during death matches. Multiplayer jostling has since evolved even further.

There are many ways multiplayer gaming is accomplished:

- **Physically on one device**: such as multiple players on a console.
- **Head-to-head:** Two or more players compete against each other in real time on the same game system. Most sports, action, and some FPS games allow for head-to-head play.

- **Via a wireless connection**: Such as a device that uses Wi-Fi, Bluetooth, etc.

- **Network/peer-to-peer:** Two or more people play with and against each other in real time on machines connected via the Internet on a wide area network (WAN) that can be created by the developer or the player. Games can also be played on a wireless network using a Nintendo Switch or mobile device.

- **Client/server:** These computer systems are big and fast enough to handle multiple users at one time. Some **massively multiplayer online** games (**MMOs**) and **massively multiplayer online role-playing games** (**MMORPGs**) use client/servers to handle the enormous amount of traffic. The **server** is the computer running the game simulation code. **Clients** are computers that connect to the server, send input from users, and display the game world to them. A system may include game servers that run the simulation, account servers that deal with player login, and database servers to store persistent game information.

- **Connected via a network:** This can be a network such as the internet—using the power of the **cloud**. The cloud allows you to connect and play remotely using any compatible device. The data transmission from the cloud to a device is known as **streaming.** Current streaming platforms include PlayStation Plus Premium, Xbox Cloud Gaming, Luna, Steam, Discord, and GeForce Now.

- **Ad hoc Wi-Fi:** This connection allows players to play device-to-device without cables or a network. It is common in mobile gaming devices, but it suffers from not being able to transfer large amounts of data and players must keep in close proximity during play.

After you decide how your players are going to connect, you need to determine what they are going to play. Three broadly different styles of play are found in multiplayer games:

- In **competitive** games, players have the same objective but work against each other. This often involves fighting to the "death," completing an objective first, or achieving the highest score. (Or maybe it's just fun to fight each other!)

- **Cooperative** games give players the same objective while (in theory) working together to achieve it. After playing *Gauntlet* with my stupid friends, I realized even a cooperative game can easily dissolve into a competitive one.

- Some matches are a **mix of both.** For example, a team deathmatch is actually both cooperative and competitive.

- **Conjugate** gameplay has players sharing the same gameplay space but not the same goals. This type of play can be found in some FPSs, MMOs and MMORPGs as dozens, if not hundreds, of players dash around the game world at the same time, each with their own agenda and motivation.

So just what are these motivations? Well, I'm glad you asked; otherwise, I wouldn't have had anything to write about for the next few pages. Look at all these game modes found in multiplayer games—some unique to the genre. You can easily combine these modes to create conjugate gameplay scenarios:

- **Death match/free-for-all:** It's every person for themselves as players battle each other for high scores or jockey for the best weapon. Usually, players all start on common ground at the beginning of a death match and gain (or lose) equipment that gives them an edge over the course of the game.

- **Team death match:** This mode has teams of players killing each other for dominance. It can even have competitive goals, where players on the same team can compete for the highest score.

- **Fighting:** Two or more fighters enter; only one leaves! It's often connection speeds, not flying fists that cause problems with fighting games. If the connection is slow in a game where split-second moves make a huge difference, that "lag" can cause gameplay to suffer. Make sure your programmer teammates are aware of predictive code solutions.

- **Survival:** Usually, the goal of survival game mode is to defeat all the enemies or survive getting from point A to B. Players of the *Left 4 Dead* series watch each other's backs in combat as well as help each other heal when in danger.

- **Area/territory control:** The player has to travel to and protect/defend a certain location from AI enemies or human players. The excitement comes from the tug-of-war struggle of attacking, retreating, and retaking an objective as players attempt to "move the line" closer to the final area. An area control map game can last hours given the right two teams.

- **Defend/king of the hill:** This type of gameplay is much like area/territory control, but one team of players is given a certain location, which needs to be defended for a designated period of time.

- **Control:** This game mode has one player become a target of the other players, either by possessing an object (like a flag or *Halo*'s oddball skull) or being designated as "it" by the game code. The player who is "it" is sometimes handicapped while being "it." This mode can be played both competitively and cooperatively with other teammates protecting the player.

- **Capture the Flag:** Each team starts with a flag. The goal is to capture the other team's flag and bring it back to your base without allowing your flag to be captured. If your flag is captured, you can't score until it is returned. This mode is a staple of many first person multiplayer shooters.

- **Race/driving:** Racing modes have players competing for position or time. Often, that competition can get nasty if players are given the means to mess with the other players during the race (such as *Mario Kart*'s power-ups). For combat races, you can use a regressive system where the player in front is the most vulnerable to attack from the other players who are coming up from behind. *Burnout Paradise* (2008) introduced the "Easy Drive" mode where multiple drivers can participate in events and socialize as they drive.

- **Team objective:** The players are given an objective, usually one that can be achieved only by working together. Games like *Defense of the Ancients* (2005) and *Love in a Dangerous Spacetime* (2015) require "all hands-on deck" in order to win the game.

- **Asynchronous:** Players play against each other, but not at the same time. Players can either take turns as with *Kind Words*, *Skulls of the Shogun*, and *Draw Something*, or they can play simultaneously without interacting with the other player as in *Dark Souls: Remastered*, *Death Stranding*, or *Real Racing 3*.

- **Gambling:** In games of chance, players play competitively or in combination to achieve the highest score (or at least beat the odds.) Avoid progressive systems where the rich get richer, and the poor get poorer.

- **Reflex:** How fast is your trigger finger? Quiz and puzzle games often have players see who's faster to determine victory, or at least give them an opportunity to use their...

- **Knowledge:** There's nothing like proving you're smarter than the guy sitting next to you on the sofa. This genre has consistently maintained its presence in video games such as You *Don't Know Jack*, *Buzz!*, and the *Scene It?* series as well as adaptations of TV game shows including *Who Wants to Be a Millionaire* and the *Price Is Right*.

- **Creation:** The multiplayer components of *Roblox*, *Minecraft*, and *Spore* consist of players visiting or interacting with another player's creations. This mode is a great way to extend the life of a game because your players create the content for you! For example, *LittleBigPlanet: Game of the Year Edition* showcased 18 brand new levels that were created by the community's top-rated player creators. A whole subgenre of "play" emerged when players of *The Sims* were given tools to make "stories" of their characters. These movies became just as popular as the game!

- **Virtual life:** PlayStation's *Fallout Shelter Online* (2019), and *Animal Crossing: New Horizons* (2020) are just a few of the games in which players can customize their virtual worlds and interact with other online occupants. What started as text-only chatrooms have become the reality described in Neil Stephenson's visionary book *Snow Crash*. (Now where's my samurai sword code?)

One more important question to ask yourself is: how dependent on multiplayer is my game going to be? For example, some games are multiplayer-only—*League of Legends* (2009), *MAG: Massive Action Game* (2010), *Hunt: Showdown* (2018)—and can't be played as a single-player experience. Knowing the answer to this at the start of the design process will impact the rest of your design.

How Many Is the Right Number?

You may be wondering how many players multiplayer systems should support. Take, for example, a melee-based fighting game like *Street Fighter*. If this type of game had more than two players, there would be all types of problems. Players would bunch up as they fought, making it hard to see individual players. Collision detection would be problematic, and it would all just devolve into mob warfare rather than a contest of skills that makes a good fighting game. On the other hand, an MMORPG like *World of Warcraft* would feel empty if it allowed only a few hundred players to roam around at the same time. So, how many players should there be? Let's look at the numbers:

- Fighting game (*Street Fighter*) = 2 players
- Fighting game (*Helldivers 2*) = 4 players
- Social games (*Uno*) = 4 players
- Action platformers (*Splunkey 2*) = 4 players
- Driving (*Burnout Paradise*) = 8 players
- VR FPS (*Gun Raiders*) = 12 players
- FPS (*Warframe*) = 16 players
- FPS (*MAG*) = 64, 128, or 256 players (depending on game mode)
- MMORPG (*World of Warcraft*) = roughly 4,000 to 5,000 players *per server*

As you can see, there is a HUGE difference between the numbers of players. Think about the interactions you want the players to have. Smaller game screens such as mobile devices can't handle more than one player—which means Wi-Fi or online solutions—and even the largest screen can get too crowded if there are too many players playing on one screen at once. Will the characters run into each other as they play? Sometimes, the number *makes* the gameplay as with the *Super Smash Bros* series; other times, it will just cause collision issues. How quickly will players move around the playfield, die, and respawn? These values can often be used to help determine player count as well. Finally, you should always "stress test" your game to see how many players it can handle before it breaks.

MMORPGS, or Hell Is Other People

The MMORPG genre has evolved rapidly to have its own set of tropes and methods of play, some of which hardly qualify as "playing" at all. Becoming familiar with these tropes and including them in your own design will not only fill out your game but also keep you competitive:

- **Buffing:** Spell casting affects not only the caster, but also the entire party. This method of play allows players to assume certain roles during gameplay. For example, if a cleric is able to prepare a healing buff (via hotkey), as players take damage, they can restore them fully to allow them to continue fighting. There are other games that use physical objects to create the same healing effect such as the large healing potion in *Dungeons of Eternity* or the Flowberry Fizz in *Fortnite*.

- **Character customization:** A huge appeal of any MMO is being able to assume the role of another character and to get lost in that fantasy life. The level of player character customization can range from preset character templates to making characters fully customizable down to sex, eye color, and nose length. Within the game, further encourage customization and let the players buy or win clothing, weapons, armor, gear, and mounts that fit the personality and class of the characters they are playing.

- **Chatting:** A text or voice chat system in your game is expected these days. Players will use MMOs as a social gathering place as much as a place to play your game. This is especially true in VR where you are interacting with real players. To not be able to talk and interact would remove the "reality" from virtual reality.

- **Crafting:** Players combine harvested, found, or bought items to create new gear and weapons. Players first need to find "recipes" and "components" for creating items to be able to craft objects. As with the ability to customize characters, let the players craft items into unique creations. The time needed to create an item depends on the power of the item or weapon. Sometimes players can craft in workshop locations or pay in virtual or real money to reduce crafting time. Create a separate screen for crafting so the players can focus on the activity. You can use skill-based minigames to successfully initiate the crafting process. Some games allow for "trial and error" style crafting, with players running the risk of destroying components if they fail in their attempt. Just don't allow players to destroy a hard-to-get or expensive crafting item. It's not fair to punish the players twice!

I made it myself!

- **Economy:** Many MMO games thrive on an economy system. Players win treasures that allow them to customize characters; buy better weapons and gear, housing, and mounts; and even buy their own castles! (Or space stations, secret HQs, and so on.) Balance earnings and buying. Make it worthwhile for players to go through the effort. Let players store loot and items in personal safes or public banks. Many MMOs have developed an economy that spills over into the real world, where players buy in-game money with real-world cash.

Howabout you *don't* kill eight of us and we'll buy you those boots instead?

- **Grinding:** As players level up their characters, the rate of their progress slows down. Slow down the rate of progress too much, and players will experience "grind." Grinding is often used to artificially extend the length of gameplay, but it can also get frustrating for players who feel they are wasting their time. Keith Burgun, designer of *100 Rouges*, has this to say: "Grinding is a low-risk activity that the player can do repeatedly for real gain. In any game that has grinding, grinding is the optimal move. It becomes not 'what is the best move' for the player but 'how much can I bore myself for my own gain?'"[1]

Here are a few suggestions on how to reduce the impact of grinding in your own design:

- If content is too similar, things will feel repetitive. Add variety.

- Players grind because they feel they can't progress due to a lack of power, abilities, or money. Make game difficulty ramp smoothly rather than steeply.

- Give players more freedom. Don't make them always follow designer-defined objectives.

- Offer more rewards. Grinding is often done in response to monetization. If players have alternative rewards to shoot for, the repetitive activity won't feel so grindy.

- Make grinding its own reward. Offer achievements or special status for making the most of an activity.

- Reduce! Make your game or your victory conditions shorter. Just concentrate on the "good stuff." Remember, if it seems too long or boring, it is!

- **Instanced dungeons:** To make MMO gaming a unique experience, dungeons can be instanced. This means content such as enemies and loot or even the level map are randomly generated to provide a different experience each time it is played. These dungeons exist "outside" the game world, allowing for several groups of players to be in the same albeit alternate versions of the dungeon at the same time. That way, players don't have to wait for the dungeon to "restock" between player interactions.

- **Item collection:** Item collection is a huge motivating factor in MMORPGs. Players create items that improve combat and other in-game abilities, especially tedious ones like crafting, mining, or harvesting. Most items fall along a rarity scheme: common, uncommon, rare, and unique. Special items can be gained only by defeating specific creatures (getting these items is known as "drops"), and seasonal items are available only at certain times of the year or by attending specific world events.

- **Open world structure:** Most MMOs feature sandbox worlds where players can (presumably) go anywhere and do anything. However, that is merely an illusion you will need to maintain for players. In reality, you will need to build the world in the way you want players to play the game. **Gating**

Not cool, dude.
Not cool.

---

[1] www.cheatcc.com/extra/pokemonshowedmehowgrindingcanbeagoodthing.html

mechanisms, such as level or gear requirements, will prevent players from traveling to places they aren't ready for. Some games allow players to wander into higher-level sections, but the humiliation they receive at the hands of the enemies will usually force them to retreat until they've reached the necessary level to tackle the area's foes.

- **Player versus player (PvP):** Players love to see how strong their characters are by killing other player characters. You'll often find this competitive mode in many MMOs including *Black Desert Online* (2015), *Secret World Legends* (2017) and *World of Warcraft* (2004). However, not everyone wants to run the risk of being randomly killed while playing. As a precaution, many MMOs have dedicated PvP servers. Another alternative is that your world has PvP combat restricted to certain locations.

- **Griefing:** When one player harasses another player by constantly killing them, that behavior is called griefing. You can create systems to penalize players for bad behavior or segregate them into friendly fire servers. Make sure your policies are clear to the players, and a warning/zero tolerance system helps keep the peace.

- **Guilds:** Players are social animals and, as a result, they form groups. Players will form parties of characters, called guilds, to explore, socialize, and run raids. As a designer, you will want to create in-game meeting places for guilds to socialize. While it requires a lot of work, you also may want to design tools to promote guilds within your game world. Useful guild tools include stat tracking, calendars for running raids, guild asset customization and communication tools. This is critical for allowing players to switch from global communication where everyone can hear them to team communication for planning tactics and giving direction. Of course, in a VR world, a team setting should be overridden by proximity. If you are in the same room as a player from the other team and you are talking, then they should hear you just as they would in the non-virtual reality

- **Player housing:** Give your players a personal space to show off their achievements, display their souvenirs, or just "park" their player character safely between game sessions. Having a home base will make players feel much more connected and "at home" in the game world, which will make it become a place they want to return to again and again.

- **Raids:** When players team up to defeat difficult game scenarios, such as storming a castle or battling a particularly fearsome enemy, they are leading raids. Players who assemble and lead a raid need to be one part strategist, one part manager, and one-part social director. As a designer, you should create scenarios that can be overcome by a variety of party configurations, and even allow for the players' creative thinking or just plain dumb luck. Creating and cultivating the legends of these raid targets will let players know that they have to marshal their forces to defeat them. Design systems that make it easy for players to share the loot after the raid is over based on each player's performance.

- **Spawn camping:** This is a practice by players who wait for an enemy or player to appear at a spawn point to kill that player. You can combat this bad habit in your level design by creating multiple spawn points, making camping locations risky to stay at for extended periods of time, or by making spawn camping locations easy to see.

- **Trading/auctions:** Because players often end up with lots of identical loot, or with items that their character class can't use, trading and auctions are good solutions to help players clear out inventory. Make sure your players can easily trade items without ripping each other off. Create locations in your game world to promote trading. Some games have auction houses, where regular auctions are held, and players can bid on items using in-game treasure. Or items may simply have a "sell back" value so players can sell the item back to the "game." Better to have 3 more gold than a low powered dagger that you will never use and that takes up space in your backpack!

Designing Multiplayer Levels

Now that I've overwhelmed you with a ton of information about multiplayer design, let's look at one of the most commonly found element of multiplayer gaming—levels.

Have you read Level 9 already? The one about designing levels? Good, because most of that information is still valid when it comes to making a multiplayer level. But there are some important differences. Here's some advice for the three stages of making a multiplayer map—planning, mapping, and building.

Planning Your Level

Keep these questions in mind as far as planning:

- **What is the gameplay?** The type of gameplay will dictate the design of your level. For example, a "king of the hill" level is going to have a central location where the teams will clash over who controls the hill, while a capture the flag is going to be broken into three zones—team one's base, team two's base, and a no-man's land where the gameplay emphasis is going to be on players racing back and forth between bases.

- **What's the story?** Why are the players fighting in this place? Knowing the story will help you design the level objects that tell the story. For example, you could tell the story of a battle in a war-torn village by using overrun barricades, a building with its wall blown out, and an abandoned tank.

- **What's the theme?** The theme should not dominate the map. Don't sacrifice good gameplay areas just because they don't fit into your theme. There's nothing wrong with combining themes (remember Mexican Pizza?). Multiplayer levels don't always have to make sense; they just have to be fun.

- **What makes your map memorable?** One of the hardest things for a new player to do during a multiplayer match is to learn the level while trying to keep alive. Memorable geometry and level objects help a player orient themselves when they spawn in. When they sees the object, they will say to themselves, "Ah-ha! I know where I am."

- **Design for all types.** Many multiplayer games have different player roles, and you need to take all of these different play styles into account. Make sure you create interesting spaces that allow each player type to do what they do best.

Mapping Your Level

Here are a few pointers on mapping:

- **Keep your map simple.** It's easier for players to understand how to get around on a simple map. Use simple shapes like squares, figure eights, and circles for paths and open spaces. Simple maps make it easier to guide your player and highlight the objective and are easy to modify if something needs to be changed.

- **Mirror your map.** Take your map design, copy it, reverse it, and paste it! Not only does it save on production time, but the players can explore their own territory and have a good idea how to get around when they enter the enemy's base.

- **Use walls.** Use walls to funnel the player toward the objective. Narrow spaces like tunnels and bridges can be used to point the player in the right direction and create stand-off scenarios.

- **Set up defensible areas.** Players should have a good idea of where they are going to fight before they get there. Show defensible areas to players as they approach it; for example, a team might have to "hold a platform" during a control point game. This way the players can scope out where the fight is going to be and plan their strategy accordingly.

- **Include a no man's land.** A "no man's land" is where the most danger and action take place—otherwise cover loses its significance. Make players risk exposure to attack if they want to pass through no man's land. Some games will offer alternative paths around or under a no man's land; however, if the other team catches on, the fighting will move to these pathways!

- **Make good use of spawn points.** The player should always have an opportunity to see another player coming but shouldn't be able to use that opportunity to ruin the fun. Give the player a chance to get out of the spawn point alive. Make it too dangerous for an enemy player to "spawn camp" in front of a team's base by making the space wide open or too hard to enter. Many games use gates that prevent enemies from entering so the player can get onto the battlefield without getting killed.

- **Make sure players can find their way around.** Use big and small level objects to help with orientation. You want to help players orient locally as well as globally. Using a weenie like a big castle will help the player know where they are when they first enter the level, but a castle becomes almost useless as an orientation tool once the player is fighting in the castle's hallways and dungeons.

- **Provide alternate routes of approach.** Can the player sneak through tunnels, rocket jump onto rooftops, swim through water, or use a zipline to get across the map? Letting the player use these alternative routes lets them feel smart and sneaky and makes game play unpredictable.

Building Your Level

Pay attention to these items for building:

- **Check collision:** When creating your gray box level, make sure there are no places where a player can get "snagged" on to the level's geometry. Be especially careful of stairs, corners, and ledges. Watch out for "seams" where the player can fall between the collision and drop out of the world!

- **Play test:** After you have your level built in gray box, play it as often as you can with as many different players as possible. Use **heat maps**—code that indicates where players go and what they do during a play session—to determine where players fight, hide, and die. Use that data to modify your map. Your goal is to create a play space in which the player will want to play everywhere, not just congregate in one place.

- **Textures:** Use clearly different textures on floors and walls so players can see the path of the floor. Be careful of textures that tessellate or look visually cluttered. Use light colored textures to create a path for the player to follow.

- **Color:** Color is another way players can quickly determine what level they are in. They will associate a dominant color scheme with each level—even if subconsciously. You can use color theory to help set the mood—green feels dank, red feels dangerous, blue feels stealthy.

- **Lighting:** Use lighting to point out objectives and passageways. Players love to hide in shadows, so create lots of shadowy overhangs, doorways, and tunnels for them to lurk in. Use the lighting of the time of day to further set the mood of your level. Just changing the lighting from day to night can give a totally different feel to your level.

- **Sound:** Use background noise to help the player get into the mood. Unless you want to put your players on edge, avoid using sounds that the player can mistake for another player like rustling trees that can be mistaken for enemy movement or explosions in the distance that can be mistaken for enemy gunfire.

The Dirty Half Dozen

The best way to learn how to make an FPS multiplayer map is to play one. Here are a few classics you should check out. Hopefully they will inspire you to make your own great multiplayer level:

- **Blood Gulch** - *Halo* (remade as Coagulation in *Halo 2*, Valhalla in *Halo 3*, and *Forge World* in Halo: Reach)

- **2Fort** - *Team Fortress Classic* (remade in *Team Fortress 2*)

- **Wake Island** - *Battlefield 1942*

- **de_Dust** - *Counter-Strike* (remade in every *Counter-Strike* game)
- **Rust** - *Modern Warfare 2*
- **Overgrown** - *Call of Duty 4*

Level 14's Universal Truths and Clever Ideas

- Design multiplayer systems for your game from the start.
- Offer your players a variety of game modes and objectives.
- The right number of players is whatever is right for your gameplay.
- Allow players to customize their characters, their objects, their world.
- New play patterns will emerge when players are given the tools to create.
- Determine what level you want players to negatively interact with other players (like PvP).
- Players will always do the last thing you expect, but sometimes that's Okay.
- A multiplayer level should not be designed like a single-player level.

Level 15
Reality Check: VR, AR, XR, and Beyond

LET'S START WITH the basics: VR means **virtual reality**. AR means **augmented reality**. MR means **mixed reality**. XR means **extended reality**...it's just a blanket term that covers VR, AR and MR.

Knowing the history of VR (and all the other R's) technology is important. It helps us understand where we've come from, what has worked and what hasn't worked, and might even inform where things can go. When I ask my video game history class when they think virtual reality was invented, they usually answer the early 2000s. But VR is much older than that! Virtual reality had already existed in sci-fi books such as *Ender's Game*, *Neuromancer* and *Snow Crash*. These classic books gave game designers a target to shoot for when determining what VR might be.

The fellow wearing this invention—the TV glasses—is Hugo Gernsback. Hugo's contributions to technology are impressive: As the creator/editor of magazines **Modern Electronics** and **Amazing Stories**, he is considered the "father of modern science fiction." Perhaps you've heard of the Hugo award; yep, it's named after him. While Hugo's TV glasses were never commercially produced, they did inspire inventors to explore the idea of portable devices that brought the audience "into the show."

One of these inventors was Morton Heilig. His invention, Sensorama, was quite impressive for 1960 technology. It gave the player the experience of riding a motorcycle on the streets of Brooklyn. The users felt the wind on their face, the vibration of the motorcycle seat, a 3D view, and even smells of the city. We'll see how it inspired later VR-related inventions.

Another attempt was Ivan Sutherland's *Sword of Damocles (1968),* a massive, head mounted display that was poised above the user's head—hence its name. The Sword was actually an **augmented reality (AR)** device where images were projected onto the lens of its goggles.

Jaron Lainer is the true pioneer of virtual reality. Lainer's company VPL Research created two important inventions: the **Eyephone** and **Dataglove**. He even came up with the term **virtual reality**! The gaming industry became extremely excited about the possibility of true player emersion. Some games were designed for the Eyephone,[1] however, the system was too expensive—the entire set-up cost $250,000. And computers of 1984 could only run at 6 frames a second; way lower than the 30 frames a second needed for convincing animation. The commercial "failure" of the Eyephone system made people think that virtual reality was just a novelty.

Nintendo took a stab at virtual reality with the **Virtual Boy** gaming system (1985). Even though it was designed by their master engineer Gunpei Yokoi, it was a flop due to its clunky head mounted system that only displayed red and black graphics and caused users headaches and neck strain.

Toy company Mattel obviously didn't learn from the Virtual Boy's failure when they released the **Power Glove**

---

[1] You can see the Eyephone and Dataglove in action at www.youtube.com/watch?v=ACeoMNux_AU.

in 1989. This controller was designed to be used with Nintendo Entertainment system and was playable with two games: *Super Glove Ball* and *Bad Street Brawler*. Mattel worked with Jared Lainer to create this gaming glove, which could detect the pitch, roll and yaw of the user. It

featured a built-in d-pad and keyboard controller. However, the Power Glove had laggy and imprecise controls. Another failure.

In the early 90's, Dr. Jonathan Waldern created the company **Virtuality** and a VR system of the same name. Like the Virtual Boy, it was big, clunky, expensive, and made most users motion sick. But Virtuality was the first true virtual reality system marketed as a gaming system.[2] It was sold to arcades around the world and received high praise upon its debut, but its crude graphics soon became dated, and the lack of software support eventually caused arcades to abandon the machines.

Atari and Virtuality then teamed up to make a home-based VR system for their ill-fated Jaguar gaming console. Their efforts resulted in a low-resolution headset of poor quality. As the result of this, Virtuality went out of business and Atari disappeared from the video game industry for the next twelve years.

Virtual World, headed by Jordon Weisman, opened the first Battletech centers in 1993 in Chicago and Yokohama. The Virtual World centers were a mix of Virtuality and Disneyland. The center I used to play at in San Diego had a beautiful Victorian themed Explorer's Lounge where players could socialize until it was their turn. Each Virtual World site featured at least 16 networked "pods" where players could battle each other locally and eventually compete against other players located at the other centers around the country.[3]

---

[2] Watch the stand-up system in action at www.youtube.com/watch?v=rVn3H93Ysag.

[3] You've got to check these Virtual World Battlepods out for yourself! https://www.youtube.com/watch?v=jdJA5C_Po4U

The pods themselves were simulators with more joysticks, controllers, foot pedals, buttons, and switches than you can manage. I played BattleTech on several occasions in the early 90's, and it was the most immersive and realistic gaming experience I've ever had. Unfortunately, in 1999 Virtual World was bought by Microsoft and the Virtual World centers closed. The pods have since been bought by collectors who bring them to gaming conventions for others to play.

Disney Quest opened in 1998 at Walt Disney World where it was billed as the "future of arcades." Guests could play VR games and ride VR rollercoasters based on famous Disney attractions. *The Pirates of the Caribbean: Battle for Buccaneer's Gold* had players piloting a boat and shooting "real" cannons at marauding pirate ships and skeletal pirates. Players of *Aladdin's Magic Carpet Ride* sat on a motorcycle style seat much like Sensorama. It vibrated while gusts of air were blown at the player. Riders wore a suspended eyephone-like helmet with built in speakers and a full range of view to simulate flying on a magic carpet. Disney Quest was well-received and lasted until 2016.

While studying computer science, USC student Palmer Luckey worked on a cost-effective VR headset. He caught the attention of programming legend John Carmack of id Software. After his graduation and five more prototypes, Luckey put his invention up on Kickstarter where it earned $2.4 million in funding. He started Oculus VR and while the team continued working on the Rift headset, the company was purchased by Facebook for $2 billion dollars.

Microsoft introduced their own AR system—the HoloLens—in 2015. They added MR in 2017, which was supported by a variety of VR headsets produced by various industry leading hardware companies like Acer, ASUS, Dell, HP, Lenovo, and Samsung. Many of these devices were at a price point as low as $299, although they required a computer to drive them. Sadly, Microsoft abandoned consumer-level MR and others quickly took over the market—in this case the Oculus.

The Sony PlayStation VR and HTC Vive headsets became available in 2016. Home VR got a boost from the global pandemic of 2019 when people were looking for an escape from the lockdown. The Apple Vision Pro and the Meta Quest series of headsets came in 2022 and 2024, respectively. Developers have embraced VR and created varied titles such as *Space Pirate Trainer* (2016), *Job Simulator* (2016), *Star Trek Bridge Crew* (2016), *Beat Saber* (2018), *Batman Arkham VR* (2016), and *I Expect You to Die* (2015).

Designing for VR

When I first started designing for VR, it took a while for me to wrap my head around what I was making. I thought "This will be easy! This is no different than a first-person camera game!" I learned that this is a common misconception. While it's true that (most) VR games use a first-person camera angle, there are some major (and subtle) differences to designing a VR game you should be aware of.

Firstly, you have to think about the playspace. There are two terms you should know: **stationary play** and **room scale play.**

Stationary play has the player sit or stand in a fixed position. This limited space can be represented by a small platform floating in space as in *Space Pirate Trainer* (2016) or at a desk or behind a small service counter as in *Job Simulator* (2016).

When designing for stationary play, you can turn those space limitations into opportunities. The game series *I Expect You to Die* (2016) came about because of a designer's frustration with limited movement in VR. They devised a game about a spy locked in a car, having to escape the death trap. The game's actions were about operating the buttons and gadgets while the player stayed seated in the cockpit of the car rather than moving around, thus removing the concern of limited play space.

In room scale play, much more of the gamer's living space is used. Early gaming systems required cameras mounted onto tripods. The tripods designated the scale of the space the player had to play in. If the player ever went outside of the virtual boundary, the game would pause or even relaunch.

Unlike a console game, the player uses their whole body to play room scale VR. If your game design doesn't have the player using their entire body, then it might not be the right design. Depending on your VR system, you might have controllers or sensors for the head, hands, body and even feet.

Because controlling a game with your body is more intuitive than using a controller, you will have to design actions that a player can perform with their body. For example, in a VR game a player swings an arm to swing a sword or a tennis racket. A player turns their head to look at the other side of the room. A player physically moves to the side to dodge being hit by an arrow. These actions must make logical sense. They should be second nature to the player. There needs to be a logical cause-and-effect to whatever the player does in the game.

As you design a VR gaming experience, consider how the player can (or can't) move their head when wearing a headset. Some headsets require wires connected to the computer, limiting the range of movement. Others allow for a greater range of movement. Consider the weight of the headset and how long a player might or might not be able to keep it on. Those headsets get heavy! Wearing a Vive headset is very different to wearing an Apple Vision Pro. Players using lighter hardware will be able to wear it longer before they feel neck and head strain. You want to consider how long the player will be able to wear the gear and when to give them breaks.

One of the differences between traditional game design and VR is designing the space. VR levels require everything in the level or environment to be in full 360 degrees. For example, if the player is standing in a square room there should be, at the minimum, something to interact with on all four walls of the environment.

However, designer Radu Anghel remarks that "you're focused on a 15-degree angle, left and right, up and down, anything outside that area gets less attention."[4] This limited range of attention, may be why many VR horror game designers take advantage of that trope "it's right behind you!!!" when creating a scare.

As you create your design, consider how you are moving the player around. As technology improves, the player has "limitless" space to play. However, there are still the real-world space considerations. Designing an engaging play experience for players who have a lot of space as well as limited play space is a challenge. You can't predict what space each player will have, so you will have to design for both cases, stationary and room scale.

Many VR experiences require the use of a controller. But rather than the sometimes-confusing configuration of analog sticks, buttons, and keys that console and computer games have, in VR, the controller is an *extension* of the player's hand. Think of the controller as an invisible hand with a finger extended. The player will need at least one way to perform simple operations in the game.

This virtual finger will be used for poking, pressing, and selecting. As the player isn't going to feel anything during the experience, (at least until haptic gloves become commonplace!) precision controls go out the window.

---

[4] https://www.toptal.com/designers/virtual-reality/designing-vr-games

Because virtual reality is trying to simulate reality, it is doubly important to "sell" the player's interaction with the world. I've found that sound and animation is critical when designing for VR. We want the player to almost feel their actions in the game. When Schell Games was designing the sword fighting game *Until you Fall* (2020), the game wasn't feeling right. They decided to focus on making the game have "one good hit." Swinging a sword and hitting a guy had to be great first. What will it be like for the player to do that? What kind of visceral feedback will they get from doing it? How will that "one good hit" feel awesome to the player? How will the rest of the game be designed around that **innermost loop**?

The innermost loop is another word for the **primary action**—the thing that the player does the most in the game. However, in VR, the primary action should consist of an action that uses broad strokes and broad movements. The controls that require simple motions are much better in VR than subtle or precise actions. I have played games where the player can switch from a hand configuration to a weapon or other device configuration with the press of a button. Keeping it clear and simple is always best with VR controls.

Character interaction is another aspect of VR that is crucial for creating immersion. Because VR characters can usually be viewed at a close range, they need to not only look great but realistically respond to the player's actions. Not repeating dialogue (having many recorded dialogue responses), having reactions that change the character from an ally to an enemy or an enemy to an ally—how they engage with the player is vital. Even pathing must work correctly. No running into walls or getting caught in geometry! You want to avoid problems that will break immersion. Character interaction is not just about realism, but it is about creating an emotional connection that makes for a great virtual reality gaming experience. Look at games like *Half Life: Alyx* (2020) or *Batman: Arkham VR* (2016) for great examples of character interaction.

Practically Unreal

Because space is often very limited, whether in stationary or room scale designs, VR designers have come up with some clever solutions to simulation moving through space.

In most games, the player can use an analog stick to move; just like in a console game. But what happens when you run out of room to move? Your character will stop at an invisible wall or even worse, pass through geometry at the "edge" of your game level. This is an unacceptable situation!

One way to solve moving in VR is "zapping." This is where the player points a reticule or a pointer (represented on the hud as a path and a targeted spot) to a location in the environment —usually past the confines of where the player can go—and when the button is pressed, the player is "teleported" to that spot.

Another option is to take control away from the player (after the spot is selected) and make the character walk to the spot instead. I prefer the walking method because it is a less jarring transition for the player. You'll find zapping in games with sneaky characters—like in a horror or shooter game, while action games tend to prefer the character movement method.

Another solution is to make the player move continuously like in a rail-shooter. This is used in swinging games such as in *Spider-Man: Far from Home Virtual Reality* (2019) or the *Windlands* series. Many people dream of flying and you can do just that in *Megaton Rainfall* (2017) and *Iron Man VR* (2020). But be careful, flying, especially tight turns in flight, can cause motion sickness. *Adr1ft* (2016) lets you move around in zero gravity as you repair a damaged space station. An advantage of that slower pace of movement is that it reduces the chances of getting motion sick. Getting motion sick doesn't even require actual movement to occur: the *perceived* motion is enough to cause it. Common symptoms of motion sickness include:

- Dizziness
- Headaches
- Cold sweats
- Queasiness
- Nausea and vomiting
- Fatigue

Many of the ways to prevent causing motion sickness are technical— such as latency issues, laggy or inaccurate tracking, low refresh rate—but this is a book about game design, not programming.

What you can do as a designer is: Give your player something steady to focus on, whether it's in the world or on the HUD or another character in the world. Avoid locations that have persistent rolling motions, like a boat moving on the ocean. Abrupt transitions or fast camera moves can make players feel sick. Camera motions and scene transitions should be slow and smooth!

And if you ever feel yourself getting motion sick, take a break, go outside and have a drink of water. Maybe call it a day and save playing for tomorrow.

If you are going to move around in VR, you need a place to do it. The same level design rules we discussed earlier still apply: Always have something for the player to do, avoid invisible walls whenever possible, make the border level look like real objects or low barriers, etc.

But in VR, you need to be even clearer than that, as a player might actually run into a real wall or object during gameplay. Some games will represent the "real world" as a grid that appears when the player steps into it or as a hard visual border that looks very different than the game environment. I don't prefer these solutions as they tend to break immersion.

The Many Worlds of Virtual Reality

Remember the *virtual* in virtual reality. It's funny how many VR games only simulate the real world while they can represent virtually *anything*. The boundaries of the game world in VR extend far beyond the confines of the box that player plays in. You can create any type of environment with any kind of interaction. For example, you can make a crazy Escher-esque room slide around with stairways and passages that extend and retract. You can be looking out the viewscreen of a spaceship onto a view that stretches through the infinite vastness of space. You can make a player climb a towering tower or dive into the depths of the sea.

When we were designing Terminator VR, we had limitless possibilities to choose from. We can make our experience take place anywhere. We can have enemies emerge from ruined skyscrapers and descending from the sky in hunter-killer ships. We simulated you flying in a drop ship and standing on a rickety rooftop. You can even look through the cracks of the floorboards to see Terminator enemies approaching on the floor below. It was a pretty exciting experience to help create something so all-encompassing.

Often interviewers will ask me "what is the future of VR?" I think that in terms of experiences and visuals, virtual reality still has far to go. I'd love to see more games that are personal, artistic expressions of the game designer. Let's see whimsical, fantastical worlds that we've never seen before. I challenge this next generation of VR creators to think outside the box and give us something that we've never seen before!

While we're waiting for that to happen, we're dealing with the genres that just work better in VR.

- **First-person shooter:** First-person shooters are great! First-person shooters are popular! However, there have already been a lot of first-person shooters in VR, so if you are going to develop an FPS for VR, you need to have an interesting hook. For example, *Pistol Whip* (2019) is a rail shooter where players fire two guns at once. In *Superhot* (2016) time moves at normal speed when the player is moving; but when the player fires a weapon, it slows to a crawl ala the *Matrix's* bullet time. Archery also works well in VR. *QuiVR* (2016) and *Battle Bows* (2023) are excellent examples of this subgenre.

- **Melee combat:** Sometimes it's just fun to bash stuff. *GORN* (2017) is bloody bashing in a gladiator pit, *Beat Saber* (2018) is a rhythm game where you are armed with two unlicensed lightsabers, and *Slap Simulator* (2021) allows you to smack around your least favorite celebrities. Watch out though, players of some of these games have been known to accidentally break furniture or even cause themselves accidental injury during play. Allow for breaks in these types of games as the action can get pretty wild.

- **Escape Room:** VR is great for creating virtual environments that the player has to escape. Some of the best of these are *Rick and Morty: Virtual Rick-ality* (2017), *I Expect You to Die* (2016), and *Escape the Lost Pyramid* (2014). Remember the basic rules of VR: give the player a lot to do, use 360 degrees, and remember that you can extend gameplay past the confines of the room without ever having the player leave that space. Think outside the box while you design within your game.

- **Hidden object:** Unlike the frantic pace of a melee combat or FPS VR game, you want to keep the pace of a hidden object game casual. *Agent Hawk* (2018) and *Red Matter 2* (2022) give you plenty of time to find the objects despite its ticking timer.

- **Tabletop game simulation:** One of the great things about playing tabletop games in VR is you can move around the table without getting out of your chair! While I find that playing board games in VR isn't quite the same as playing their analog counterparts, there are some games that have come up with creative solutions and even reimaged games away from the tabletop. *Werewolves Within* (2016) moves the classic game of werewolf out of the living room and out to the dark. It's loads of fun and dripping with theme. *Catan VR* (2021) simulates the classic Eurogame but enhances it with animated elements and a thematic play environment. You can even build your own games in Tabletop Simulator![5] (2014)

- **Walking simulator:** While I still maintain that walking is not gameplay, this gentle genre emerged in the late 2010s. *VR Walking Simulator* (2021) lets you walk through a quiet forest and occasionally snap photos of the wildlife while *Everyone's Gone to the Rapture* (2015) has you stroll interrupted with the mystery of "where has everyone gone?" These types of games use the level to tell their stories, so make sure you use all of the tricks including posters, environmental objects and animations.

- **Horror:** Horror is a very common genre in VR. There are survival horror games like *Arizona Sunshine* (2016), *Resident Evil 7: Biohazard* (2017), and *The Walking Dead: Saints and Sinners* (2020) where the player shoots hordes of enemies (usually zombies), but VR also gives the designer an opportunity to be more atmospheric. You can create creepy experiences to freak out players (especially YouTube reviewers)! Whether you explore a haunted mansion in *Phasmaphobia* (2020), *Layers of Fear* (2016) or just stay at home in *Alone?* (2016), you are going to get scared! Remember, scary games rely heavily on lighting, atmosphere, and pacing. There needs to be a build up to a scare, and you don't want your scares to be back-to-back. Creeping dread is best, where the player knows that something bad is going to appear or happen, but they don't know when!

- **Sports:** There are lots of sports games in VR from golf to boxing, basketball to bowling. Racing is well represented, too. When designing sports games, remember that you don't need to be 100% simulated. There will be times where the game should be on the player's side—a golf ball will roll around the hole before going in. A basketball might do the same with a hoop. Creating these moments of "fake tension" makes the experience more dramatic.

- **Simulation:** Personally, I don't understand why someone would want to simulate working at a job in a video game, but I have to admit that games like *Job Simulator* (2016), *Cooking Simulator* (2019), and *Accounting +* (2018) are ridiculous fun and a hoot to play. These games concentrate on "wacky" controls—ones that are purposely difficult to operate such as oversized hands, imprecise controls or slippery or bouncy objects. The key to these is to keep things light and slightly out of the player's control. They will expect chaos to happen or even better, encourage it with their own actions!

Real Life, but Better

As VR equipment became more accessible, developers like The Void, Dreamscape, and SPACES used VR to create **location-based experiences** (LBEs). In an LBE, you don VR headsets and wear backpacks housing computers. Often you would use a controller or even a

---

[5] If you want to learn more about making tabletop games, I suggest my book *Your Turn! The Guide to Great Tabletop Game Design* (Wiley, 2023).

custom hand-held device such as a gun. You then walked through a physical environment, which was sometimes laid out like a maze in a Halloween haunted house or sometimes like a large empty soundstage. Over the entire play space was an array of cameras that tracked you as you walked through the environment. You could encounter ghosts, xenomorphs, terminators, or even Darth Vader himself in *Ghostbusters: Dimensions* (2016), *Alien: Descent* (2016), *Terminator Salvation: Fight for the future* (2018) and *Star Wars: Secrets of the Empire* (2017).

The difference between an LBE and traditional virtual reality was that you interacted with real-world props, control panels, hydraulic platforms, even mist and scent sprayers that brought touch, motion, and smell to the experience.

One of the simplest but best LBE VR experiences is *Richie's Plank Experience* (2016), which simulated walking between two skyscrapers using nothing but VR and a wooden plank. The tension created from this simple simulation really freaked out some players. They would drop to their knees to safely crawl across the plank. Others just flat-out refused to walk across it. It was a great lesson in the power of virtual reality! Some other lessons I learned were:

- The player is just happy (and amazed) to be in the location. Being in a full-VR environment is amazing to most players but being able to fully move around in one is even better. Don't overwhelm your player with too much activity, they're just trying to take in what is all around them.

- Keep the player's activities simple. Pull a trigger. Press a button. Pull a lever. Step on marked space on the floor. Single actions.

- Keep distances short in reality. Because of the heavy gear players have to wear, they tend to walk in short shuffling movements. Be especially careful about things like stairs or uneven surfaces. If you do have them, make sure they are represented in the virtual world so that players don't trip or stumble on them.

- Be careful using transitions between scenes or locations that could cause disorientation. I find that having your player walk through a "magic portal" (or a simple doorway) is less jarring.

- Bigger is better. Imposing skylines, giant monsters, flying dragons in the sky. A Stay-Puft Marshmallow Man. Anything that will awe your player. Plus, it's easier to aim at a giant enemy than a little one.

LBEs are magical experiences. They really brought the best of VR and the best of theme parks together. Sadly, the majority of the major LBE companies closed in 2019. Enclosed spaces and equipment that had to be fastidiously cleaned didn't fare well during a global pandemic. Expensive operating costs didn't help either. I don't know if LBEs will be back any time soon, but the genie is out of the bottle, and when they do return, I'm sure that they will be better than ever.

Augment This

Where virtual reality and LBEs bring you into a virtual environment, **augmented reality (AR),** or **mixed reality (MR),** brings the game into the user's environment. To see the augmented reality, you need a layer (usually a glass screen, a smart phone's camera, or the lens of goggles) between your eyes and the real world.

An AR experience uses sensors, cameras, and algorithms to scan the environment and then generate images and characters who are "smart" enough to interact with these real-world items. If you are playing an AR game in your living room, the game can recognize where the furniture is located and could have Pikachu actually standing on your coffee table. AR games can be played anywhere, which makes them a challenge to design since you'll never know where the player will be.

Early AR, such the *AR Games* (2011) for the Nintendo DS 3D system, required a card with a special image on it to help the software "lock on" to a position. The character and other game play elements were centered around the card. If the player moved too far away from the card during gameplay, the images would disappear, and the game would pause until the player moved back to the card again. *Start the Party* (2010) used PlayStation's Eye Toy camera peripheral to view the players on their tv screen. Digital characters and items could be interacted with during the game play. Personally, I found the end result to be very charming.

When mobile phones introduced GPS, developers like Niantic saw new opportunities. Their games *Ingress* (2013) and *Pokémon Go* (2016) not only made millions of dollars, but created millions of fans who would travel to real-world locations like parks and statues in order to capture a Pokémon or capture territory for their team. I played Pokémon Go during that magical summer of 2016. It was pretty neat to see dozens of people all working together as they searched for Pokémon in the real world.

Designing an AR game comes with its own challenges. While developing an AR enabled apps, I learned a few important things:

- Introduce what an AR item or creature looks like early on in the experience. Avoid trying to make your objects and creatures look too real. Players need to know the difference between what's real and what's virtual in order to interact with them.

- Work with your software engineer to make sure that object mapping is as accurate as possible. That accuracy can be key to selling the illusion that the item or effect is happening in the real world.

- Make sure the player knows the parameters of the AR experience. Nothing breaks immersion faster than when the augmented elements disappear on screen.

- Keep the motions required to operate augmented elements to simple motions. A swipe. A tap. A circular swirl. I wrote *Swipe This! The Guide to Great Touchscreen Game Design* that is an entire book about how to interact with virtual objects that you might want to check out!

- Keep play sessions on the short side. There should be no quests that take an hour to complete. Shorter sessions give the player an opportunity to take a break as well as help avoid the mobile device running out of battery during play!

Pokémon GO was the most successful of these types of AR experiences, but it didn't always deliver that "Pokémon" experience users wanted—like nurturing a Pokémon or having them fight other players' characters. I believe that AR has a lot of potential as an entertainment medium, but it needs to be the right application of that technology. AR is just going to get better as time goes on. Perhaps *you* will help create the next great AR experience.

The X Factor

XR or **extended reality** is often found in workplace applications rather than gaming. XR experiences that emphasis training, education, therapeutic treatments, and data exploration and analysis. I could write a whole book on the topic, there is a lot to cover. Instead, here is just one example of how XR is entering the marketplace:

XR can be found in stores where customers do virtual try-ons of clothing. Lego Stores used XR technology to allow a customer to place a box next to a screen to see what the set inside was like. Maison Valentino had virtual try-on displays. A customer would get scanned and then presented with a selection of fashion looks without having to try on a stitch of clothing. These technologies are creating more personalized, memorable shopping experiences.

XR experiences are often static displays that don't require the level design or mechanics that games do. What is important is the experience's UI. Simplicity of controls and user feedback is of primary importance. Design interfaces the same way you would for VR. Everything will be operated by the user's real hand. Think of the interface as a big smart phone.

Many XR experiences incorporate features that are found in video games, even if the products themselves aren't games per se. **Gamification** is the term often used by the clients of these XR experiences. They want to make their products more like games, because people like games. Gamification adds game features to something that doesn't traditionally have rules, gameplay or a win/lose condition. This is where knowing game design comes in useful. The same ideas and concepts were used in the creation of these XR designs. However, you must remember that the users of these XR experiences aren't traditionally gamers. They're just regular people. However, if you pull off an interesting interaction, the experience will seem like "magic".[6]

Reality Is the Best Virtual World

The first **artificial environments** started with gardens in Victorian England. They influenced the creation of American theme parks in the 1950s, which in turn influenced the themed restaurants and shopping malls of the 70's and 80's. Even if you choose not to make your living making digital games, you can apply the fundamentals of game design to these real-world places.

A great example of a real-world game is *A Pirates Adventure: Treasure of the Seven Seas* in Adventureland at Walt Disney World, Florida. The designers of that game really paid attention to helping the player find their way to a quest (they gave them a map as well as directions).

---

[6] As author Arthur C. Clarke said, "Any sufficiently advanced technology is indistinguishable from magic."

The quests were located relatively close to each other so the player didn't get too tired walking from one to the next. They designed the puzzles to be simple and easy to understand and execute such as fire a cannon or show a glyph to an idol. They had the "payoff" for the quest to be broad and clearly visual since there are so many distractions in the park, you don't want your player to miss seeing the big moment. I highly recommend studying attractions such as this to learn from the professionals![7]

Other places offer **LARP** or **live-action role playing** experiences, where you can pretend to be a wizard or a cowboy for a day. In Knott's Berry Farm's *Ghost Town Alive* you can help live-action actors solve their problems, vote for the mayor of the town or even plan to rob the bank! At Universal Studio's *The Wizarding World of Harry Potter*, you can buy a robe and a magic wand to create magic around the land—thanks to Bluetooth and RFID technology.

In 2010, the hotel chain Great Wolf Lodge purchased *MagiQuest,* another live-action role-playing game where players use their wands to battle against magical monsters and solve challenges. There are even bosses to fight like in a video game. *Artemis Spaceship Bridge Simulator* is a LARP that travels around from convention to convention. It takes place on the "real" bridge of a star ship. *True Dungeon* is an LARP event held every year at the Gen Con gaming convention in Indianapolis. This exciting experience features actors, challenging puzzles, giant monsters and role-playing where each player character has a set of skills or actions that they can perform based on their class (barbarian, wizard, rogue, etc.).

The Happiest Places on Earth

Theme parks have been inspiring game designers for generations. If you have the means, I highly recommend visiting as many of these as you can. Not only are they enlightening and educational, but they are fun! Here are some themed places around the world you can visit:

- **Disneyland, Anaheim, California, USA:** The grandfather of theme parks, Disneyland uses its space much more impressively and efficiently than its other versions. See my talk[8] to see how it's been inspiring game designers for decades. And don't forget to check out Trader Sam's at the Disneyland hotel, which is packed with story and surprise!

- **Ghibli Museum, Mitaka, Tokyo, Japan:** This park has several replica locations from the classic animated films such as *Kiki's Delivery Service, Princess Mononoke*, and *my Neighbor Totoro.*

- **Universal Studios, Orlando, Florida:** While the Hollywood, Japan, and Bejing versions have similar attractions and attributes, the Florida Park connects the two Harry Potter-themed parks with an immersive Hogwarts express attraction.

---

[7] You can watch a walkthrough of *A Pirate's Adventure: Treasure of the Seven Seas* at www.youtube.com/watch?v=g_zLi39jzFI.

[8] www.youtube.com/watch?v=P4uPwhSqW8Q

- **Efteling: World of Wonders, Kaatsheuvel, Netherlands:** Open a few years before Disneyland, Efteling started with a fairy tale forest and has grown into a magnificent theme park, complete with original fantasy characters, attractions, and shows.

- **Meow Wolf Omega Mart at Area 15, Las Vegas, Nevada, USA:** This unique attraction not only has a supermarket filled with whimsical items you can buy, but it has a secret hidden behind its walls that can take literally days to explore!

- **Warner Brothers World, Abu Dhabi, UAE:** This theme park is completely enclosed (to protect it from the heat) and features beautiful recreations of the worlds of DC Superheroes, Looney Tunes, Scooby Doo, and more!

- **Puy de Fou, Les Epesses France:** A massive forest location built around a real castle that features epic and immersive stage shows including medieval jousting, a Roman chariot race, and a Viking attack on a village.

- **College of Wizardry, Czocha Castle, Poland:** Spend a week in a real castle[9] roleplaying as a wizarding student.

But you don't have to travel the world to see an artificial experience. Garage "Haunters" do it every Halloween! Heck, give me a few rolls of black plastic, a couple of black lights, a fog machine, a music player, and a plastic skeleton, and I can create an artificial environment that could scare you silly![10]

---

[9] This is especially exciting if you come from a country where there aren't real castles.

[10] I have been making haunted houses in my garage for decades. I've gotten so good at it that I once scared a person off their feet, another was too scared to move, and a third was so scared, they threw up. I felt bad about that last one.

Level 15's Universal Truths and Clever Ideas

- Everything old is new again.
- VR is about a place, not necessarily the player.
- Consider the player's physical space when designing for VR.
- Keep VR controls broad and simple.
- Let the player's imagination do the heavy lifting.
- Design and include methods to prevent players from getting motion sick.
- Remember that LBE players are dazzled by the world they are in, so keep their activities simple.
- Consider the real world when designing for AR.
- The rules of game design work in the real world, too!

Level 16
Everybody Wins: Monetization and Marketing

Instead of loving people and using money, people often love money and use people.
—Wayne Gerard Trotman

FIRST, A DEFINITION: **monetization** is a series of strategies employed by the developer to try to make players pay additional money past the player's initial purchase.

Next, some history: Game developers have always been happy to separate the player from their money. This philosophy has been with us since the dawn of commercial video gaming: if you wanted to keep playing a game of *Pong* in 1972, you put in another quarter. You could buy "add-ons" and "expansion packs" for games like *The Sims* (1989) and *Sonic & Knuckles* (1994) that would expand play or add content into existing games.

When computers and gaming consoles became internet-enabled in the late 90s, developers added **downloadable content** or **DLC** to their game's stores. This DLC could be anything from new units in *Total Annihilation* (1997) to extra levels like in *Metal Gear Solid VR Missions* (1999) and *Star Wars: Knights of the Old Republic* (2003) to horse armor in *Elder Scrolls IV: Oblivion* (2006). Around the same time, **microtransactions**—very inexpensive upgrades or DLC that costs as low as .49 cents—became popular with South Korean gamers in titles such as *QuizQuiz* (1999) and *MapleStory* (2003). Soon after the Apple app store opened in 2009, microtransactions became ubiquitous to off-set the cost of free games that were offered on the platform.

Monetization may be used by a developer for many different reasons. Some use it to allow players to extend their play time or improve their gaming experience. Others use it to extend the life of the game past its initial "life span." And yet others use monetization to recoup their cost of production or to make a profit after the game has been initially released. Methods employed include:

- **"Premium" pricing:** In the old days, we used to just call this "the retail price." But times have changed, and the traditional price of a game now means that it is special. Developers will list their game at a premium price often because of scale of the game (i.e., a AAA game) or it might have an expensive IP attached and the publisher wants to earn that money back. As of this date, premium pricing for games ranges between $39.99 to $89.99 USD. This has been traditional pricing for video games since the 80's, which is why your parents would complain that video games cost too much. However, I firmly believe that video game developers deserve to get paid.

- **Pay-to-play:** Just as arcade players fed quarters into games to continue play, modern mobile gamers feed dollars into their devices to buy continues. In this method, players pay for energy or credits to keep their game going, so they don't lose their score, ranking or status they'd earned during the game. Or you can buy more credits to keep playing the game if you are grinding toward a goal or reward or enjoying playing the game!

- **Product placement:** Starting with Pepsi and Canon camera billboards in *Pole Position* (1982), developers have been happy to "sell space" to advertisers within their game's levels and environments. This in-game advertising can take many forms from displays of Coca-Cola cans in *The Coca-Cola Kid* (1985) to "wearable" Air Jordan IX's for your *Fortnite* character. President Obama's campaign advertised on billboards in games like *NASCAR 09, NBA Live 08,* and *The Incredible Hulk* during his 2008 electoral campaign. If you go this route, you will want to consider the genre of game as some genres are more appropriate for product placement than others. For example, it's perfectly fine to have them in sports, FPS or platformer games but less appropriate to use in an adventure or educational game.

- **In-game advertising (the other kind):** There are a variety of ways your ads can be displayed. A **banner ad** is a graphic that runs above or below the play area of your game. You can create a **commercial** for your game—a short video that interrupts gameplay—that acts as a "gate" for your player. The player must watch the ad in order to progress or if they want some sort of reward. Some ads are even optional, incentivizing the player with some sort of reward (usually in-game currency) for watching it of their own volition! This is a great option to offer players who have run out of credits or turns!

Or you could have **sponsorship**, where a company pays to advertise within your game such as the ads displayed on the walls of the hockey rink in *Hockey All Stars 24* (2024). Regardless of the style used, in-game ads are the #1 way that a developer can earn revenue from their game. However, used too much, they can create ad fatigue. I won't tell you how many times I had to watch an ad for *Royal Match* (2021). It was so annoying!! So, when pop-up ads started to clutter up mobile device games, the developers came up with a sneaky new trick: they would remove the offending ads for a small fee!

■ **Virtual goods:** The earliest virtual goods were sold to players of multi-user dungeons who realized that it was sometimes cheaper to pay for an item than to earn it. With the success of *World of Warcraft's* virtual economy, the eyes of developers were opened to the possibilities—and profitability—of virtual goods. Virtual game sales in some games were so profitable that the developers were able to offer their core games for free. How much can virtual goods set you back? Anywhere from .49 cents for a (discounted) weapon in *Team Fortress 2* to a virtual planet in *Entropia Universe* that will only set you back $6 million in real-world money.

■ **Downloadable content (DLC):** Originally, downloadable content was free. It was just a way for developers to get new content to customers of their game. **Promotional codes** were the most popular of these early delivery methods. These were codes that the player could type in to unlock content that was already part of the game's code. Developers soon learned that players wanted everything associated with the game and started charging for it. Costumes and skins, new weapons and vehicles, levels and gameplay modes, music, brand new storylines...every type of game content was fair game in this new marketplace. It remains a staple of modern gaming where they usually can be bought in a **store** that is part of the game's UI.

■ **Merchandise:** T-shirts! Stuffies! Stickers! Pins[1]! There are so many items that can be sold to players who love your game. Especially if you are promoting your game at a conference or convention, why not have merchandise to sell to your fans?

Just be aware that dealing in merchandise can be a real hassle to store and transport (especially t-shirts; they get heavy!). You can always rent a storage shed or warehouse for your merch but sometimes you could spend more on rent than the money you'll make selling them.

You can always sell them online on your game's website, although dealing with shipping can be a hassle, too. And if something gets damaged in shipping, your customer often demands a refund or a new item. Just remember that you will also have to pay taxes at the end of the year on all of those items sold, so make sure to keep careful financial records.

---

[1] The PAX chain of conventions (PAX East, PAX West, PAX Unplugged, PAX AUS) have created a whole collecting subculture around the buying and trading of pins.

Some developers (and many publishers) feel that a monetization system is necessary for a game to be competitive in today's market. Other game designers feel that monetization systems ruin a gaming experience. Players either love 'em or hate them. You've heard about the success stories: *Candy Crush Saga, Clash of Clans, Honor of Kings, Roblox*…. But what about the others?

I've also seen games cancelled due to monetization systems that were poorly thought through, as in the case of Supercell's 2012 *Battle Buddies,* which was a shooter where you had to buy your guns! Or even worse, look at developer Mikengreg. Despite achieving 200,000 downloads with their game *Gasketball,* the developers ended up homeless and had to borrow money to survive. Terrible! The cause? A poor monetization plan.

Back to Business

Let's not make that mistake, shall we? Instead, let's consider what kind of business model you are going to use to make money. There are plenty to choose from:

- **Trial:** A free version is severely limited in scope. It's usually just a few levels—just enough to give players a taste of the game in the hopes that they buy the "premium" version.

- **Freemium:** Freemium is the best-known monetization model. This unlimited trial or "velvet rope" model lets players play without paying. While the players can play most of the game, key features are missing. At a certain point, players can pay for a "premium" version of the game.

  The freemium model has been in the running ever since Nexon made a splash with its freemium game *KartRider* in 2005, but it really gained steam with *FarmVille* (2009). When playing Farmville, players could pay to speed up game processes. They could speed things up by recruiting real-world friends from the players' Facebook lists— which became a huge pain when all of your friends started asking you for help. The other way was to pay a small fee to complete the task. Why wait when you can build your farmhouse (or whatever) immediately? When *FarmVille* gained 50 million players and $100 million in profits,[2] the industry took notice, and this monetization scheme became the new model.

- **Free-to-play (F2P):** These games are free to download, but if players want to avoid grinding or to progress faster, they can pay for more currency, power, or time. *Smurf Village, Simpsons Tapped Out,* and Zynga's *-Ville* series all follow this model.

- **Downloadable content (DLC):** We just talked about this kind of content that improves, extends, or enhances the gamer's experience. Some of the most popular DLC are vanity items like *Team Fortress 2*'s hats, *Fortnite*'s costumes and dances, or full-blown play experiences like *Grand Theft Auto IV's Ballad of Gay Tony* or *Marvel Spider-Man: The City That Never Sleeps*.

- **Season pass:** Most commonly found in AAA console games and in mobile games, the "season pass" offers a bundle of content ranging from new episodes to weapons to exclusive vanity items to small amounts of in-game currency offered for free or at a reduced cost. While intended to extend **player retention** (the time a player spends playing a game) often season passes are offered on the first day of a game's release, ensuring that players will have plenty to play after they finish the core game.

- **Membership:** Membership grants players benefits not available to regular players. Players gain access to special treasure, costumes, minigames, or other experiences. Often, these experiences are shown to non-member players to entice them to join. Memberships often offer to remove annoying ads that interrupt gameplay.

- **Premium:** The full version of the game is often sold at a "premium" price. Even when players pay full price, the game can still sell them DLC, memberships, and other in-game purchases.

- **Subscription:** Subscriptions ask for regular payment—usually month-to-month. The challenge to the subscription model is to make sure you continue to add content, so players feel as though they are paying for something worthwhile. *World of Warcraft* is one of the world's largest subscription games with 7.25 million subscribers.

Cashing In

So, you've convinced your players to pay into your monetization plan. Great! But just what are you giving them for their money? Here are some things your players might want to pay for:

- **Chance:** If players have an opportunity to improve their chances of success, they will pay. Whether it is improving a percentage of something happening in the game or the frequency of something appearing (like rare items appear more often) or whether even

[2] http://tech.fortune.cnn.com/2009/10/26/farmville-gamemaker-zynga-sees-dollar-signs

if it's a downright guarantee that something will happen, everyone likes to *know* they are going to win, rather than "leave luck to heaven."[3]

- **Customization:** Whether it's decorating their virtual house, having an exclusive avatar or wearing a virtual hat, players love to express their identity through customization. This is a great opportunity for using other intellectual property. The game *Fortnite* allows players to dress up as some of their favorite characters from movies, TV, anime, cartoons and comic books. And when another player sees me playing as Boba Fett, you can bet they're going to get jealous. Many times, these types of customization options are offered for a limited time, making players rush to buy them for fear of missing out.

- **Convenience:** Today's players have less time to play games. And as they say, time is money. So instead of waiting for that pumpkin to grow or for a character to finish that chore or for that treasure chest to unlock, why not just pay to speed things up? Just buy a few extra coins or credits or cronch berries or whatever and pay to finish the job. Some games give players the option to have friends help (what a hassle!). Make sure the benefits are clear and what you are offering is too good to pass up!

- **Exclusivity:** Rare items and experiences are prized by many players. Appeal to their vanity and status by creating limited or expensive items. Then other players will see these items and want to buy them, too! Give your levels of rarity cool code names and special colors to indicate their specialness. Here are some examples of more commonly used rank terms in order of their quality:

  - Poor, Apprentice, Inferior, Junk
  - Common, Normal, Standard, Consumer Grade
  - Uncommon, Expert, Superior, Industrial Grade
  - Rare, Magical, Restricted, Unlimited, Superb
  - Epic, Artisan, Unique, Very Rare, Classified
  - Legendary, Mythical, Super-Rare, Fresh, Covert
  - Ultra, Artifact, Promo, Exotic, Limited
  - Infinity, Heirloom, Exclusive, Mythic Rare

- **Progress:** Stuck on a level? Want to keep playing? Why not pay to progress! Economist Ramin Shokrizade lists two different gates to progression: "soft gates" and "hard gates." Players eventually can pass soft gates by grinding (playing a level or doing a task over and over and over again). However, a player can also pay to accelerate the process. With hard gates, the players have no choice but to pay. A common technique is to make players pay to pass a hard gate only to find that a more expensive hard gate lies beyond.

---

[3] "Leave luck to heaven" is the translation of the Japanese phrase "Nintendo" – a company who, ironically, was one of the last major publishers to embrace monetization. They finally succumbed with *Super Mario Run* (2016) and *Fire Emblem Heroes* (2017).

Because players already paid to pass one hard gate, why *not* spend a little more for the next one, right?

- **A Bargain:** You can offer your items cheaply—.99 cents for a virtual item? That's a bargain!! And no one can resist a bargain, right? Granted, some people feel that offering games and virtual items for that cheap is what is killing the video game industry—items being priced so low that their creators cannot possibly make a profit from them...but "killing" the industry is such strong language! "Hurting" is probably a better term, perhaps. What do you think?

- **Prestige:** If you come riding into Stormwind City wearing your best purple glowing armor, you are gonna make everyone jealous! You show up to the game with that digital card signed by freakin' Samuel L. Jackson, you know that people are going to look twice. You announce to the entire server that you've given your bestie a virtual ring that cost ninety-nine real world dollars, you'll get their attention. Game developers know that there are some players out there that will pay top dollars for extra exclusive virtual items. As they say, if you charge 1 million dollars for something, you only need to sell it once![4]

Money Is the Root of Something Something

Let's face it. There is a shady side to monetization. Companies want players to play for years, not just months, and monetization can keep players coming back because the more the players pay, the more invested in the game they feel. These consistently spending players, known as "whales," are the targets of **coercive monetization**, techniques designed to get players to spend even when they don't want to. I'm not condoning using these techniques in your games, but it's good to at least know about them:

- **Currency obfuscation:** There should be a difference between your in-game currency, which is earned by the player, and premium currency, which is used to buy content using real money. For example, *Puzzle and Dragons* (2012) uses coins as its in-game currency and magic stones (or eggs) as its premium currency. Players defeat monsters to earn coins to pay for items in games and use real money to pay for stones to buy premium (including more coins!). Simple right? Even more confusing are the rates of exchange: 1600 Microsoft points costs $19.99. So how much is each point worth? And if games cost 1200 points, what can you spend your remaining 400 points on? Anything? And because I now have leftover points, I'm going to have to buy more points to afford something else! See? If you keep prices just confusing enough, buyers won't be exactly sure how much they are spending.

---

[4] Unless you want more than 1 million dollars, I guess.

- **Bundling: Bundles** are groupings of items offered at a discounted or lowered price to incentivize purchase. For example, a bundle in *Marvel Snap* may offer players a bundle of 3000 credits and one "premium mystery variant" card for $24.99 USD. They may also offer a bundle that consists of an exclusive card variant, 1200 gold, a new title, 1000 credits, a unique icon and 155-character boosters for the same price. Which begs the question, which bundle is a better bargain? If there appears to be a "better" bundle to purchase, then audiences will be more likely to buy that one.

  Bundles also get confusing when in-game currencies get involved. If the player can't figure out the conversion rate from real money to in-game, then they might not determine whether a bundle is a bargain or not.

- **Ramping:** Ramp the game's difficulty to the point where players *need* to buy boosts to progress. *Candy Crush Saga* (2013) has an extremely sharp difficulty spike that forces the players to spend if they want to succeed. This is known as the **Pay-To-Win** strategy.

- **Rewarding:** Players are tempted to make a purchase with the promise of more rewards in the future. *Jetpack Joyride's* counterfeit machine gave the player double coins for each run they played. *Marvel Snap* gives free credits daily to players. *Monopoly Go* has *Daily Rewards* (rewards for continuous days of play); play seven days in a row to earn a prize. Their *Endless Bargains* tier awards two tiers of rewards before asking for a $3.99 payment to unlock three more tiers of rewards, one paid, two "free." The cost of the tiers increased with each level and *Endless Offers*: that worked similarly to Endless Bargains but offered bundles of rewards instead of just a single one. These techniques give the impression that players are getting a good deal, and they might be, but they are often used to get players to spend more than they might have originally purchased.

- **Games of chance:** Many times, players are offered an opportunity to play a game of chance at the end of a round or as a side game to extend play or earn more in-game currency. These are mini-games like a **wheel of fortune, slot machine, matching numbers, cash-grab booths, gashapon machines, whack-a-mole,** and others. The model of these kinds of games has moved away from players actually losing and instead winning varying degrees of prizes. For example, you might win a small prize that doesn't extend play, or you might win a big one that allows you to keep going. Sometimes, the game will give the player a small win to entice them to play again in hopes of winning a larger one.

- **Fun pain:** Zynga founder Roger Dickey promoted a monetization concept that he called "fun pain." He said you need to provide both fun and pain to the players. For example, in *FarmVille*, the constant clicking players do to perform tasks is a "painful" action that requires time and effort, but eventually yielding the "fun" result for players. Dickey warned that too much clicking would drive players away, too! Designing fun pain is a delicate balancing act![5]

---

[5]For more Roger Dickey, check out his video about how to monetize games at vimeo.com/32161327#.

- **Gacha:** Named after the **Gashapon** toy vending machines originally found in Japan, is a prize, reward or surprise that is concealed in a capsule or box packaging. The player buys the capsule without knowing what is inside but having some idea of the types of prizes they can win. Sometimes, you get something you desire; other times you might get something you already own. In-game collections are often made up of virtual items obtained from Gacha. There are several techniques associated with Gacha.

  - **Spins/Pulls:** The player has a limited number of times they can "pull" a Gacha from the machine. Additional pulls can be purchased with in-game currency or real-world currency. Sometimes, the player might earn additional spins during the pull process—in the same way that a pinball player can randomly earn an extra play once the game is over.

  - **Near Miss:** The player almost gets the item they desire and is motivated to do "just one more time" in order to try to win it. The feeling is they were so close they are sure to get it the next time. This, of course, is a false assumption created by the game.

  - **Pity system:** If the player has bought Gacha several times without getting the "good" prize, the good prize will be awarded to the player to keep them buying. Another situation would be if a mini game such as a wheel of fortune rolled to a "miss" but at the last minute clicked back over to win. A moment of tension is created in which the player thinks they might lose and then they win at the last minute. In crueler games, the opposite of this might occur.

  - **FOMO (Fear of missing out):** Gacha are offered for a limited time and if the player doesn't buy it during this time period, they might not ever get it.

- **Loot Boxes:** A monetization system that first appeared in 2004, **loot boxes** are virtual items that can be opened with keys purchased using in-game or real-world currency. Inside the box is a variety of items ranging from weapons, armor, and equipment, to skins, sprays, hats, trading cards, and other cosmetic and collectible items. Loot boxes are usually graded by rarity. For example, the contents of a common box are less exciting than the contents of a rare box. Some loot boxes have a spectrum of rewards and as the player purchases more loot boxes, the rewards the player already owns are removed from the list of rewards the player can gain, thus incentivizing the player to get more loot boxes in order to get what they really want.

The controversy over loot boxes reached a head in 2017, when players of *Hearthstone* and *Star Wars Battlefront II*, among others, complained that in order to be successful at playing a game, loot box purchases needed to be made, thus changing the emphasis to pay-to-win; the focus of the gameplay changing from skill to money. Since then, loot boxes have been less popular among game developers.

- **Membership:** If a player joins the game's club/guild/rewards program, they will get extra benefits during the game. For example, each month *Call of Duty Mobile* offers several tiers of season passes. The first, known as a "Battle Pass," rewards players skins, weapon blueprints, calling cards, and additional Call of Duty Points (CP) that could be used toward the player's next in-store purchase. A Premium Pass membership allows players to unlock even more content—especially weapons and cosmetics. The Battle Pass Subscription grants extra rewards during each season along with a 10% boost to the player and weapon XP, discount coupons and limited discounts on crate (loot box) pulls. This constant flow of bonuses and rewards keeps players engaged far longer than a single reward ever could. And since there are new seasons of content, it incentivizes players to either keep coming back to pay for it again and again or join the subscription for a discounted rate.

- **Extra Slots:** In games where the player is offered limited reward slots, the player can pay to unlock a "third slot." The player can be charged for this to happen on a one-time or permanent basis. Players can often access the third slot by joining a membership program.

- **Unlocks:** This method prevents a player from playing without paying a cost. This can be really odious if used incorrectly. As a "bad" example, *Batman: Arkham Origins* (2013) was a free-to-play download, but it wouldn't let players start the game unless they paid a 99-cent unlock fee. Players who downloaded the game felt tricked. They would have preferred to know about or even pay the .99 cent fee ahead of time rather than getting ambushed by it.

- **Reward removal:** Another popular trick is to threaten to remove rewards unless players pay. Placing a big ol' timer (only three days left!) forces players to decide; buy or not buy? (That is the question!) It's easier to get players to make digital payments during the heat of the game rather than before or after when they have time to think about exactly how much money that bushel of Smurfberries cost. Another trick is to give players so many rewards that they can't hold them all and so they must pay for more space! Sneaky!

As you can see, there are downsides to all these models. Players feel as if they are being taken advantage of when the game doesn't let them progress without paying. They are constantly being asked to pay for extras they don't want or need. Or they might feel like they have to pay for access to the full game experience even after paying for the product. Or, they might not be able to afford their higher tier/more expensive options. These situations can create bad feelings toward the game and the publisher.

Designing It In

Monetization systems require a lot of work to create, and require the creator to really understand how monetization works. It demands a lot of attention to get right and can ruin a game experience if applied too heavily or lightly. This all sounds scary, but not to worry; we will navigate these tricky waters together.

The first thing you want to ask yourself is: How important is the monetization system to your game? For example, some games lean heavily on monetization and won't let the player progress without it. Other games will make it optional, letting the player choose when to spend money...if at all. Making this decision at the start of the design process will impact the rest of your design.

Give monetization systems lots of attention early in the design process. Don't leave them to the last minute. You can exploit some aspects of these systems to your benefit in all aspects of your entire design. But you say "I'm a game designer! I'm busy designing a game, and now you want me to design a game that makes money? What happened to a game *just being fun*?"

Well, for better or worse, times have changed, so if you want to work as a game designer these days, it helps to know how to design in monetization. That's ok, I'm here to help you through this process. If you want to succeed at monetizing your game, here are some proven tips and tricks.[6]

1. **Plan your monetization strategy:** Pick the type of way(s) you want to monetize. Do you want to sell continues once a player has run out of plays? Do you want to sell custom skins or cards or levels? Can the player speed up the time it takes for something to build or unlock? Once you know the answers to the gameplay questions, you can pick the right strategy for the game. The game should come first.

2. **Choose the right game monetization model:** It makes more sense to use a timed/unlock system if you are building a castle, than by watching commercials. It makes more sense to make the player watch an ad if they want to continue playing. Find the right model that fits your game. Ludo narrative dissidence exists even in advertisements and stores for a game! Follow the same rules you would as you would for storytelling in your game.

---

[6] I am legally bound to mention that there is no guarantee on anything.

3. **Design a game that needs monetization:** Some games don't need monetization, while others benefit or even thrive from it. A CCG or puzzle game or an RPG is a much better fit than an adventure game or a horror game. Design in "high value" features that improve the gameplay. Think about what you as a player would find worthwhile and choose those features. Don't just put something in because you think it will earn you money.

4. **Optimize your game for retention and engagement: Retention** means that you are keeping players playing your game. The goal is to keep players coming back over and over again. How do you do this? By giving them what every player wants…variety! Often, several of these retention strategies are employed in a single game.

   - **Daily rewards:** Players get free things (gold, credits, buffs) for playing every day.

   - **Limited time items:** Items change every so-many hours, so if you don't get it during that time period it's gone (but most likely it will be back). A small counter keeps track of the countdown until the item is gone to drive **FOMO** (fear of missing out).

   - **Season Pass:** An extended time period (such as a few weeks or a month) where players can pay a small amount of money to try to earn special rewards within a limited time span. Once the time span is over, however, the rewards are no longer available.

   - **Weekly specials:** Offer special deals to your players on days when players are less likely to play.

   - **Leaderboard:** Players compete for the top spot for bragging rights or exclusive or limited time rewards.

   - **In-game events:** Special events that the players can participate in and do a variety of activities, from modifications to the core gameplay to completely different styles of play for a limited time. Often themed prizes are attached to these events to act as proof that the player attended the event.

5. **Communicate with your players:** Players lead busy lives, and there's a lot of entertainment competing for their attention. That's why you've got to get their attention first! **Push notifications** can be sent via text to remind players of events, bargains and deadlines that are running out. Send out **email updates** informing them of any changes made to the game or promotions coming up. YouTube videos, blog posts, and any other way you can reach your audience is good. An engaged audience is one that keeps playing your game and coming back for more!

Regardless of what method you use, the key to good monetization is keeping in the good graces of the players; Use the power of monetization for good (keeping the game going) and not for evil (exploiting the players). Player perception colors that opinion and that perception can quickly change, which results in the "evil pay to win microtransaction game by greedy devs" stereotype. However, capitalism doesn't have to be all bad. There are still many ethical ways to monetize:

- **Provide alternative ways to earn.** Let players realize there are multiple paths to reach their goal. Paying will provide the quick path, but they can play longer to achieve the same results.

- **Warn players that your game costs money to play.** Let players know what they're getting themselves into from the start. Sometimes, you can turn around players' opinions if they are really enjoying your game and feel it "deserves" to be supported.

- **If they pay, provide discounts.** Use bundling, early player adapters, and membership to give your players benefits and save them some money. They're more likely to spend if they feel that they're saving money.

- **Let the players back out of the pay option.** Don't lock players into paying. Let them back out if they get cold feet or make a mistake. They will be much more likely to spend in the future if they know they aren't going to regret doing so now.

- **If you must have advertisements**, make sure that they are relevant to the player. Gamers are much more likely to tolerate watching an advertisement related to gaming (a new game, a game accessory or gaming service) than one not related at all.

People can lose their head when it comes to money, so it's always best to treat others the way you'd want to be treated. If you think your monetization method is taking advantage of your players, perhaps it's time to rethink that plan. Your players will appreciate your thoughtfulness in the long run.

How come there isn't more art in this chapter?

Because we asked them to pay $0.99 an image.

beep boop

Marketing: A Million Voices Yelling "Look at Me"

Marketing is how you go about promoting your game. Marketing, in the past, was something done by a team member who was dedicated to doing that job. But let's say you've designed and developed a video game. How can you help with marketing it? How are you going to let people know about it?

In "the old days" there were lots of ways you could easily advertise a video game...on television, with radio ads, in gaming and genre magazines, on the back pages of comic books, in the newspaper, The Electronic Entertainment Expo aka E3... Most of those methods are gone.[7] But sadly, almost all of those traditional ways to market your game don't exist nowadays. Bummer.

As a game designer at a big developer or publisher, I barely ever was involved with marketing. There were whole departments at the publisher who did this. But sometimes I was called upon to help the marketing department. Some of the ways that I helped included:

- **Make playthrough videos:** As someone who had played the game many times over and knew where all the "good stuff" was—the stuff that made the game look cool and exciting—I was often called upon to play the game so it could be recorded for promotional videos. If you watch the trailers for *Pac-Man World*, *Maximo: Ghosts to Glory*, and *Maximo vs. Army of Zin* on YouTube, you'll see my awesome game playing skills in action!

- **Write ad copy:** As someone who likes to write, I was always happy to help write the text found on the back of the box. But even though video game boxes aren't as common as they used to be, you can still help write the text for the blog or website, the game description on Steam or for the Nintendo eShop or the Microsoft Store.

- **Help design the game's box cover:** If you are a visual artist, you can help design the game's cover! When I was a creative manager at THQ, I was asked to help design the cover for *Drawn to Life: The Next Chapter* for the Nintendo DS. Because of my familiarity with the game that I knew what was most important about the game—which characters and the player actions—needed to be highlighted on the cover.

- **Hype up the game:** Magazine articles, blog posts, podcasts, TV interviews...any public facing way that you can promote your game helps. Post about your game on LinkedIn, Facebook, or Instagram. Make a short TikTok video of you working on the game or showing gameplay. Interview your teammates about working on the game. People love to see "how the sausage is made"—warts and all![8]

---

[7] Well, comic books are still around. And thank goodness, otherwise, I'd have nothing to read on Wednesdays!

[8] Ick! Who wants to eat a warty sausage?? Gross!

There are many other ways you can spread the word about your game. If you happen to live near a college or a gaming store, you could hold demos where people come and play your game. It's a great way to get feedback.

You could submit your game to a festival, where it might end up being featured with other games or who knows, you could even win a prize!

You could attend a convention and spend some money to rent a table or create a booth to promote your game. There's a big list of all the gaming conventions all over the world at videogamecons.com/calendar/.

If you do get a booth at a convention, I recommend attending that convention first (usually the year before), so that way you know what you are in for. You can understand how booths are set up and how much space you'll have. You can figure out how to design your booth to move players in and out as they play the game. You don't want your booth to get clogged up with people! Also, you will be spending all day on your feet, so spend a little extra for a padded floor. You can rent these kinds of things (along with chairs, tables, tablecloths, power strips, TV monitors, and more) from a company that is affiliated with the convention center.

You will also need signage for your booth. Game logos are usually the best, but you can make cut-outs of your characters or posters of your games or, if you really want to spend the money, you can have a costume of your character made to greet your players as they come to your booth. You can figure out what merchandise you want to have available.

Creating, preparing and operating a booth at a convention takes a lot of time and is a lot of hard work. The bigger the show, the harder it will be for your booth to stand out. I recommend looking at other attendees' booths for good ideas! You can also do a lot of this online as well. Lots of people who go to conventions take photos of them and share them online. There are plenty of ways to get ideas.

Catch and Release

A lot of game creators asked me to include a section on releasing a game. The reality of the modern gaming market is that as there are smaller game design teams, everyone on the team should help get the word out about your game. Getting people to know about your game can be critical to its success.

Pre-release is the time before your game comes out. Starting at least one year from your game's release, you want to build an **audience**. An audience are the people who you want to educate and get excited about your game. Your goal with anything shown during pre-release is three-fold. Make your audience *aware* and get them *interested* and *excited*.

You want to show something that is unique, attention grabbing, even a bit mysterious. Many developers start with a **teaser trailer,** which is a 30-second-long video that shows either a bit of the lore of the game or flashes of gameplay. Or, they might show a **trailer,** which is a video showing a couple of minutes of gameplay or part of the story. This trailer needs to show off the game's beauty, a unique gameplay mechanic or how exciting your game is to play.

You can also release a few images of your game that include a title, a character, a screenshot or two. However, keep this in mind: Whatever you release out into the world will a) be out there *forever*, and b) will (hopefully) spark the interest of those who see it. Then your audience will ask questions that you need to be prepared to answer. Questions like:

- What's the gameplay?
- What's the story?
- How much of this is "faked" for the video?
- What's the gameplay?
- How much will the game cost?
- What system is this playable on?
- What's the gameplay??!!

All of these questions are okay, because when someone asks a lot of questions, it means that they are interested. Which is good! But you will need to be able to answer these questions with the materials you release to your audience, whether it's your own website, a press-release, or an interview with a podcaster or webmaster.

The real challenge with marketing your game is "rising above the noise." Steam estimates that *fifty* new games are released *every day*! That's *forty-nine* other games that you are competing with, just on the day that you release. That doesn't count all of those other games...as well as older games that are already on Steam!! So, if the competition is so stiff, just how do you get attention for your game? As near as I can tell, you need at least these three following things:

1. A good title
2. A bangin' video
3. Great gameplay

We've already learned how to come up with a good title earlier in this book and hopefully, it has taught you how to create some great gameplay, so let's talk a second about the video. Again, this used to be something that a trained professional would do. There are plenty of talented video editors out there and they're worth the money you'd pay them. But if you need to go "on the cheap" and do it yourself, here are a few things to keep in mind:

- **Always be moving.** The character in the game should always be moving, whether it's running, sneaking, fighting, driving...whatever. Never have a character "just standing there," even if you are trying to show off how beautiful the character model or the world is. If you need to have one of these "beauty shots" in your video, then have the camera move instead. At least there will be some motion in the image.

- **Cut on the action.** This means that when you make an edit, edit near or around action. Don't wait too long afterward so the viewer isn't watching a character just running around or standing in place.

- **Show the character.** Many videos just show the back of the character as they run through the game world. But people like looking at faces. If you can, rotate the camera around to show the front of the character. It can be a little tricky to control the camera and get a character to execute a jump or swing at an enemy, but it can be done.

- **Quality sound.** Nothing says "amateur production" more than poor sound quality, especially when it comes to narration. You need to invest in a quality microphone (I use a Blue Yeti microphone) and edit your sound with a program like Audacity or SoundForge.

Just because you've released your game doesn't mean you can just sit back and count your money. You need to follow up your game with **publicity**! This means getting your playable game to reviewers and social media influencers. Make sure your game's build is something you can easily send on-line. You will want to compile your build into an application that is easy for the player to install and play.

You should also talk about your game. If you have friends with gaming podcasts, ask to be a guest around the time of your game's release. Or, reach out to your favorite gaming podcast and ask them if you can be on their show to promote your game. Be sure to reach out to them before your game comes out, because they often will book guests months in advance.

Write about your game online and get your friends to share your posts and blog articles. Make sure to share lots of pictures of the game—and of you making the game! I once chronicled the creation of a game that I was making, and by the time the game was ready, I had many people interested in buying the game just because they had heard about it online.

You might want to submit your game to a **contest** or a **festival**. Many of these have submission fees, but if you win in a category, the exposure can definitely help when it comes time to release your game. Here's a list of a few festivals from around the world that you can submit your game to:

- A MAZE: https://2021.award.amaze-berlin.de

- DevGAMM: https://devgamm.com/spring2021/devgamm-awards/

- Digital Dragons (free): https://digitaldragons.pl/indie-celebration/indie-celebration-2021-registration/

- The GDWC: https://thegdwc.com

- IGF: https://igf.com

- INDIECADE: https://www.indiecade.com/submissions/

- INDIGO: https://indigoshowcase.nl/indigo-award/

- Pixel Awards: https://www.pixelheavenfest.com/pixel-awards-europe/

- Nordic Game Discovery: https://www.bigfestival.com.br/nordic-game-discovery-contest-en.html

When you are ready to release your game, **throw a party**! Making a game is a lot of hard work, and finishing it is something that should be celebrated!

Level 16's Universal Truths and Clever Ideas

- Decide how dependent your game will be on monetization.
- Design monetization systems for your game from the start.
- Don't ignore the power of coercive monetization.
- Consider the concept of "fun pain" in your monetization system.
- Design ethical monetization systems.
- Use multiple methods for player retention.
- Build an audience before you release your game.
- The key to social media is consistency.
- Gaming conventions are a great way to see how others promote their games.
- Do whatever you can to get attention for your game!
- Celebrate your game's release!

Level 17
Some Notes on Music[1]

WHEN THE IMAGINEERS were creating the *Star Wars Star Tours* attraction at Disneyland, they initially intended the experience to be "realistic." The audience would hear only the sound of the Starspeeder 3000 and the pilot's dialogue. However, when they tested the attraction, something didn't feel right. Without the classic theme by John Williams, the attraction just didn't seem like "Star Wars," so the music was added in.

Music brings a lot to any entertainment experience, be it a theme park attraction, movie, or video game. But it also requires a lot of work and coordination between many members of a team, which contributes to the reason music and sound are usually left until late in production. This is a mistake. Sound and music can bring so much to a game that leaving it until to the last-minute means missing out on some great design opportunities.

Music and sound in gaming have come a long way in a short time. Back in the 1970s and 1980s, arcade and console programmers had only electronic beeps and boops to play with. Even with those limitations, game creators were able to create some simple but memorable musical themes (or even just jingles) for games like *Pac-Man*, *Donkey Kong*, and *The Legend of Zelda*. Sound advances happened with almost every system; voice synthesizing and MIDI format audio meant that music became lusher. However, game creators were limited because sound and music files took up a good amount of memory on cartridges.

The big jump in game music came with CD media games. Starting with Red Book audio (Red Book being the set of standards for CD audio), music in games began to sound just like any other recorded music, and it was possible to store more of it on the CD. As games moved onto DVD media, the biggest problem with sound and music (storage space) was no longer an insurmountable issue. Nowadays modern PC and console games use streaming sound (MP3s or console-specific formats and decompressed as needed by the sound chip). Emphasis shifted from the programmatic issues with music and sound to what to do with it creatively.

Pitch Perfect Design

The first question you need to ask yourself when thinking about music design is, "What kind of music do I want?" There are really two answers to this question: licensed or original.

Licensed music is previously recorded music that can be "licensed" for use in a game for a fee. While music publishers own the rights to the recorded music, companies that work on behalf of the publishers, including the American Society of Composers, Authors, and Publishers (ASCAP) and Third Element, negotiate licensing deals. Game publishers usually handle the job of obtaining the rights to music licenses and negotiating deals.

How the heck do you draw a picture of licensed game music?

Because video games currently don't generate royalties once published, game publishers will negotiate **one-time buy-out fees** for music licenses lasting over a period of seven years to "life of product." Licensing fees can range from $2,500 to more than $30,000 a song. The more popular and prestigious a song is, the higher the licensing fee. I don't want to think how much the licensing fees were for *The Beatles: Rock Band* (2009).

If the song you want for your game is too expensive for your budget, don't fret; there are still plenty of options. You can license a less-expensive cover version of a song. This was done in the first *Guitar Hero* (2005). Or, you can find a similar sounding but less expensive song at a music library. In fact, libraries are great if your game calls for a wide variety of musical styles or requires incidental music, like that heard on a radio or in the background of a bar scene.

Your other option is to use **original music.** Original music is a composition that is created specifically for your game. Unless you can compose, perform, and record your own music, I suggest hiring a music director to work with your team.[2] Not only will create the music, but they can also handle the resources required for performing, recording, and preparing the music for your game. Even though that's a lot of work, a game designer still has plenty of prep work to do before even getting to that stage.

I Know It When I Hear It

I find it helps to be able to talk to a music director in their own language, even if you can't write music, play an instrument, or carry a tune. You just have to know what you like and have an opinion about it! Provide examples of what you want for your composer: try to cut out as much of the guesswork as possible. For *Maximo: Ghosts to Glory*, I gave the composer a mix tape of music from movie soundtracks and songs I thought would be appropriate for the game's levels. While they say that "a little knowledge is a dangerous thing," I have found it useful to develop a musical vocabulary, so you are speaking the composer's language. Doing this will make it that much easier to request changes when you know what to listen for and what it's called.

Here are a few **musical terms** I have found useful to know:

- **Accent:** Emphasis placed on a beat to make it louder or longer. As in "please place more accent on the drums."

---

[2] That is, if you don't already have a music director working on your team.

- **Beat:** The "pulse" of the music. Music is measured in beats. Music can have fast beats or slow beats.

- **Chord:** Three or more tones played at the same time to create harmony.

- **Instrument:** An object that produces music. Synthesized music replicates the sounds instruments make. The choice of instrument can greatly change the theme and mood of a piece.

- **Mood**: The "feel" or theme of a musical piece. The mood of a musical piece can be based on emotion (fear, excitement), action (sneaky, combat), or even location (tropical, Russian). Mood is created by instruments and changes in tempo and beat.

- **Octave:** This is the interval between one musical pitch and another with half or double its frequency. One octave up has twice the pitch; one octave down has half the pitch. You will likely be telling the composer to bring something "up an octave" or "down an octave" to make it sound higher or lower pitched.

- **Pitch**: The highness or lowness of a tone. A tone's pitch can be adjusted either higher (to sound like the Chipmunks) or lower (to sound demonic). A tone's frequency is adjusted to add variety into game sounds without creating new sounds. For example, a sword clanging on metal can have its frequency changed so the player doesn't have to hear the same sound over and over.

- **Rhythm:** The controlled movement of music in time. Ravel's *Bolero* builds in rhythm to a frantic conclusion.

- **Tempo:** The rate of speed of the music, which can range from very, very slow to very, very, very fast. There's even a specific tempo for walking speed called *andante*!

- **Theme:** The "heart" of the musical composition. Usually, a composer will come up with the theme first and then "flesh it out" to fit the length required. For example, John Williams created the *Raiders of the Lost Ark March* when Steven Spielberg couldn't decide between which of two themes that he liked better...so he had Williams combine them!

- **Tone:** The sound or characteristic of a particular voice or instrument.

- **Upbeat:** The last beat of a measure but can also refer to making the music sound happier, friendlier, or faster.

- **Volume:** The softness or loudness of the music.

Music with Style

Now that you can communicate with your music director, you need to consider the genre of your game. What style of music do you want for your game? A traditional route would be to use the style of music generally associated with that genre. Say you're making a sci-fi game. Do you want orchestral music like John William's score from *Star Wars*, something like Vangelis's synthesized music from *Blade Runner*, or do you want to go old school with 1950s' theremin[3] music in the style of the original *The Day the Earth Stood Still*? Feel free to go in another creative direction: how would a sci-fi game feel with a hip-hop soundtrack? Or a trance soundtrack? Or polka?

Creating a **temporary soundtrack** (or "temp" soundtrack) for your game will cut down on the guesswork for your composer and give them clear examples of what you want. Finding music is incredibly simple compared to the past, when we had to scour our CD collections or go into "the field" with microphone and recorders to get samples from the real world. But with the advent of iTunes, YouTube, Spotify, Pandora, and other music-finding websites, assembling tracks is a breeze: put in a couple of keywords and you'll get hundreds, if not thousands, of results. You can have your team's programmer insert this temp music into your game during production, but keep in mind there is always a danger that your team will really start to like (or hate) the temp tracks and complain if they are changed! Also, **make absolutely sure** you don't leave any music in your game that you don't have a license for. You may have to pay big money to use it or scrap all that work!

And the Beat Goes On...

Next, prepare a list of your musical needs. To determine this, figure out how many levels/environments/chapters/racetracks/unique encounters your game has. Each one of these levels will require **background music** or the **soundtrack** of the game, literally, music that plays in the background as a kind of audio backdrop for gameplay.

Traditionally, background music is themed toward the level. Spooky music on the haunted house level, medieval music for the castle level, jungle drums for the jungle level—you get the idea.

Background music tracks usually run for a few minutes and loop over again to save space in memory and composition time. Work with your music director to make sure the transition

---

[3] Have you ever heard that strange "weee-ooooo-oooooo" music in a 1950s sci-fi film? Odds are it was created using a theremin, which is an electronic instrument that is played without using any physical contact. You can hear a theremin here: www.youtube.com/watch?v=JzRb1OVpat0.

between the beginning and the end of the song sounds correct and isn't marred by silence or an awkward change in tempo.

The next question to ask is whether you want—or more realistically, you can afford—to have background music on every level. You may have to reuse tracks throughout the game. For example, in *Maximo vs. Army of Zin*, we had two songs created for each world and alternated between them so players wouldn't have to hear the same song twice in a row.

Instead of having a straightforward song-per-level system, you may want to work with your sound programmer and music director to create a **dynamic score** instead. In this method of scoring a game, music is broken up into themes that are played when a certain situation arises. For example, dynamic music can kick in during combat to make a fight feel more exciting and fast paced. The main theme music will come back once the fight is won.

Dynamic scoring is similar to the music convention **leitmotif,** in which a specific character or scenario has a specific musical theme associated with it. One of the most commonly known leitmotifs is from the *Star Wars* films. Darth Vader, Luke Skywalker, Yoda, and the Princess Leia/Han Solo romance all have unique themes that play whenever the characters are on-screen. If more than one is on screen, it's up to your composer to switch between them without making it sound too jarring.

Hey! Sweet theme music!

The most commonly encountered dynamic score themes include:

- **Mystery:** The player has entered a new and mysterious locale. A little bit of mysterious music can help set the mood.

- **Warning:** Sinister or menacing music plays whenever the player is entering a hazardous area or about to encounter enemies. This type of theme can be found in many horror games.

- **Combat:** Exciting music plays whenever the player is engaged in combat.

- **Chase/fast movement:** Chased by dinosaurs? Pursuing villains? Giant boulder hot on your heels? A fast-paced chase theme will make the action feel even more exciting.

- **Victory:** Be sure to sonically reward your players, even if it's a "sting" (a very short piece of music) to let players know when a fight is over, and they are victorious or to celebrate a successfully accomplished event in the game. *The Legend of Zelda* games have some great examples of rewarding players with music.

- **Walking:** While most games play "walking" music, I believe that if you play slow music, the player is going to move slowly.

Here's a tip: if you make the music's beat faster than the player can walk, it will motivate the player to move faster. In other words, remember this **very important thing**:

ALWAYS MAKE THE MUSIC MORE EXCITING THAN THE ACTION ON-SCREEN

Don't forget to budget for music for your title screen, pause/options/save screen, game-over screen, or any bonus or minigames your games may have. Your opening theme is very important: it's the first piece of music players hear and sets the stage for the rest of the game. I suggest using your best piece of music for the start screen to really get players excited about playing your game.

Environmental effects are the music of the world around us. Locations have their own special background sounds, a graveyard at night sounds very different from a city during lunch hour. Sometimes, music can just be too overbearing or feel wrong for certain environments or games. Combining environmental effects with a dynamic score to punctuate action can be very effective. In *Maximo: Ghosts to Glory*, the hub levels were designed to have environmental effects to help players get into the mood of the locations while the gameplay levels had more traditional background music.

Diegetic sound is when sound comes from a source within the game level. For example, a song is playing over a radio. And in some cases, the player can turn off the radio or even change the station! Diegetic sounds can be the player's footsteps, a smack when the player hits an enemy, a "bong!" when a player strikes a gong in the level.

Non-diegetic sound is when the music plays over the action. For example, weird theremin music plays when your character enters a space station. It's perfectly okay to use non-diegetic music in your game, in fact it's the most common way music is used. Non-diegetic music or sound can even be used to communicate a message or story point to the player, such as when the game has a **narrator**. *The Stanley Parable*, *LittleBigPlanet* and *Bastion* all have narrators that instruct the player and comment on their actions as it happens; making the narration feel more relevant to the player.

When is a sound not a sound? When it's **silence.** Silence has a powerful effect on the listener. Often sound is used judiciously to indicate that something special is happening to the player or the world. It can be used to indicate great speed (when the music drops off as the player engages the boost in *Burnout*), intense action moments (as in "reflex time" in *F.E.A.R.*), suspense, or even a character's failed attempt at humor.[4]

Sounds Like a Game to Me

Next, assemble a list of sound effects. Develop your sound effect lists as you develop the move sets of your characters and enemies. Start by cataloging the basic sound effects for your main character:

---

[4] Usually accompanied with the sound of crickets—so I guess it isn't silent after all.

- **Movement:** Start with the sounds for walking and running on specific surfaces like stone, gravel, and metal, and splashing through water to make your character feel grounded in the world. Jumping, landing, rolling, and sliding all need sounds, too to let players know they've pulled off the moves.

- **Attacks:** Making swings and kicks "swoosh" will make them sound more dynamic. Make unique attacks sound distinct, like Pac-Man's "eating a ghost" or Mario's jump/stomp.

- **Impacts:** A nice meaty "whack" will make a punch or kick feel more powerful. Weapons, spells, and explosions all need dynamic and loud sounds to let players know they've hit something or someone. Don't forget object reaction effects like breaking wood, shattering glass, and clanging metal.

- **Weapons:** Guns bang, swords clang, and laser blasters "pew pew!" The bigger the weapon, the bigger the sound effect. Your weapons should sound as unique as they look; for example, the iconic hum of a light saber matches its distinctive visual.

- **Hit reactions:** "Oomph!" "Ow!" and "Aarrgh!" may sound funny while you are recording them, but they are some of the most important sounds in the game. Whenever players get hit, they need to know it and the sound will clue them in.

- **Vocal cues:** Need to communicate with the players? Use your character. Having your hero say, "What's this?" when he spots treasure or "That's better!" after being healed will not only let players know what's been accomplished or is possible, but also provide a chance to add some character to your character. Don't forget effort cues, such as grunts of exertion when pushing moveable blocks and pulling stubborn levers.

- **Death:** Nothing says "you're dead" better than a good blood-curdling scream. Make sure you account for all the horrible ways to go, from a groan when getting slain to the gurgle of death by drowning to a long scream when plummeting off a cliff.

- **Success:** Use sound effects to indicate success to your players. Play a "sting" to let players know they've won and don't forget to have your character celebrate vocally with a "woo-hoo!" or "yeah!"

If you need temporary sound effects (while you are waiting to hire a professional sound designer), I suggest buying CD libraries from sound-effect providers like *Sound Ideas*[5] or *Hollywood Edge*.[6] Their libraries have sounds for things you can't even believe anyone would ever need such as cougars sneezing or the hum of a nuclear reactor. They even have sound effects from some of the most popular Hollywood movies and TV shows. Even if you don't have a dedicated sound effects designer on staff, sound effects are useful tools to have around the studio. Be prepared to spend many hours trying to find "the right" sound effect.

You can also find many sound effects online for free (though, of course, you should always check for copyright and so on—better to be sure than on the end of a lawsuit later). However, even with all these great resources online, sometimes you just can't find the effect you need. This is the reason I turn to sound editing tools like *Sound Forge*[7] or *Vegas*.[8] With these programs, I can quickly and easily mix together two or more sounds to get an idea across to a sound effects designer.

Decide whether you want your sound effects to be realistic or cartoony. This choice will generally be set by the theme of your game, but sometimes there are exceptions. Realistic sounds make the world feel grounded in reality, but sometimes the sounds can be too subdued. Cartoony sound effects are exaggerated and great for "video game-y" things like extra lives and treasure collection, but sometimes they are a little too "on the nose," and they risk taking the player out of the game's world.

---

[5] www.sound-ideas.com

[6] www.hollywoodedge.com

[7] www.magix.com/us/music-editing/sound-forge

[8] www.sonycreativesoftware.com/vegaspro/audioproduction

Make sure your sound designer is using sound to its greatest potential. Make sounds go "up" in pitch and tempo to make something sound positive, like collecting an extra life or completing a task. Make sound effects go "down" to reinforce negative and failure situations.

Sometimes, your sound designer will have to "sweeten" a sound effect because the real-world version just doesn't sound right. For example, I have found that breaking bones never sound right; they sound more like dry twigs cracking. Instead, my team "sweetened" the effect with the sound of a bowling ball cracking into pins.

When you are creating attack and reaction sound effects for your characters, work with your animators to determine **timing.** You want to make sure your sound effect doesn't last longer or end before the animation does. After you determine the animation's timing, create the sound effect to fit. Make sure your sound programmer knows what frame of animation the sound effect is supposed to play on.

Sounds can be used to give the player a warning or clue to something else in the game. The whistle of a falling bombshell can give the player enough of a chance to dive for cover. A crackle of electricity or ominous thrum of magical power will give the player pause when approaching a protected doorway. A player can search for an item like a lost pocket watch or misplaced cell phone by following the sound of its ticking or ringing.

Be careful not to have too many sounds playing at once. To prevent sound effects from creating cacophony, you will have to prioritize them. Your sound programmer can help you designate sounds into three categories: **local, distant,** and **priority.**

- **Local sound effects** play when the player is close to the source of the sound effect. This may be a babbling brook, a ticking clock, a ringing phone, the hum of machinery, or the growls of an enemy. As the player gets further from the source, these sound effects fade away.

- **Distant sound effects** are sounds that the player can hear even if they are far from the sound's source. These include explosions, a wolf's howl, approaching vehicle engines, or the ominous thrum of a tower o' doom.

- **Priority sound effects** are sounds that will always play regardless of where the player is. These are sounds that provide the player gameplay feedback, including loss of health; collection of treasures/goodies; score or combo increase; power-up or countdown timer; successful enemy hit; death; world interaction such as landing, collision, or weapon impacts; and footsteps/swim strokes/wing flaps.

- **Dynamic music** and **dynamic sound** are crucial to some game designs. Having sound come from a specific direction or source will help make your game world feel more real. This is more critical in VR where direction of sound can matter.

You can design your game to make these types of sound be a huge part of your gameplay. When playing *Fortnite*, I listen for gunfire in the distance to determine where adversaries are. I listen to the different types of reports to get an idea of what weapons they might be using. When I close in, I listen for the sound of breaking walls or footsteps to help me figure out how close my enemies might be. I find the sound in the game makes my play session thrilling and filled with tension!

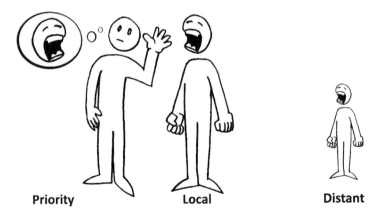

Priority   **Local**   **Distant**

Orchestrating it all

Here's a production related tip: When naming files for production, give your music and sound cues descriptive but short names so your teammates don't have to guess what they are. For example, music for level 2 of your game may be called Lv2Song.wav, and the sound file for a variation on a robot enemy's blaster shot may be roblast2.wav.

Sound not only is effective for communicating what is going on in the game, but also can be used for gameplay. Whole genres of games are centered around music and sound, from *Dance Dance Revolution* (1998) to *Band Hero* (2009) to *Dark Echo* (2015). When creating sound-based and music-based gameplay, don't rely completely on the sound. Create visuals to echo the music and sound. You can never provide too many clues for the players, and you get the benefit of creating gameplay that can be played by impaired players.

- **Short-term memory games** like *Simon* (1978) require players to memorize and repeat a short piece of music. It helps to have a visual component to the gameplay, not only to help players remember which notes to play but also to accommodate deaf (and tone deaf) players.

- **Rhythm games** like *PaRappa the Rapper* (1996) *Taiko: Drum Master* (2004), *Rhythm Heaven* (2008), the *Guitar Hero* series, and the *Tap Tap* series require players to keep the beat in time to the music. Many of these games require or come with specific peripherals resembling instruments from guitars to maracas. When designing rhythm games, make sure you account for player fatigue. This is doubly true for games that use motion controllers or dance pads. You don't want to give your players a heart attack! Provide mandatory breaks between songs and levels so players can catch their breath and keep playing.

- **Pitch games** have players sing in order to match a song's pitch. These games require a microphone to play, as seen in the *SingStar* or *Karaoke Revolution* series of games.

- **Music creation games** blur the lines between music creation tool and game. *Electro-plankton* (2005) and *Fluid* (1998) feature charming player characters and dynamic on-screen activity; however, their end goals are not to win but to create and enjoy.

Other music games defy classification. *Vib-Ribbon* (1999) creates platform-esque gameplay based on whatever CD players insert, creating different play experiences with every game. *Rez* (2001) is a classic rail shooter with an added layer of players creating complex electronic music with each enemy they destroy. *Battle of the Bands* (2008) is a rhythm game in which players play a musical tug-of-war (from disco to country, for example) as they launch attacks at each other. *Crypt of the NecroDancer* (2015) is a rogue-like rhythm game and *Hi-Fi Rush* (2023) is a 3D platform/action game where combat happens on the beat.

As you can see, there are plenty of ways to integrate music and sound into gameplay. Don't neglect them; they're an important tool for a designer to use.

Level 17's Universal Truths and Clever Ideas

- Determine sound needs early in production. Don't wait until the last minute.
- Learn how to "speak musician" to communicate your desires to the composer.
- Communicate important game actions to players using sound effects and vocal cues.
- Don't use music and sound effects that you don't have the rights to use.
- Use music to move the game's action.
- Use leitmotifs to help tell your story.
- Determine proximity and timing of sound and music to make it feel more realistic and interactive.
- Silence can be as powerful as music.
- Use music and sound effects as gameplay (but make sure you have accompanying visuals for sound-impaired players).

Level 18

No One's Going to Watch Them Anyway

YOU'VE ALL EXPERIENCED this: You are all ready to start playing a game, you press start, and then you are forced to watch a 20 minute cutscene of story. Arrrgh! I just want to play the game!!!

A cutscene is an animated or live-action sequence used to advance the story; create spectacle; provide atmosphere, dialogue, and character development; and reveal clues that players would otherwise miss during gameplay. Players often have no control over the game while a cutscene plays.

I find cutscenes to be a double-edged sword. On the one hand, they usually look fantastic, allowing your game world and characters to be shown in a way that may not be reproducible in the game engine. On the other hand, however, there is a history of many cutscenes being too long, not necessary to the story, or a downright chore to watch. Many players will skip through cutscenes (if the game gives them

Why can't it just GET TO THE GAME?!!

the option to do this!) to "get to the game." To avoid this, you should first ask yourself this **very important thing:**

CAN THE ACTION BE DONE WITH GAMEPLAY?

Since cutscenes are very expensive to make, it's best to use them judiciously. I say "cutscenes are best saved for kissing and blowing things up" for these reasons:

- You can create more emotion in a cutscene because you have direct control over all the elements.
- Collisions in games just don't look as good as they do in a pre-rendered movie. Two characters kissing (or holding hands or whatever) just looks a lot less awkward.
- It's often better to take control away from the player so they can get swept up in the story or blown away by the spectacle.
- Explosions look awesome when they are pre-rendered.

A Cut Above

Just as there are many ways to make movies, there are many ways to make cutscenes: full-motion video, animations, flash-animated sequences, prerendered cutscenes, puppet shows, and scripted events.

- **Full motion video** (or **FMV**) cutscenes were popular when video games were first being published on CD media. Titles like *Wing Commander III: Heart of the Tiger* (1994), *Command and Conquer* (1995), and *The Horde* (1994) employed live action cutscenes featuring Hollywood actors and production values. An outside production company usually produces FMVs because they require all the resources of motion picture production.

  During the mid-1990s, FMVs became so popular that several systems dedicated to playing **interactive movies** were produced. Early game systems like the 3DO Interactive Multiplayer, PlayStation, Philips CD-I, and Sega Mega CD (as well as PCs) specialized in games with extensive or playable FMV sequences, such as *Night Trap* (1992), *Sewer Shark* (1992), *Phantasmagoria* (1995), and *Psychic Detective* (1995). Even though DVD media can easily handle the file size of the videos, FMVs have become less popular with game developers these days. They're usually deemed too expensive to produce for something the game's audience may not watch.

- **Animated cutscenes** or **full-motion animations (FMAs)** offer a stylistic alternative to FMVs. A cell-animated or stop-motion-animated cutscene is converted into a video format that the game's engine can play, and it is then shown during the game's title and story sequences. Players have no control over the game during these sequences. Due to the involved production, generally long shooting time, and cost, animated cutscenes are scarce in video games. However, there have been many gorgeous examples of animated cutscenes, such as the *Neverhood* titles (1996), *The Curse of Monkey Island* (1997), and the *Professor Layton* series (2007).

- **Flash-animated sequences** are created in Adobe Flash, which, due to the use of still images and simple movement, lends the animation a distinctive visual style that often resembles graphic novels. *Batman: Arkham Origins Blackgate* (2013) and the *Sly Cooper* series use this method for storytelling. Sadly, Flash was terminated in 2020, but it's stylistic form lives on.

- **Pre-rendered cutscenes** are created using high-resolution versions of the game's character models and environments, with cinematic cameras to create dynamic and dramatic choreography, imagery, and storytelling. Players have no control over the game during these sequences. With enough money, time, and manpower, these pre-rendered cutscenes can look spectacular. Check out any Blizzard title, Final Fantasy series game, or Namco fighting game to see what I mean.[1]

- **In-game cinematics** or **"puppet shows"** use in-game assets such as characters and environments to create cutscenes. They are called puppet shows because the characters in early versions of these cutscenes moved unnaturally, giving an impression of marionettes. Visually, they are only distinguished from gameplay by the use of a cinematic camera. Puppet shows can be noninteractive or allow players limited character and camera movement (such as looking around with the main character's head) as seen in *Assassin's Creed* (2007) and the *Call of Duty: Modern Warfare* series.

- **Scripted events** are similar to puppet shows where in-game assets are used to create animated sequences, but here players are allowed limited to full interaction with the game during the sequence. Since their inclusion in games such as *Half-Life* (1998), *The Operative: No One Lives Forever* (2000), and the *Medal of Honor* series, scripted events have become the preferred method to convey story without upsetting the pace of gameplay. They are quite common in FPS, VR, and action games, but if these events are not properly choreographed, players run the risk of missing or not seeing the event. They can also get repetitive if players have to experience them repeatedly due to dying before the event's objectives can be completed.[2] Here are a few ways to make sure your players are watching your scripted event:

  - Have your events activated only when the player character is actually looking at or facing the scripted event.

  - Build your level geometry to "frame the scene" so players get a clear view of the action.

---

[1] During the production of *Tekken 3*, I remember the game's Japanese producer proudly telling me that the game's spectacular cinematics were the work of just two animators. He then told me that both of the animators ended up in the hospital due to exhaustion!

[2] This often leads to the "Groundhog Day" phenomenon, where players feel as if they are caught in a time loop having to live out the same sequence of events over and over again.

- Move the camera around the environment to give players an idea of its layout and space.

- If you have a mobile camera, be sure to start your event from the player's POV or position. This is particularly important for cutscenes that use the in-game camera to show events like geometry changing position or when giving hints about puzzle elements or revealing enemies. You should use the camera to always show a clear cause and effect, such as "pull this lever and that door opens."

The good news is that you can now determine which type of storytelling device is best for your cutscene. The bad news is that you now have to write it.

How to Write a Screenplay in Eight Easy Steps

Because there are so many books on screenwriting, I'm not going to even attempt to go into the detail they do. If you're interested in reading an in-depth analysis on screenwriting, I suggest the following books:[3]

- *Screenplay: The Foundations of Screenwriting* by Syd Field (Dell, 1984)

- *Story: Substance, Structure, Style and the Principles of Screenwriting* by Robert McKee (It Books, 1997)

- *Screenwriting 434: The Industry's Premier Teacher Reveals the Secrets of the Successful Screenplay* by Lew Hunter (Perigee Trade, 2004)

Since you are reading this book and not one of those, here is a quick-and-dirty guide to teach you how to write your screenplay like a professional, to be used by storyboard artists, animators, or voice actors:

Step 1: Outline your story. If you don't know the beginning, middle, and ending of your story, you won't know what the heck you're writing. But you already learned how to do this back in Level 3, right?

Step 2: Break down your story scene by scene to determine which characters are in each scene and what locations they take place in. This information is going to be important for staging as well as asset-creation purposes. You may not be able to have 10,000 Orcish warriors charging over a hill in a puppet show cutscene. You may want to play around with the order of your cutscenes. Maybe you want to start with a flashback because there is more action in a later scene than in your first scene. For example, in *SpongeBob SquarePants: Atlantis SquarePantis* (2007), we started the game at the end of the story

---

[3] Do me a favor and read them AFTER you've finished this one. Okay?

because it was the scene with the most action, and we wanted the game to start with a high-action scene. I find it better to start with a bang to grab the viewers' attention.

Step 3: Determine which scenes of your story are going to be cutscenes versus being told through gameplay. I prefer to tell as much of the story as possible through gameplay because this is what players will be doing the most—playing the game.

Don't make players watch something they should be doing. It's always better to have the players do than watch.... Wait a second; that's a **very important thing**. Let me try that again:

IT'S ALWAYS BETTER TO HAVE THE PLAYERS DO THAN WATCH

Step 4: Write your scenes and dialogue. Determine what needs to happen and what needs to be said. Try to communicate your scenes with action more than with words. Write to entertain. It doesn't hurt to be funny either. What you do need to be, however, is brief. As Shakespeare once said, "brevity is the soul of wit." Or in other words, **keep it short.** Don't bore with a lot of yapping or technobabble.[4] Try to get your point across in as few words as possible. I used to treat writing dialogue like a game of "Name That Tune." "George, I can write that dialogue in 12 lines." "Oh yeah, well, I can write that in eight lines or less." "Write. That. Dialogue!"

Step 5: Write your script in the official screenplay format. If you are going to be a writing professional (hey, you're writing a video game, so guess what? You *are* a writing professional), you'd better learn to do it the way the pros do. Every other entertainment professional uses this format, so there's no reason to reinvent the wheel. Here's a simple style guide:

```
SCENE #. INT./EXT. (choose one) - LOCATION - TIME OF DAY
CAMERA ANGLE
Describe the setting, introduce CHARACTERS in ALL CAPS, highlight
  any ACTION in ALL CAPS too.
CHARACTER'S NAME
(actor's direction goes in parenthesis)
Dialogue is written here. Keep it brief.
```

That's pretty much the basics of screenwriting format! Plenty of screenwriting formatting programs like *Final Draft* or *Movie Magic Screenwriter* are available if you want to save time pressing the Tab key on your keyboard.

Step 6: Read your dialogue. Dialogue often sounds great "in your head" when you've written it down but sounds strange or clunky when it's read aloud. Expect to rewrite (and rewrite and rewrite) your dialogue.

---

[4] Yes, *Metal Gear Solid* series, I'm still looking at you.

Step 7: Let it simmer for a day or two. Often you will get new ideas or think of better ways to write scenes or snappier dialogue. Have others read it and give you their feedback. Try not to hover too much over them as they do it.

Step 8: Prepare your script for voice actors using a spreadsheet program like Microsoft Excel. "Break out" the characters' dialogue line by line because this is the way voice actors read and record their dialogue. Having the actors' lines isolated will make it easier for them and you to get through what they need to read without having to page through a lengthy script. Make sure to retain scene numbers on your spreadsheet. Remember to give each line of dialogue a file name so the sound engineer has something to name each sound file when cutting up the session tracks. This will be the same file your programmer uses to put the track into the game. Here's an example:

Cold Steele VO Script: Jake Steele dialogue (Actor TBD)

File Name	Dialogue	Notes
Opening_01_01	Those terrorists have hidden from us for too long, Montoya.	Opening cinematic
Opening_01_02	Well, they're about to get a taste of COLD STEEL.	Place emphasis on "cold steel"
Opening_01_03	Saddle up, amigo. We're going hunting.	
Opening_01_04	Heh. You can say that again.	
Opening_01_05	Montoya! Noooooo!	Montoya is killed by terrorist
Cutscene_01_01	Just because you've got me trussed up like a Thanksgiving turkey doesn't mean you've won, Von Slaughter.	
Cutscene_01_02	I wouldn't give you the map even if I did have it... Ungh!	Jake is slapped by Von Slaughter at end of line
Cutscene_01_03	Go ahead, sucker. Do your worst.	Hurt but not defeated
Jake_Climb_01	Unnnh!	Climbs mountain
Jake_Climb_02	Umphf! Umphf!	Alternative climbing take
Jake_Collect_01	Come to papa.	Collects pick-up or cash
Jake_Collect_02	This will come in useful.	Collects pick-up or cash
Jake_Collect_03	Heh heh.	Collects pick-up or cash
Jake_Health_01	Oh yeah, that's the stuff.	Drinks health tonic
Jake_Health_02	That was a good one.	Drinks health tonic
Jake_Yell_01	Yaaaaah!!	Jake's charge move
Jake_Yell_02	Here I come, suckers!	Alt charge move
Jake_Victory_01	Take that, sucker!	

File Name	Dialogue	Notes
Jake_Victory_02	Boo-yeah! That's what I'm talkin' about!	
Jake_Hit_01	Ow!	
Jake_Hit_02	Oomph!	
Jake_Hit_03	Aarrgh!	
Jake_Death_01	Yaaaaaaaah!	Jake falls off cliff
Jake_Death_02	Ung! Ooooh!	Jake is shot and drops to his knees
Jake_Death_03	Not again! Uhhhhh!	Alternative death take
Jake_Death_04	YAAAAAAAAAAAAAAAAAA!	Burned to death

As you may have noticed from this example, VO (which stands for **voice over**, btw; and **btw** stands for **by the way,** btw) scripts have a lot of "YAAAAAAAAAAAAAA!" and "Oomph!" and "Unngh!" in them. Voice actors read these lines literally, so write this dialogue the way you want it to sound. There's a big difference between "Arg!" and "Aaaargh!" to voice actors. One's a pirate, and the other is a death rattle.

If you're not sure how to spell a grunt, hit reaction, or death cry, I suggest reading comic books. They're filled with all sorts of onomatopoeic[5] words like "POW!" "CRASH!" and "AIIEEE!"

Finding Your Voice

Now that you've written your script and broken it out,[6] you might find it helpful to record a **temp track**, like I do. This is a track of moderately talented amateur actors and team members (such as you) reading the lines for the purposes of determining audio file size and length. All you need to record a temp track is your script, a willing actor, a decent microphone, computer software that can record audio, and a quiet place that doesn't echo to record. Try to do your

---

[5] That's a fancy way of saying "It's spelled like it sounds."

[6] A "break out" is actually an industry term for converting a screenplay into this type of formatting for voice over actors.

best to read each line the way you will eventually want it performed by a professional voice actor. However, it's a bad idea to animate a character's lip sync to a temp track: the actor's performance will end up very different than that of the temp actor. You should use temp track audio only for timing and blocking purposes.

Speaking of **voice actors,** while *you* could play the part of Jake Steele, international terrorist hunter, you really should hire a professional actor for the final game. I've had the privilege of working with dozens of VO actors over the years and believe me, there is a HUGE difference in the performance you get from an actor versus an amateur. You want the best for your game, right? So, hire an actor...or two...or three...or a dozen. But before you can hire an actor, you're going to need to hire a **voice director.**

Voice directors will help you cast your game's characters based on the character descriptions you give them. Make sure you're accurate with what you send and don't be vague. If necessary, give your voice director the name of an existing actor you imagine would be perfect for the role. Who knows, you may even be able to get that person for the part![7] The voice director will book the studio time and help you get the best rate. They will help you schedule your time to get the most recording time with your actors. The voice director will direct the actors during the voice-over sessions and work with the sound technicians to get the best quality results.

As you get ready for the voice-over session, send the script to the voice director. It doesn't have to be the final draft, but make sure you let the voice director know that you will be bringing changes to the script with you. On the day of the voice session, be sure to bring the following:

- Extra physical copies of the script.

- A highlighter, for calling out lines to the actors in the script during the session.

- A ballpoint pen or pencil, to make notes and to keep track of changes to the script. (Trust me, there will be changes.)

- Images of the characters the actors are playing. Bring whatever you can to give each actor an idea of what the character looks like. In many cases, VO actors will play several parts in your game (the voice actors union allows an actor to portray up to three characters in one game), so even if it's "drooling alien no. 2," bring an image to help the actor bring that character to life. And send that image ahead of time to the voice director as well to aid in casting.

---

[7] This happened to game developer Tim Schafer, who thought he could never get Jack Black to play the lead in *Brütal Legend*.

- A book or handheld game. "Hurry up and wait" is the motto of the entertainment industry. There is always plenty of downtime as actors and sound technicians prepare for the session. Keep out of their way, but don't wander off too far.

- Provide beverages and snacks. Voice sessions can last all day if not all week. According to the voice actor's union, you need to provide a meal for your talent if your session lasts a whole day. Even though all you're doing is sitting and listening to actors all day, it can still be exhausting!

If you aren't the game writer/designer, make sure your writer/designer is on hand when it's time for the voice-over recording session, too. Very often, there will need to be script rewrites, and the actors and voice director don't always know the context of the line. You may need something very specific for your game: don't leave it up to someone else. Not that there's any problem with improvisation. Giving actors free rein to create great additions and alternate takes on your script will give you plenty of material to work with, and the actors enjoy doing it, too. If they enjoy working with you, they will want to work with you again in the future.

Check. Check 1. Sibilance! Sibilance!
Is this thing on?

And finally, **have fun!** Remember, you are getting paid to sit in a room listening to actors say lines that you have written! It doesn't get much better than that!

Level 18's Universal Truths and Clever Ideas

- Your cutscenes should fit the style, budget, and schedule of your game.
- Learn and write your script in the standard screenwriting format.
- Start off your game with a bang to draw in the audience.
- It's better to have the players do than watch: tell your story using gameplay.
- Allow the players to skip cutscenes and don't make them watch these scenes over and over again.
- Keep your cutscenes short to save players' time and your money.
- Save your cutscenes for big spectacular moments and intimate ones. Use cutscenes for kissing and explosions. Do everything else in gameplay.
- Professional actors make a big difference. Use them whenever possible.
- Break out your actors' material when preparing for voice acting sessions.

Level 19
The Play's the Thing

AS A GAME designer, you are going to play your game many times over. I have lost track of how many hundreds, if not thousands, of times I have played a level during the development of a game. I'd play a level over and over and over and over again because I was trying to make it "just right." You will play your game so many times that you will become the world's best player of your game—until you hand it over to the QA team or get it into the hands of the public. They will always end up being better players than you for some reason!

But playing a game to test something—such as a fix to the geometry and testing a combat animation—is very different than **playtesting** your game. To understand the need for play-testing, you need to understand the concept of **systems** first.

Thinking in Systems

You see, a game is nothing more than a system. And a system is a series of interactions.[1] Playtesting evaluates those interactions to make sure that they are doing what they need to be doing. So, let's talk about systems.

Systems are made up of four things:

- Stocks
- Flows
- Dependencies
- Feedback Loops

---

[1] The following concepts come from the book *Thinking in Systems* by Donella H. Meadows (Chelsea Green Publishing, 2008).

A **stock** is something you can count. An element you can measure. It's measured as a physical quantity and it's usually a noun word, but not always.[2] A stock in a video game can be anything from the number of coins that are spread throughout a level to the player's score in the game. It can be the amount of health or ammunition a player possesses. It can be a lever or button on a control panel, or it can even be the player's position in space relative to some other object or position.

The goal of a game is usually to fill a stock. A stock could be points, rank, the player's physical position, resources, objectives, ammo, or health. You don't want to lose your stock because that often ends the game. For example, if you lose all of your health, you die (if you're on your last man), and thus you lose the game. Don't die if you don't want to lose.

Stocks tend to change over the life of the system. They go up, they go down. The trick is often not to let them go "too" down. In a game, your health goes down, then you find a health potion or a med kit, and your life goes back up. Some jerk shoots you and your health drops back down again, etc. You get it. You've played games.

Flow is the process that impacts the value of the stock. By adjusting the rate of the flow, you change how quickly or slowly the player can change the value of the stock. If you make health potions too limited, then the player won't be able to gain health—especially if that jerk shoots you again! But if you make med-kits plentiful, then the player can raise their health back up after they've been shot. Make them too plentiful and it won't matter if a player gets shot because it will be simple for them to gain health again. And the game will go on forever!

Flow comes from an "infinite" **Source** (usually represented on a diagram by a cloud.) This source can be something invisible and magical to a player like a spawner that generates treasure, ammunition, enemies, or resources. Sometimes, sources are other stocks like a magic potion bottle or a fountain that the player can drink from to regain their health.

There are all sorts of different relationships of stocks and flows in a game. Points (stock) lead to scoring (flow). Health potions grant healing. Position is changed by movement. Ammunition is a quantifiable pick-up item. *As a player*, you cannot choose to directly control the amount of stock. But you may have control over the rate of the flow. But as a *game designer*, you control both.

These are what I call "knobs" —controls that the game designer can use to adjust different elements of the game, such as pacing, difficulty, length, and mood. These all contribute to the concept known as **balance**. But we'll be talking more about that in a bit.

---

[2] We've learned that game development is always full of exceptions!

Something that a game designer can create is a stock that has multiple flows. For example, you could have a magic fountain that requires a bottle the player fills with healing potion. The player can then drink from that bottle to regain their health. They can always return to the fountain to refill their bottle. These are how **fetch-quests** are often organized.

SOURCE   **FLOW**   **STOCK**

At this point, your author pulls up a chair and says, "I forget to define what a fetch-quest was." It's when a character in the game needs the player to get something (to fetch it) and bring it back to them for a reward.

Let's say an NPC needs an item, but you can only get that item by first getting a different item for a second NPC. In this case, the stock is the item, and the flow is the player moving all over the game map to find the items to bring them back to the NPCs. You can chain these stocks and flows together for as long as you'd like or until the player gets sick of running errands for non-existent characters!

A stock can also have multiple flows. In fact, there are **positive flows** and **negative flows** in games. If our stock is points, then we can have ways to gain points and ways to lose points. If our stock is moving, then we can have forward movement and negative movement in the form of knockback, slippery slopes, or giant fans that push us backward. When ammunition is our stock, picking up more ammo is a positive flow, while shooting our ammo is a negative flow! Negative flows don't have to be a negative thing, they can just be part of the process of playing the game!

DEPENDENCY   DEPENDENCY   STOCK   STOCK

FLOW   FLOW

SOURCE

Dependencies are factors that affect the rate of flow. Any flow can have a dependency. For example, a magic spell might have a **cool-down** that takes three seconds. The cool-down represents the time between uses. These cool-downs are there to prevent a player from

spamming[3] the action—repeating it several times to gain an unfair or unwanted (by the designer) advantage—like being able to kill enemies too quickly, thus removing the challenge and fun from the game.

Dependencies are applied to stocks and flow to create heightened situations or variety to the game. If the stock is position and the positive flow is movement, the dependency is the speed of movement. If the stock is ammunition and the negative flow is shooting, then the dependency is weapon type. If the stock is the enemy's health and the positive flow is damage, then the dependency is the level of the enemy.

Here's a mindblower. The value of a stock can itself, be a dependency. This is known as a **Feedback Loop.** When a source flows into another stock, which itself can be a dependency based on the flow of stock, that flow itself is a dependency of the flow back into that stock! Here's a less complicated way of thinking about it. When the player takes damage, the HUD indicates that the player is losing health. They have to go find med kits (instead of engaging enemies, which cause more damage to the player) to raise their health back up.

---

[3] The origin of the term "spam" is fascinating. It originally comes from a canned lunchmeat (ham in a can) called SPAM that was part of the emergency rations sent to the UK during WWII. Britons of the 1970s were familiar with the lunchmeat, especially the audiences of the popular comedy TV show *Monty Python's Flying Circus*. In one particular sketch, a couple is at a restaurant. The waiter rattles off all the choices available and all of them have SPAM in them. One particular menu item is "Spam, spam, spam, spam, spam, spam, spam, spam, baked beans, spam, spam, spam, and spam" while a chorus of Vikings sings "spam, spam, spam, spam..." in the background. It's very silly. During the early days of the internet, trolls would cause trouble by repeatedly typing or copy-and-pasting the same words over and over again in a thread (including "spam") to try to get attention or just be a nuisance. Computer nerds (who were also *Monty Python* fans) started to refer to the practice as "spamming"—the term used when you were bombarded with text over and over again. It evolved again to mean getting lots of unwanted things online such as junk emails, which we now refer to as "spam email."

Creating good feedback loops is the goal of a game designer. They are what we are trying to achieve with our systems. There are two types of feedback loops: The **reenforcing loop** and the **balancing loop.** Both types inform the player whether they are doing well or not. A game that

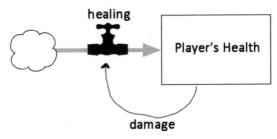

"feels good" has a good feedback loop. The most common example of a feedback loop is a glass of wine.

Wine starts in a barrel in the cellar (a stock) and is brought to the player (flow) by a waiter (dependency). The waiter pours (flow) the player a glass of wine (stock), which is consumed by the player (flow) ending up in the player's body. However, the player can only hold so much wine (stock) before they either get drunk or vomit (reinforcing loop). The reinforcing loop is the feedback the player receives that tells them to "keep going" or when to stop.

In a reinforcing loop, the flow changes in the same direction as the stock. The higher the stock, the higher the flow. "Garcon, more wine!" The lower the stock the lower the flow. The waiter says, "we are out of wine" and therefore you don't get to keep drinking. Believe me, it's for the best.

Reenforcing loops create the gameplay of the game. They are the interactions of the player and the game's system. They are tools (those knobs) that we game designers have to adjust the gameplay. In a boss fight, the harder the fight, the more ammunition you use up, and thus the harder the fight becomes as the player struggles to find more ammo. In Monopoly, the more properties you own, the more rent you collect, the more you force your opponents into bankruptcy.

Reinforcing loop systems have drawbacks. This is known as the "rich get richer" phenomenon. For example, you are playing a game like Monopoly. The person who is doing the best will continue to do well as they gain more and more property, allowing them to drain the other players of money by charging them rent. Meanwhile, the player who is doing badly will keep doing badly because their money is going to rent so they can't afford to buy property. The losing player realizes that they will never win, which is a real "feel bad" moment for the player. We want to avoid this.

A Delicate Balancing Act

A Balancing Loop is what game designers use to balance the system. The flow changes in the opposite direction of the stock. The higher the stock, the lower the flow. The lower the stock, the higher the flow.

For example, in *Tetris*, the better you score (high stock), the harder the game becomes (change direction of flow). In *Mario Kart*, if you are in the back of the pack (low stock), the safer you are from being hit by a blue shell (change the direction of flow). This is an example of **rubber-banding**, the catch-up mechanism I mentioned in Level 13 of this book.

Balancing loops are how a game designer balances a game, which is to say, to make a game feel fairer to the player. When a player complains about a game, they often complain about the game's balance, the way the game feels too unfair to the player. If the game is too difficult, or if the player loses (health, lives, points, status, progress) too often, they will complain! Oh, how they howl! THIS GAME IS BROKEN!!! This is why we must properly playtest our games often in order to gain an unfamiliar perspective on our game.

Emergence, Eschmergence

Game design is an **iterative process**. This means a game's features are tested over and over again to make sure they is doing what they need to do. This is part of the reason video games take so long to make. Because the bigger the game gets, the more systems the game has, and thus the harder it is for the designer to "see" the entirety of the game. This is known as **obfuscation.** Game designers can actually use obfuscation to hide how a system works, such as a randomly generated treasure chart in *Diablo IV*. It's hidden from the player, but we are delighted when we finally get "something good!"

Obfuscation leads to **emergence**, which is when something surprises the player because they didn't expect it to happen. Emergence is one of the feelings that we strive to create as game designers. It surprises and delights the player, which is great! You can create emergence by having a system so complex or so hidden from the player that they just don't see the inter- action coming. To the player, it seems like an accident or an unpredictable result, but it's all predictable.

However, some game designers believe in **emergent game design.** They believe that game- play will "just happen" if the player is given a set of gameplay tools and a chance to play with them. This is a foolish way to work. First of all, it's called "design" for a reason. Everything in the game is there for a reason. Because you (or a programmer or artist) created it. There's no randomness in games. There are random systems but those are designed, too! Now there might be fun, interesting, and unexpected things that might happen if you throw a bunch of mechanics and interactions together in a hope that players will "find the fun," but those products are **toys**, not games.

Emergence is what the game designer DESIGNS, and only what a player EXPERIENCES. Emergence DOES NOT EXIST for a game designer, only for the player. Creating systems and understanding how they work together is what the job of designing is! If you take the time to think about how your game systems relate to each other, the outcomes of those relationships can be predicted. I knew a game designer who was working on a game with 64,000 different systems. When I asked him if he knew the result of every interaction, he said if I know what the system does and how it interacts with another system, I can predict the outcome.

However, if the game designer isn't keeping track of the game's systems and the game's systems get so big that they aren't predictable, this is how bugs are introduced into a system. The designer failed to see the connection within the system. By the way, if the unexpected interaction is bad, it's a **bug**.[4] If it's something accidentally good, it's a **feature**.

Games must be tested over and over again to make sure there are no bugs, and that the player is able to interact with the game the way the game designer wants them to. Here are some things to look out for to avoid bugs (and even features!):

- Level geometry needs to be positioned in the right place, that it helps guide the player through the level, look appealing and not have bugs, such as a gap where the player can drop through the world!

- Combat systems need to have fast animations that respond quickly to the player's command. An attack needs to do just enough initial damage to not immediately kill an enemy but keep it alive just long enough to be a challenge. The enemy needs an animation or an effect to indicate that damage has been taken. The player needs just enough health to survive an encounter with the enemy and not die immediately—unless you are intentionally designing a difficult game like an *Elden Ring* or *Mega Man 9*.

- A match three game needs to have great feedback so it's noticeably clear when the player has selected pieces on the board. They have effects that respond to that selection and even more effects if the player has made a successful match. It needs to be clear what the next successful match might be.

Up to the Test

Question: When should I start playtesting?

Answer: The minute you have something on your screen.

Remember, game design is an iterative process. This means you will be constantly testing your game. Testing should be done from the very start. The more you test, the more (a) you will find problems to fix, and (b) you will "find the fun."

---

[4] A bug is a malfunction in the computer, which were originally caused by real bugs that found their way into the hardware. The first recorded instance of a bug causing a technical malfunction occurred in 1947, when engineers working on the Mark II Aiken Relay Calculator, an early computer at Harvard University, found a moth lodged in the machine's hardware.

"Find the fun" is an interesting albeit troublesome concept. It is true that the emergence of unseen systems will create fun situations, I've experienced myself. For example, I was playing *Grand Theft Auto 3* and having a wonderful time stealing cars and driving them all over the city. As I recklessly drove my stolen car around, I gained more "wanted stars," which made more police cars chase after me. Pretty soon I had a fleet of police cars after me. If you've ever seen the ending of the original *Blues Brothers* movie, it was like that. There was one street that had an extremely large pothole in it. I had accidentally run my car into this pothole more than once, so I knew that any car that drove into it wasn't coming out. With an armada of police chasing after me, I headed toward "pothole street." I ditched my car as I drove directly into the pothole and stood back to watch the spectacle. There must have been thirty police cars that drove into that pothole, piling up higher and higher. It was a glorious carnage! Because I knew the pothole was there (feature) and that cars would get trapped in it (feature), and because I knew I could get a whole bunch of police cars to follow me if I stole a car and drove it around (system), I knew I could create the awesome police car smash-up. (fun!) It was a predictable but obfuscated part of the game. Did the developers know it was there? Maybe. Perhaps that's why that pothole was there.

However, I don't recommend using "find the fun" to design your core gameplay. It's a phenomenon that really only occurs after testing. If you find fun as you playtest, great! But don't rely on it to make your game fun. We are designers. What we create is designed. Randomness is just a happy accident.

Play's the Thing

Did you know there are four distinct types of ways to playtest? The first is **Solo Playtesting**. As you create your game, you will be testing features. This type of testing checks to see if something works. Does the grey box level I created guide the player around? Does the scripting I did on the moving platform move the platform at the speed and distance I set it to do? This type of testing makes sure that things work as expected. I have a few tips when playtesting your own work:

1. **Play the level.** I've met game designers who don't play their own game. They will build their levels in an editor and fly around in God-mode to check what they've made, but they will not play the game as the player experiences it. To me, this is crazy sauce! You need to experience the game as the player will experience it.

2. **Play with the "knobs."** If you have scripted elements in your game, I always suggest playing with the knobs to see what the extremes are. That is, see how fast a moving platform can move before a character can't stand on it. See how far a player can jump or fall before they take damage. Find out how many times a player must attack an enemy before the combat gets too boring or repetitive. By understanding the extremes, you can learn what feels good. This is how you balance gameplay, by adjusting and readjusting. It's an ongoing iterative process. But, by the end of the project, you will have a "feel" for what works and what doesn't in the game. You should be running on instinct as well as knowledge just in time to finish up.

3. **Play the game backward.** If your character (or vehicle) can turn around, there's a good chance that a smart aleck player will turn around and drive backwards. Make sure that geometry looks good from this new angle, and that spawners and triggers can be tripped from this direction. A game might even crash if someone drives into a place where they aren't supposed to go. The solution? Either make it work or don't let them do it. Some games have a timer that, if you go somewhere you aren't supposed to be, your character dies or is reset to the starting position. It will hopefully stop them from playing "the wrong way" or going where you don't want them to go.

4. **Play like an "idiot."** Designers have a bad habit of playing the game the way it is supposed to be played. They therefore fail to see a problem, a sticking spot, or some other issue in the level or with the gameplay. The solution? Jump around. Run against geometry repeatedly. Go where you aren't supposed to go. Run along the edges of the world. Speed run the game. Run past enemies rather than engage them. When you play unpredictably, you will replicate how the public might play your game and find issues you would have otherwise missed.

5. **Play all of the versions.** Games will often get ported—or translated—onto other game systems. A PC game might get ported over to a Playstation 5 version. You need to play your game on every system that it goes on. Don't assume just because something works correctly on one version that it will on another.

Once things work the way you want them to, enjoy that moment. While things seem perfect, know that they aren't, which is why you should start the next type of testing:

Team playtesting is when you get your teammates to play your levels or try out your gameplay features. You might be tempted to tell them how to play your game, but you should resist this. You will learn more about what is wrong with your game if you just sit back, shut up, and observe how they are playing the game. Hilarity will ensue. They will mess up all types of things. They will break your game. You will resent them for it but repeat to yourself, "Game design is an iterative process."

Try to test only one or two features or levels at a time. Don't overdo it and make your team-mates play a marathon session. Even better, play with a group of your teammates, so they can also see all the things they need to fix. The artist will see the geometry that has a slight gap in it or a texture that isn't quite aligned properly. The programmer will realize that the jump physics still feels a bit "floaty," or the AI of an enemy could use a wider detection radius. Make sure that someone (you) takes lots of notes. Remember, you aren't playing the game at this point, only your teammates are. You should only be observing what their reactions are to the game.

You might want to make this type of team playtesting part of your daily or weekly routine. Remember, designers tend to get "designer blinders" when they work alone. Having your teammates "remove" them is helpful for you. Also, leave your ego at the door. Your team-mates are criticizing the game, not you. You are not your work.

Once you have the game in a showable state, it's time for the **friends and family playtest.** It doesn't have to be your actual friends or family, just people who haven't played the game before who will give you honest feedback about it. This is really where you want to take notes. Even better, you might want to video record this. If you can afford to record the screen AND the player, that's the best. You want to record the screen to show how the player is playing the game and where they are making mistakes. You want to record the players to see their reactions to the gameplay. Again, don't make the gameplay session too long. Have a clear idea of the **goals** that you want to test before you even plan the session. Goals you might want to test include:

- Can the player find their way around the level? Can they find the exit?

- Can the player solve the game's puzzles? Are they too hard? Too easy?

- Is the combat too hard? Too easy?

- Can the player determine what the story of the game is?

- Can the player determine what the objectives are?

- Can the player understand the UI and successfully navigate the game's interface?

Once they get done playing, you will want to give them a questionnaire, *like the one you'll find in the back of this book in Bonus Level 4*, that asks them about their play experience. There are no wrong answers, only their perception of what their experience was. If enough people say that something in your game is a problem, then swallow your pride and admit that it's something that needs to be changed—even if it will be hard to do.

It's easy to fixate on the negative but remember that play testers are rooting for you. They want the game to be the absolute best that it can be. Listen to what they have to say and strongly consider their feedback. Here's a pro-tip: *You don't have to use any of their suggestions. You* decide what is right or not for your game. Listen politely to the tester, and you can ignore what you feel is inappropriate.

Finally, you are ready to test your game with the **general population**. This is showing your game off at a festival or at an industry event. You have no idea who will show up to play your game (It might be me!), so, treat everyone with politeness and respect, even if they smack talk your game! This isn't the place to get feedback, although you will observe things if you are paying attention. The best thing you can do at a big event is watch your game being played and answer the players' questions about the game. This is marketing as much as it is playtesting. Remember, whenever you show off your game, you want to do it in the best light possible!

Level 19's Universal Truths and Clever Ideas

- Games are systems.
- Systems are composed of stocks, flows, dependencies, and feedback loops.
- These elements are how a game designer controls the feel and interaction of a game.
- Play with the "knobs" to understand the highs and lows of the system.
- A game that feels "good" has a good feedback loop.
- Balancing loops are how we make a game feel fair to the player.
- Game design is an iterative process.
- Emergence DOES NOT EXIST for a game designer, only for the player.
- Obfuscate game play systems to create variety and surprise for the player.
- "Play like an idiot" to find edge case problems and outlier issues.
- You need to have your game played by other humans.
- When playtesting, just shut up, sit back, and take notes.

Level 20
And Now the Hard Part

CONGRATULATIONS FOR MAKING it this far. You've learned a lot about game design and systems and mechanics and enemies and cameras and all of the nuts and bolts of a game. You have learned how to communicate your game idea using a one-sheet or a ten-pager or a GDD (or whatever method works best). Hopefully, you are packed full of knowledge and the proud creator of a great game idea! But what do you do with that game design? It needs to be turned into a game. One of the things you need to do to make that happen is make a **pitch.**

The Pitch

It takes a lot of money to make a video game. If you are independently wealthy, then great! You are all set[1]! However, if you are like the rest of us,[2] you will need money. In order to convince someone to lend you the money to make that game, you are going to need a pitch.

---

[1] If you are independently wealthy, please get in touch with me! Authors don't earn much, even ones who are game designers!

[2] Poor.

A pitch is a streamlined, easily digestible version of your game design document. It contains everything that's great about your game without being too long-winded. It needs to convey the excitement of playing your game only by stirring the audience's imagination. It needs to show how original your game is without committing to a single line of code. A good pitch gets the idea of your game across quickly and efficiently. That's a lot for a single presentation to do, but I've seen good pitches that have resulted in deals with a publisher.

To start making your pitch, you'll want to use a slide presentation program like **PowerPoint** or **Keynote** to create your pitch document. This is not because you will be giving your pitch in a board room,[3] but because it's the quickest and easiest way to create a game design pitch. Just recently, I was told on Tuesday that I had to have a pitch presentation ready by Friday. It seemed like a short deadline, but thanks to a presentation program and some pre-created artwork, I was able to make the deadline with plenty of time to spare![4]

If you have already created a one-sheet or a GDD for your game, a pitch presentation should be pretty easy to create. You've already created all the information about your game! I have a handy outline I use to create pitches in presentation software. Each point represents a slide in the software.

- Slide 1 - Title screen with logo
- Slide 2 - Game outline
- Slide 3 - Gameplay examples
- Slide 4 - How your game will be awesome and what makes it different from others
- Slide 5 - Competitive products
- Slide 6 - Some information about yourself and your team including contact information

That's mostly what you need. The presentation should be around six to twelve slides. You can go longer, but not many people have the patience to sit through that. I've said it once, and I'll say it again: shorter is sweeter.

Remember the basics of making presentation slides such as choosing a font that you can read easily—something **sans sarif**—without sarifs. Or, don't put too much information on one page. Another basic is, don't create a "wall of text" for the audience to read. Or, everyone loves pictures, so put at least one picture on a slide.

---

[3] Although sometimes you might!

[4] I am a professional. *grin*

Personally, I always strive to create a pitch that is nothing but pictures. See if you can pitch your game using as little text on the slide as possible. The best pitches are peppy and move along fast. Just like a video game. And just like in a video game, your audience likes **variety**. I don't like to repeat using images on different slides, and I don't like having my audience stare at the same image for too long.

Because many game pitches introduce new worlds, characters or game play concepts, I find that **concept art** is very important to a successful pitch.

I am reminded of when George Lucas pitched *Star Wars* to movie producers. They just didn't understand what he was trying to create. It was too weird. Too unlike anything that had come before it. Too ahead of its time. It wasn't until he brought in Ralph McQuarrie to create concept art that producers understood what Lucas' vision for the film was. I often look at McQuarrie's artwork to see what story points Lucas was trying to tell the producers. Together (there are twelve images McQuarrie originally painted) they tell a complete story of the key points of the movie.

Whenever possible, I hire professional concept artists for my pitches. I find that comic book artists also make good concept artists, and they're easier to find. However, good concept art can be expensive—often in the $500 to $3000 price range—and thus an obstacle to some (indie and student) game developers.

If you have the talent yourself, why not create the art yourself? There are plenty of art software packages at a variety of prices available: **Adobe Photoshop** (www.adobe.com), **GIMP** (www.gimp.org), **ClipStudio Pro** (www.amazon.com/dp/B07DYSR1QH), or **Procreate** (apps.apple.com/us/app/procreate/id425073498).

There are alternatives. You can search **Google Images** for inspirational images that you can place into your pitch. Or you can use AI programs like **MidJourney** (www.midjourney.com)

or **NightCafe** (creator.nightcafe.studio) to create quick placeholder images. Make it very clear to your audience that this AI art is placeholder images and that you plan on using human artists for the final game art. Human artists need jobs too!

No matter what type of artwork you use, make sure the art is *representative* of the vision you are trying to get across. You are trying to create a **tone** in your pitch. Don't create confusion between the images and the game play. For example, if you are making a serious military shooter, don't use cartoony images in your pitch. That's another form of ludonarrative dissidence and you don't want to confuse your audience.

No One Cares About Your Stupid Little World

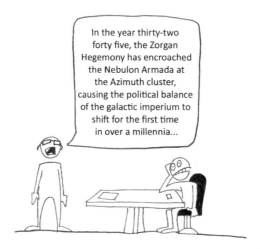

I once sat through a pitch where the presenter started telling us the intricate machinations and politics of his fantasy world. The minute that happened, I tuned him out. It was too much information to process at once. Many modern and student game designers love "lore"—background stories about the characters and the world. Maybe they're frustrated novelists or screenwriters who want to use games as a medium for sharing their creativity. Maybe they want to show off how creative they are.

A pitch is not the time or place for lore. While worlds are fun to create and inventing a world's details is important to making the world feel real, realize that *nobody cares about your world*.

All the audience cares about is THE GAME PLAY. I didn't care who the Nebulons were or what the significance of a Galactic Imperium was. I just wanted to know how the GAME IS PLAYED. Keep that lore to yourself...for now.

Here are some rules of thumb when pitching:

- **Pitch the right people.** You need to consider to whom you are selling your idea. Too many times, coming out of a pitch presentation, I've heard, "That was a great pitch, but we'd never publish that type of game." This is sad, because if the developer had taken a little time to do some research about the publisher, that situation never would have happened. You don't want to waste your time (not to mention the publisher's). Some publishers publish only certain genres of games. Don't pitch a family game to a publisher that specializes in hardcore action games. That said, many publishers do publish a wide range of titles, and their company objectives may change. Timing is everything. There are many stories of someone pitching a certain type of game exactly when a publisher was looking to publish that type of game. You never know!

- **Pitch in a controlled environment.** You can never be sure where a pitch presentation is going to take place, but you want to pitch your game in a location where the audience's attention is on you and your presentation. Do what you can to have control over where the meeting takes place. Work with your target audience to ensure that your pitch takes place in the right setting. For example, pitching a game on the show floor of a convention like PAX (East or West) or New York Toy Fair is much harder than in a private meeting room, where you can have some quiet and the full attention of your attendees.

- **Be prepared.** Just as with any other type of performance, you need to practice. Practice giving your pitch in front of your peers. Invite them to give you feedback on content as well as your performance. Don't be afraid to access your inner actor. You will be telling the story and the narrative of your game to the publisher, so you want to get the publisher's team as excited about your game as you are excited to make it. If someone on your team is better suited to speak in front of a group, have that person give the presentation instead—with your supervision, of course. You should still be present at the pitch to help answer questions and fill in details. You want your game to shine in the best possible light, and you have only one chance to impress. Make sure your computer is compatible with any type of setup, and always bring backup data on a flash drive or disc. I have seen presentations stop cold because the sound wasn't working correctly. Bring plenty of copies of documents. Knowing how many to bring is a little harder to predict because the number of attendees can be unpredictable. Here's another situation to consider: would you still be able to make your pitch if the power went out? So, as the Boy Scouts say, be prepared.

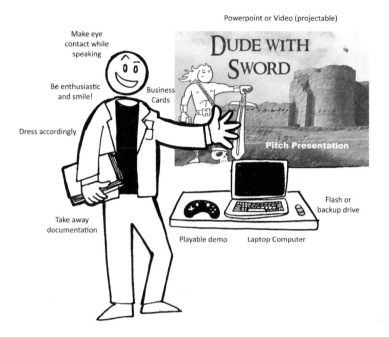

- **Know your project inside and out (and then some).** Even though your game hasn't even been made yet, you should know everything you can about it. Publishers will ask questions to try to poke holes in your design. It's not that they're malicious; they're just looking for topics that may cause trouble after the game starts production. Or, they might be excited about your design and want to hear how great it will be. Be able to talk about your game in depth but remember not to go on and on. You don't want to drown your audience in detail unless they ask for them. If you don't know an answer to a question, it helps to say, "I'd like to hear your thoughts on that."

- **Keep the focus.** Production teams sometimes bring in several pitch ideas in an attempt to find out what the publisher is interested in. I'm not sure I agree with that strategy. Having more pitches means that (a) the meeting will go on longer, (b) less time will be spent on each game presentation, and (c) you may not get consensus on which idea is the best. There will always be one idea that stands out from the others, so why muddy the waters? I say let the attendees concentrate on that one idea. You may have to revisit the publisher to pitch another game idea. If you do present several ideas at a pitch meeting, make sure all the presentations are of the same level of quality.

- **Maybe you need a team.** If you are pitching more than one game idea, you might want to take a page from the great developer Double Fine. Tim Schafer, who usually did all the pitches, instead had a team of three different designers pitch their individual ideas. As an audience member, I appreciated that because I was able to put a different face to each game, and each person's presentation style was different, which made each pitch its own unique experience.

■ **Pitch to represent.** Even if you don't have a great game pitch or truly original idea, but you have a great piece of technology or a prototype gameplay mechanic, it may not hurt to present it to a publisher. Sometimes, a publisher has a license but hasn't picked a studio to develop it into a game. Sometimes, timing and good luck play just as much a part of the pitch process as having a great game idea and strong presentation. In my many years working at a publisher and hearing scores of video game pitches, I have developed the "pitch equation:"

GAME DEMO > GAME DESIGN DOCUMENT > PRESENTATION > PITCH

Game demos are a lot of work. If not planned for properly, they take time away from the production of the main game. They can really disrupt the flow of your production and can lead to crunch time: long hours trying to get content into your game. *However*, demos show you are serious about making your game and allow potential publishers a chance to get their hands on code, which sometimes is the best way to sell your game.

In fact, I will go as far as to say that a playable demo is *critical* to the success of selling your game. Is it a guarantee? No way. But I have been in pitches with the best deck ever and a publisher will still say "do you have a playable demo?" Saying "no" in that situation can feel frustrating and embarrassing.

If you have a playable demo, there's no reason for the publisher to doubt that you can make the game. Do yourself a favor, if you are going to pitch a game, make a demo.

Who's Paying?

When the game industry started out, developers programmed games in their garages.[5] These young game creators soon formed companies like Atari, Activision, and Sierra, and eventually sold their games around the world.[6] As gaming took off, many of these developers evolved into publishers, manufacturing their own games, gaming consoles, and eventually hiring other development teams to create games for them.

In the mid-80's, as consoles became the dominant system for playing video games, the publishers gained more control over what games were made. During this time, you could still create and distribute your game without a publisher...but only if it was on a computer, not a console. While there were some digital distributors like Stardock, it was mainly publishers

---

[5] Richard Garriott (*Ultima* series), William Anderson (*Disney's Aladdin, Cool Spot*), and Danielle Bunten Burry (*M.U.L.E., The Seven Cities of Gold*) all got their start by creating games at home and selling them packaged in plastic baggies to local computer stores. These homebrew efforts launched the careers of many early game creators.

[6] Or, they were existing companies like Nintendo, Namco, Sega, and Konami who got into the video game business.

who controlled major releases, as they were the ones who could afford to invest the capital necessary to develop console games. When Internet-enabled consoles became the norm, publishers started to offer downloadable content as add-ons to their retail games. In 2002, Microsoft and the Valve Corporation started digitally distributing games through the Xbox Live and Steam platforms, changing the way players purchased games. Sony, Nintendo, Origin, and other digital distributors soon followed suit.

The real game changer came in 2008 when Apple launched the App Store. Developers leapt on board and after a few early successes,[7] the new gaming gold rush was off and running. It's been a while and things have cooled down, but the success of digital distribution has opened up many new markets for game developers:

- **App stores:** Apple's App Store. Google Play. Android Market. Amazon's Kindle store. All of these distributors of downloadable mobile games offer appealing alternatives to their console counterparts. Overall, it is cheaper for a game developer to submit a game to these app stores. These stores take a smaller cut in the profits and have less restrictive submission guidelines than their console publisher counterparts. However, you are competing with hundreds of thousands of titles in an already over-saturated market. How do you stand out from the crowd? Simple. Be awesome.

- **Digital Distribution:** Digital distribution platforms, such as Valve's Steam, Microsoft's Xbox Live Marketplace, Sony's PlayStation Store, GameStop, and Nintendo eShop deliver games right to the device and at any time of day or night. They offer everything from the smallest indie games to the latest and greatest AAA titles.

- **Crowd funding:** Launched in 2009, Kickstarter created a platform where game developers (as well as inventors and artists) could get their projects funded by the donations of individual contributors. Soon, other crowd-funding sites like Indiegogo and GoFundMe cropped up, giving developers new ways to earn capital. While funding isn't guaranteed, successes like *Broken Age* (2014), which earned $3.45 million from over 87,000 backers within a month, and *Wasteland 2* (2014), which earned $2.93 million, make crowd funding an appealing option.

- **Web hosting:** When Flash was at its height, there were several web hosting sites. Popular games like *Bejeweled*, *Plants vs. Zombies*, *Robot Unicorn Attack,* and *Peggle* got their start as web games. Many of these sites were swallowed up by corporations and publishers. Only a few remain: Kongragate, Newgrounds, and Adult Swim Games host free-to-play games created by all levels of developers; from amateurs to veteran game creators.

---

[7] *Trism* (2007) earned $250,000 in the first two months of release and was one of the App Store's earliest success stories.

- **Traditional publishers:** These are the EAs, the Sony Computer Entertainment, the Nintendos, the Activisions. Sure, you could walk in off the street with a great game demo, but unless you have an agent or manage to get a meeting with a business developer, the chances of success are slim. Usually, publishers like to work with established talent or their own development teams. However, if you do get a meeting, you will need a killer demo and/or pitch presentation.

But before you publish your game, you need to let people know that you make games. Create a portfolio website. One that shows off your design drawings or you map layouts. Take screen captures of your level layouts and post them on art showcase sites like Deviant Art (www.deviantart.com), ArtStation (www.artstation.com), Instagram, or any other social media platform of your choice. Create short video walkthroughs of your level designs and post them to YouTube. You need to show people what you can do.

Video Games Is a Haaaard Business

Making video games may sound like fun and games, but it is a lot of hard work. It takes lots of effort and hours to design and create a game. Even after all that hard work, a game that may seem to be a "sure hit" may get poor reviews or mediocre sales. There are plenty of examples of well-made and fun games that received great reviews and still did badly when it came to sales. Sometimes, the publisher may not be able to finance the promotion of the game to the level you believe it deserves. Sales projections may be set at levels that the game just can't reach.

It's not all the publisher's fault though. Sometimes team members may not put their best work into the game; family and health issues may distract them from their jobs. God forbid, your lead designer or a key team member gets sick or dies during production.

When Reality Gets in the Way

Remember this very important thing:

VIDEO GAMES ARE MADE BY PEOPLE

These things happen, so you want to give your game a fighting chance to be the best possible. Most games that go badly are the result of bad planning. Here's a list for troubleshooting your game during production:

- Don't overpromise content and bite off more than the team can chew.

- Plan ahead. Prepare for team illnesses and vacation. Prepare for hardware failure, brown-outs, or other technical issues.

- Try to lock down design and content as soon as possible. Constantly changing content in the pursuit of perfection will eventually wear down your team and may even kill your game.

- Players will always find ways to break your game, so make sure to play the game the way they would. Don't just play the game the way it's "meant to be played." Do unusual things and bang on the game until it breaks. Then fix it and keep working.

- If you are creating an international version of your games, make sure you account for sensitive cultural differences. For example, Titan Studios, the creators of *Fat Princess* (2009), had to redesign the cartoony four-fingered game characters to have five fingers for the game's release in Japan.[8]

- Beware of **designer blinders**, the phenomenon that happens when you are too close to your game. It results in game creators thinking their game is too easy or half-baked elements are "good enough."

    1. **Imagine that you are the "first player."** This can be tough to do but try to imagine what it would be like for someone playing your game for the first time. Are you giving players all the feedback they need to play and understand what's going on? Are you giving them enough excitement and fun?

    2. **Be objective.** Look at your game with the "10,000-foot view," an objective looks at everything in your game. Use tools like beat charts and outlines to identify weak spots in your design.

    3. **Try to break the game.** Do things you wouldn't normally do. Often designers get so used to playing a game the way it is supposed to be played that they forget that players might play their game another way. Put yourself in someone else's shoes.

    4. **Compare your game to other games.** Does your game make you feel the same way other games do? If not, what is it about that other game that you like that yours doesn't have?

    5. **Tell your game's story.** As you play the game, you are creating the game's narrative. Does this narrative match with how you want the players to play the game?

---

[8] There are at least three explanations to why the four-fingered visual is considered taboo in Japan. Yubitsume is the practice performed by members of the Yakuza—the cutting off at the knuckle of the pinkie finger as atonement. The resulting mutilated hand has the appearance of having four fingers. The number four, pronounced Shi, also means death. It's an unlucky number, much like 13 is in Western cultures. The Burakumin are a social class that is still met with discrimination. The four-fingered sign was used to designate Burakumin (because they often worked with four-legged animals) and became a derogatory gesture. Modern Buraku activist groups have sued over the use of the four-fingered sign in Japanese media.

6. **Iterate on your game design in all stages of production.** This one is super important, so I'm going to write it in all caps to make sure you don't miss it: ITER-ATE ON YOUR GAME DESIGN. Game design is an iterative process. Like a samu-rai sword, you must break and reforge your game until it is strong and powerful. (Did I already use this metaphor? I forget.)

7. **Get feedback.** We've talked about the four types of play testers. You will want feedback from all of these groups. But don't get mad at them when they tell you something you might not like to hear. Many times, they are right. If people feel strongly enough about something to complain about it, there is usually a legiti-mate reason they are complaining, and you should address it. Don't forget to have your loved ones play your game. They are the most complimentary (because they love you!) and are the best people to gauge whether your game is fun or not.

8. **Use a focus group.** These are people who are picked to play your game for a par-ticular reason: they like action games, they play games a certain amount of time a week, or they might be of a particular age or sex. They are often paid to play your game and give their opinions. There are a few things to be careful of. Sometimes, one person in the group will become the "alpha;" that means this person's opin-ions carry more weight than the rest of the group and they can steer the group's opinions. Other group members might not be brave enough to voice their own opinions, even though that's why they're there! Make sure everyone gets asked questions. Another problem with focus groups is if the group members are being paid for their opinion, they might feel as though they need to say something nice about your game. You want honesty, not flattery. Lastly, just because you are pay-ing people for their opinions, that doesn't mean they're right. Take all focus group feedback with a grain of salt.

Problems with games will happen. And sometimes you will have made something that just doesn't work or that isn't as fun as it sounded on paper. When this happens (and it will hap-pen), my advice is: **If it doesn't work, throw it out.**

Don't be precious with your ideas. They're a dime a dozen. But when you do throw something out, have a backup plan in mind. Don't make throwing away work a habit. It's better to plan things to help anticipate problems than to waste work. Wasting work means wasting time. Wasting time means wasting money. Both time and money are limited resources for a devel-oper. It's better to get rid of good ideas; that means you have too many good ideas! You can always use them on the sequel.[9]

---

[9] S.I.F.S. ("save it for the sequel") was a popular saying at many of the studios where I worked.

Cutting content happens in every game. But the more you cut during preproduction, the less you will have to cut during production. Make sure you are cutting content for the right reasons. Don't cut or change content that connects and has an impact on multiple game systems; otherwise, you will be asking for trouble.

One other note about game design: **Beware of pride.**

Game designers can get quite possessive about their designs. After all, they have poured their hearts and souls and even their dreams into them. However, pride can get in the way of making choices that are best for the game. As a creative manager, I have seen designers get argumentative when defending gameplay that just isn't fun, controls that just don't work, ideas that just aren't that good. Most designers want to make decisions about game design themselves. They want to feel ownership of the design. I understand that emotion, and I don't fault others for that, but some of the choices made early in the game's design might end up causing issues or being things that might have to be changed or removed later.

Of course, the problem is that no one likes to be told that their ideas aren't good or that their game play isn't very fun. This is a tricky situation to navigate. If this issue does arise, be diplomatic and approach the topic gently. Try to suggest a solution, or even better a way to get your fellow designer to come up with a solution. If they just aren't getting it or refuse to compromise, often you might have to just let it go and live with the consequences.

Remember, the most important thing about game development is getting the game done.

Vertical or Horizontal?

I don't want to go too much into game production (that subject could fill an entirely different book), but you should consider how to build your game before you start making it. Having a solid plan of attack will avoid a lot of problems in the long run.

Some teams create a **vertical slice** that acts as a demo to be shown to publishers and a template for the rest of the game. A vertical slice is a level or sequence of your game that has been designed, built, and polished to the highest level of playability possible. When creating a vertical slice, you need to start with a grey box level but instead of stopping there, you continue to develop the level until it has the highest quality of controls, camera, visuals, gameplay, code, effects, and audio that the final version of the game will have. Usually, the target is 80% of the final game quality.

May I have another vertical slice, please?

Although experienced teams can create vertical slices in as little as a matter of months, it is a very time-consuming process that can lead to **crunch time**—long working hours that can be very stressful to the team as they rush to create, insert, and test content into the game. In fact, any poorly planned production plan will lead to crunch time, whether you are making a vertical slice or diving right into making the entire game.

CRUNCH TIME IS BAD!

If you have to crunch, something is wrong with your game development. I have seen many young game designers think that doing crunch time is a noble thing. They believe that working long hours and late nights means that you really care about the game. **You're making a game, not saving the world**, so don't sacrifice your health, your sanity, and your life to make it.

Crunch time is often caused by bad planning, but it can be caused by other things. Here are nine ways to help you avoid crunch time:

- **Schedule.** Creating a schedule of all the work required to make the game will help you determine how much time it will take to make a game. You know what tool will help you determine how much work there is to do? That's right, your game design document.

- **Do the hard stuff first.** Often people are scared to do the hard stuff. This might be a tricky camera system, a complex collision system, or a complicated design. However, doing the hard stuff is the point where you run into trouble. If you tackle the hard stuff early on, you can do the things you know you are good at later in production. Don't put off the hard stuff!

- **Allow for revisions.** Your GDD will help the team determine what work there is to do, which is why it's important to keep it up to date. You wouldn't want anyone to work on anything you don't need, right?

- **Make up your mind.** If you keep changing your mind, you won't know what to do. One game I worked on redesigned an enemy character ten times! That's a lot of wasted time and effort. If you decide, stick with it and live with the consequences.

- **Communicate.** You'd think that a team of people working toward a common goal would want to talk to each other. However, that's not always the case. Egos, differences in opinion, thoughtlessness, and even fear of doing the wrong thing can get in the way of everyone making a great game. Don't be afraid to communicate with your team; let them know you are willing to talk and, more importantly, listen to them, too. If something bad has happened, talk to your team. The sooner you can resolve the problem, the better.

- **Don't put off meetings.** Sure, they can be long and sometimes boring, but don't put them off. Show up on time and set a time limit. Keep your meetings centered on just a few topics to avoid distractions. Try to keep the meetings on topic and make sure they don't turn into meandering stories, shouting matches, or long debates. Provide snacks to keep people's energy up and offer pens and paper so they can track their ideas. Also, don't have meetings if you don't need one. If you don't have an agenda for the meeting, then you probably don't need a meeting!

- **Expect delays.** Life happens. Your teammates get sick, take vacations, and have important life events. Teammates go on honeymoons. Kids are born. Grandparents die. Pets die. Life is going to get in the way of making your game. Just roll with the punches and keep moving forward. Most of all, be sympathetic to your teammates. Even if you don't have kids of your own, have some understanding for those who do. Be a mensch.

- **Plan for learning.** It takes time for someone to learn something new. An artist might have to learn a new plug-in; a programmer might need to learn a new way to write code. As a designer, you should always be learning new tools, playing games and learning new ways to make your game better.

- **Plan for mistakes.** Humans make mistakes. It's going to happen. You might overwrite a document file you had been working on for days (it's happened to me), you might give an artist the wrong image to model (it's also happened to me), or you might edit the wrong file and check it back in (yes, I've done this too!). Let your teammates know you made a mistake immediately. Don't try to hide it. Just do your best to avoid mistakes, use version control and other fail safes, and try to recover from the mistake as quickly as you can.

A **horizontal layer** is another alternative to game production. The team members bring "up" all elements of the game, from beginning to end, at the same time in **gray box** form. When your team is creating gray box levels, geometry is roughly built, and character animation assets are mostly placeholders. Details such as texturing, effects, and sound are generally absent at this point. After all game assets have been play tested and approved, the team can move on to the next step of "prettying up" and polishing the game even further.

It may not look like much now, but you've got to imagine it with stone walls, the skull torches, the spike-filled pit and the goblin henchmen...

The hardest thing about presenting gray box gameplay to other team members (and publishers and marketing partners and so on) is that it requires them to **use their imagination**. Don't laugh! Even in a creative industry such as making games, that ability is rarer than you'd think. The trick is to not let these people get the wrong idea about your game. Make sure there is concept art on hand to help communicate these visuals before they are in the game. What's great about this type of iteration is it gives the team a chance to play around with the game and discover what's great about it. If bouncing off enemies' heads turns out to be more fun than punching them, it's not too late to adjust the design to compensate for the gameplay.

Expectations of the Game Designer Position

So, what is the job of being a game designer actually like? There's really no one answer to that question. It depends on what stage the game is in (concept, pre-production, production, post-production, or release) and what tasks need to be done. The game's schedule dictates a lot of what my day-to-day activities are. A few of the tasks I will do as a game designer include:

- Think up and write down the basic idea of the game
- Create pitch presentations and pitch the game at industry events or in meetings
- Collaborate on the game's design and review other designer's work
- Develop and write the game's story
- Develop and design the character's actions
- Develop and design levels, mechanics, and enemies
- Discuss the game's design with fellow team members
- Draw level maps and create grey box versions of them in-engine
- Playtest the in-game levels and game play
- Script mechanics and the camera in-level
- Write dialogue and direct voice actors
- Write marketing copy for the website, press releases, or back of packaging

These are just some of the tasks I've done on a game! I have found it is best to be the person in the room who raises their hand and says, "I'll do it!" It's the best way to gain experience, and it will make you a much more valuable team member.

What to Do for an Encore?

Congratulations! You've designed and created a game! If your game does well (either critically or financially) or if your publisher can afford to pay you a second time around, you may get to make a sequel.

Publishers like sequels. Sequels are safe(r) bets. A proven intellectual property (IP) that doesn't need to be explained to the audience. "If you loved the first one, you'll love the second!"

It's easy to understand why a safe bet is appealing to a publisher, but it's not without its problems. Sequels often seem to represent a missed opportunity. Some teams just "phone in" or rush to make their sequel, creating retreads of the last game. Sequels should be treated as an opportunity to get it right.

The first time you make a game, you are limited by several factors: you have to build a team, build an engine, figure out just what the heck this character and the gameplay are going to be, get the whole thing to work and actually be fun, and then hope that the audience is going to like and buy it. After you've finished that, you've licked the hard part—especially if you've sold well enough to warrant a sequel. You should start your preproduction with the driving desire to make the game perfect.[10]

For example, after finishing the first *Maximo* game, I went to my producer with a list of 40 things I thought were broken and needed to be fixed in the sequel (to my delight, I was able

---

[10] Okay, odds are you will never obtain perfection, but it's not a bad goal to target. Then again, it didn't help *Duke Nukem Forever*, did it? That game took 14 years to develop, took two development studios to complete, and when it finally released in 2011, it was criticized as being "out of date."

to get 39 of those requests fulfilled!).[11] We wouldn't have had the opportunity to make that better game if we didn't have a chance to make a sequel.

Besides, if there were no sequels, there would be no *Super Mario Odyssey*, *Legend of Zelda: Tears of the Kingdom*, *Angry Birds Journey*, *LEGO Fortnite*, *Hades 2*... you get the idea. Here is some advice on making a video game sequel:

- Use the "spine" of the original game as a basis of your gameplay design for the sequel. Take everything that was good in the first game and improve on it. Take everything that was bad and throw it away. This advice seems like common sense, but it's not all that common. Things like lousy camera, control, and gameplay mechanics are "justified" by teams because they were in the first game. Just because they were in the first game doesn't mean they were that good. Don't be afraid to cut out the bad bits. If it's better than the original, no one will complain.

- Don't let the players down. They expect all the good things from the first game to be in the sequel, and you shouldn't be disappointed. For example, if your audience loved the wall-running mechanic in your first game, then by all means, keep the wall-running in the sequel. Don't make the players have to re-earn or, worse, rebuy things they could get free in the first game. In *Maximo vs. Army of Zin*, players started with all the major moves from the first game and earned brand new ones in the second. It only made sense that Maximo would have known how to do all the things he learned in the first game!

- Name it something other than "*GameName 2*." Names are really important to a game. Giving your sequels titles that are exciting, mysterious, or cool will further your game's fiction rather than reduce your games to a numbered outing.

- Always introduce something new. This may seem to be pandering to marketing, but make sure there are five new things in your game for the back of the box, preferably new gameplay concepts to bring something fresh. Also, try to introduce at least one new hero and villain to the franchise. Remind the players that this is a new experience, not just a rehash.

- ...But don't make it too new. In *Maximo vs. Army of Zin*, we didn't realize that the players wanted to fight more supernatural enemies. We had them battling clockwork creatures instead. The fans were unhappy because we had deviated from what they liked in the first title. My friend, project manager George Collins, recommends that every sequel should be **"30/70:"** 30% new material and ideas and 70% based on the original game. It's not a bad formula to follow.

---

[11] Although the first *Maximo* game sold better, I still think the second one is a better game.

If you get a chance to make several sequels, you have an opportunity to create more change. Don't let your franchise get stale. Why not try doing something wildly different? This, of course, requires buy-in from your publisher and marketing department, so it can be tricky to pull off. I've worked on franchises that were in their 5th, 8th, or even 16th incarnation and sometimes a completely new direction is what is needed to shake things up.

Level 20's Universal Truths and Clever Ideas

- Demo > GDD > pitch presentation > pitch outline.
- Cater your pitch to the right audience.
- Be prepared for any technical problem.
- Know your game completely to answer any questions your audience might have.
- Practice your pitch in front of an audience.
- Video games are made by people: schedule in "people issues," both good and bad.
- Remove designer blinders any way you can.
- Build games using either horizontal layer- or vertical slice-style production. Pick one and go!
- If something doesn't work in your game, throw it out, but try to plan ahead to avoid this issue.
- Avoid crunch time with responsible design goals and detailed production planning.
- Use the 30/70 rule when creating sequels: repeat all the stuff that was great in the first game but throw out everything that didn't work.
- Don't let legacy keep your sequel down. Take a hard look at what can be improved from the first game.
- Don't let the players down.

Level 21
Continue?

Time to Level Up!

So, let's see.... You've thought up some game design ideas, you've written some game design documents, you've made (and eaten?) some chili, and you've pitched your game.

Congratulations! **You've leveled up!**

And just as in games, you're just getting started. Now, it's time for you to learn firsthand that making video games is the best job in the world. Do me a favor: as you make your own games and move forward with your game design career, keep this book in your backpack. Or satchel. Or purse. Or on your deck...somewhere within reach. I hope it will be helpful the next time you get stuck on a problem, or maybe it will provide a little inspiration from time to time.

Finally, always remember these very important things:

- **You're only human.** You're going to make mistakes. You are going to experience doubt. You are going to run out of ideas (temporarily). When those things happen, don't be too hard on yourself. Take a break. Get out of that chair and stretch your legs. You're making video games, not performing heart surgery. No one is going to die if you don't get it done today. Your health and your sanity come first.

- **Always be fair and generous.** Give credit where credit is due. Let people know when they're doing a good job or when you're having fun working with them. Try mentioning one thing you like about their work before going over the list of things that need fixing. It never hurts to be a thoughtful and decent person. This is a relatively small industry, and word gets around very fast when you don't play nicely with others.

- **Keep learning.** The world is filled with so many wonderful things, who knows what will inspire you to make a game? Read a book, take a class, watch a YouTube video, and talk to another human being. Keep your mind open to new things and good ideas will come!

- **Always keep playing games - even the bad ones.** Play all the games you can. "Being bored" is impossible in this modern world.... There are always new games, new types of games being created. Play all the games! If you are young, play older games. If you are old, play the new hotness. Don't ever turn your nose up at a game. Never let someone else play the game for you. Stop watching those videos about video games and start playing video games. You need to put your hands on the controller to understand how a game feels and plays, and you need to understand why it is good or bad. That's the only way you are going to develop your own taste for games, which will help make your games stand out from all the others.

- **Do what you love for a living.** If you can't get up in the morning and look forward to what you will do during the day, you shouldn't be doing it.[1] Follow your passion. Remember that not many people get to make video games for a living, so enjoy every minute of it.

You're still here?
The book's over!
Go design your own video game!

- **Don't be scared.** Don't be afraid to share your ideas with other people. Sharing will get people excited for your idea. But don't stop with the idea, it's the execution that matters. Also, you don't need to be working for an AAA company to work in games. Game designers make games. If you make games, you are a game designer. Don't wait for someone to "invite you to the party"—throw your own damn party!!

- **Give something back whenever you can.** If you have knowledge, share it! Once you've been working in the game industry for a while, share what you learned. Answer a fan's letter, mentor a younger coworker, teach a class, give a lecture, or lead a discussion group, write a blog about making games, or even write a book. You never know where giving something back will lead you, but it always ends up someplace good.

It did for me.

---

[1] My father, Anthony Rogers, gave me that advice when I was a teen...and it's one of the best bits of advice I've ever received.

Bonus Level 1
The One-Sheet Sample

THE DOCUMENTS SHOWN on the following two pages are examples of one-sheets that can be used as templates for creating a concept overview. The one-sheet template is a very important document, not just for the team and managers to "be on the same page" with the project priorities and objectives, but also as a tool to pass on to management, marketing, sales, licensors, and others to get them excited about your game when you aren't there to do the job yourself.

Ultimately, the style in which you create the one-sheet doesn't matter as much as the information on it. The first example is a text-only version, whereas the second example adds images. No matter the format you use for your one sheet, the key is to keep it short and informative.

You should reiterate the points on the one-sheet every time you talk about the game. You'll know when it eventually sinks into your teammates. That is when you propose a new design feature, and they reply "That doesn't fit with what the one-sheet says," and they're right. Don't be insulted; consider it a victory! (We designers need to take them where we can!)

Farm Wars (title) concept overview

XBOX LIVE/WII WARE/PS3 Download (Game platform)

Target Age: 15–21 (target audience)

Rating: E10

Game Summary: Farmer MacDonald has a farm... and those animals are fed up! Tired of being exploited, the animals build cybernetic death armor and attack! Farmer MacDonald must fight frenzied waves of killer cows, sinister sheep and crazed chickens to protect his produce. Sell your crops to upgrade the farm and buy weapons! Farm as well as you fight otherwise you'll "buy the farm!"

(Include the beginning, middle and end of the game story, give an indication of the game play style, the player's objectives and elements.)

Game Outline: Players create and maintain a basic farm, plants and cares for crops during the *Farming Round*. Enemies attack during the *Battle Round*. Harvest and sell remaining produce during the *Selling Round*. Use profits to buy new seed, rebuild your farm and upgrade your weapon in the *Buying Round*. After a *Season* (4 sets of 4 rounds), the player fights a boss to progress to the next Season. Later seasons will feature weather that will affect farming, selling and battle rounds.

(Don't go into great detail, but it needs to be more in-depth than a summary.)

USP (Unique Selling Points)

- RTS action meets farming simulation!
- Build and breed unique farm, weapons and crops. Hundreds of combinations!
- Over 50 weapons from a simple hoe to the DeathBringer 3000!!
- Fight hordes of enemies and bosses!
- Multiple game endings based on player's performance.
- Multiplayer "Barnyard Brawl" battle mode.

Use USPs highlight cool and unique features—game play style, game modes, single or multiplayer, technology innovations, cool features. There shouldn't be more than 5–7 of these.

Similar competitive products:

- Farming: Farmville and Harvest Moon series
- Defending: Tower Defense and Lock's Quest

Choose competitive products that are successful, recent or very well known - preferably all three.

A Compelling Story, A mystery that unfolds thru cinematic and puppet story sequences

Excitement! Fun! Heroic!

MAXIMO VS The ARMY of ZIN

A Single Player Combat / Action Game!

The Sequel to Maximo: Ghosts to Glory

Maximo's appearance reflects his status!

MAXIMO:

TEEN (Violence) Rated

- **More Heroic** - Maximo has to save others not just his own skin!
- **More attack moves!** Cool Combat Motions & combos, simple to command!
- **Get Stronger!** - Build up your character with the new experience system to gain effective and powerful abilities, armor and new weapons!
- **Responsive movement and combat feel** - Satisfying to play controls
- **Customize your character** with unique boxers and abilities!

Maximo's character image:
- He's Brave, Heroic and Impulsive!
- He's a man of action! Physical in nature.
- Will always do the right thing even if it's to his disadvantage.

Maximo's telling character traits:
- He is always holding a sword
- He fights even in his underwear
- He has Death as a companion

THE ARMY OF ZIN

Unique, marketable and Very Cool

- **Created by the famous artist Susumu Matsushita**
- **Enemy Variety** - Different size, shape, movement and method of attack and defeat.

FUN TO PLAY AND EASY TO GET INTO!

The Zin Legend....
500 years ago the Army of Zin attacked! The forces of man rallied and in a great and terrible battle the Zin were defeated and placed in the Great Vault. There they tick away the centuries waiting to freed so they can march once more.

Collect Death Coins to play as DEATH!

Innocent and not so innocent characters for Maximo to interact with and rescue!

Grim finally shows his true nature as the reaper, an invulnerable and unstoppable floating force!!

Keep collecting Koins to buy unique items!

Unexpected game play situations, enemies and story twists!

The Second Saga Begins...

Eight months have passed since Ghosts to Glory and Maximo and Grim have searched in vain for Sophia... Their search is suddenly interrupted when they encounter a maiden menaced by a strange "clockwork" monster...

Jump over obstacles and beat the crap out of stuff with style!

The Besieged village:
This once peaceful village is bombarded into ruin by the army of Zin. Maximo must search out the mysterious Gearmaster who lives in the dark forest.

Cool dark atmospheric stylized creepy environments!

The Haunted Forest:
Maximo must brave the horrors of the haunted forest where even the trees don't want him to leave alive. Maximo learns about the Zin from Tinker, the cute and intelligent Gearmaster, before being abducted by Lord Bane.

Hazardous obstacle courses and physical puzzles!

The Crystal Mountains:
Maximo will have to cross teetering bridges and crumbling paths to reach Castle Hawkmoor and the great Vault. Maximo duels with his old rival, the Baron, to gain access to the Great vault.

Active environments that move and change as you smash stuff!

The Dead Sea:
The Dead Sea has been sucked dry by the Zin Fortress and the mysteries of the deep uncovered. Maximo must battle his way to the Soul crusher.

The Zin Fortress:
Maximo must survive the grinding gears to rescue Tinker, destroy the soul crusher and the soul stones that power the Army of Zin.

Bonus Level 2
The Ten-Page Design
Document Sample

UNLIKE THE ONE-PAGER, which should be kept to one page, the ten pager is more like a set of guidelines than a strict policy.[1] It's more of a "ten pointer" than a ten-pager, but you can dedicate a page a topic.

What's important is that you include all of the broad strokes of information. Make sure your document is accessible and exciting to read! The goal is to use this document as the foundation for both your GDD and the slides of your pitch.

---

[1] Kind of like the pirate's code.

Page 1: Title Page

Include a graphic if possible, a title (preferably a logo), your contact information, the target platform, the target audience, the target rating, and the expected shipping date.

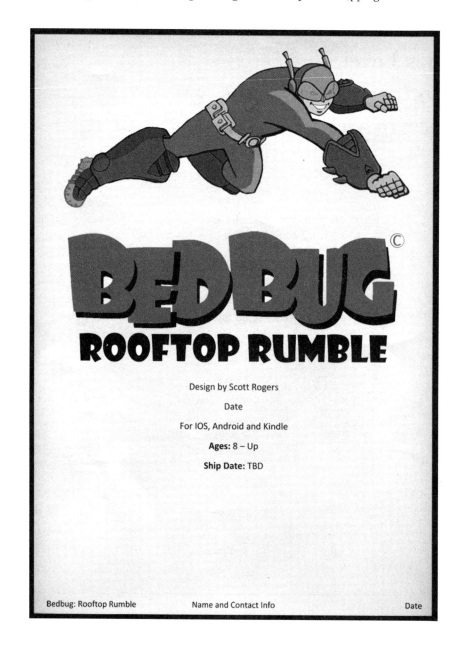

BED BUG©
ROOFTOP RUMBLE

Design by Scott Rogers

Date

For IOS, Android and Kindle

Ages: 8 – Up

Ship Date: TBD

Bedbug: Rooftop Rumble   Name and Contact Info   Date

Page 2: Story and Gameplay

Outline the story (beginning, middle, and ending) mentioning the setting, the characters, and the conflict. Give a brief description of the gameplay and some of the cool and unique things a player will do in the game.

Game Story Summary: Bedbug, the leaping lawman, protects the citizens of Silicon City from the forces of evil. Unbeknownst to him, **Player One**, the couch jockey of crime, has "leveled up" Bedbug's arch-villains using his holographic video game technology; turning the bad guys into a super-powerhouses! Can Bedbug run fast enough, punch hard enough and jump high enough in this endless runner/jumper?

Game Flow Outline: Bedbug: Rooftop Rumble is a side-scrolling endless runner/jumper that finds Bedbug, the single-father superhero dashing across the rooftops of Silicon City. Using Bedbug's jumpin' boots, the player can launch themselves into the air to avoiding hazards and break height and distance records. The player punches out criminals and rescues citizens to earn Pow! points. Earn enough Pow! to execute super-moves or earn the assistance from favorite Bedbug characters like Captain Superior, Blue Tiger or Elvira. Watch out! Super-villain bosses will attempt to stop the leaping lawman, forcing the player to change tactics if they hope to survive. Players can defeat bosses and earn (or purchase) Bug Bytes to restock their utility belt with power-up items that aid them in their never-ending fight against crime! Players can try to improve their high scores and post them to Game Center. Or compete against friends in "Duo Duel" mode.

Bedbug: Rooftop Rumble — Name and Contact Info — Date

Page 3: Character(s) and Controls

This page is where you provide answers! Who does the player control? What is their story? What can the player do that is unique and special in the game? Does the player ever play as more than one character? Can the player adjust their character? Does the player do these actions with a controller, hand-actions, or a single finger (in the case of touch-screen controls)? Show a control map if applicable.

CHARACTER: As a child, **Buddy Sprang** wanted to be a superhero when he grew up but a tragic accident resulted in an injury that confined him to leg braces and crutches. Turning to computer programming and the internet, Buddy created a search engine he sold for millions. Using his newly earned fortune, he built jumpin' boots that allow him to not only walk but jump as high as a building and kick hard enough to dent steel and shatter concrete. He spends his days taking care of his daughter, Elvira and nights as **Bedbug**; striking terror into the hearts of criminals who fear the Bedbug's bite!

CONTROLS: Bedbug: Rooftop Rumble use the following touch-controls to play:

- Bedbug **runs** constantly, requiring no player input, but Bedbug will slow down if he takes damage or runs into an enemy or obstacle.
- **Tap** the left hand side of the screen to **uppercut**. This allows Bedbug to jump over obstacles and leap high into the air. Upgrade his Jumpin' Boots for higher jumps.
- **Tap** the right hand side of the screen to **punch**. Punch enemies to defeat them and collect Pow!
- **Tap** both the left and right hand side simultaneously to **block**.
- **Tap** on a utility belt pouch to use an equipped **gadget**. Players can equip up to four utility belt gadget during one game session. Each gadget is a one-time use power-up.
- Bedbug automatically collects Bug-Bytes and Super-Helper power-ups. Players can spend Bug-Bytes for gadgets and upgrades. Super-Helpers are one-shot advantages to help Bedbug – from summoning the destructive power of Captain Superior and the flashing claws of Blue Tiger to the healing aid of his daughter Elvira.

Bedbug: Rooftop Rumble   Name and Contact Info   Date

Page 4: Gameplay Overview

What game genre is your game? What is the primary action of the player? What awesome things does your character do? The gameplay overview should give the reader a brief idea of the flow of your game. Break the information into bullet points to convey it ever faster and clearly.

GAMEPLAY: Bedbug: Rooftop Rumble is an endless runner, where the player automatically runs from left to right over the rooftops of Silicon City. Along the rooftops, he will find criminals to fight, innocent victims to rescue, Bug-Byte chips to collect and super-villain bosses that bar his way. But the action doesn't restrict itself to the horizontal plane! Bedbug uses his Jumpin' Boots to launch himself up the sides of buildings, dodging hazards and enemies as he goes.

All of the controls in Bedbug: Rooftop Rumble are optimized for touch screen play. A simple tap can make Bedbug punch, jump, and block or use one of the gadgets from his utility belt.

As Bedbug defeats bad guys – from muggers and bank robbers to costumed criminals – the player will earn Pow! Once a player has collected enough Pow!, the player will be attacked by one of Bedbug's super-villains. Unfortunately for our hero, all of the baddies have receive high-tech upgrades from Player One, turning them into holographic versions of famous video game enemies. Bedbug will have to keep on his toes and the player will have to change tactics with each boss encounter if they want to survive.

But Bedbug isn't without his tricks. Players can either collect Bug-Byte chips or spend real money to buy gadgets for Bedbug's utility belt. Flash pellets temporarily stun enemies. Bug-bite zapper causes more damage. Snacks can restore health. The player can also collect Super-Helper power-ups that summon help from Bedbug's family and fellow superheroes – from the Blue Tiger's spectral claw attack that clears the screen of enemies to a simple hug from Elvira that restores all of the player's health.

The levels in Bedbug: Rooftop Rumble are programmatically generated – changing up enemy placement, mechanics, hazards and background art to keep things fresh for the player. The player can try to beat their best time (and display it in Game Center and at Google Play Games) or fulfill the requirements of over 50 achievements to earn more Bug-Bytes.

DUO DUEL MODE: Players can compete against each other in Duo Duel mode: an asynchronous game mode where players take turns "ghosting" each other's moves for points. Think of it as a game of H-O-R-S-E with far more punching, jumping and super-villains!

Bedbug: Rooftop Rumble	Name and Contact Info	Date

Page 5: Gameplay Overview (continued)

Sometimes, your game is so awesome that you need a second page to describe how cool it is!

GAME WORLD: It's bad enough that the rooftops of Silicon City is a dangerous place filled with hazards like sparking electrical wires, swinging crane arms and treacherous drops but it's also a haven for ruthless criminals who prey on the innocent. Fortunately for the citizen of Silicon City, Bedbug patrols these rooftops.

Leaping from building to building, the leaping lawman helps those in need and battles crime no matter where it shows up – whether on the urban sprawl of downtown to the smoky rooftops of Little India to the gleaming spires of the Cassandra Building.

When play shifts to vertical leaping sections, the player will jump past hazards like dropping plant pots, flocks of pigeons and open windows – some hiding criminals while others show amusing vignettes of city life and cameos from Bedbug supporting characters.

As the player's run continues, the locations will randomly change to prevent the scenery from getting boring – shifting in color and lighting to indicate to the player that they are making progress.

Bedbug: Rooftop Rumble   Name and Contact Info   Date

Page 6: Gameplay Experience

Here's where you write about the overall feel of the game. What is it like to play? What emotions and moods are you trying to convey? How is the gameplay going to be presented? How is the story going to be told? (Cutscenes? Text? Level design?)

GAME EXPERIENCE: After the Bedbug Games logo, the player is taken to the start screen. The player will have three options: Shop, Play and Duo Duel. Shop allows the player to buy Bug Bytes, power upgrades and gadgets for the utility belt. Duo Duel starts the two-player competitive mode. Play starts the game.

A short cut scene shows Player One in his lair vowing revenge on Bedbug. The camera pulls back to reveal he is speaking to all of Bedbug's greatest foes. Then Player One presses a button on his gamer glove which shoots out a beam of energy and imbues the villains with a mysterious power. Cut to Bedbug running along the rooftops – this is where gameplay begins.

The world and characters of **Bedbug: Rooftop Rumble** isn't grim like *Batman: Arkham Origins*, but it isn't a parody like the *Middle Manager of Justice*. The overall feel of the game and its world is of a classic American comic book from the 70's and 80's. The stakes are high, the danger is real even if it's from super-villains wearing holographic armor based on classic video game characters. That's not to say there isn't room for humor in the game. The reaction of an enemy getting defeated by an attack or super-move could be look or sound funny, as long as it doesn't descend into the realm of silliness.

The music in **Bedbug: Rooftop Rumble** should be up-tempo and heroic – either orchestral or rock. It should be something you never get tired of hearing even after the 100th time a player attempts to break their distance record.

Bedbug: Rooftop Rumble   Name and Contact Info   Date

Page 7: Mechanics and Modes

Break down some of the gameplay mechanics and play modes. Is there multiplayer? Are there mini or micro games? Let us know!

GAME MECHANICS: These are some of the hazards, purchasable gadgets and collectable items available to the player.

HAZARDS: The rooftops can be a dangerous place for even a superhero! In addition to enemies and super-villains, here are some of the hazards that our hero faces:

Sparking neon signs	Collapsing walkways	Falling flower pots
Smoking chimney tops	Whirling air conditioners	Flocks of dangerous pigeons

GADGETS: Fortunately, Bedbug's utility belt is packed full of gadgets including:

- Steel gauntlets – does double damage to enemies
- Smoke pellets –
- Flash bomb - temporarily stuns criminal enemies
- Bug-bite taser - zap baddies and earn double the Pow!
- Boot Boosters – gives Bedbug a longer and higher jump
- Jamming device – reduces projectile accuracy by 50%
- Nighty-night gas pellets - knock out an entire screen of enemies
- Kevlar body suit – provides 25% protection from melee damage
- Nomex body suit – provides 25% protection from projectile damage
- Snacks – replenish 25% health
- Tech magnet – makes bug bytes easier to collect

SUPER-HELP: At random intervals, Bedbug can collect Super-Help Icons. Super-Help icons instantly summon Bedbug's family and allies

Captain Superior: The leader of the Super Battalion upstages Bedbug again by zooming in and attacking enemies before Bedbug even gets near them. Be sure to collect the resulting Pow! or you might lose it!

Blue Tiger: This mystical member of the Super Battalion unleashes the power of his spectral tiger gem, creating a flurry of claw attacks that does major damage to all enemies on screen.

Vampire Bat: The late-night avenger unleashes his flock of bats that collects all Pow! and Bug Bytes pickups for a short period of time.

Battle Girl: This princess of patriotism uses her mystical spirit shield to protect Bedbug temporarily from any damage.

Mistress Mind: The mistress of mind-control mesmerizes all enemies on screen, stunning them and leaving them easy targets for Bedbug to mop up!

Elvira: Bedbug's daughter arrives for a big hug – that replenishes all of the player's health.

Bedbug: Rooftop Rumble   Name and Contact Info   Date

Page 8: Enemies and Bosses (If Applicable)

While it doesn't hurt to weave descriptions of enemies into the gameplay and story, sometimes you need to call special attention to a particularly exciting or dramatic character. What makes your enemies unique? How does the player interact with them? How does the player defeat them? What does the player get from defeating them?

If you have no enemies in your game, you can use this page to describe the game's core conflict. How will the players be challenged and how will they overcome it?

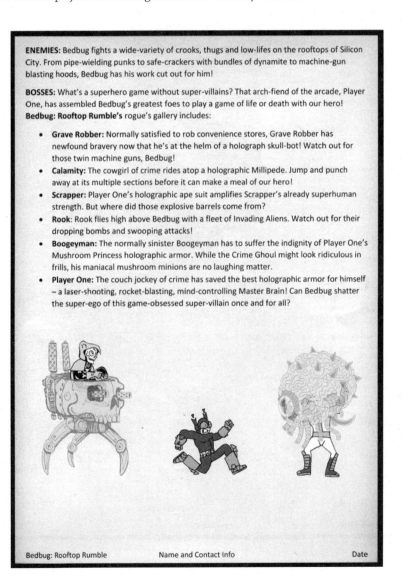

ENEMIES: Bedbug fights a wide-variety of crooks, thugs and low-lifes on the rooftops of Silicon City. From pipe-wielding punks to safe-crackers with bundles of dynamite to machine-gun blasting hoods, Bedbug has his work cut out for him!

BOSSES: What's a superhero game without super-villains? That arch-fiend of the arcade, Player One, has assembled Bedbug's greatest foes to play a game of life or death with our hero! **Bedbug: Rooftop Rumble's** rogue's gallery includes:

- **Grave Robber:** Normally satisfied to rob convenience stores, Grave Robber has newfound bravery now that he's at the helm of a holograph skull-bot! Watch out for those twin machine guns, Bedbug!
- **Calamity:** The cowgirl of crime rides atop a holographic Millipede. Jump and punch away at its multiple sections before it can make a meal of our hero!
- **Scrapper:** Player One's holographic ape suit amplifies Scrapper's already superhuman strength. But where did those explosive barrels come from?
- **Rook**: Rook flies high above Bedbug with a fleet of Invading Aliens. Watch out for their dropping bombs and swooping attacks!
- **Boogeyman:** The normally sinister Boogeyman has to suffer the indignity of Player One's Mushroom Princess holographic armor. While the Crime Ghoul might look ridiculous in frills, his maniacal mushroom minions are no laughing matter.
- **Player One:** The couch jockey of crime has saved the best holographic armor for himself – a laser-shooting, rocket-blasting, mind-controlling Master Brain! Can Bedbug shatter the super-ego of this game-obsessed super-villain once and for all?

Bedbug: Rooftop Rumble   Name and Contact Info   Date

Page 9: Expandability and Replay

What extra cool stuff makes your game even more appealing? How will the game be supported past its initial release? What incentives are there for the player to keep playing the game?

BONUS MATERIALS: Players that download **Bedbug: Rooftop Rumble** will also get a digital copy of Bedbug #1. This exciting 32 page comic features the origin of Bedbug, three additional Bedbug adventures, four who's who guides to Bedbug's greatest allies and enemies and never-seen before artwork.

ACHIEVEMENTS: Each game, **Bedbug: Rooftop Rumble** players can attempt to earn three achievements. New achievements replace older ones when collected. There are over 30 achievements that will challenge the player's skills, endurance and patience!

- **Crime Smasher:** Defeat 100 criminals
- **Combo Artist:** Get a 100 hit combo
- **Punching Bag:** Get knocked out 100 times
- **Block Master:** Block 200 attacks
- **Friends for Life:** Collect all six Super-Help icons in a single game
- **Blow Back:** Deflect a dynamite bundle back into its thrower
- **Pow! Procurer:** Didn't miss collecting a single Pow! during a game
- **Fully Loaded:** Purchase all utility belt gadgets

Bedbug: Rooftop Rumble   Name and Contact Info   Date

Page 10: Monetization

How will your game make money past the initial purchase? What types of in-game items can the player buy? Describe why the player would want to make these purchases. Will the player pay to bling up their character, gain temporary power, unlock more levels, or be able to purchase something else? Or...will the initial game be free with in-game purchases and/or add-ons available?

MONETIZATION PLAN: While **Bedbug: Rooftop Rumble** will be a paid game ($1.99) Players will still be able to make in-game purchases. There are no hard gates within the game, rather the player will be able to collect and spend two currencies in the game: **Pow!** and **Bug Bytes.**

POW!: Players earn Pow! every time they defeat an enemy. The bigger the baddy, the more Pow! is rewarded. Players must collect Pow! by tapping on it or collect it with a power-up, gadget or Super-Help ability. Earn enough Pow! to unlock Boss Fights and new gadgets.

BUG BYTES: Bug Bytes are small microchips that are collected throughout the game. Players can also earn Bug Bytes by defeating bosses. Use Bug Bytes to purchase gadgets, one-shot boost power-ups and special costumes. Players can visit the in-game shop to purchase packages of Bug Bytes (at .99, 4.99. 9.99 and 19.99 increments) or a one-time purchase Bug-Bite Zapper ($1.99) to double the Pow! yielded from defeating a bad guy.

Bedbug: Rooftop Rumble   Name and Contact Info   Date

To sum things up for the ten-pager, its content acts as a starting point for both you, as you design the game, and for the reader. It should provide a framework that you will eventually use for your GDD, so that you aren't starting from a blank page.

The ten-pager should excite readers so that they will want to learn more about your game!

Bonus Level 3
Game Design
Document Template

THE FOLLOWING PAGES are a template for creating a game design document, or GDD. This GDD is skewed toward an action, adventure, platform, RPG, and shooter style game. However, most of the elements listed in the template can be adapted for any style of game. For example, if you are designing a driving game, you will substitute character for vehicle. You will describe what the different vehicles are and the differences in how they are handled, how they maneuver, and what obstacles they will have to avoid/overcome. You get the idea.

Don't feel like you must fill in every detail of information while creating the GDD, but it is better to have areas of the design roughed out than to not have them at all. I tell the developers I work with that a "To Be Determined" is better than nothing at all. You are trying to capture the scope of the work necessary to complete the game. You can always come back to it later.

Remember that a GDD is a living thing: everything in it is liquid and might change due to anything from technology limitations to production time realities.

In the end, this template should be a guide to help you get started, but what matters most is that your team understands what your game design is about so that they can make it. If you need to provide images for your teammates to understand your vision, then use them. Links to videos work, too. If listing everything in bullet points is easier for them to read, then do that instead. Your goal is for your teammates to read the darn thing. Communicate the idea as best you can.

COVER

(Insert evocative cover image here)

YOUR GAME'S TITLE

Document version number (keep this current!)

Written by (your team name here)

Point of contact (producer or lead designer with email address)

Date of publishing

Version number

Footer should always have:

Copyright Company Date   *Page number*   *Current date*

GDD Outline

Table of contents: Remember to keep this current.

Revision history: Update this information with publishing dates and track which author updated the material.

Game goals: Why should the audience/reader care about your game?

- **Game's "high concept"**—Provide a brief (elevator pitch) description of your game. What is the game's genre?

- **Who, What, How?**

  - **Who:** Who is the player playing as?

  - **What:** Provide an overview of the gameplay. What is the game about?

  - **How:** Explain how the game will be unique. Mention "back of the box" features.

- What platform is the game for? What audience (rating) is the game for?

Story overview: Remember to keep this description short and frame it in the context of the gameplay. What are the beginning, middle, and ending? List locations the player will visit and characters the player will encounter. What is the central conflict of the game? How are you communicating the story?

Game controls: Provide an overview of the controls, including a control map. List specific moves the player will be doing, but don't go into detail on the actual moves...yet.

Technological requirements: Keep this brief as many of these features will be included in the game's technical design document (TDD).

- What tools is this game going to use?

- How are camera, physics, bosses, and so on going to be done? Will they be implemented by programmer? By designer? Hard coded? Scripted?

- What design tools is this game going to use? List level creation and scripting tools used.

- Proposed tools for cheats. Include controls for level, invulnerability, camera, and other gameplay related cheats.

- For PC games, include a section covering target specifications of the computer needed to run the game. This would list information including the minimum CPU speed, RAM, minimum graphical abilities, required peripherals, and so on.

- **Front end of the game:** Indicate what credit screens will be shown when the game is first turned on including:

- Publisher
- Studio logo
- Licensors
- Third party software manufacturers
- Legal screen

Attract mode description (if applicable): Give a description of what in-game material will be shown if the game is left idle on the start screen.

Title/start screen: What is the first impression of the actual game? Include the following:

- An image of the title/start screen and any associated animations or graphics
- A list of what selection options are available to the player
- How the player interfaces with the options (cursor, d-pad, and so on)

Save/load file: Describe how a game file is saved and loaded. Include information about what naming conventions (such as how many characters) are available to the player.

Player options: Include image, sound and music, and player interface details. Describe connecting links to options including:

- Video settings
- Audio settings
- Music settings
- Subtitle settings
- Contrast tool
- Alternate control settings (reverse joystick, feedback on/off, and so on)
- Accessibility options (brightness, color blind adjustment features, and so on)

Game flowchart: Show how all the screens from the "title/start screen" to "game over" connect to each other.

Loading screen: What does the player see when the game is loading? What images or information is presented? Are there player tips or trivia displayed?

Game camera(s): Call out any specific camera types.

- What kind of camera is used in the game? (First person, third person, isometric, forced scroll, locked camera, and so on.) Is more than one camera used in the game?

- Description of logic system for camera. Include the following:

  - Game-specific situations requiring unique cameras

  - Camera troubleshooting guide with examples of what camera will do when encountering problems

HUD system: Include wire-frame illustrations of how the information will be displayed on screen. Include all associated imagery such as health/status, power/fuel, money, ammunition, timers, maps/radar, speedometers, lives/continues, targeting/reticles, or special views like "predator-vision."

Player character(s): Provide information about the playable and non-playable characters found in the game. Use concept art to show these characters. What is their relationship? Does it change over the course of the game?

Can the player modify their character? What features can be adjusted? Create a wireframe of the interface and what happens when players change features.

Player metrics: List and detail the metrics of the player's character pertaining to movement, combat, content-sensitive actions (QTE), health, player death, and idles.

Player skills: List the player's skills and how they evolve over the course of the game. Use a tech-tree to illustrate player growth.

Weapons: Describe the weapons that the player will use. Their size. Their damage values. Their ammo types. Their rate of fire. Do they have a sight or scope or thermal vision? Do they have recoil that affects the player's aim? Can they be modified? How does a player equip or switch a weapon? Describe effects such as cool down, poison, freeze, flame damage, and so on. What lore does it tell?

Player inventory: How does the player store and access equipment, weapons, armor, quest items, spell books, and so on. Create a wireframe to illustrate how the HUD will operate.

Combat: Describe and/or illustrate all of the player's combat moves and actions including combos. List the different weapons available and how they are used, including for melee and ranged. Provide a weapon tech tree showing the types of weapons players can earn over the course of the game. Also list ranges and damage values and types for each weapon as well as how the player equips, reloads, and changes weapons. Illustrate how lock-ons and targeting systems work.

Power-ups/state modifiers: List all power-ups and state modifiers. Use illustrations to show how they are activated as well as what their effect and durations are.

Health (if applicable): Describe how health is gained, lost, and tracked on the HUD. How will players know if their health is low?

- **Alternate states:** Describe any alternate states the player will experience (stunned, poisoned, turned into a baby) and how the state might alter the player's controls, vision, and so forth.

- **Lives** (if applicable): Explain how lives are earned and lost and what happens when the player runs out of lives.

- **Death** (if applicable): Describe what happens when death occurs. Is it perma-death? List situations that require specific animations (fire, drowning, etc.) and how does it affect controls, view, or anything else. What does a game over screen look like? What penalty is there for dying?

- **Checkpoints system:** How does the game keep track of checkpoints/save spots? How does the player access them in the HUD? How does the auto-saving system work?

Scoring (if applicable): Assign point values to actions (such as collecting items or defeating enemies) and describe what happens when players reach milestones. How do players earn bonuses or modifiers from chaining or combos?

Leaderboard setup: Is there a leaderboard or ranking system? How does it work? What happens when someone rises or lowers in the rankings?

Achievements and objectives: What objectives can players complete to level up, unlock items, or change their status? Are there visual badges for completion? What do they look like? Where on the HUD/screens are they displayed?

Gashapon: Can players collect gashapon during the game? What kind of system does the player interact with to earn them (vending machine, slot machine, etc.)? Where can the player display the gashapon they collect? Are there in-game bonuses for collecting sets of gashapon?

Rewards and economy: Describe the game's monetary system (systems) and how money is earned, spent, and saved (if appliable). List items that can be purchased and how much they cost. Wireframe how the shopping interface works. Describe any storekeeper characters (if applicable) and how the player interacts with them.

Vehicles (if applicable): What vehicles are used in the game? Can they be upgraded or customized? Provide images. How does the player control each vehicle? What are the metrics for the vehicle and how do they differ from the character's metrics? How do the vehicles interact with the world, enemies, and power-ups in the game? Can they be destroyed? How does the player enter and exit the vehicle? Does the vehicle require a different camera system? What abilities does the vehicle have?

Game progression outline: Provide an overview for each and every game level. Create a beat chart for the entire game. Show how gameplay and story intertwine. Indicate the introduction of major gameplay and story elements including abilities, weapons, enemies, bosses, rewards, quest items, puzzles, or plot twists.

World overview/level select/navigation screen: Provide images and a control scheme showing how the player will navigate these screens. Is it an overworld that uses the player character? Is it a map that the player uses a pointer? List world locations and where they lead to as well as what characters, enemies, quests, or other things are associated with them. Are animations required for these screens? List them. Provide music direction for each world area.

Universal game mechanics: List mechanics that will be found throughout the game. Always include images of each mechanic and hazards. List things like moving platforms, breakable items, interactable objects, and puzzle elements. How will the player interact with them? List what animations, sfx and vfx, are needed for each one.

Game levels: List each of the levels (or themes of levels) mentioned in the world overview. Include their name, a visual description, major gameplay elements, enemies and bosses found there. List items and quests associated with the level. Include what time of day is represented. Describe the training level and what skills the player will learn. Suggest color guides and music to set the mood.

Hub level (if applicable): Describe the hub/overworld level. How do players move from it to other levels? Will there be load times? What does the player see if there is? How can the player save and load from the hub? Are there specific locations or characters found there?

General enemy rules: List the behavior types (patroller, hunter, flyer, and so on) and how their AI operates. Describe spawn parameters. List interaction rules (detection, combat, conversation).

Level-specific enemies: Provide an image and name of the enemy and where it appears (world and level) in the game. Show its scale in relationship to the player character. List all movement and attack patterns. List the damage it causes (and how such as melee, ranged, and so on.) and any other effects (knockback, theft, and so on.). List health and what reward it provides when defeated. Describe how it is introduced to the player. Create an animation, sfx and vfx, list for each enemy.

Bosses: Provide an image and name of the boss and where it appears (world and level) in the game. Show its scale in relationship to the player character. List all movement and attack patterns. List the damage it causes (and how such as melee, ranged, and so on) and any other effects (knockback, theft, etc.). Call out weak spots. List health and what reward it provides when defeated. Describe the location where it is fought and what other special mechanics or hazards are required. Describe how the boss is introduced to the player. What lore will they provide? Create an animation, sfx and vfx, list for each enemy.

Non-player characters: List the non-player characters in the game and where they will be encountered. Provide descriptions (gender, race, age, etc.), images, personality and what is their relationship to the player. How does the player interact with them? Suggest voice types for dialogue. What lore will they provide?

Quest items/Puzzle object sets: List any plot relevant quest items or puzzle pieces. How do players interact or inventory them? How are they used in the context of the game? If they can be examined, does that require a different camera?

Minigames: List the types of minigames found in the game. Provide illustrations of each game type. Describe how to play them and what their control schemes are. List how pre-existing game mechanics can be used, and which mini games require unique mechanics. List what levels/worlds they are found on. What rewards do they provide?

Monetization scheme: Will there be monetization in the game? What is the currency? What will it be spent on? Create a list of the items that a player can buy. Describe alternate skins and add-ons. How can the player spend real-world money to buy items? Wireframe the store interface. What benefit does it provide the player? What is the suggested pricing of the items?

Cutscenes: Are cutscenes used in the game? When do they appear? What form (pre-rendered, puppet show) do they take? Write a script of each cutscene in screenplay format.

Music: List all music needs. Describe the feeling or mood evoked for each piece. List where the music will be used. Don't forget music for the title, pause, and option screens as well.

Credits: Include the names and job titles of the team. Including photos of the team at work are optional.

Bonus materials: This is where easter eggs and concept art galleries are mentioned. Commentary, interviews, deleted material, documentaries, and gag reels.

Appendixes: This is the place for long lists including player animation, enemy animation, sound effects, music cues, cutscene scripts, in-game text, and voice-over scripts.

Bonus Level 4
High-Concept Pitch Presentation

Slide 1: Title Page

Start with a compelling image and logo that sums up your game.

Put the date of the presentation on the PowerPoint or Slides so the people you present to will remember when the meeting took place.

For author credits, use the studio's name. Remember no one makes a game by themselves.

Include contact information such as e-mail address or phone number.

Slide 2: Company Profile

Briefly outline who you are, what you've done, and how long you've been doing it. This is a great place to showcase the covers of any games your studio's created.

Obviously, you can skip creating this slide if you are presenting to your peers.

WHO ARE WE?

Bedbug games president, CEO, lead designer and janitor Scott Rogers has been making games since 1993 and is responsible for such classic titles as *Farm Wars, Relic Raider, Super Magic Guy* and the smash hits *Dude with Sword* and *Dude with Sword 2* - which combined have sold at least one unit.   Maybe.

Slide 3: Target Specs

This slide covers the very basics of the game. What genre of game is it? What is it rated? Who is the audience? How long does it take to play?

Slide 4: Game Story

Who is the player character (if applicable) or what are they controlling? What is the game's story (if applicable) or the game's story genre? What is the main conflict?

Don't forget the beginning, middle, and ending of the story. If there is no story, what is the game's theme?

Slide 5: Game Features

Why should the audience/readers care about your game?

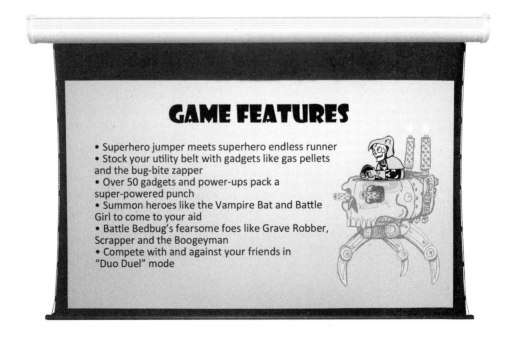

Slide 6: Gameplay Summary

This slide should briefly summarize the gameplay. What is the primary action? What is the camera view? How will the play build in challenge over the course of the game? What are the different gameplay environments? What are the super-cool features of your game? What are the "hooks" that make this game unique? You should mention unique play modes. You might need several slides to cover these topics.

Slide 7: Gameplay Details

Dive into the interesting gameplay details. Your goal is to describe what it is like to play the game. Dedicate specific slides to unique or cool features to highlight how they improve the gameplay and add to the experience.

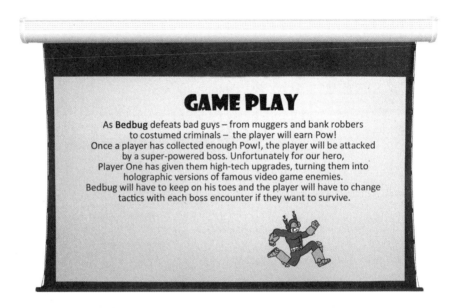

GAME PLAY

As **Bedbug** defeats bad guys – from muggers and bank robbers
to costumed criminals – the player will earn Pow!
Once a player has collected enough Pow!, the player will be attacked
by a super-powered boss. Unfortunately for our hero,
Player One has given them high-tech upgrades, turning them into
holographic versions of famous video game enemies.
Bedbug will have to keep on his toes and the player will have to change
tactics with each boss encounter if they want to survive.

GAME PLAY (CONT)

Bedbug isn't without his tricks. Players can either collect Bug-Byte
chips or spend real money to buy gadgets for Bedbug's utility belt.
Flash pellets temporarily stun enemies. Bug-bite zapper causes more damage.
Snacks can also restore health. The player can also collect Super-Helper
power-ups that summon help from Bedbug's family and fellow superheroes
from the **Blue Tiger's** spectral claw attack that clears the screen of enemies to
a simple hug from his daughter **Elvira** that restores all of the player's health.

Slide 8: Monetization and Download Strategy

How are you going to extend the life of the game beyond release? What is the monetization model? Give examples of how players can purchase items and how the purchases impact gameplay.

Slide 9: Production Specs

Share the production plans here. How large is your development team? How much time will it take to create the game? How much is it going to cost to make the game?

Bonus Level 5
Playtest Questionnaire

THE FOLLOWING ARE suggested questions you could ask your play testers after a playtest session. Remember to always take notes or record the player's feedback.

- What was your goal while playing the game? How did you try to achieve it?
- Explain why the victorious player won.
- What was the story of the game?
- How much time did you feel like you were playing?
- Did the game consistently provide interesting decisions to make?
- To what extent did you feel like you were in control of the outcome of the game?
- Did anything hold you back from accomplishing your strategy or plans within the game?
- While playing, were you ever confused, frustrated, or bored?
- What struck you as particularly unbalanced?
- What was your least favorite part of the game?
- Were there any rules or instructions that you felt were unclear?
- Did the theme match the gameplay?
- Is there anything you feel needs to be added to the game?
- What other games have you played that you feel are comparable and why?
- Did you have fun?
- What was your favorite part of the game?

- Would you play the game again?

- Would you recommend the game to others?

- How much would you expect to pay for a game like this?

- Is there an email you would like to be notified at when the game/Kickstarter goes live?

Bonus Level 6

Achievement Unlocked: Exactly Like Making Chili

(Feeds 6-8)

Ingredients:

Two chicken breasts, boiled then shredded

¼ cup of extra virgin olive oil

1 sweet onion, finely chopped

1 30 oz. can of Navy beans

1 30 oz. can of Black beans

1 30 oz. can of Pinto Beans

1 30 oz. can of whole kernel corn

1 30 oz can of Tomato sauce

1 14.5 can of diced tomato

2 diced green chiles

1 packet of chili seasoning

Lime juice

Salt

Pepper

Instructions:

1. Heat olive oil in a large pot over medium heat. Add onion to the pot and sauté for about 5 minutes, until the onions soften and become translucent.

2. Stir in a packet of chili seasoning.

3. Add one half of the navy beans, one half of the can of black beans, and one half of the pinto beans to a blender and puree. **Don't drain the cans;** you want the liquid!

4. Stir pureed beans into the pot.

5. Add tomato sauce, diced tomatoes with green chiles, and whole-kernel corn to the pot, draining only the corn.

6. Add shredded chicken to the pot.

7. Mix in the remaining navy, black and pinto beans, then stir to combine.

8. Let your chicken chili simmer over medium heat until fully heated through, about 15 to 20 minutes. Although the longer it simmers, the better it will taste.

9. Add the juice of 1 lime.

10. Season with salt and pepper to taste.

11. Spoon chili into serving bowls

12. Serve with any of the following:

Tortilla strips

Shredded Monterey Jack cheese

Sour cream

Hot sauce

Index

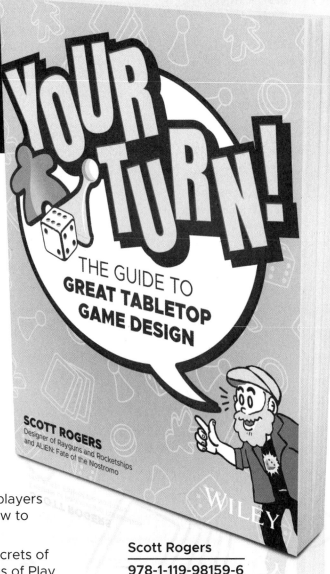